BREAKING THE BARGAIN:
PUBLIC SERVANTS, MINISTERS, AND PARLIAMENT

In *Breaking the Bargain*, Donald J. Savoie reveals how the traditional deal struck between politicians and career officials that underpins the workings of our national political and administrative process is today being challenged. He demonstrates that the role of bureaucracy within the Canadian political machine has never been properly defined, and that the relationship between elected and permanent government officials is increasingly problematic. In effect, Savoie argues, the public service cannot function if it is expected to be both independent of, and subordinate to, elected officials.

While the public service is attempting to define its own political sphere, the House of Commons is also in a state of flux. The prime minister and his close advisers wield ever more power, and cabinet no longer occupies the policy ground to which it is entitled. Ministers, who have traditionally been able to develop their own roles, have increasingly lost their autonomy. Federal departmental structures are crumbling, giving way to a new model that favours the sharing of policy and program space. The implications of this functional shift are far-reaching, having a deep impact on public policy, government operations, and, ultimately, individual and institutional accountability.

Drawing on a wide range of sources, including published and unpublished government documents and extensive interviews with present and former government officials, Savoie provides important historical background and clear analysis of the realities facing ministers, deputy ministers, and members of Parliament. Comprehensive and insightful, *Breaking the Bargain* makes a significant contribution to contemporary debate on governance and the potential for political reform in Canada.

DONALD J. SAVOIE holds the Clément-Cormier Chair in Economic Development at the Université de Moncton.

DONALD J. SAVOIE

Breaking the Bargain

Public Servants, Ministers,
and Parliament

UNIVERSITY OF TORONTO PRESS
Toronto Buffalo London

© University of Toronto Press Incorporated 2003
Toronto Buffalo London
Printed in Canada

ISBN 0-8020-8810-4 (cloth)
ISBN 0-8020-8591-1 (paper)

∞

Printed on acid-free paper

National Library of Canada Cataloguing in Publication

Savoie, Donald J., 1947–
 Breaking the bargain : public servants, ministers, and Parliament /
Donald J. Savoie.

 Includes bibliographical references and index.
 ISBN 0-8020-8810-4 (bound)   ISBN 0-8020-8591-1 (pbk.)

 1. Administrative responsibility – Canada.   2. Ministerial
responsibility – Canada.   3. Canada. Parliament – Reform.
4. Civil service reform – Canada.   I. Title.

 JL75.S384 2003   352.3'5'0971   C2003-902494-6

University of Toronto Press acknowledges the financial assistance to its
publishing program of the Canada Council for the Arts and the Ontario
Arts Council.

University of Toronto Press acknowledges the financial support for its
publishing activities of the Government of Canada through the Book
Publishing Industry Development Program (BPIDP).

To those who showed me the way in
public administration:

Professor J.E. Hodgetts, for the light
Gordon Robertson, for the wisdom
Jack Manion, for the values
Gérard Veilleux, for the insights
Louis-J. Robichaud, for the inspiration

To my wife, Linda, for making it possible, and to our
children, Julien and Margaux, for the reality check

Contents

Tables

Preface

A public-opinion survey, conducted in January 2002 by Leger Marketing, ranked twenty professions in terms of trust. Politicians obtained the lowest rating of all – 18 percent – trailing car salespeople at 23 per cent. Nor is it only the public that holds this view. Members of Parliament (MPs) themselves no longer hesitate to voice criticism of their own institution. Surveys also reveal that career public servants do not enjoy the respect from Canadians that they once did. Moreover, notwithstanding several major reforms introduced over the past twenty years, the most urgent task still facing the federal public service is to establish a sense of purpose and direction and to modernize its operations. Disillusionment with the capacity of government to deliver what it promises and to operate efficiently, and disillusionment with the role of MPs and with the apparent inability of Canadians to hold government officials and their programs accountable, have become the hallmarks of our national political and administrative institutions.

Whatever the cause of our discontent, the literature has and continues to look at these issues separately. The same can be said about practitioners. Public servants have been trying to reform their institution independent of Parliament, and MPs are discussing reforming their institution with little reference to the public service. I have become convinced that what is really at issue is the whole machinery of Parliament, cabinet, and civil service. The total configuration, not bits and pieces, is what should concern Canadians as they seek to improve their system of governance.

Students of public administration have all too often accepted Woodrow Wilson and Frank Goodnow's theory of the division of politics and administration, which was advanced in the hope of separating respectable administration from dirty politics. A central purpose of the theory is to establish separate and distinct spaces for political actors and career officials. The machinery of government has also been built around the notion of having space so that both politicians and career officials can get their work done and be held accountable. Perhaps because of this theoretical perspective and the recognition that politicians and career officials perform vastly different tasks and are governed by different values (for example, the political world places a premium on visibility, while civil servants have traditionally valued anonymity), scholars and practitioners have all too often focused on the executive and neglected Parliament and the electorate or vice versa. This partial view in turn probably explains why Canadians have not paid sufficient attention to how the institutions work together.

I take a comprehensive look at Canada's federal political-administrative institutions in this book. The risk I take is that this approach will not satisfy the specialist of the House of Commons, cabinet, and/or the civil service. Indeed, the specialist will invariably have a more intimate knowledge of the workings of the relevant institution than a comprehensive perspective could ever produce. But the risk is well worth taking if it encourages more research on how Canada governs itself. I also assume that the political system has changed, should be changed, and can be changed. I do not, however, accept that Canadians can transfer bits or pieces of another political system to its own, and I believe that adapting the Westminster-style parliamentary system to accommodate changing circumstances offers the best promise for Canada.

In this study, I also seek to go beyond describing what exists in order to offer suggestions to strengthen Canada's national political and administrative institutions. I readily admit that we social scientists are much better at asking questions and at pointing to shortcomings than at formulating recommendations about how to improve things. We prefer exploring the reasons why things are as they are rather than speculating about how things should be. In seeking to explore how things should be, I run the risk of lecturing citizens, politicians, and civil servants on how things should work. That, I want to stress, is not my goal. My objective is quite modest – to launch a debate on the workings of political and administrative institutions and try, as best as I can, to offer insights on how Canadians can better govern ourselves. As the reader will see, there is no magic bullet at hand. The best that we can do is to probe, ask questions, offer *des pistes de solutions*, and encourage Canadians to think about their Parliament, government, and public service. If this volume accomplishes this goal, then I will have met my objective.

I incurred many debts in writing this book. Several of my friends – all accomplished students of government – read an earlier version and made many comments and suggestions for improving the manuscript. They are Peter Aucoin, Nick d'Ombrain, Evert Lindquist, B. Guy Peters, Peter Russell, and Cynthia Williams, as well as my first professor of political science, Philippe Doucet at the Université de Moncton, and my last professor, Nevil Johnson at Oxford. I want to single out Nick d'Ombrain for his willingness to share freely with me his considerable knowledge of the machinery of government, for his advice throughout the planning and writing phases, and for his detailed comments on earlier drafts of this book.

I also owe a special thank you to a good friend, Mel Cappe, high commissioner for Canada in London, for hosting a luncheon attended by leading British academics, journalists, and staff of the House of Commons, which enabled me to test some of my findings and conclusions. Mel Cappe also provided invaluable insights into the workings of the machinery of government in a subsequent discussion, which helped me enormously in revising the manuscript.

I also want to state with more than the usual emphasis that without the co-operation of cabinet ministers and senior public servants, both current and former, and several members of the House of Commons, this book would not have been possible. They all made time available to endure my questions, and all were generous with their recollections and insights. Many went further and, as the reader will see, offered me documents to review and draw material from for the purpose of this endeavour. No student of government could have been better served. I would also not wish to suggest that they necessarily agreed with the findings presented here. All the defects of the book are mine.

I started writing this text at Nuffield College, Oxford, in November 2000 and finished it while I was again visiting Nuffield in November 2002. The college library staff was very helpful on both occasions. I spent the academic year 2001–02 at Harvard and at Duke as a senior Fulbright scholar, which enabled me to concentrate all my time and energy on this project. I want to thank the Fulbright Foundation for its support.

Ginette Benoit typed this book with willingness and dispatch; I am most grateful to her for her help. Joan Harcourt read and reread the manuscript and made numerous improvements. I also want to express special thanks to the staff at the University of Toronto Press – particularly to Virgil Duff.

As always, my family accepted with good cheer my decision to write another book, knowing full well that it would consume much of my energy and interest for a few years. For this reason, my sincere thanks go to Linda, Julien, and Margaux for their continued understanding, support, and, above all, patience.

BREAKING THE BARGAIN:
PUBLIC SERVANTS, MINISTERS, AND PARLIAMENT

1

Introduction

The Bargain Then and Now

This book explores the territory between elected and permanent government officials – a kind of no man's land. To be sure, this territory has been visited before, but it remains disputed terrain, not least because the role of bureaucracy within democracy has never been properly defined.[1] It is expected to be both independent and subordinate to elected officials and, as well, politically sensitive but not politicized. Thus the territory is fraught with uncertainty, if not pitfalls.

The Traditional Bargain

On the face of it, the theory on bureaucracy and democracy is quite straightforward: the civil service in a parliamentary system based on the Westminster model has no constitutional personality or responsibility distinct from the government of the day.[2] It is ministers, not permanent government officials, who have the final say, because ultimately they are the people accountable to Parliament and the public. The minister is responsible for everything done in the department, and everything done in the department may be the object of parliamentary scrutiny.[3] One can hardly overstate the importance of the doctrine of ministerial responsibility to Canada's systems of government, both federal and provincial. The Privy Council Office declared as recently as 1993 that the doctrine constituted 'the cement of our system of government.'[4] Former Prime Minister Joe Clark, a widely respected parliamentarian for the past thirty-five years, stated in 1977, when he was leader of the opposition, that 'if we destroy the principle of ministerial responsibility, we destroy the system of government which we have in this country.'[5]

At the same time, many politicians, civil servants, and students of government, in Canada no less than in the United States, still somehow cling to Woodrow Wilson's call, made 115 years ago, for an apolitical public administration built on the premise that politics and administration could and should be separated. Wilson maintained that politicians should establish policies and that administrators should run government programs. He went on to argue that the 'administration lies outside the proper sphere of politics. Administrative questions are not political questions. Although politics sets the tasks for administration, it should not be suffered to manipulate its offices.'[6] The dichotomy was important, he felt, not simply for establishing efficient administration but also for strengthening democracy itself. To separate the two realms would constitute a powerful counterweight to 'centrifugal' democracy, since it would create an apolitical public service. More to the point, it would set up a distinct space in which career officials could function.

Bureaucracy, possibly more than any other public institution, has had little in the way of clear guidance to shape its development, at least in Anglo-American democracies. Whether by design or not, the architects of political order and national constitutions have paid little attention to the administrative side of government. In Britain and, by ricochet, in Canada, the matter was resolved by declaring that the civil service had no constitutional personality. Thus the relationship between politicians and career civil servants relies on practice and tradition, not on rules. Practice and tradition suggest that career officials propose, ministers dispose, and career officials execute. But this axiom no longer rings as true as it may have forty years ago. To many observers, modern government, with its overcrowded policy agenda and complex policy issues, has considerably weakened ministers' ability to dispose of matters with a full knowledge of the facts and the alternatives.[7]

But even countries with a long history of written constitutions have neglected the role of bureaucracy. In the case of the United States, for example, James Q. Wilson writes that 'the founding fathers had little to say about the nature or function of the executive branch of the new government. The constitution is virtually silent on the subject and the debates in its constitutional convention are almost devoid of reference to our administrative apparatus.'[8] Canada's consolidation of its Constitutional Acts is no less silent on the role of bureaucracy. 'The Executive Government and Authority of and over Canada is ... vested in the

Queen ... [and] ... there should be a Council to aid and advise in the Government of Canada, to be styled the Queen's Privy Council for Canada; and the persons who are to be members of that Council shall be from time to time chosen and summoned by the Governor General and sworn in as Privy Councillors, and members thereof may from time to time be removed by the Governor General.' It says little else on the matter and nothing at all to guide the work of ministers with their permanent officials. Even the Constitution Act of 1982 remains silent on bureaucracy and its role and responsibilities. Thus, much as in Britain, the role of bureaucracy in Canada is to be sorted out somehow by having ministers be responsible to Parliament for the policies and activities of their respective departments and career officials responsible for administration. The fathers of Confederation thought that they had settled the matter once and for all when they wrote in the British North America Act that Canada should have 'a government similar in principle to that of the United Kingdom.' In brief, they wrote the constitution according to the British notion of responsible parliamentary government and grafted to it a federal structure based on the American model.

One can assume that the architects of the political order believed that democratic control would be exerted through a line running from ministers to all those who would exercise power in the name of the government. The lines of accountability would thus be clear: they would run from official, to minister, to cabinet, to Parliament, to voters. One can also only assume that, if for some reason the lines of accountability were ever to break down, Canada would, in the British tradition, somehow muddle through and sort things out if and when it became necessary. The belief underpinning this view is that if one establishes a process to hold ministers accountable, then the substance will take care of itself. That is, the focus of accountability is on processes and mechanisms rather than on the substance, and if everyone respected process then there would be no reason for accountability to break down.

In the absence of formal rules, politicians and public servants some time ago struck a 'bargain,' or an understanding, over their respective duties to guide mutual relations. This traditional bargain has over the years helped shape how power is distributed and controlled in modern society. Under the arrangement, public servants exchanged overt partisanship, some political rights, and a public profile in return for permanent careers, or at least indefinite tenure, anonymity, selection by merit, a regular work week, and the promise of being looked after at the end of a career that did not require paying close attention to their own material self-interest. Politicians meanwhile exchanged the ability to appoint or dismiss public servants and change their working conditions at will for professional competence and non-partisan obedience to the government of the day.[9] The traditional bargain in a parliamentary system based on the Westminster model casts career officials as political eunuchs. This stands in contrast to the Basic Law of 1949 in West Germany, which called on public servants to be loyal to the constitution rather than to the government of the day.

Still, the traditional bargain under the Westminster model has a valuable component. A permanent career and anonymity enable career officials to provide fearless advice to their political masters – to speak truth to power. This function, according to a widely circulated task-force report on 'Values and Ethics in the Public Service' produced by senior federal officials in 1996, 'may involve telling ministers, in confidence, things they do not necessarily wish to hear.'[10] It also means that career officials must always give *l'heure juste* to their ministers and provide their best professional judgment and advice. Thus the architects of the political order sought to establish distinct spaces for politicians and bureaucrats. Ministers would decide policy; career officials would provide fearless advice on policy matters but then implement whatever policy decision ministers would make and administer programs in an apolitical manner.

The notion of distinct spaces (roles, spheres, or areas of jurisdiction) permeates Canada's national political and administrative institutions and defines the relationship between politicians and career officials and how government departments operate. Canada has, for example, a constitution that spells out in fairly detailed terms which level of government is responsible for what. Early students of federalism, including the authors of the Federalist Papers, stressed the importance of space in establishing a federal system. K.C. Wheare provided a working definition of federalism in 1963: 'by the federal principle, I mean the methods of dividing powers so that the general and regional governments are each, within a sphere, co-ordinate and independent.'[11] The same can be said within a national government. Parliament plays a distinct role, and occupies a different space from cabinet. In turn, cabinet has its own distinct role, and so have individual ministers within their departments. The same is true again about government departments, which hold responsibility for a given sector, and so it goes down the line, with every career official occupying a specific office with specific policy or program responsibility and having a specific job description. This is expected to work on the basis of a traditional bargain that has never been written down.

Politicians and public servants have been largely left on their own to define or update the bargain. Political theorists have paid little attention to the issue. C.B. Macpherson's widely read Massey Lectures, *The Real World of Democracy*, for instance, scarcely touch on bureaucracy. This is even the case with his lecture on 'Liberal-Democracy as a System of Power.'[12] In brief, theorists appear to assume that the role of bureaucracy is to be the neutral implementer of legislative policy. Robert Dahl, for example, argues that one of several conditions for democracy is that 'the orders of elected officials are executed.' He does not, however, elaborate on how this condition can be met, other than to observe that 'the extent to which this condition is achieved is perhaps the most puzzling of all to measure objectively.'[13]

Problems with the Bargain

Recent Canadian studies of democracy have dealt with referenda, the Charter of Rights, freedom of the press, and political participation – but, again, not with bureaucracy.[14] It appears that political scientists, in Canada, as elsewhere, regard bureaucracy as just one centre of power or influence and believe that there is no compelling reason to single it out for special consideration.

It is now becoming clear, however, that things are not well on this front and that muddling through has become extremely difficult, if not impossible. If nothing else, the plethora of reform measures introduced during the past thirty years or so indicates that government at some point became too bureaucratic, too hierarchical, too remote, or perhaps too 'something' without having a proper sense of what that something was. Some politicians believe that 'bureaucrats' have come to dominate the policy-making process without being accountable for their actions.[15] Indeed, by the 1970s many politicians and their advisers claimed that permanent public servants were running governments and that their apparent deference to politicians was pure pretence. In addition, it appears that the theory on bureaucracy and democracy is being rejected by the very people who were designed to benefit the most from it – ministers. Sharon Sutherland writes that 'the evidence is found in the number of cases in which ministers have passed the blame to public officials unnecessarily, and in various ways the system is being forced to run at cross purposes with itself.'[16] In brief, the traditional bargain between politicians and public servants is coming unglued, and the space that was once established to determine who is responsible for what is no longer clear. This is true virtually everywhere in Canada's federal machinery of government, and the implications are far-reaching.

For one thing, it became obvious by the 1980s that confidence in government was in decline. Canadians told public-opinion surveys throughout the decade that 'they had less confidence in the public service than in any other institution, save for the trade union movement, politicians and more recently the tobacco industry.'[17] A federal government–commissioned research report based on extensive opinion surveys rang the alarm bell in 1995. It revealed that 'general attitudes to government have deteriorated. Most Canadians are cynical and hostile to government. There is a widespread belief that governments are self-serving, inefficient and ineffectual.' It added that it was important to distinguish between popularity and legitimacy. It explained that the government of the day was 'clearly quite popular [but] popularity is, however, more ephemeral and elastic than legitimacy ... There is ... a long road back to re-establish trust in government.'[18] In their review of the Charlottetown Accord referendum of 1992, four leading political scientists claim that in 'consolidated democracies' such as Canada 'party and parliamentary institutions seem under siege ... for frustrating popular will and bottling up the very urge to democracy.'[19] Bluntly put, the problem is this: the executive is perceived to be dominating Parliament, and the civil service is believed to be dominating the executive.

Leaders of the Canadian civil service have also acknowledged that government institutions still confront problems of legitimacy, even after far-reaching cuts in spending and operations. Jocelyne Bourgon, former clerk of the Privy Council and secretary to the cabinet, observed in 1999: 'There is no doubt that democratic institutions have fallen into some degree of disrepute; some 32 percent of Canadians do not believe that government is a positive force in their lives. Voter participation in the 1997 election was at the lowest level since 1925.'[20] Little did she know then that the turnout in 2000 would be even lower. Two MPs from the governing Liberal Party voiced deep concern over the 5 per cent drop in turnout for the general election in 2000: 'The drop confirms years' worth of academic admonitions, politicians' anecdotes and pollsters' findings, all warning that Canadians are disengaging from the political process ... a consensus has emerged that the time to reinvigorate Canadian democracy is now.'[21] There are many problems that need to be addressed – not least, the notion that governments have become so big that they defy effective co-ordination, grow undirected, display little accountability, and permit only marginal public influence on decision making.[22]

Governments, including the Canadian government, have not sat idly by while public confidence in them has waned. Ottawa has introduced a host of reform measures to modernize government operations, particularly since the early 1980s. However, it has sought, by and large, only to fix the boiler room of government. That is, it overhauled operations and delivery of services in the belief that this was where the problem lay. It is revealing to note that the country's political institutions, at least when compared to the civil service, have been left pretty well intact. The movement to 'reinvent government,' which has enjoyed considerable popularity in recent years, has been restricted to reinventing bureaucracy, not political institutions. Of course, the reforms did affect the relationship between elected and permanent government officials. Without putting too fine a point on it, they sought to recast civil servants as entrepreneurs and citizens as clients, but they did not reinvent politicians. It takes only a moment's reflection to appreciate that the strategy, if successfully implemented, would have altered the territory between politicians and permanent officials.

To be sure, there was a fairly widely held consensus in political circles evident as early as the late 1970s and early 1980s that bureaucracy was part of the problem in society, no longer part of the solution, and that it was at least partly responsible for the problems of legitimacy confronting governments. Bashing bureaucracy came into fashion throughout the Western world, and Canada was certainly no exception. The civil service stood accused of many things: it was bloated, cumbersome, uncreative, lethargic, and insensitive. One observer wrote: 'among the more affluent and better educated, one of the few things that unites the left and the right is their common disdain for bureaucrats.'[23] Aaron Wildavsky, a leading student of public administration in the twentieth century, concluded that bureaucracy was now only for the brave.[24] As for reforming government operations, politicians and senior civil servants would set the agenda, and they too left no doubt as to where they believed the problem lay.

In some instances, the 'generals' in Canada and elsewhere actually began to shoot on their troops. Conservative Prime Minister Brian Mulroney spoke about giving 'pink slips and running shoes' to bureaucrats.[25] Paul Tellier, Canada's top public servant for most of the Mulroney years and himself the architect of significant reforms, voiced some harsh criticism of the federal civil service in 1992, shortly after he left government. He revealed, among other things, that while in government he spent too much time answering 'irrelevant questions from individuals who were just trying to justify their existence inside the bureaucracy.'[26] In the United States, President Ronald Reagan declared that he had come to Washington 'to drain the swamp,' while it is said that Margaret Thatcher 'detested senior civil servants as a breed.'[27]

It also appears that the doctrine of ministerial responsibility has been tossed aside when convenient. Civil servants have learned the hard way that their ministers will not necessarily protect them in times of crisis or when they find themselves embroiled in controversy. For instance, when it became public knowledge in the early 1990s that Mohammed Al-Mashat – Iraq's ambassador to the United States – had been admitted to Canada as a landed immigrant, minister after minister declared regret. Significantly, the government claimed that officials had handled the process from start to finish. The fact that 'ministers are ... responsible for decisions taken in the departments of government'[28] was not raised as an issue, at least by ministers of the day.

In this instance, ministers showed no remorse in pointing the finger at officials. Some must have concluded that the doctrine of ministerial responsibility simply stood in the way of holding accountable those responsible for the decision. What is wrong, they seemed to ask, in opening up the process and establishing exactly what happened, how it happened, and who made it happen?[29] If ministers were not 'responsible,' then permanent officials were. Ministers perhaps felt that the doctrine of ministerial responsibility served only in this case to inhibit 'accountability' and attempts to sort out who was 'responsible.' Clearly, ministers decided to redraw the lines of accountability. The Al-Mashat case revealed that they no longer accepted fully the doctrine of their own responsibility. In fact, Joe Clark, who sang the doctrine's praises in 1977, hummed quite a different tune fifteen years later: 'A minister cannot be held responsible for matters that concern him if he was not informed.'[30]

What about Wilson's doctrine of an apolitical public service? Scholars have long challenged the division between politics and administration. For example, Paul Appleby argued back in 1949 that 'public administration is policy making' and that 'administrators are continually laying down rules for the future, and administrators are continually determining what the law is, what it means in terms of action.'[31] Luther Gulick wrote: 'every act of public servants is a seamless web of discretion and action,' and 'discretion can be found at all levels of the organization.' He added that the 'degree of discretion is more pronounced in badly organized and poorly directed administrative units.'[32] Even Woodrow

Wilson in time repudiated his division of realms. It seems that it was based on a misreading of German sources and that he never meant to argue for a complete separation.[33] But a myth was born, and the civil service found it salutary.[34] It removed public administration somewhat from partisan politics and even from politicians. For example, Canada's Civil Service Commission (CSC), which sought to place appointments to the civil service outside the hands of politicians, came into being some twenty years after Woodrow Wilson published his paper. Thus the establishment of the CSC and the merit principle created in law a space belonging exclusively to career officials.

In addition, although the much-maligned distinction between politics and administration has never fitted well in Canada's system of government, it survives, *faute de mieux.* The essential feature of the Canadian system is the clear division between politicians and civil servants on the one hand and the close relationship between policy and administration on the other. Moreover, Canadian politicians continue, publicly at least, to embrace the political–administrative dichotomy and hence the need for politicians and career officials to occupy distinct spaces. This explains, at least in part, why Ottawa has introduced management reforms in recent years. Indeed, much of the new public management (NPM) movement, which has enjoyed high visibility in Canada, as elsewhere, since the early 1980s, is built around this belief and the notion that private-sector management practices are superior to those found in government. 'Steering,' in David Osborne and Ted Gaebler's world, is a matter that belongs properly to the politicians, while 'rowing' belongs to the civil servants.[35] In any event, Canadian prime ministers from Pierre Trudeau to Jean Chrétien have consistently declared their intention to govern and to establish policy, but to let the managers manage.[36] The establishment of special operating agencies (SOAs) and the new food-inspection and revenue agencies are obvious attempts to separate the two functions. Every management reform introduced by the Canadian government since the late 1960s has been built around the theme of 'letting the managers manage.'

The relationship between civil servants and politicians is of course central to the process of governing. Each partner represents an essential component of governing in a democratic regime. The political component represents democratic legitimacy and the dynamic element of policy change. Politicians may be hazy about the procedures required for getting things done in the public sector, but they generally know, or ought to know, what they want the policy outcomes to be. The civil servants, in contrast, represent stability and expertise. Democratic ideologies place a premium on stability, and democracies invariably turn to rules and processes to achieve it.[37] Civil servants, even in governments that recruit them for general ability, rather than for their expertise in a particular policy area, gain expertise through experience. In time, they become well able to advise ministers about how to achieve their policy goals.

But there are problems on this front as well. Politicians may applaud NPM in their speeches, but their actions often suggest something else. There is evidence in Canada and elsewhere that politicians have sought to redefine the space belonging to career officials in order to check their influence. One of the earliest students of public administration, Max Weber, wrote that 'under normal conditions, the position of a fully developed bureaucracy is always overpowering. The political master finds himself in the position of the dilettante, who stands opposite the expert, facing the trained official.'[38] As formulating public policy and making government decisions became more complex, political masters, one can only assume, became more dependent on the advice of expert or career public servants. As they became more dependent on public servants, they probably became suspicious of their growing influence. Some politicians began in effect to look at the permanent public service as a kind of entrenched aristocracy within a democracy. This attitude in turn explains why politicians have of late sought, through various means, to strengthen their own hand in shaping government policy and decisions. It is now clear that public servants no longer monopolize the policy advisory function as they once did. They face competition from several quarters. In a number of instances, the political staff has been expanded. There are also a growing number of partisan strategists *cum* policy advisers operating on the periphery of the government structure. Party pollsters are also advising political parties, including those in power, on policy. There is a growing array of research institutes, or think tanks, always at the ready with policy advice. Some former senior public servants have written about the increasing importance of the 'political arm of government' that has been put in place to counter the 'bureaucratic arm.'[39]

In any event, NPM also seeks to weaken the bureaucratic arm. It is rooted in the public-choice literature, which argues that bureaucracies are inefficient at least in part because sponsors and hence clients have so little influence in shaping policy and programs or in deciding whether they should be continued or scrapped. A central feature of the movement is its strong emphasis on empowering 'customers,' 'consumers,' and 'clients.' Proponents believe that this will lead to a new public-service culture and break down the formal systems of control that lead civil servants to overly cautious behaviour and maintenance of the status quo. Customers, unlike citizens, will force bureaucrats to deal directly with their complaints and shed new light on the weak points of government policy. Bureaucrats will also have to deal with the public's views about what they ought to do.

Turning citizens into customers changes governance and the relationship between politicians and civil servants. Quite apart from the resulting debate over the possible loss of equity in the provision of public goods, the bringing together of 'empowered' front-line government employees and 'empowered' customers will also embolden people at the bottom of the organization and on the front line.[40] Carried to its logical conclusion, it should mean privatization of some state functions, provision of some public goods and services in a commercial fashion (for instance, make or buy) and a commitment to give citizens (read: 'customers') greater choice in public services (through vouchers). More important, perhaps, it signals yet one more attempt to separate administration from policy. Smaller government would enable politicians to understand the machinery of government and the policy process more quickly. Separating policy from administration would also enable them to focus their energy and their limited time on broad policy issues and away from administrative matters and details. Politicians might regain the upper hand in shaping policy and promoting change. Finally, turning citizens into customers means that career officials must now share with the general public a space that they once occupied with limited interference in administering government programs.

NPM's goal is to break down formal systems of control and instil a new 'bias for action' in government bureaucracies. Empowering front-line employees also ensures a leaner, more frugal government, since it moves towards more simple organization, with departments and agencies concentrating on 'their core business' or on their programs. The goal is nothing short of changing the culture of the civil service and the attitude of its mandarins and making it exceedingly difficult for the Sir Humphreys of this world to continue to exercise undue influence.

How Do We Govern Now?

It appears that public servants will in future have to use what powers they have in a somewhat different manner. Both within government and between government and the civil service the hierarchy of the past simply does not appear to be acceptable. This may well call for a new relationship. More specifically, the spaces once occupied by politicians and career officials are being redefined.

In any event, the reader may well have already concluded that existing theories on the relationship between politicians and permanent officials are now hopelessly dated. If our current system works, it is only because both groups somehow make it do so. But notwithstanding their good will, there are all too many visible cracks in the system. The Al-Mashat case is but one of many suggesting a basic flaw. Still, in contrast to that case, the HRDC scandal that dominated the media for the better part of the year 2000 revealed that some ministers are still prepared to play by the rules of ministerial responsibility. Jane Stewart, in charge of the department when the scandal broke, accepted ministerial responsibility and never once 'tried to slough off any blame on the real culprits – her predecessor, Pierre Pettigrew, who was the minister when the problems developed, and senior bureaucrats such as Mel Cappe who was the deputy minister and responsible for administrative matters.'[41] One could have pointed further back to Doug Young, who was minister when the Canada Jobs Fund, the program under review, was conceived and introduced. It was Young who insisted that MPs be consulted in the decision-making process – something that Woodrow Wilson would not have approved. But, despite her decision to play by the rules, Stewart was subjected to 'a year from hell,' and many observers insisted that we had witnessed a breakdown in accountability.[42] She was a victim partly because 'democratic rules are ill-defined, ambiguous, self-contradictory and controversial' on the role of bureaucracy.[43] Jean Chrétien had declared during the 1993 election campaign that his ministers, unlike Mulroney's would accept full responsibility for things done in their departments. But he changed his tune in 2002, if not earlier, when his government and some of his ministers were accused of mismanaging public funds and government contracts. He stated boldly, 'The cheques are not signed by the ministers. The verifications are not signed by the ministers. It's signed by the bureaucracy.'[44]

What should be done with the established doctrine and principles that guide relations between politicians and permanent officials? The purpose of this book is to answer that question. More specifically, it explores what are arguably the most important theoretical questions in public administration today: who should decide, how should these decisions be justified, and how should decision makers be held to account?

The underlying assumption is that we need to reconsider the relationship between politicians and career civil servants. First, perhaps because it relies on practice rather than on rules, political scientists have paid scant attention to it. The literature offers a multitude of studies on all facets of new public management but virtually ignores how politicians and career officials should now work together. In addition, politicians have shown little interest in the workings of the public service other than, from time to time, criticizing bureaucracy. Second, government works today in a manner fundamentally different from when current practice took shape. Indeed, virtually every aspect of governance has changed dramatically since ministerial responsibility and the traditional bargain between ministers and bureaucrats emerged. The media, 'e-government,' globalization, the size of government, the complexity and overlapping of public-policy issues, among other things, have changed how government decides. The clerk of the Privy Council and secretary to the cabinet wrote in 2001, in his annual report to the prime minister on the state of the public service of Canada: 'We are moving away from a traditional model of public service based on hierarchical, directive management.'[45] The notion of space that had guided the work of government departments since before Confederation seems obsolete. Although it is not yet clear precisely how the new model will work, one can assume that it will or should alter the relationship. Thus understanding the relationship is useful, whether or not changes are in order.

Political and administrative institutions reflect what E.E. Schattschneider calls 'organization of bias.'[46] The bias in Canada's machinery of government has been to establish what we might now call distinct spaces for ministers and public servants somehow meshing their fields together at the top in a 'no man's land.' Has practice in recent years, albeit by stealth, moved towards a new model that does not recognize boundaries or space? Mel Cappe envisaged a world of 'public servants without borders' and looked forward to the day when he could go to the lobby of the National Arts Centre and verify his income tax calculations with Revenue Canada, renew his driver's licence and forward an e-mail to a local politician all on a single portal.[47] This new world transforms how government organizes its activities and how Canadians can hold policy makers accountable. Career officials must also adapt if the borders melt away and 'no man's land' moves down further in the bureaucracy and even out to non-governmental actors.

This book will also test several hypotheses:

- The notion of space that seemingly underpins how the House of Commons, politicians, and the public service go about their work and how accountability is apportioned is giving way to a new approach to governing.
- Although government, ministers, and public servants were never completely separate, it was considerably easier forty years ago to delineate policy and management tasks, particularly inside but also outside government.
- Ministers and public servants used to operate under a traditional bargain that gave the public service more opportunity to focus on the long-term interests of the country, however broadly defined, and to challenge the views of ministers in confidence. Civil servants now tend more to anticipate the wishes of the prime minister and of strong ministers and to protect their political interests.
- Political and policy actors have lost the sense of the traditional space that they are expected to occupy. MPs no longer call the government to account; ministers are not making policy; the prime minister, the Prime Minister's Office, the Privy Council Office, and a handful of senior ministers now fill more functions than they should; and the public service is increasingly uncertain about its role in policy and management.
- The traditional bargain between politicians and career civil servants now operates under severe stress and strain.
- While the bargain still applies, both sides have reverted to cheating to work around it.
- Governments indiscriminately added functions, tasks, and accountability requirements to the machinery of government without rewriting the traditional bargain.
- Governments now tend to concentrate some policy and decision-making authority with a few key officials, who carry an unmanageable burden, but they also defuse authority on other issues to the point that accountability evaporates.

Outline of Study

Part I (chapters 2–4) offers a historical perspective. Its purpose is to provide the background for what follows, because both students and practitioners of Canadian politics and public administration have lost sight of the origins of these institutions. We know that the architects of Canada's machinery of government looked to Britain and, to a much lesser extent, to the United States. One of their central purposes was to create a non-partisan civil service and to distinguish it from the political arena. In this sense, they created two distinct realms – political and administrative. Chapter 2 reports on how this system took form in Britain and Canada, including the departmental structure and the position of deputy minister.

We then explore in chapter 3 how the traditional bargain between ministers and career officials took shape. The bargain calls on public servants to provide the government of the day non-partisanship, loyalty, impartiality, discretion, and professionalism, in return for anonymity and security of tenure. Hierarchy is a crucial part of ministerial responsibility and the traditional bargain. It enables ministers to reach, if necessary, into the hierarchical bureaucracy and secure an explanation for why things have gone wrong. The doctrine of ministerial responsibility underpins the traditional bargain, although Canadian policy makers have stood by it more religiously than have their British counterparts.

There was a golden age in the mid-decades of the twentieth century when the Canadian civil service was held in high esteem and its work was valued, by both politicians and the public. Chapter 4 reports on this era and describes the village-like atmosphere in which it flourished. Ministers knew that they were in charge and welcomed the advice of senior career officials. Both sides occupied distinct spaces. Deputy ministers knew their departments well and, with their associates, prepared policy proposals for their ministers. Ministers decided what was politically saleable and what was not. They would take departmental proposals to the cabinet table and discuss them with their colleagues. Government was small, and everything of any consequence was brought to the attention of deputy ministers and ministers. Trust in government's ability to act appropriately was high, and there were precious few voices calling for access-to-information legislation.

Somewhere along the line, governments and their civil services came under heavy criticism. Governments grew substantially, and policy- and decision-making processes became far more complex. Politicians began to direct criticism at public servants. A new breed of politicians, who believed that non-elected officials had become too powerful in shaping policy, began to take charge. The traditional bargain was set to be transformed. Not only were career officials believed to have too much power, but royal commissions and task forces argued that they were largely deficient in their management skills.

Part II (chapters 5–7) examines the extended crisis of the 1980s and 1990s. Chapter 5 shows how policy makers diagnosed the patient. To be sure, the voices heard towards the end of the twentieth century suggested that there was plenty wrong with government, and there appeared to be no shortage of things to fix. Political parties were losing members, and surveys revealed that most Canadians held federal politicians of all stripes in low regard, viewed government programs as wasteful, and saw bureaucracy as inefficient. Societal changes also had a major impact. The collapse of deference, the emergence of new media and the growing belief that one person's opinion was as good as the next affected the bureaucratic elite.

Politicians pointed to bureaucracy as the central problem. In Canada, as in other Anglo-American democracies, governments set out to make public servants more responsive to their policy directions. The relationship between ministers and senior career officials changed. Deputy ministers were no longer drawn from departments in which they had spent their careers. Central agencies, such as the Department of Finance, the Prime Minister's Office, the Privy Council Office, the Public Service Commission, and the Treasury Board, deal with all policy areas and oversee the 'line' departments, and so experience in a central agency, notably in the Privy Council Office, has become a virtual prerequisite for deputy-level appointments. Accordingly, deputy ministers today are much less familiar with the department that they lead than was the case some forty years ago. At the same time, a new management vocabulary began to emerge. The business model and related themes such as 'empowerment' came to dominate government operations by the 1980s. Senior officials would no longer be administrators, principal officers, senior finance or personnel officers, or assistant directors. They would henceforth be managers, and citizens, clients. The change in vocabulary was a signal that career officials had their own management space, where centrally prescribed financial and administrative rules and regulations would give way to business practices and more flexible organizational structures.

Chapter 6 reports on a new policy-making model that forces career officials to look outside their departments when shaping new measures. The policy process is now porous and embraces many actors. The ability to arrive at a stable consensus, to secure understanding from the relevant sectors of the public over proposal actions, requires a 'horizontal perspective' that is as important as the substance of the policy itself.

There is now a veritable army of policy consultants, research institutes, think tanks, and lobbyists that has moved into the world of policy advisory once occupied by career officials. It has transformed policy making in Canada. 'E-government' has also further 'opened up' the process. New information systems are 'horizontal' by design and capable of penetrating all sorts of 'boundaries' in government. The machinery of government was also reformed to include partisan policy advisers to work in ministerial offices to counterbalance the influence of public servants.

The desire of politicians to create a new management space for public servants based on the business model was destined to run headlong into problems, and chapter 7 reports why. The department's senior manager – the deputy minister – is asked to wear many hats. Deputy ministers now have to spend the bulk of their time on 'horizontal' policy and management issues. In addition, while politicians may during election campaigns stress the need for better management, once in office they become preoccupied with political and policy issues, and management invariably takes a back seat.

Successful deputy ministers today have developed a capacity to detect and manage emerging political crises. In addition, the nature of their work has changed, and their role as 'negotiators' and 'networkers' dominates their agenda. In brief, their perspective is now more horizontal than 'vertical.' As well, many outside actors now have access to the management space in government. The media, through access-to-information legislation, have a ring-side seat to management decisions and measures. Several parliamentary agents not only have a *droit de regard* but have also become legitimate observers, if not actors, in management. It is virtually impossible for the business-management model to operate in this environment. This becomes even more evident when one compares performance and accountability criteria for senior managers in the public and the private sectors.

Part III (chapters 8–10) considers where we go from here. Chapter 8 looks at the role of members of Parliament – at how they get elected, their interests or preoccupations in office, and their status and role in the new system of governance. Canadian MPs, more than their counterparts in other Westminster-type systems, see their role as working on behalf of their constituencies. To do this, however, they must move in on program administration and hence on career officials.

Legislation is increasingly drafted in broad and enabling terms designed to provide maximum flexibility in the implementation stages. But flexibility comes at a cost. Legislation no longer clearly lays down the parameters within which public servants must operate. But other changes, notably in the tabling of spending estimates, have redefined the relationship between Parliament and program administration and also enlarged the program space occupied by career officials. MPs need the capacity to function effectively in this new scheme of things.

Chapter 9 asks whether Canada can turn back the clock to the days when the traditional bargain flourished. It explores the forces that have redefined the making of public policies and the delivery of government programs and services. The impact is being felt virtually everywhere in government – from the establishment of new agencies and arm's-length foundations to the application of the merit principle in staffing senior executive positions.

Chapter 10 explores potential reform of political institutions to accommodate a 'porous' and consultative policy-making process. The challenge for Parliament is to modernize its instruments to hold accountable a government that increasingly operates without space. How can we enable governments and their officials to define their work and responsibilities in such a way that we can hold them accountable?

Information for this study comes from a number of sources, including published and unpublished government documents. Several senior government officials made available information and material that helped me enormously in preparing questions for the interviews and in completing my research.

As part of the research for this book, I interviewed forty-five present and former government officials, including cabinet ministers, members of Parliament, deputy ministers, heads of crown corporations, and middle- and lower-level government administrators. I conducted off-the-record interviews to elicit candid comments. I did not draw representative samples, which would have been impractical for the study. The interviews were largely unstructured, and I tailored many to the position of the respective respondent. Accordingly, except for one question that I put to all deputy ministers, I did not pose a series of common questions to interviewees.

PART ONE

Foundations

2

Creating a Non-partisan Civil Service

When Lord Durham visited the British North American colonies in the late 1830s to review the political impasse between Upper and Lower Canada, he witnessed at first hand the sorry state of the civil services of the two Canadas, and he did not mince words in passing judgment on their capacity. He discovered 'a most disheartening scene of administrative incompetence.'[1] He in fact discovered two civil services that neither were civil nor constituted much of a service, and permanence would become a central feature of the civil service only in the next century.[2] At the time of his visit the two civil services were not actually civil because there was little to distinguish them from the political arena. Indeed, Canada wove together the political and the administrative worlds into a seamless web, which predetermined their relationship. Elected and non-elected officials occupied the same space. They were not much of a service: there was no body of full-time salaried people, and basic functions of government were left either unattended or in the hands of unpaid amateurs. Even the crucial administration of justice was in urgent need of repair.

Durham could just as easily have argued that there was simply no administration, competent or otherwise. The executive lacked control over the use of funds for public works and ad hoc commissions were put in place to deal with individual projects. There were also few administrative rules and regulations that applied across government. One contemporary observer wrote: 'There was a scene of confusion and riot of which no one in England can have any idea. Every man proposes a vote for his own job; and bills are introduced without notice, and carried through all their stages in a quarter of an hour.'[3] Corruption was widespread, and chaos ruled. The situation cried out for action. The reforms introduced by Durham and his contemporaries were far-reaching, and they are still being felt today.

This chapter looks at the forces and events that have shaped the Canadian civil service. In his *Pioneer Public Service* (1955), J.E. Hodgetts designated the period 1841–67 as the 'formative years,' arguing that few students appreciate the extent to which decisions, both by ministers and by officials, determined many present practices. He added, 'The intricate give and take between the political non-technical minister and the technically trained specialist ... [has] been the constant concern of the administrator: a different time, a different place has simply shifted the emphasis a little one way or the other.'[4]

Decisions taken during the formative years were important. But the struggle for responsible government and for domestic control of administrative matters was not the only force shaping the Canadian civil service. There were others, some peculiar to Canada. For example, developments in Britain very often directly affected Canada's civil service. Together, these forces provided the basic elements of Canada's political and administrative institutions – departments and deputy ministers, the cabinet system, and anonymous civil servants – all explored in this chapter. In short, they guided development of the traditional bargain explored below in chapter 3. They also gave rise to a civil service that could boast an impressive list of accomplishments in the last century both at home and abroad, perhaps most notably in its 'global era' (chapter 4).

Departments and Deputy Ministers

Lord Durham, Hodgetts tells us, found no one in government or anywhere else capable of assuming responsibility to deliver government services. Rather, a hostile legislature insisted on overstepping the proper limits of parliamentary interference in order to show the executive that it was quite independent.[5] 'At the top of the hierarchy Durham could discover no real heads of departments who were capable of assuming both individually and collectively responsibility for administrative services. A Governor owing responsibility to the Colonial Secretary, an atomized Executive Council tendering discordant secret advice to the Governor who need pay no attention if he so desired; a Legislature swinging rudderless in the full tide of its own passion tied to the unstable mooring of the colonial electorate; uncivil and unfruitful squabbles between Governors and Assemblies, resulting often in hopeless deadlock; and, finally, a group of poorly informed Whitehall departments, with snail-like pace passing references on colonial matters back and forth, issuing detailed instructions, sometimes over the head of the Governor, to officials of their own choice who were responsible for administering local services.'[6] If nothing else, it was apparent that reformers needed to start from scratch and essentially build a system of governance. Indeed, it would have been impossible to strengthen the executive without taking into account the role of the legislative branch. Responsible government would require a new system of governance that would outline who was responsible for what.

Durham himself had insisted on a number of initiatives, and the British colonial secretary, Lord John Russell, laid down three basic 'rules of administration' as a pre-condition for responsible government.[7] First, 'the executive should be charged with the administration of the Public Revenue and ... the Representative Assembly should check and control abuse, profusion, or misapplication.' Second, 'every office should be so constituted that all proceedings carried on in it should be a matter of daily record and proceedings should, when requested, be laid before the Assembly.'[8] Third, the functions of departmental heads should be clearly laid out and the incumbents be made directly responsible for the conduct of public business.[9] This was a tall order for the two Canadas in 1840 – and for the other British colonies. The challenge was so great and the agenda so ambitious that the more important question for the reformers was where to start. They would commence where most people setting out to reform the public sector usually begin – with money and with administrative processes in government departments. The reformers embraced the view that the executive should initiate money matters and that unity of command should guide administration in departments.

British influence informed virtually every major development in the rise of the Canadian civil service. Those charged with implementing the findings of the Durham Report and implementing the Act of Union of 1841 looked to the British model for inspiration. There was of course a constant flow of both correspondence and money between the colonies and the Colonial Office in London.

Still, the North American colonies and their bureaucracy had to deal with something that British civil servants did not: geography. They had to come up with ways to provide services over a vast territory. They had no choice but to experiment with decentralization. This is difficult enough in mature governments with well-oiled administrative and financial processes already in place. For the pre-Confederation civil service to decentralize operations while creating a departmental structure was an extraordinary challenge. The fact that they were unable to look to Britain for guidance here did not help matters. As a result, major problems surfaced in regional and local offices. Hodgetts writes that 'it would be a tenable thesis that the history of the developing federal civil service reveals a gradual curtailment of powers delegated to local agents ... and has tended to place a few key officials under an unbearably heavy burden.'[10] The political and administrative difficulties associated with this decentralization gave rise to an institutional memory that, I believe, lingers still.

Quite apart from the problem posed by geography, pioneer civil servants had to establish Canadian control over administrative matters and to develop suitable machinery of government. Again, Durham had views on both matters: Britain should stop asserting a kind of 'absentee control' over trivial local matters, as it caused unrest and administrative inefficiency, and Canada should adopt the British departmental form, with 'responsible' ministerial heads.[11] He argued that it was possible to maintain some degree of colonial dependence in conjunction with promoting local self-government via a clear division of responsibility – a kind of colonial responsible government. However, autonomous local control required machinery of government able to provide services efficiently and to hold people accountable for their decisions.

The building blocks of Canada's public administration and its working relationship with ministers have their roots in the reforms of 1841–67. These too came mostly from British experience. British practices were evident at almost every turn – in parliamentary control of the public purse, in public accounts and the public accounts committee, in the preparation of annual estimates, in the definition of an audit function, and in departmental structure.

Lord Sydenham, the first governor of the new united colony, is credited with introducing cabinet government to Canada. Adam Shortt reports that Sydenham 'initiated his personally selected cabinet into the mysteries of cabinet government, dependent for its life upon retaining the support of the majority of the legislature ... He organized and maintained for the first time in Canada a government party.'[12] As in Britain, new central agencies, as we now call them, were established to co-ordinate government operations, and Canadian officials had the 'British Treasury as [the] model in trying to strengthen the Inspector General's Department.'[13] A Civil Service Act, including provisions for an Examining Board, was enacted in 1857, two years after Britain had passed similar legislation. The list goes on.

The most important legacy, according to Hodgetts, was the departmental framework. There was widespread belief in the early 1840s that responsible government would, without a clear departmental structure, be fraught with danger or impossible. As a result, the government grouped functions within departments, established unity of command, and put in place a hierarchy of responsibilities. The central, twofold purpose was to enable career officials to define their responsibilities and do their job and to enable politicians to hold them accountable.

Canada's Civil Service Act of 1857 was inspired by similar reforms in Britain following the Northcote–Trevelyan report. Northcote and Trevelyan summed up the problem that they wanted to resolve: 'Admission into the Civil Service is eagerly sought after, but it is for the unambitious, and the indolent or incapable that it is highly desired. Those whose abilities do not warrant an expectation that they will succeed in the open professions, where they must encounter the competition of their contemporaries, and those whom indolence of temperament, or physical infirmities make unfit for active exertion, are placed in the Civil Service, where they may obtain an honourable livelihood with little labour, and with no risk.'[14] Their report made four key recommendations: entry into the civil service through open competition and examination; promotion on merit, based on proper assessments prepared by superiors; a distinction between intellectual and mechanical labour; and measures to unify the civil service, including a common basis of recruiting.[15] Canadian reformers emulated the British report but made no attempt to distinguish between intellectual and mechanical labour.

However, both the British and the Canadian acts and resulting civil-service commissions had very little impact at first on recruitment. The commissions never received the power to compel departments to submit candidates for examination, and the tests were non-competitive. As well, Canada's act was conveniently put aside for staffing positions above the most junior, clerk-level positions. As well, success in the basic entrance exam (which did not have rigorous standards) did not guarantee employment. The government would simply pick and choose those to be hired, as earlier, on the basis of partisan politics. In 1857, for example, 688 took the test and 516 passed, but fewer than 10 per cent of the successful applicants were hired. Thomas D'Arcy McGee, a leading politician, in 1863 urged repeal of the Civil Service Act 'in the interest of country and the civil service.'[16]

But the act did have an impact over time. Some sixty years later, a new Civil Service Commission, this one with teeth, was established. This act would separate the political from the administrative world in staffing permanent government positions. In addition, the 1857 act contained a provision peculiar to Canada that was applied to all departments and that still applies. It coined the term 'deputy minister' – a permanent, co-ordinating head in each government department. By contrast, Britain has permanent secretaries, and the United States, under-secretaries, assistant secretaries, or directors. All Canadian departments soon appointed a deputy minister. Thus, along the lines recommended by Woodrow Wilson, the minister would look after politics and broad policy areas, and the deputy, administration.

The term 'deputy minister' is misleading in that it suggests that the permanent head can play a partisan political role and assume complete authority to act in place of the minister. This is not the case. Still, the position has evolved since 1857 and now sits unchallenged at the top of the departmental bureaucracy. Deputy ministers, like permanent secretaries in Britain, are the administrative and permanent heads of departments and do not usually leave when the government changes. Few observers would have predicted in 1857 that the position that the reformers were establishing in statute would come to dominate public administration in Canada. Deputy ministers would forever stand at the gate between things political and things administrative and would in time assume an extremely heavy workload.

But progress on the staffing front was tentative. Staffing remained patronage-ridden for at least fifty years after Confederation, with promotion based on seniority. The merit principle was considered too complicated or controversial. One British official summed up the difference well: 'seniority is a matter of fact, while merit is a matter of opinion.'[17]

A sizeable part of the bureaucracy was expected to provide services that paid for themselves – an approach that appeared again in the 1990s. Some departments were expected to 'make ends meet' and to cover their expenses by charging for their services so that, 'almost until Confederation, many services were maintained by contributions from the interest concerned.' For example, 'the Culler's Office ... supervised the grading of timber and supported by direct levies made upon the timber dealers; the Emigration Office met most of its costs by charging an immigrant head tax ... The Fisheries Branch of the Crown Lands Department was at first financed entirely by the licence fees and fines it collected.'[18] However, this approach had fallen out of favour by 1867.

First, policy makers argued that failure of an essential government service to generate sufficient revenues one year could jeopardize it the next. As well, essential services often generated indirect benefits to society as a whole. Immigration, for example, helped everyone, not just new arrivals, and so society as a whole should bear the cost. Second, a number of legislators argued that this approach seriously inhibited Parliament's ability to control government operations and to hold ministers and departments accountable. Revenues could cover expenses, and thus Parliament would not need to determine the 'true cost' of services or how and why public funds were actually spent. Also problematic, senior civil servants running programs designed to be self-supporting could enjoy a degree of independence from politicians. This system allowed them to create and operate their own space outside the purview of Parliament and thus to be accountable to no political institution.

The political struggle for responsible government in the two Canadas is well documented. Responsible government was first introduced in Nova Scotia in 1848. In 1849 in the united Canada the principle of cabinet responsibility became accepted practice. However, as we saw above, responsible government, self-government, and cabinet responsibility required an organized and coherent civil service to support the executive. The buck would no longer stop in London or with the colonial governor and his secretary. As local politicians took control and became accountable for their decisions, they needed a coherent departmental structure as well as appropriate administrative and financial procedures. Only then would Parliament be able to assume its proper role as protector of the public purse and hold the executive to account for its actions.

Canada's basic government structure, the development of a civil service, and its relation to politicians did not develop in isolation. As we saw above, Westminster and Whitehall provided the model for Canada to emulate. W.A. Carrothers wrote in the very first issue of the *Canadian Journal of Economics and Political Science* that 'it is to be hoped that before long we shall, in all of the provinces, have developed a permanent civil service of high character and efficiency, which will carry on its work regardless of the party in power. There is no doubt that the efficiency of government service in Great Britain is to be attributed largely to an efficient permanent civil service. Were this evil remedied in Canada, a great many of the charges of corruption on the part of governments would disappear and, incidentally, there would be a greater respect for government, on the part of the Canadian people.'[19] Two separate realms were being created – one for the party in power, the other for the permanent public service. The

Whitehall model would alter the relationship in Canada between senior civil servants and their ministers. No longer would senior civil servants owe their appointments to the patronage of a minister. This change would promote senior civil servants' allegiance to the public service as an institution rather than to the views of a particular minister. In turn, this sea change would give rise to a departmental culture and to a departmental perspective based on a store of knowledge and experience.[20]

The Cabinet System

The broad outline of Canada's cabinet system, including the principle of ministerial responsibility, was set in nineteenth-century Britain. For our purposes, there are two issues: how the cabinet system in a parliamentary government operates and how it took shape.

Sir Ivor Jennings writes that 'the House of Commons and the Cabinet are the instruments of democracy [so that] the prerogative of the Crown and, to a lesser degree, the powers of the aristocracy, have been subordinated to public opinion.'[21] These instruments took shape over time rather than as a result of a single event, and so practices became conventions and precedents became the governing rules.

Historians regard Sir Robert Walpole (1676–1745) as Britain's first prime minister, although the title was first used in an official document only in 1878, when Benjamin Disraeli signed the final instrument of the Congress of Berlin. Walpole established the precedent that a minister needed the confidence of Parliament, no less than of the sovereign, to continue in office. Before Walpole and arguably for some years after him, the government was really the sovereign's government and the ministers were his or her ministers, in the sense that both the first lord of the Treasury and the master of the House were servants of the sovereign. But when Walpole resigned in 1742, after he lost the confidence of the Commons, he set in motion a series of events that would give rise to a minister who would stand 'primus inter pares.' Walpole also, according to Harold Wilson, created for the premiership what Walter Bagehot would later attribute to cabinet – 'a position of a hyphen which joins, a buckle which fastens, the Legislative part of the Executive to the Executive part of the State.'[22]

Walpole resigned office under pressure from the House, including some of his own colleagues. He left, but his colleagues remained in office. Thus the Commons had removed a minister, but not the ministry. Some forty years later, in 1782, King George III invited Lord North to form a government after the opposition had successfully attacked the whole ministry and its policies. North told the king that the whole cabinet, except for the lord chancellor, would have to resign before he would form a new government. The king agreed, and those who were removed stayed together 'in a nascent opposition [and] the nineteenth-century party system began to emerge.'[23] This development ended the legislature's ability to pick and choose policy by overthrowing a combination of parliamentary groups. It also signalled ministerial responsibility – the collective responsibility of the cabinet to the House.

Historians credit William Pitt with creating the office of the prime minister, since he was the first to hold the position in a sense that it would be recognized today. He became the effective head of cabinet, picked its members in consultation with the sovereign, and ensured that government policies were accepted by his cabinet colleagues and were collectively recommended to Parliament.[24] Thus Pitt's ministers became his ministers rather than the king's. It was only natural that anyone invited to become the sovereign's chief minister would want a say in deciding which member of Parliament was to be invited to hold a cabinet position. The need to hold a collective front in Parliament, and at times against strong public criticism, meant that the chief minister would wish to pick ministers with similar political views and policy preferences. For this reason, political parties grew and secured an increasingly important role throughout the nineteenth century, both in Britain and later in Canada.

It became widely accepted that parliamentary government and indeed democracy itself would function best if there were both a minority and a majority in Parliament. Further, groups of MPs ideally should have shared objectives and expectations. Thus parties competing for power would become a central feature of parliamentary government. Jennings explains that 'the democratic system implies an appeal to the people by contending parties supporting different policies ... and if there be no Opposition there is no democracy.'[25]

Political parties and party government became necessary when the government required parliamentary majorities to survive rather than relying on the support of the crown. In Britain, the process began in the mid-eighteenth century and became fully developed between 1832 and 1867, while in British North America it began to emerge in the 1840s.[26] Thus there is a direct link between the rise of party politics and the principle of ministerial responsibility in Britain and the development of responsible government in British North America.

The gradual shift of power from sovereign to Parliament and cabinet would have significant implications. Ministers were now part of a team and no longer the personal choice of the sovereign. No matter how competent a minister, and regardless of the sovereign's confidence, he had to resign along with the rest of the cabinet when his party lost power or the confidence of the Commons. This development transformed the struggle for power. And, leaving aside legal and technical niceties, the fact that the monarch no longer constituted the executive necessitated new relationships and processes. Bagehot wrote succinctly that the 'Queen must sign her own death warrant if the two Houses unanimously send it up to her.'[27] Earl Grey meanwhile explained that parliamentary government meant that 'the powers belonging to the Crown ... be exercised through Ministers who are held responsible for the manner in which they are used ... and who are entitled to hold their offices only while they possess the confidence of Parliament and more especially of the House of Commons.'[28]

In parliamentary government, 'the people' are represented by the House of Commons. The government and its general policy require the confidence and approval of the House, and, in the final analysis, the sovereign and cabinet must give way to the Commons. Political parties appeal to the electorate, and election outcomes decide the composition of the House, which determines the party origin of the cabinet.[29] The difficulty lies in applying what Grey describes as 'the first principle of our system of government – the control of all branches of the administration by Parliament.'[30]

Democratic control within a parliamentary system is mainly conventional. The key convention is the concept of ministerial responsibility: in Grey's words, 'all holders of permanent offices must be subordinate to some minister responsible to parliament.' Are ministers responsible to someone or somebody, for decisions or activities, or for both? What are collective cabinet responsibility and individual ministerial responsibility? What is the origin of the doctrine? Where does the civil service fit in?

There are three basic components to the doctrine – the collective responsibility of the cabinet, the individual responsibility of ministers, and the anonymity of public servants. Most students of public administration believe that the doctrine must come as a package, that it is not possible to favour one of the three components and discard the other two to suit a particular circumstance or issue.[31]

Henry Parris observes: 'A person is responsible to someone for something [and] ministerial responsibility is an ancient feature of English government and this sometimes obscures the fact that neither the some-one nor the something have remained constant.'[32] Parris explains that ministers became responsible to the crown and to the political nation in medieval times and to the law courts in Tudor times.[33] But the doctrine evolved again during the Victorian era to become a central feature of government. By then it had come to signify 'in ordinary parlance the responsibility of ministers to parliament, or, the liability of ministers to lose their offices if they cannot retain the confidence of the House of Commons.'[34] The doctrine leaves no doubt that the government is sub-ordinate to Parliament and that ministers are accountable to Parliament.

In turn, however, Parliament does not give orders or directions to per-manent officials, and it has no direct control over any department. Put differently, MPs should not attempt to govern unless they are members of the cabinet. Thus two distinct domains, or spaces, emerged – one for ministers to govern and the other for the House to hold the govern-ment to account and, if it so desires, to remove the government from power. There are several reasons for this formula, including the fact that, traditionally, acts of the executive properly belonged to the mon-arch or the executive. In any event, it is difficult to imagine how a body of 301 members (in Canada) representing several political parties could possibly make decisions on a day-to-day basis. The proper role of the House of Commons then is not to govern but to act as a public for-um, to be the country's leading deliberative body, to focus opinion, to criticize government, and to hold ministers accountable. This theme becomes central in Part III of this book.

Geoffrey Marshall and Graeme C. Moodie explain that the govern-ment's collective responsibility means that it has to 'submit its policy and defend its policy before the House of Commons and to resign if defeated on an issue of confidence. The defeat of any substantial bill should be regarded as a loss of confidence.'[35] One can speculate on what prompted Lord North in 1782 to ask George III to remove all ministers, except the chancellor, when invited to form a new cabinet. It may be that he wanted a fresh start and that he truly felt that the Commons had lost confidence in the whole ministry, not just in one or two ministers. But some historians suggest that early cabinets favoured the collective ele-ment mainly because it protected them against the monarch, who other-wise could pick ministers off one by one to produce a more pliant group of advisers.[36] However, cabinet solidarity has, in more recent times, strengthened the prime minister's position, enabling him or her to force the hand of a recalcitrant minister – to accept a policy or leave. The flip side, of course, is that the doctrine enables a government to function. As Sharon Sutherland explains, the government 'would not be able to govern as one administration if the cabinet's membership could be changed by the House of Commons exercising an authoritative veto on individual ministers.'[37] Still, it is ironic that the collective element of ministerial responsibility was established some 200 years ago to attenuate the king's power, while today it strengthens the prime minister.

Jennings sums up the individual responsibility of ministers: 'Each minister is responsible to Parliament for the conduct of his department. The act of every civil servant is by convention regarded as the act of his minister.'[38] Marshall and Moodie elaborate by pointing out that the minister is the 'constitutional mouthpiece through which departmental actions will be defended or repudiated and from whom information is to be sought.'[39] Only the minister can speak for the department to the House, which in turn must look to the minister to secure answers about departmental policies and activities. This element of ministerial responsibility is particularly relevant to our purpose, because it links the political and the administrative. Sutherland observes: 'The central feature of individual ministerial responsibility for administration is that [it] offers a timeless focal point for legal, political and administrative responsiveness.'[40] The genius of the doctrine is that it offers accountability through time: the current minister is responsible for 'all' activities of the department, past and present. Accordingly, the House of Commons can look to the present minister to seek answers about what may have gone wrong in the past.

Civil Servants: Neither Seen nor Heard

What about the role of civil servants? The reverse side of ministerial responsibility is the permanent status enjoyed by civil servants. It is widely accepted that career civil servants in a parliamentary system should avoid the limelight. Thus the 'space' that they occupy was designed to be private, and they are to do their work with the least amount of public visibility possible. The department speaks before Parliament and the public with one voice – that of the minister. 'The good civil servant is neither seen nor heard. The one who is made fully visible has failed.'[41] This is a key part of the relationship between politicians and career officials.

The duty of civil servants is tied solely to the government of the day.

Although they should never be asked to do anything unlawful, they have an unconditional duty to serve ministers loyally. It is the ministers, not the permanent officials, who decide what information should be made available to Parliament and when it should be released. In brief, civil servants are servants of the crown – that is, of the executive – not of Parliament.

Again, in line with British experience and the development of parliamentary government, no single event defined the role of civil servants in Canada, which adjusted and evolved to deal with changing circumstances. Permanence is a case in point. It became a central feature in Canada only in 1918, when nearly the entire civil service and virtually all appointments were placed under the Civil Service Commission. But, as we saw above, there had been steps towards permanent status, even before Confederation.[42] Indeed, while patronage tied to first appointment continued until 1918, it became accepted practice that most such appointments, once made, were permanent.

As in Britain, it was in the nineteenth century that Canada made the transition from a civil service based on office to one based on salary. Civil servants had previously provided services and looked for opportunities to increase fees or levels of services to generate more revenues for themselves and, at times, for their staff.[43] A new culture emerged with salaries – relatively modest remuneration compared to the commercial world, and no profit from area of responsibility. The public 'ought unquestionably to be served as cheaply and as is consistent with being served with integrity and ability.'[44] Indeed, for a long time the moral authority of the civil service was based on its ability to be parsimonious with public funds. One of the basic goals of the civil service, until at least the 1960s and the Glassco Commission, was to do things as cheaply as possible and, if at all possible, to avoid spending. Demanding administrative and financial rules in all government departments, from the Depression to the Glassco report, ingrained this approach.[45]

Permanence for civil servants, as we saw above, also developed over time in both Britain and Canada. It arose because of the increasing complexity and volume of work in government and the need to do away with political patronage in staffing.[46] Permanence does not mean simply holding on to a job for a long time. Rather, it means keeping a position through change of government, a concept that appeared with the arrival of responsible government.

The rationale for a permanent civil service appears in the opening pages of the Northcote–Trevelyan Report: 'It may safely be asserted that, as matters now stand, the Government of the country could not be carried on without the aid of an efficient body of permanent officers, occupying a position duly subordinate to that of the ministers who are directly responsible to the Crown and to Parliament, yet possessing sufficient independence, character, ability and experience to be able to advise, assist, and to some extent, influence those who are from time to time set over them.'[47] The report was tabled in Britain in the 1850s, at a time when political leaders came and went quickly; thus a permanent civil service was postulated as a counterbalance to the impermanence of politicians. It also constituted the key that enabled civil servants to advise ministers as they saw fit. Permanence would thus entail a higher standard of conduct, forthrightness, discretion, and loyalty to whatever government was in power. This too became a significant part of the traditional bargain.

To ensure that career officials could advise ministers without fear or favour they also had to be shielded from attack – and hence forgo public praise. An institutional culture developed in which civil servants avoided the limelight and public praise to the same extent that ministers would seek to pursue it. Thus separate arenas emerged for the politicians and for the civil service. The first would need approval every four years or so and provide political legitimacy to the public policy process. The second would be permanent and show loyalty to the government of the day.

Permanence finally triumphed in Canada for good with the implementation of the Murray Report of 1912 and revisions to the Civil Service Act in 1918. There was one question left to resolve – how far up the hierarchy was permanence to go? In Canada, the matter was settled early, with the deputy minister's position. In short, permanence and the connection between civil servants' anonymity and ministerial responsibility are key to Canadian government.

The civil service and its building blocks, including ministerial responsibility, are a product of their time. The term 'civil servant' was first used in India to distinguish the role from that of the military servants of the East India Company. In time, however, it also came to signify a distinction between the political and the partisan versus career civil servants.

The doctrine of ministerial responsibility thus was born in a different era. Ministers could readily accept responsibility for policy decisions, which were clearly *their* decisions and *their* policies. Similarly, they could, if they so wished, dominate administration in their departments. Henry Parris writes that 'the early nineteenth-century minister, if he was also a man of business, bestrode his department like a colossus. His duties were both political and administrative, but he worked within a system which enabled him to give much time to the latter.'[48] For example, Lord Palmerston was secretary of war from 1809 to 1828, and there was no issue too small to escape his attention, including 'the disposal of one unserviceable horse.'[49] He retained his capacity for detail after he went in the 1830s to the Foreign Office, where he 'read every report, every letter and every despatch received ... down to the least important letter of the lowest vice-consul. What is more, he answered them.'[50] Little wonder then that ministerial responsibility made eminent sense.

Things were no different in Canada. Sir John A. Macdonald was asked as minister of the militia in July 1862 to explain the absence of three officials in the department – one who suffered from epilepsy, another who had lost his eyesight, and a third whose delicate health made attendance impossible.[51] The Murray Report, tabled in 1912, observed that ministers 'have too much to do and do too much ... [and] Cabinet business ranged from questions of the highest importance ... down to the acceptance of a tender for the erection of a pump.' Murray concluded with the Wilsonian view that 'the business of a minister is not to administer, but to direct policy ... the carrying out of this policy ... should be left to his subordinates.'[52]

The simplicity of government operations allowed ministers this picayune attention to detail. The civil service borrowed heavily from the structure of the army and the navy in building its organization. Government departments had a 'series of levels of authority and command, each answerable to those at a higher level and able to give orders to those at a level below them.'[53] An era of limited government and a pyramid chain of command made it easy for departments to speak with one voice to the minister and hence with one voice to Parliament, the public, and other departments.

Nor did nineteenth-century ministers have to spend much time dealing with the media. There were only a few newspapers, and the era of the 24-hour-a-day electronic media was still 100 years away. There were no paid lobbyists and precious few interest groups demanding access to ministers. The time was ideal for the development of cabinet government, ministerial responsibility, and anonymous civil servants – all the elements of the traditional bargain.

The nineteenth century left another valuable legacy: the rise of political parties and the belief that the best government would emerge from a conflict between parties – one in government and at least one other in opposition. The one in power would constitute the government, and the one in opposition would oppose, criticize, and be available to assume power. Sir Norman Chester points to a significant related development: the conflict over power 'placed emphasis on government secrecy, not disclosing any information that might be of use to the opposition.'[54] The notion of anonymity and the loyalty of civil servants would take on added importance for the party in power, and it would not die easily, even with the arrival of more activist governments. Clement Attlee, Britain's Labour prime minister from 1945 to 1951, stated bluntly: 'No Government can be successful which cannot keep its secrets.'[55] Attlee's views still resonate in Canada in senior government circles. Prime Minister Jean Chrétien echoed them when he chaired his first cabinet meeting in 1993.[56] Gordon Robertson, former clerk of the Privy Council and secretary to the cabinet, writes that 'the whole basis of cabinet government rests on privacy or full discussions will not be possible.'[57] Thus the traditional bargain would place a premium on secrecy and managing confidential information.

Conclusion: A System that Worked

The basic principles guiding the civil service seem perhaps hopelessly dated and in urgent need of an overhaul. Gordon Robertson observed in 1968 that 'the unitary, homogeneous, aristocratic environment of eighteenth and nineteenth-century England in which it [our system of government] was developed was about as different from the circumstances of Canada today as it could be. The problem is how to adapt the system to cope with a different place and time.'[58] The situation has changed even more since 1968.

Constitutional purists, however, argue that the basics including ministerial responsibility, have stood the test of time. They ask, if ministers are not accountable to Parliament for the actions of their officials, then who should be? If officials are to be held directly accountable for their actions, then they need ways to defend themselves publicly when accused of incompetence. The purists also ask, if ministerial responsibility is so outmoded, why has no one offered even 'an initial draft of a new version more appropriate to modern times?'[59]

By its nature, the House of Commons exerts a negative rather than a positive control. Ministerial responsibility makes the minister 'blameable' for both policy and administration, and the minister in turn can reach into the hierarchical bureaucracy and secure an explanation for why things have gone wrong as well as how to make things right. The point, as Herman Finer explains in his classic essay, is that the views and advice of civil servants are to be private and their actions anonymous: 'Only the Minister has views and takes actions. If this convention is not obeyed, then civil servants may be publicly attacked by one party and praised by another and that must lead to a weakening of the principle of impartiality.'[60]

Were this latter situation to prevail, then the concept of permanence would stand on shaky ground. In contrast, jettisoning anonymity, permanence, and secrecy in order to modernize government operations would necessitate invention of a new civil service. For this reason, constitutional purists make the case that one cannot pick and choose elements of parliamentary government to suit a particular purpose without putting at risk the whole system. Given all the above, one can easily appreciate why and how the traditional bargain between politicians and public servants over their respective duties took shape to guide mutual relations. It established separate realms for politicians and for career officials but made accountability clear by having ministers responsible for both policy and administration in Parliament. Notwithstanding the constitutional purists, the traditional bargain today operates on shaky ground. The next chapter explores this issue further.

3

The Traditional Bargain

The Fathers of Confederation embraced the British constitution as the model to guide Canada's political development, and the British North America Act (BNA) of 1867 was British in spirit and design. The goal was to write as little as possible in the constitution and to establish representative democracies for the national and provincial governments based on parliamentary principles. The British constitution is to a large extent the product of various historical events from the Magna Carta (1215) to the development of political parties in the eighteenth and nineteenth centuries. Accordingly, it is made up of statute law, common law, and conventions. Parliament would stand unchallenged to create laws for all aspects of collective life and constitute the one polity to provide the continuing source for authoritative action for society.

Canada would go as far as it could in embracing the British model, but there were limits. The Fathers of Confederation also, however reluctantly, looked for guidance to the United States – another nation that grew out of British colonial status. The first limit on the British model was the need to design a federal system, like that of the Americans. Thus, the BNA Act provided for both parliamentary government at the national level and a division of powers between the two levels of government, thereby limiting the supremacy of Parliament. Other developments have further shifted Canada away from the British model. The Constitution Act of 1982 and its Charter of Rights and Freedoms have moved many issues to the courts, where Canadians can test legislation for its constitutionality. The desire to borrow from both the British and American models prompted noted Canadian historian Kenneth McNaught to observe that Canada has 'produced a unique sense of ideas, structure and custom that defies the model maker.'[1] He added that the resulting pot-pourri of 'ideas and customs' could make a contemporary analyst 'about as secure as a goose on shell ice.'[2]

But there are normative ideas associated with bureaucracy. How has Canada dealt with accountability? To what extent does Canada live by the doctrine of ministerial responsibility? How have recent British experiments in public administration affected Canada? The purpose of this chapter is to answer these three questions.

Accountability in Canada

A senior Canadian government official once observed that accountability is the 'hole in the doughnut' – everything done in government should be linked to accountability, but we are no longer certain what its requirements are or should be.[3] A federal task force on values and ethics chaired by a deputy minister revealed in late 1990 that its agenda came to focus on 'issues of responsible government and the accountability of public servants.' The report added that 'many public servants assume, rightly or wrongly, that the principles governing the relationships between themselves, ministers and Parliament are shifting, but they do not yet understand what the new principles are to be, and they assume that these shifts may alter the old deal under which the public service previously operated, in ways that remain as yet obscure.'[4] Many students of government agree that the current framework of accountability is not at all clear.[5] John Uhr, for example, comments on the 'endless quest – the search for the accountability of public administration.'[6]

Still, some observers argue that the doctrine of ministerial responsibility remains clear enough and that it should not only provide all the necessary answers, but also define how ministers and public servants can work together. Sir Ivor Jennings argued that the Westminster model provides for the clear division of roles between politicians and public servants and between policy and administration. Ministerial responsibility informs both relationships.[7]

There are certain basic requirements of the doctrine of ministerial responsibility and accountability. Geoffrey Marshall writes: 'Ministers, as the Crown's servants, carry on the executive government of the country. They accept legal responsibility for the use made of the royal prerogative and for the advice that they give to the Crown. They are politically accountable to the House of Commons both collectively and individually. They must by convention resign if defeated in the Commons on an important policy issue. A minister, as head of a department, should resign if he is found to be at fault in the running of it or if important errors are made by civil servants under his control which are of such a kind that they imply inadequate supervision by the minister.'[8] How does one draw a line between collective and individual responsibility? What constitutes an important policy issue? How does one figure out if an error is important or not? How does one possibly demonstrate whether ministerial supervision was adequate in an age of sprawling bureaucracies and complex decision-making processes? Why say 'should' rather than 'must' resign? Marshall points out that the doctrine was a constitutional convention and that its meaning and application were not rigid and changed gradually without formal legislative action.[9]

The traditional bargain between ministers and career officials runs along the following lines: public servants report and are accountable either directly to ministers (in the case of deputy ministers) or through superiors in a hierarchical arrangement. When public servants appear before parliamentary committees or speak publicly through the media or public speeches, they do so on behalf of their ministers. They are servants of the crown, whatever the statutory provision for their employment.[10] Accordingly, career officials are expected to provide to the government of the day non-partisanship, loyalty, impartiality, discretion, and professionalism in return for anonymity and security of tenure.

This arrangement requires a great deal of discipline on the part of career officials. Public servants, as we saw above, lose some political rights and should not have a public identity, given that the civil service has no constitutional personality separate from the government of the day. If the public servant cannot accept this requirement on any given issue, he or she should resign. Career servants must channel advice upwards in confidence. Accordingly, the shroud of secrecy that embraces cabinet deliberations applies to the public service as a whole. Since the minister is responsible for departmental policies and actions, this secrecy enables him or her to control the facts of the situation and all public comment. This arrangement serves both ministers and public servants well. It enables ministers to manage a public controversy or the elaboration and announcement of a new policy initiative. Career officials are often expert in their own policy areas and have inside knowledge of how a policy took shape, but they have no public persona. Ministers never have to fear being eclipsed by their own officials. In addition, career officials can produce and provide fearless advice for their ministers.

Hierarchy is a crucial feature of the doctrine. Government agencies and departments have historically been organized in a clearly defined hierarchy of offices, with clear lines of authority and subordination. John Stuart Mill argued in his *Considerations on Representative Government* (1862) that responsibility is provided best and work done best if all functions of a similar subject are allocated to single departments.[11] This notion has guided the development of Canadian machinery of government from the beginning. The new Dominion government established, for example, a Department of Agriculture in 1867. Despite employing only 27 people, it had clear responsibility for the sector. In this sense, the government defined an area of responsibility, labelled it agriculture, and housed there all responsibilities for the sector. Government departments have been and continue to be organized in this manner. They are hierarchical, and they contain units that provide services, manage finances, and so on. Departments organize units and officials hierarchically, laying out boxes on an organizational chart, and a clear chain of command runs down from the minister through the deputy head to the lowest level of officials.[12] The machinery of government also defines a specific position for every unit and for every public servant. Departmental units are assigned responsibilities in the organizational charts, as are public servants, through job descriptions.

Much as in the military, in the civil service hierarchy establishes lines of authority so that commands can be transmitted, and it allows a 'calculability of results for those in positions of authority.' Hierarchy also provides the 'governed' a clear line for appealing 'the decision of a lower office to the corresponding superior authority' and, as Mill argued, enables a variety of activities to be brought together in one organization.[13] In Canada, as in Britain until recently, existing departmental structures added new activities and new offices rather than creating new agencies or departments. Government departments and agencies in Anglo-American democracies showed remarkable stability during the twentieth century. Finally, hierarchy enables a minister, who is 'blameable' for both policy and administration, to reach down into the bureaucracy to secure an explanation for and to find solutions to problems.

But career public servants are also well served if their views and advice to ministers and their actions remain anonymous. They must exercise discretion. Again, as Herman Finer explains: 'If this convention is not obeyed, then civil servants may be publicly attacked by one party and praised by another and that must lead to a weakening of the principle of impartiality.'[14] As already noted, the public service draws its permanent status from the doctrine of ministerial responsibility.

Bureaucrats, no less than politicians, value secrecy and confidentiality, particularly under the Westminster model. Peter Hennessy, a keen observer of Whitehall, believed that 'secrecy is the bonding material which holds the rambling structure of government together. Of all the values incorporated into the culture (of the civil service) secrecy is primus inter pares. It is the very essence of good government, of private government carried beyond the reach of the faction of political party, the tunnel-vision of pressure group. The rule is that the fewer people who know, the better, including insiders.' Of all the rules in government, 'secrecy is the most sacred.'[15] Things are not much different in Canada.

Why is this? Max Weber provides an answer. He maintains that bureaucracy by nature seeks to increase the influence of the professionally informed by keeping its knowledge secret. He explains: 'Bureaucratic administration always tends to be an administration of secret missions in so far as it can, it hides its knowledge and action from criticism. ... The concept of the official secret is the specific invention of bureaucracy ... In facing a parliament, the bureaucracy, out of pure power instinct, fights every attempt of the parliament to gain knowledge by means of its own experts or from interest groups. Bureaucracy naturally welcomes a poorly informed and hence a powerless parliament.'[16] But some observers argue that the notion of secrecy and confidentiality came into fashion long before a bureaucratized public service existed.[17] The military and the monarch's advisers traditionally valued secrecy. In Britain the privy councillor's oath, which dates back to 1250, requires that members 'keep secret all matters committed and revealed unto you, or that shall be treated of secretly in Council ... and will keep the same until such time as, by the consent of His Majesty, or the Council Publications shall be made thereof.'[18]

Secrecy and confidentiality have also permeated government operations in Canada. They begin at the top: members of the Privy Council swear: 'I will in all things to be treated, debated and resolved in Privy Council, faithfully, honestly and truly declare my mind and my opinion. I shall keep secret all matters committed or revealed to me in this capacity, or that shall be secretly treated of in Council.' Gordon Robertson writes: 'The fear that confidentiality might not continue to have the same rigid and unalterable observance stood in the way of having a Cabinet Secretary, an agenda or any minutes through several decades of Cabinet operation.'[19] Accordingly, both ministers and career officials value secrecy in government operations and in the making of policy.

Weber's view that bureaucracy tends to hide its knowledge is correct, but not just because it seeks to protect its own self-interest. Ministers equally value secrecy and confidentiality. Many consider confidentiality key to their political survival. For them, loose lips sink not only ships but governments. The Privy Council Office, in a rare publication on the machinery of government, reports that 'the possibility lurks behind every question put to a minister [in question period in the Parliament] ... that the answer could weaken the minister's or the government's position, even resulting in parliamentary or public enquiries.'[20] Opposition parties are always ready to pounce on any perceived weaknesses, any whiff of scandal, any potential dissension in cabinet, or any administrative miscue to weaken the government. Question period provides the ideal forum for opposition MPs to score political 'points.'

One can hardly overstate the role of question period – a recurring message of this book. Again, if the government is unable to control the information generated by the bureaucracy, it will soon find this out in question period. British sociologist K.G. Robertson writes: 'Where administration is clearly subordinated to elected representatives, then information becomes an important element in the political struggle for office and therefore something which governments will seek to control.'[21] Robertson's point resonates more in a Westminster-style parliamentary system than in a U.S.-style presidential system. The Westminster model concentrates political power in the hands of the executive, which sits in the legislature. In a U.S.-style system, the separation of powers diffuses political power and controls it by limiting its scope and countervailing its operation. Because the executive and Congress share power, each branch has access to its own information about policies and programs, and the executive does not stand daily before the legislature to answer questions.

In Canada, ministers must continually ask not only whether departmental activities are responsible and technically sound, but also whether they can withstand scrutiny in question period. Question period thus speaks to the core function of the House of Commons, which is 'first to uncover and then to magnify the complaints of the electorate so that the government hears the signals from the political market and positions itself to respond in such a way as to keep the loyalty of that market. The state of political and administrative readiness, so central to the democratic effectiveness of our system, depends on ministers attending closely to the small and great events.'[22]

Ministers and their departments cannot always predict queries in the daily question period. The government invests considerable resources in the Prime Minister's Office, in other central agencies (such as the Privy Council Office and the Treasury Board), in ministers' offices, and in line departments, trying to anticipate which issues will surface in question period. The media can always be counted on to provide ample grist for the opposition mill. A leading item on the evening news or a headline story in the *Globe and Mail* or *Le Devoir* is a sure signal to prepare responses. Opposition MPs, however, do not only mine media reports to expose government shortcomings. They may, for example, use stories from a constituent about misadministration or constituents' grievances against a junior government official to try to force a minister into making a damaging statement, which will embarrass the government.

Central agencies and departments go to great lengths to brief every minister on questions that might be asked. Career officials must constantly be on the alert. Briefing notes are prepared every day Parliament is in session, and no effort is spared in preparing ministers for daily question period.

The introduction of the television camera to question period has changed government operations. It has opened a forum once reserved only for MPs, media representatives, and a handful of people sitting in the public galleries. TV now transmits the activities of the House, when it is sitting, to virtually every Canadian home every day, and ten-second clips from question period will often be the leading item on the evening news. A veteran observer remarked recently that television has turned question period into 'a staged cockfight that has little to do with real policy debates. It is only about partisan politics, about scoring political points and making ministers look good. It requires a tremendous amount of preparation and it makes bureaucrats much more risk averse.'[23] John Crosbie, a senior minister in the Mulroney cabinet, writes: 'What television has done is to elevate Question Period from being the focus of the parliamentary day to being, in the public mind, the entire parliamentary day and Question Period is a forum for the Opposition.'[24] Career officials confirm that preparing briefing material for their ministers for question period consumes an inordinate amount of their time and energy.[25]

Politics is a survival game, and longevity in office is its own reward.

Long-serving politicians claim that minor issues and administrative matters, unless carefully managed, can come to dominate the public policy agenda, receive a great deal of media attention, and damage a government or torpedo the career of a minister. These issues, they argue, can inflict greater damage than a big public-policy issue such as free trade, the public debt, or the future of health care. Examples include Erik Nielsen's 'tunagate' crisis, John Crosbie's comment 'Pass the tequila, Sheila,' and Don Johnston's remark about the posturing of opposition MPs during televised question period.[26] Jean Chrétien had more difficulty in question period concerning his intervention with a crown corporation over a loan to a hotel in his riding than in handling all his government's decisions to deal with the deficit in the mid-1990s.

How does one play the survival game? Chrétien maintains that the 'art of politics is learning to walk with your back to the wall, your elbows high. ... It's a survival game played under the glare of light. If you don't learn that, you're quickly finished.'[27] Information is critical in the art of politics, and, for the government, the less that opposition parties know about government operations and programs the better. The adversarial format of Parliament and the fact that the role of opposition parties is to oppose, to criticize, will invariably place a premium on the control of information. What about the role of career officials, given that they are the keepers of information on government operations? According to Chrétien, 'The press wants to get you. The opposition wants to get you. Even some of the bureaucrats want to get you.'[28]

Senior career officials understand very well the doctrine of ministerial responsibility and the need for loyalty to the government and are quite prepared to play by the rules. Indeed, they spend a great deal of their time managing visible and invisible errors on behalf of the government. Visible errors are those made in question period and taken up by the media. Invisible errors are unknown to people outside government or ignored by the media. One official explains: 'There are many, many errors or problems that never become a full-blown political crisis or even a crisis at all. Sometimes we are able to manage them, but more often we simply get lucky.' He added that his role in managing invisible errors 'is to fall on hand grenades. Our role here is to manage problems so that they do not become unmanageable political crises.'[29]

The result is that the battle lines under the traditional bargain are clear: on one side are the opposition parties, always on the lookout for errors, the opportunity to show ministers and their departments in a bad light, to find a chink in the government's armour; on the other side is the government, trying as best it can to avoid or at least to camouflage errors and to protect ministers so that it can shape the public-policy agenda to its political advantage.

One measure of success for senior officials is how well their ministers perform. The general view is that if the minister looks good, so does the department. In addition, deputy ministers constitute a virtual club in Ottawa circles, and peer pressure matters. Deputy ministers do not wish to lose face before their peers, and this factor promotes close collaboration among them. How does one lose credibility in the club? Certainly, all deputy ministers prefer walking into their breakfast or luncheon meetings knowing that their minister is in no political controversy or difficulty. All pride themselves on being able to keep their minister out of trouble. This has become a key criterion for success within the club, as indeed it is to the centre of government. If a crisis develops, club members may wonder if their colleague could have prevented it. When he or she has been able to keep the minister from embarrassment in the media or in question period, the club's praise is unstinting. One deputy minister observes: 'I have never lost one minister and I have worked with several. One of my colleagues has lost every single minister she has ever worked with. That tells you something.'[30]

Senior officials stress loyalty to the government. According to the 1996 task force on values and ethics in the federal public service: 'Loyalty to the public interest, as represented and interpreted by the democratically elected government and expressed in law and the constitution, is among the most fundamental values of public service.'[31] Loyalty to the government has become an important part of the corporate culture at the most senior levels in the public service. Career officials who cannot accept this value either quit (as did Gordon Robertson when Joe Clark's government came to office) or are shunted aside, if not fired. In 1982, Neil Fraser, a public servant who criticized metrication and the proposed Charter of Rights – neither of which was related to his job or his department – was fired. The government later successfully defended the action in court.[32]

One can point to numerous cases when career officials were warned to keep information or their own views on policies within the department or at least within government or risk reprimand. Senior officials cannot protect the government while others down the line leak damaging information to the media or the opposition parties.

In the course of research for this book, I came across an exchange of correspondence between senior officials at the Canadian International

Development Agency (CIDA) that speaks directly to this point. The material dates back to the early 1980s, and the officials involved are no longer with the government. One of the agency's directors met with a journalist from the national television network CTV to discuss a project in Haiti. The agency had a consultant's report stating that the project was successful and recommending another phase. The journalist claimed that the project was a 'mess' and that a private foundation was carrying out similar work with far greater success at a fraction of the cost. He also had a report supporting his view. The journalist and the CIDA official exchanged reports, the journalist apparently agreeing to destroy the CIDA document after reading it. Meanwhile, the CIDA official began to question the viability of the project within the agency. The television network went to air with a documentary quoting the internal document. The official was called on the carpet for giving an internal document to a person outside the agency. He was told in no uncertain terms that his 'behaviour was unacceptable' and was suspended from work without pay for one day. More significantly, his career development came to a sudden halt. Ministers and career officials may occupy different worlds, but career officials know full well that they must not only work away from the media, but must take great care not to create embarrassment for their ministers or the government.

Government officials have always been expected to maintain discretion about policy issues and sensitive information. In August 2001, the government rejected a request to allow civil servants to appear before an all-party committee of MPs examining federal access-to-information legislation. The prime minister vetoed the request because the committee did not have proper parliamentary standing. The chair – a Liberal MP – was concerned that a 'task force of bureaucrats' would forward proposals 'more concerned with keeping information secret than making it public.' Moreover, the government was in court over challenges to the Access to Information Act, and its House leader explained that 'anything these officials say could be seen as having an impact on the court process.'[33] In the end, career officials did not appear before the committee. In any event, most civil servants will make every effort to avoid being drawn into a public debate over a policy issue.

Canada's access-to-information legislation broke new ground when it was introduced in 1985. Ottawa circles called it Trudeau's gift to Mulroney. That is, Trudeau would not have to live with the consequences of the legislation produced by his government, but his successor, Brian Mulroney, would.

The central purpose of the act is to provide a 'right of access' for Canadians to information under the control of any government institution. It adds that 'exceptions to the right of access' should be both limited and specific and, further, that decisions on disclosure 'should be reviewed independently of government.'[34]

As senior officials had predicted when the act was proclaimed, the impact of the legislation has been profound. For one thing, it has generated a demand for good political 'firefighters' in Ottawa and has made policy people cautious. Giles Gherson, former policy adviser in the Human Resources Development, explains, 'To address the access to information issue ... I saw myself that officials are extremely leery of putting things on paper that they wouldn't like to see made public or find its way to the media, several months later, that could be embarrassing to the minister.'[35] Conrad Winn, a pollster, argues that access to information has seriously inhibited the ability of government departments to ask the right questions when commissioning a survey: 'The bottom line for the average public servant is don't embarrass the minister, that is the surest way to have your career stopped or slowed down. If you have polls that ask all kinds of questions that would reveal the truthful complexity of what people think ... then [the polls] will inevitably show the public doesn't like something the government does.'[36] Hugh Winsor, a *Globe and Mail* journalist, readily admits that the media often take advantage of access to information to get at a story. But, he argues, they do that 'not so much to find out what the people dislike about the government ... but to try to get an advance look at what the government's agenda might be ... [and] at the next budget or the next Speech from the Throne by making an access to information request about a public opinion survey which is being commissioned.'[37]

Government officials in both central agencies and line departments readily admit that access-to-information legislation has made them reluctant to commit their views and recommendations to paper. They fear that this could well appear in the media and force officials to support or defend them in public. This eventuality flies in the face of the traditional bargain, since the views and advice of civil servants are to be private and their actions anonymous. One senior official at the Treasury Board Secretariat observed recently: 'We are now all sitting ducks. I cringe when I write an email because I never know whether it will appear on the front page of a newspaper six months down the road. It is possible now for someone to ask for all exchanges, including emails, between senior official X and senior official Y. We can no longer blue sky or have a playful mind. We no longer have the luxury of engaging in a frank and honest debate. It is now very difficult to put down on paper – be careful, minister, there are problems with your ideas and what you want to do, ministers.'[38] One can assume that this leads to less disciplined thinking as strong memoranda give way to Powerpoint presentations. One can also assume that there is less room for critical thinking. Ironically, because 'Be careful' types of advice, if given at all, are no longer committed to paper, advice has become less transparent. In addition, officials attempt to attenuate the impact of the legislation to protect their ministers and their policy advisory and administrative roles. In a detailed review of the application of the legislation, one student of public administration reports that 'requests that were identified as sensitive, or that came from the media or political parties, were found to have longer processing time, even after other considerations were accounted for.'[39]

Access-to-information legislation has also helped the media become much more aware of how government works and to identify administrative miscues. John Crosbie writes that the legislation has added to the 'woes of politicians on the government side. It gives the media and other mischief-makers the ability to ferret out snippets of information with which to embarrass political leaders and to titillate the public. In the vast majority of instances, embarrassment and titillation are the only objects of access to information requests.'[40] Journalists have also used the legislation to uncover administrative foul-ups and miscues. For example, the *Globe and Mail* reported on 29 June 1994 that documents disclosed under access to information show that the 'monthly charge [to the government] for cellular phones and services was $874,000 the previous December which translates to at least $10.4 million a year.' The article revealed that 'approximately 280 cell phones were assigned to the Privy Council Office, despite a change of government and promises of cost-cutting.' This particular access-to-information request had been made after a minister had told an opposition member that it was 'too expensive to find out what cell phones were costing.'[41] In this instance the request was intended to secure information about the government as a whole, not about a department. Several such requests surface every month, necessitating competent firefighters in Ottawa.

The government has sought to fight back as best it can. An example: the Chrétien government decided to go to court to deny access to the prime minister's agenda, which accounts for his whereabouts. Before the legislation was proclaimed it was relatively easy for journalists or academics to secure information for research purposes, and a number of them did so.[42]

Access-to-information legislation may have enabled the media, the general public, interest groups, and opposition parties to open up the private space of the government and career officials. It may well have made government more transparent in some ways, but it has also transformed the policy advisory process and government operations.

More British Than the British: Ministerial Responsibility

The Fathers of Confederation wrote in the BNA Act that Canada should have 'a government similar in principle to that of the United Kingdom.' Government in Canada, as in Britain, has evolved a great deal since then. The pull of the United States (in the case of Canada), the growth of government, the arrival of the electronic media, the information economy, and the development of new approaches to public management have produced a sea change in Canada, as in other Anglo-American democracies.

However, one can still easily see the British influence in Canada. The two systems have many things in common, including

- parliamentary government
- a cabinet system linking the legislative, executive, and administrative arms
- a cabinet drawn from the legislature
- an adversarial theatre at the political level, combined with collective, collegial, and usually consensual decision making in the executive branch, operating in relative secrecy
- vigorous media operating outside government influence
- a strong commitment to responsible government

The British and Canadian parliaments function generally in the same fashion: neither seeks to govern, and both are designed to 'secure full discussion and ventilation of all matters.'[43] They provide the basic framework for exercise of the power of the public purse and for the cabinet and public service to operate and to be held to account for their policies, decisions, and activities. But there are also important differences. Canada has been far more devoted than Britain to the Westminster model.

Question period is a case in point. In Canada, the prime minister is expected to attend whenever he is in Ottawa, and his participation is carefully scrutinized by the House and the media. In contrast, the British prime minister is expected to appear only once a week in the House to answer questions. In Canada, party leaders decide who will be asking questions in question period. In Britain it is the Speaker.

C.E.S. Franks, one of Canada's leading students of Parliament, writes that 'the Canadian question period is unique. For forty-five minutes opposition members attack the government. Most questions are of the have you stopped beating your wife yet variety.'[44] As we saw above, in Canada the objective of question period, more often than not, is to catch ministers off guard, to surprise them with queries about administrative foul-ups, and to take advantage of any opening to embarrass a minister. Question period is a free-wheeling, unpredictable, spontaneous affair. In Britain, the bulk of the questions are written, and there is usually advance notice of several days, during which ministers and their staff can work on answers. Thus much of question period in Britain is a 'ponderous dance, in which in effect the ministers give carefully phrased replies to questions at least a week old.'[45] Supplementary questions are permitted, and they can be unpredictable and potentially difficult for ministers.

In Britain adoption of accounting officers has produced, compared with Canada, a somewhat softer version of the doctrine of anonymity. Franks writes: 'Full and personal responsibility of the Accounting Officer remains central to the British system of financial control and accountability, and indeed good management generally, and the position and the practices which have developed around it establish a clear and firm division between the responsibilities of the public service and those of the minister. The Public Accounts Committee holds the Accounting Officers answerable and accountable. The unequivocal assignment of responsibilities to the Accounting Officers gives effective identity to the civil service as a corporate body with interests, procedures, and accountability to Parliament outside and, unless expressly over-ridden, independent of ministerial responsibility. These put the Accounting Officer a long way from doctrines of anonymity and responsibility to Parliament through the minister alone.'[46]

In Britain, a permanent secretary (the equivalent of a deputy minister in Canada) is the department's accounting officer unless the function has been assigned to a second permanent secretary or to another senior permanent official.[47] As a result, the permanent secretary is directly accountable to Parliament for the legality and efficiency of departmental spending.[48] Thus the permanent secretary performs the same functions as Canada's deputy minister but also renders accounts to Parliament and is accountable for them to the House's Public Accounts Committee. The Treasury makes it clear that the accounting function is important. A Treasury directive suggests that if a minister wishes to initiate a course of action involving a transaction that the accounting officer believes would 'infringe the requirements of propriety,' the accounting officer should record in writing his or her objection. If the minister still insists on proceeding, the accounting officer should seek written instruction from the minister to take the action in question.[49]

The Canadian government has consistently resisted having accounting officers. Several observers, including a Royal Commission on Financial Management and Accountability (1979) and a parliamentary committee, have urged their adoption, but without success.[50] The Privy Council Office (PCO) has explained its unwillingness: 'As government has learned through the blurring of individual responsibility by the imposition of central controls, responsibility shared tends to be responsibility shirked. Formal and direct accountability of officials to Parliament for administrative matters would divide the responsibility of ministers. It would require the establishment of firm practices governing the sorts of questions for which ministers as distinct from officials would be answerable, and this would be reflected daily during Question Period. Experience indicates that such distinctions are artificial and that Parliament prefers not to recognize the informal division between the answerability of officials and of ministers for the very reasons that ministers are constitutionally responsible and that the extent of their answerability is defined by political circumstances.'[51]

In short, the PCO wants always to have someone on the hook – the minister. In question period, MPs need not make any distinction between policy and administrative matters, so that everything is fair partisan game. Indeed, officials still subscribe fully to the view that the minister remains responsible for everything done in the department and that everything done in the department may be the object of parliamentary scrutiny. That is, the minister is accountable for both policy and administration. A former senior PCO official spoke out publicly: 'Our system of government is set up to ensure that ultimately such a distinction cannot be made – that politicians are responsible for administration as well as for policy.'[52] However, senior officials also appear before Parliament's Public Accounts Committee, without their ministers, to review financial and administrative matters. But Ottawa has refused to go the extra step and formally recognize or designate a senior official as the accounting officer. In both systems, the House decides when an issue passes from the technical or administrative realm of the career official to the political realm of the minister.

Building a Half-way House?

Margaret Thatcher launched a series of reforms shortly after she came to power in 1979. She hit Whitehall like a storm: the 'Thatcher revolution' dealt with every aspect of government, from policy to administrative decisions. Her various reforms were far more ambitious and had a far greater impact in Britain than those of Mulroney and Chrétien combined had in Canada.

There is one crucial Thatcher reform, however, that we need to highlight – her Next Step initiative. This had its origins in the report *Improving Management in Government: The Next Step* (1988). The document made the case that the work of civil servants is dominated by the demands of ministers and Parliament. It also offered a number of general observations, including one that the machinery of government itself – together with continuing demands from Parliament, from the media, and from the public – had worsened 'ministerial overload.' Too little attention was being paid to results, and too much to expenditures and activities. As well, there were relatively few external pressures demanding improvement in performance.

The report's most significant finding, however, was that the civil service was 'too big and too diverse to manage as a single entity.' This situation had led to the development of machinery of government that 'fits no operation effectively.' A unified civil service had given rise to a straitjacket of controls and rules. Controls existed on recruitment, dismissal, choice of staff, promotion, pay, hours of work, accommodation, organization of work, and even use of communication equipment. The authors pinpointed five critical issues confronting management in the civil service: 'First, a lack of clear and accountable management responsibility, and the self confidence that goes with it, particularly among the higher ranks in departments. Second, the need for greater precision about the results expected of people and of organisations. Third, a need to focus attention on outputs as well as inputs. Fourth, the handicap of imposing a uniform system in an organisation of the size and diversity of the present Civil Service. Fifth, a need for a sustained pressure for improvement.'[53]

The proposed solution was to reorganize the work of individual departments so that the job to be done received a higher priority than the centrally conceived rules and controls. The focus in future should be results, not process. The report put forward a radical proposal: agencies should be established to carry out the executive functions of government within a policy-and-resources framework set by ministers and the relevant department. Managers of agencies would receive substantial freedom to manage operations as they saw fit, but they would be held 'rigorously to account for the results achieved.' The report argued essentially that if government operations were allowed to operate at arm's length from ministers and from the Whitehall culture, then one would soon see a 'release of managerial energy.' The goal was nothing short of redefining the way the 'business of government' was conducted.[54]

The report also addressed ministerial responsibility. Prime Minister Harold Wilson in 1966 had directed the Fulton Committee not to deal with this issue in its review of the civil service. Thatcher issued no such instruction. The 1988 report argued that ministers should be fully accountable for policy, but not for day-to-day management decisions. It insisted that there was nothing new in this suggestion, since there were already a number of government functions carried out at arm's length from ministers. These included the review of tax cases and regulatory functions. The solution lay in an accountability framework that was tailored for each agency. The underlying principle, however, was that heads of executive agencies should be delegated authority from ministers for managing the agencies 'within the framework of policy directives and resource allocations prescribed by ministers.'[55]

Thatcher accepted the report's recommendations as 'a major step in the reform of the civil service.' New agencies would be created, she explained, and 'each will have its own Chief Executive, responsible for managing day to day operations.'[56]

At the last minute Thatcher had a change of mind on accountability. She told the Commons the day the report was released that 'there will be no change in the arrangements for accountability.' Officials interpreted her statement to mean that there would be little difference between agencies and departments – indeed, Sir Robin Butler, head of the Home Civil Service, did not even think that 'it would be necessary to revise the rules on civil servants giving evidence to select committees' of Parliament.[57] He wrote: 'No doubt this is because ministers, ... made it clear that any constitutional changes to redefine ministerial responsibility were out of the question as were any suggestions to end Treasury controls over budgets, manpower and national pay bargaining.'[58] In short, Thatcher wanted new wine but in the same bottle.

The government's final decision was to make agency heads 'additional' accounting officers, so that permanent secretaries would remain accounting officers for the whole of their areas of responsibility, including the agencies. However, even cabinet and Treasury officials were quick to recognize that, for all practical purposes, agency heads would act as accounting officers for their agencies' work, and would answer for it before the Public Accounts Committee. This is precisely what has happened.

By 1996, 126 executive agencies (EAs) had been created, mainly by carving chunks of 'operational' or 'administrative' activities out of ministerial departments and setting them up as distinct agencies, organized along businesslike lines. Each agency has a chief executive and operates within a 'framework agreement' (quasi-contract) with its parent department. This document specifies the agency's objectives, performance targets, and budget. The targets are revised annually and published. The chief executive's performance-related pay is usually linked, at least in part, to his or her achievement of the EA's current performance targets. EAs remain technically within their parent departments.

Although the government insists that the creation of EAs does not imply any fundamental constitutional shift in the doctrine of ministerial responsibility, there have been a number of serious disagreements between ministers and EA chief executives. The best-publicized have involved the prison service and the child support agency. These appear to demonstrate that the line between policy and operations cannot always be clearly and confidently fixed, but that it can move about in quite a volatile fashion, depending on the media and political interest in particular aspects of an operation. One observer explains: 'Even if agencies have different kinds of targets, financial (productivity), efficiency and quality, the enquiry shows that financial targets are given a much higher priority.'[59]

The purpose of creating EAs was to free government managers to focus more on management and less on 'ministers' and 'Whitehall,' or the bureaucratic culture. It was envisaged that some day the civil service would consist of a small core engaged in policy work, supporting ministers and managing departments, with the bulk of civil servants working in relatively independent executive agencies, delivering services. Thatcher made the Next Step initiative her own and instructed her ministers and the senior civil service to make it work. Thatcher was 'not for turning' on major issues, and the Next Step was no exception. She attached a great deal of importance to the initiative and insisted on having a direct hand in its implementation. The result is that today about 75 per cent of the British government has been transformed into executive agencies. The government explained that the new agencies would 'operate in a businesslike manner with the flexibility necessary to achieve agreed bottom-line targets.'

Canadian officials looked to Britain for inspiration when they created Special Operating Agencies (SOAs). However, SOAs are only a pale imitation of British executive agencies. In Canada, the agencies remain subordinate to their parent departments. In addition, their heads report to the deputy minister of their department, rather than directly to the minister, as in Britain. Accordingly, the impact on the civil service has been insignificant. The agencies cannot be said to have created a culture or promoted values different from the public service as a whole. Their leaders and personnel are selected much as are those of a regular government department.

There has been some confusion about the nature of an SOA. One deputy minister described it simply as 'a bureaucratic version of a halfway house. It is neither a jail, nor is it total freedom. It is part of a department, yet separate from it.' He added that SOAs 'are still very much part of the federal family. Staff in agencies are still public servants. SOAs still report to the department, to the Minister and to the Treasury Board.'[60] The secretary of Treasury Board wrote: 'SOAs are not quasi-Crown corporations. They remain a distinct part of the home department, albeit with enhanced operational authority.'[61]

SOAs have met with little success. The lines of accountability were never properly defined, and it quickly became apparent that deputy ministers were 'far too busy with their own jobs to give much time to SOAs.'[62] It is unclear how to evaluate them. It is not clear why SOAs were established in the first place. The government itself was not at all certain as to why. One government official writes: 'Several different perspectives inspired the establishment of the initial five SOAs. Some viewed the initiative as a way of delaying pressure to privatize or as a halfway station to privatization. Others viewed SOAs as a pilot project or laboratories for public sector reforms ... Yet another perspective [is that] the SOA concept offered a prototype for the public service (similar to Executive Agencies) in the United Kingdom ... (Over time) the rationale for the initiative became even more cloudy.'[63] We do not know if programs under SOAs are better managed than they were in traditional government departments.[64]

The SOAs, however, did serve as a laboratory. They tested the willingness of ministers and senior officials to separate policy and operations and to see new units attempt to do things differently. They also forced reconsideration of ministerial responsibility and led to a decision to leave well enough alone.

Government officials report that establishing SOAs was to provide the first clear break with the traditional control-and-command model and to launch a culture that emphasizes management practices rather than program administration. In brief, the objective was to increase managerial flexibility and efficiency. The Treasury Board Secretariat made it clear that SOAs should be 'business units oriented to good management' and should promote more 'business-like services, improve service to the customer and demonstrate concern for efficient management.' For SOAs to function properly, it was necessary to 'separate policy from day-to-day operations.'[65] The board, however, never tried to square this approach with the PCO's view that ministers are accountable to Parliament for both policy and administration.

The SOA initiative did not attempt to deal with ministerial responsibility. Unlike in Britain, where there is a direct relationship between the agency head and the minister, in Canada the deputy minister remains the key point of contact. Treasury Board simply reported that 'no change is contemplated in the current accountability relationship.'[66]

There were other problems. Unlike in Britain, where the head of an agency is the chief executive officer (CEO), in Canada the CEO is a department's deputy minister, while the head of an agency is the chief operating officer (COO). This places the deputy minister in a conflict between the department's rules and the agency's. There are all kinds of incentives for a deputy minister to favour the department over an agency that is continually striving to secure arm's-length status.

The biggest complaint one hears, however, is that SOAs have changed precious little, if anything. Central agencies still exercise control, and formal rules and guidelines still apply. The basic accountability structure remains intact, and few administrative units are now asking for agency status. They see no reason why they should, given that the rules do not change a great deal with agency status. Neither fish nor fowl, SOAs soon petered out. In 1993 there were fifteen SOAs employing only about 3 per cent of the public service, but later some were disbanded or reincorporated in their home departments (for example, the Canada Communications Group).

In more recent years, two high-profile new agencies have brought related activities under one roof. The Canadian Food Inspection Agency (CFIA) deals with the regulation of animal, food, and plant health and with consumer safety vis-à-vis the labelling and packaging of food products. The Canada Customs and Revenue Agency (CCRA) replaced Revenue Canada. The new agencies, unlike the SOAs, enjoy separate employer status under the Public Service Staff Relations Act, although employees remain federal public servants. This change and other financial changes are designed to give the agencies more elbow room in personnel and financial management. But, as Michael Prince observed about the CFIA, these agencies, like the SOAs, do not constitute a bureaucratic revolution, shaped as they are 'by the conventions of parliamentary accountability, ministerial responsibility and merit public service.'[67] The government of Canada has been extremely reluctant to experiment with the machinery of government and to tamper with the traditional accountability structure.

The establishment of the CFIA and the CCRA simply moved nearly about one-third of the federal public service away from centrally pre-scribed administrative rules and procedures. The government solved its 'bureaucratic problem' by walking away from it, given that it did not apply whatever solutions it came up with for the two agencies to all the public service. In addition, the fact that the House of Commons or its committees did not seriously question this development suggests that parliamentary scrutiny is not working well.[68]

Conclusion: The Real Thing

The government of Canada has stood firm on the doctrine of ministerial responsibility, the anonymity of career officials, and the traditional bargain between politicians and career officials. Indeed, Canada has hunkered down and stood by the Westminster–Whitehall model more devoutly than even Westminster and Whitehall have. Britain's Next Step agencies, for example, have institutionalized assignment of responsibility and accountability to career officials.[69] Australia and New Zealand have followed suit. All three countries have taken to heart Geoffrey Marshall's point that ministerial responsibility is a 'constitutional convention and that its meaning and application [are] not rigid and that they [can] change gradually over time without formal legislative action.'[70] Not so Canada.

Canada chose not to experiment with the agency model to the same extent as Britain, New Zealand, and Australia. The jury is still out on the success of the model. It depends, it seems, on the question being asked and on who is asking the question. Some argue that the agencies operate more efficiently than traditional government departments. Others, however, insist that there is little solid evidence to suggest this and, further, that accountability in executive agencies is not at all clear, as it is in traditional departments.

One potential benefit of the agency model is that it can better define the management space available to government managers. It is designed to remove centrally prescribed administrative controls and to increase managerial flexibility while, to the extent possible, removing programs from the policy-making process. But, at least in Canada, and it appears elsewhere, the agency model has not strengthened accountability in government or improved relations between ministers and career officials, not to mention relations between both groups and the House of Commons. Ministers have, through their actions, shown time and again their uneasiness with ministerial responsibility. The reasons for this are varied and may have little to do with the agency model. One could point to a now much more complex policy and decision process and to misunderstanding of the doctrine itself. Whatever the reasons, recent developments appear to have left Canadian ministers and career officials as secure as a goose on shell ice as they go about their work. But this has not always been so. There was a time when the traditional model worked extremely well in Canada. The next chapter looks at this era and considers how and why the model ran into problems.

4

Life in the Village

There was a golden age when the Canadian civil service was held in high esteem and its work was much valued by politicians and the public. It was known for its frugality, its professionalism, its loyalty to the government, and its capacity to serve without drawing attention to itself. Senior career officials also had a well-honed capacity to work with ministers. Indeed, one rarely heard criticism from either side about the other. The environment was ideally suited for the traditional bargain to flourish. Ministers knew that they were in charge, and they welcomed the advice of the senior mandarins. Senior career officials, meanwhile, sought to serve their ministers well and did not hesitate to be forthright in their advice, even if the advice was not always welcomed. Politicians and career officials knew and respected the fact that they occupied different spaces. Meanwhile the media, the general public, and organized interest groups, to the extent that these existed, would honour the respective responsibilities occupied by both politicians and career officials and allow them to work in relatively secrecy.

This golden age is described as a 'small village' in Hugh Heclo and Aaron Wildavsky's 1974 study of the British civil service, *The Private Government of Public Money*.[1] Village life, however, became unpleasant by the 1970s in both Britain and Canada. Politicians began to voice their criticism publicly about the work of their civil servants. A new breed of politicians viewed the policy advisory role of the civil service as somehow deeply illegitimate. Bureaucrat 'bashing' became fashionable in political circles, in the media, and in academe. Politicians wanted a different public service, although it was not at all clear just what kind of public service they were after. Still, it became evident that the traditional bargain guiding the relationship between politicians and career officials was operating under tremendous stress and strain. This chapter looks back to that golden age, when the traditional bargain worked with hardly a hitch, and at life in the village; it then looks at the challenges of the 1960s and 1970s and at the turmoil of the 1980s.

The Golden Era

There was a time, not long ago, when Canada's civil service was regarded as one of the best in the world. In *The Ottawa Men* J.L. Granatstein documents the kind of civil service that served the Canadian government between 1935 and 1957. One can make the case that the golden era extended to the early 1970s, albeit with some difficult moments during the Diefenbaker years (1957–63). The period was characterized by a relatively small, not-well-paid civil service that shared a profound belief that public service was a civic virtue, a vocation.

On size, Granatstein writes: 'Through the Second World War and well beyond, most of the key officials had offices in the East Block. Indeed, it is now difficult to believe that in this building so much political and bureaucratic power was concentrated. The Prime Minister, the Clerk of the Privy Council Office, and the Under-Secretary of State for External Affairs all had their offices there ... The officers of the Department of External Affairs, the staff of the Prime Minister's Office, and the Privy Council Office, were also located there. Finance was close by.'[2]

It is difficult to appreciate how the machinery of government could possibly function with so few people. In 1873 Prime Minister Alexander Mackenzie had no secretary and answered all correspondence himself.[3] In 1909 the newly created Department of External Affairs was entirely housed above a barber shop in Ottawa.[4] Gordon Robertson reports that the 1950 federal–provincial conference involved only about 75 officials: today the same conference would involve about 375.[5]

On remuneration, Granatstein writes that 'salaries were low ... Robertson was negotiating trade agreements ... wearing suits that were shiny with use.' He adds: 'Of course, they wanted a comfortable salary, but almost all would have remained at their posts without it.'[6] He reports that 'they felt a duty to serve their country and its people. If that sounds trite and pious today, it is only because our age is more cynical.'[7] Senior civil servants believed that they were serving a collective purpose that transcended their own personal interest. This constitutes a key element of the traditional bargain. This conviction, we are also informed, 'helped to alter the way Canadians lived, acted and thought about themselves.'[8]

But the mandarins clearly understood that they possessed only a 'power of a sort.' Granatstein explains: 'The Ottawa Men lacked the ultimate power that comes from the ballot box: the power to move men. All the mandarins had, essentially, was influence on politicians.'[9] Career officials knew this intuitively, as did ministers. Granatstein argues that this explains why senior public servants such as C.M. Drury, Lester Pearson, Jack Pickersgill, and Mitchell Sharp eventually left for partisan politics. They appreciated that politics and the civil service occupied different territory. Those civil servants who stayed were driven by one objective – to serve 'their minister well.'[10]

On public policy, Canadians emerged from the Second World War determined never to permit another depression of the kind witnessed in the 1930s. By war's end, the public's belief in government's ability to intervene and to manage the economy was high. Large latent demand and rapid population increase, combined with the realization that government's management of the war effort had been successful, allowed government carte blanche to expand. Canadians had learned that governments were able, in moments of crisis, and when moved by an all-consuming goal, to lead the country to high levels of economic activity and employment. Not only had the Allies won the war, but unemployment had fallen to zero, yet prices had been held down. Growth of productivity and real gross national product (GNP) accelerated, inequalities among social groups diminished, civilian consumption actually increased, there were no balance-of-payment crises, and foreign exchange rates remained stable. When the war ended, everyone was prepared for measures to avoid a return of the Depression years. But the expected severe economic downturn did not materialize, and the measures proved unnecessary. Still, governments (in particular, the federal government) were now convinced that they possessed a new arsenal of economic policy to achieve high employment and generally to manage the economy.[11]

Canadians also believed that they had in place the required machinery of government to produce the right mix of public policies. Politicians knew that they were in charge and welcomed the advice of the mandarins; both groups knew each other well and were comfortable with one another. Mitchell Sharp, a senior deputy minister who later became a senior cabinet minister, observed a particularly strong relationship between the minister and his deputy minister. He explained that the deputy minister and his associates prepared policy, while the minister decided what was politically saleable and what was not.[12] The centre of government, or central agencies, did not play a strong role in policy advice until the late 1960s or early 1970s. The minister would take a document to cabinet and talk about it with his or her colleagues, who would collectively decide whether or not to give a green light to the proposal. There was little input or second guessing from central-agency staff and limited interdepartmental consultation. The process served both ministers and civil servants effectively.[13]

The process worked well largely because it was simple and straightforward. The role of the media then was to be a narrator or an independent observer reporting and commenting on political events. It is now, of course, a major political actor in its own right. Television and its tendency to offer a ten- or thirty-second clip on the evening news to sum up major policy issues, or, more often, to report on something gone awry in government, have changed government operations. The media have become far more aggressive and less deferential to political power. Some observers suggest that the Watergate crisis in Washington in the mid-1970s was a defining moment, and not just in the United States. Neither Granatstein nor Gordon Robertson made much reference to the media. Their books leave one with the impression that the media in that earlier era were very much on the outside, looking in.

But there were other factors. The Office of the Auditor General was considerably smaller than at present, and its role much more modest in scope. It tabled an annual report, based on financial audits. It never hesitated to point out waste in government spending and anyone playing fast and loose with the public purse. But comprehensive and value-for-money audits, which are much more subjective and controversial, had yet to see the light of day.

Politicians and bureaucrats ran their distinct worlds as closed shops, keeping important information off limits to outsiders. In any case, Canadians had little interest in getting inside information. Trust in government's ability to do the right thing was high. There were precious few voices calling for access-to-information legislation. Nor did politicians and bureaucrats have to concern themselves with affirmative action programs or official languages legislation. It was a world akin to a small village, where everyone knew everyone else, recognized their own place in the general scheme, and knew how to get things done without fuss.

The village was a relatively stable community. Civil servants were career officials in the true sense, and they were there for the long haul. Long service was expected, and it provided a continuity in policy making that is not seen today. As Granatstein reports, 'Robert Bryce's career extended from the end of the Depression into the 1980s, if one considers appointments and advisory roles.'[14] Bryce was no exception.[15] Deputy ministers by and large quietly retired with their public-service pension, happy in the knowledge that they had served their country away from the limelight.

Life in the Village

One of the vivid images in *The Private Government of Public Money* involves 'village life in the civil service.' Canadian civil servants and their political masters shared a common set of values – much as would the inhabitants of a small village. This integrated, elite culture was in part a result of common social backgrounds and common patterns of socialization in school and university. Although villages may have had different perspectives on governing and policy, and different career motivations, the two groups actually were very similar in outlook. In particular, they shared a common interest in governing their societies and in ensuring that the existing system did not change significantly.

While the 'village' was small, male-dominated, elitist, and conservative, it was effective. The common background of the participants helped make this possible, as did their belief that a consensual policy was better than an imposed one. In that era, even in nominally adversarial political systems, such as any operating in the British tradition, consensus tended to prevail, with little substantial policy change from one government to the next. That absence of sharp policy difference made the ideal of a politically neutral civil service attainable, given that all the potential political masters would be seeking the same broad goals, or nearly so.

The comfortable life in this political–administrative village had a number of characteristics. First, there was mutual respect among the inhabitants, and the civil service was thought of as a partner and, more significantly, as an ally of the political executive. In the Westminster model, the village system tended to be more closed, permitting private negotiations and agreements among the parties involved. Further, civil servants' political neutrality made the village mentality secretive. Mutual respect was in part a function of a second characteristic – mutual dependence. Each partner understood that it needed the other to reach its own personal and collective goals.

Another aspect of this mutual dependence concerned policy. Ministers tended to understand that they were amateurs in the policy business and therefore had to rely on the advice of their civil servants, if they were to make good decisions. The politicians, of course, also brought a great deal to the relationship, especially legitimacy, derived from their connections to the electoral process and to Parliament. Although most government decisions, including the making of legislation, was done by the bureaucracy, all that activity was legitimated in the popular mind by the ministerial connection with the public.

Policy making was also a straightforward affair. The deputy minister was the key player, and anything of consequence was brought quickly to his office. The village was sufficiently small that there was no need for an elaborate consultative process to assess options. The relevant deputy minister might simply have lunch with a handful of interested individuals in other departments to explain or sort out a game plan. Gordon Robertson wrote that, when the Ottawa policy process became more complex, more formal, and more consultative, 'I was sceptical of the idea of a minister trying to put forward all possible solutions to a question. Many so-called solutions would be straw men, put in to observe the rule but really to be knocked down. It also was likely to mean that no solution, even the best, would be totally worked through if three or four had to be given equal treatment.'[16] Senior officials had traditionally provided the knowledge and expertise and outlined the policy prescription to the minister, who would take it to cabinet. Ministers would accept the proposed solution, give it political legitimacy, and then 'sell it' to Canadians.

The traditional bargain between politicians and their civil servants flourished in the village – relatively low pay and anonymity in exchange for security, respect, and influence over public policy. The civil servants committed themselves to a public-service ethos in which they received much of their gratification from their sense of service and from the respect that they received within the system. This made their participation in the policy process more palatable to politicians, who by and large did not consider them self-aggrandizing or threatening.

The rather cosy relationship gained legitimacy from the widespread belief that government was a positive force for improving the economy and society. The civil service was respected. Further, economic growth funded 'treble affluence,' in which the nation's total resources, private resources, and public resources could all increase simultaneously. An increase in public programs did not have to mean a reduction in private consumption, in contrast to the seeming zero-sum calculation of today.

The relationship assured that politics and policy change were largely a matter of rational decision making. The post-war years saw new techniques, such as program budgeting, being introduced to allocate public funds more rationally – a 'best' way to allocate resources could produce a Pigovian optimum for public expenditures. Availability of resources and the absence of budget constraints facilitated rational choices.

Although the village was very comfortable, it also provided substantial benefits for society at large. First, although it offered governance of a certain complexion, it did produce successful governance. A well-developed organizational memory assisted its competence. Career stability meant that civil servants would remember a long line of past policies and their fates. The system also allowed them to offer unwelcome advice to decision makers. Their tenure and the respect that they enjoyed permitted them to advise a minister that he or she was heading in the wrong direction. That advice was not always heeded, but it was very probably given.

Life in the village produced predictability for society. Citizens knew what to expect from government, almost regardless of what party was in office. This predictability reflected the ideological consensus of the time and a general sense that government was successful, and centrist civil servants served as enforcers. The fact that the Liberal Party held power from 1935 to 1957 also encouraged close collaboration between ministers and career officials. Granatstein writes: 'In the Liberal hegemony, it was a relationship marked by mutual regard and trust, and that on balance served the nation well.'[17] Still, career officials were aware that while it was very important for them to be aware of politics, they could not put the interests of the Liberal Party ahead of the public interest.[18] Yet the arrival of Conservative John Diefenbaker in power in 1957 proved to be a difficult moment for village life. Diefenbaker, however, very quickly came to rely a great deal on the advice of Robert Bryce, a career official.

Gordon Robertson, who worked under prime ministers King, St Laurent, Diefenbaker, Pearson, and Trudeau, describes the changes in the working relationship between politicians and civil servants from 1941 to the 1970s.[19] At first, 'government was small and departments were tiny,' and everything of any consequence was brought to the attention of deputy ministers and ministers.[20] Lester Pearson, then a senior official at External Affairs, became exasperated with the kind of details requiring a ministerial signature. He wrote a memorandum in October 1941 to his deputy minister asking how he was 'going to show the Prime Minister how to win the war and make the peace if you have to spend two hours each day talking about the cost of Désy's table linen or the salary of the newest stenographer.'[21]

In summary, the village that provided a home for civil servants and politicians was small, accessible, comfortable, and an effective mechanism for governing. The doctrine of ministerial responsibility worked well, and politicians and civil servants had a strong working relationship. But things started to change in the environment of politics, in the nature of political leadership, and in government operations. A different model of governing began to emerge by the 1980s, after several decades of crisis, outlined next.

Civil Service under Siege

The role that governments played in society fell out of favour in many Western countries during the early 1970s, and a slowdown in economic growth coupled with rising inflation gave birth to a new and dreaded phenomenon, stagflation. The confidence of many of those reared on the merits of Keynesian economics began to sag as they discovered that, contra Keynes, the scope and cost of government kept growing in good economic times as well as in bad. By the late 1970s, a good number of countries were witnessing double-digit inflation and a growth in the costs of government that outstripped growth in the economy. The standard Keynesian response of increasing government spending to deal with rising unemployment appeared ever more inappropriate in the face of inflationary pressure and growing government deficits. Observers began to write about a crisis of 'governability' or 'governmental overload.' Political parties favouring a greater role for government in society and increased public spending were losing public support. For instance, in California, a grass-roots movement in 1978 successfully championed Proposition 13, a measure designed to limit taxation and, by extension, government spending.[22]

One concern was related to the apparent inability of governments to deal simultaneously with unemployment, inflation, balance of payments, and debt. Another extended to the apparatus of government itself – specifically, the bureaucracy, which to many now seemed a barrier against, rather than a vehicle for, progressive change. Those who still argued against tampering with the machinery of government and its 'armies' of entrenched officials were dismissed by both political left and right. Even people who had supported the ideas and social welfare programs of leaders such as Franklin Roosevelt, Clement Attlee, Harold Gaitskell, T.C. Douglas, and Adlai Stevenson were now calling for changes to the apparatus of government.[23]

Public servants came under attack virtually everywhere in the Western world. Even the British civil service, long a role model for its Canadian counterpart, came under heavy fire. The transition from a highly respected institution to a widely criticized one is best exemplified by the work of the Fabian Society, an organization devoted to spreading socialist principles. In 1947 the society declared that 'we have in Britain what is probably the best civil service in the world.'[24] By the late 1970s the society produced a highly critical report and called for major changes.[25]

In 1968 the Fulton Committee declared that the British civil service remained the product of the nineteenth-century Northcote–Trevelyan report. It found the service ill-equipped to meet current challenges. It provided its own list of discontents: too few skilled managers; not enough communication with the community; inadequate personnel management; too much emphasis on the 'amateur' or the 'generalist'; and insufficient responsibility and authority for scientists and specialists.[26] Both politicians and civil servants, the report argued, were seeing stable regularities giving way to public impatience with the capacity of government to introduce and manage change – any kind of change. Although the government had directed Fulton not to deal with the matter, his report also challenged ministerial responsibility.[27]

Canada had its own Fulton exercise – the Glassco Commission, which tabled its report in 1962. The commission looked to management and argued that the 'ponderous system, virtually unchanged in the past thirty years, is regarded by many as the price that must be paid under democracy in order to hold public servants properly accountable.'[28] However, 'the system in place no longer did the job.' Size appeared to be the key problem. What was a relatively simple government organization in 1939 'has become today a complicated system of departments, boards and commissions engaged in a multitude of different tasks. Obviously, the methods found effective for the management of the relatively compact organization of the prewar days cannot control without extensive alteration, the vast complex which has come into being in the past twenty years.' The government's financial controls seemed too cumbersome, with a wide variety of 'checks, counterchecks and duplication and blind adherence to regulations.'[29]

The Glassco Report recommended sweeping changes to existing programs and their funding, rather than concentrating on proposed increases, as in the past. It avoided dealing with ministerial responsibility, as did the government in its response. The government accepted most of the Glassco recommendations.

It is clear that government grew substantially throughout the 1950s, 1960s, and 1970s, and government decision making became far more complex. Total federal spending in 1950–51 totalled $2.4 billion; in 1960–61, $6.7 billion; in 1970, $15.3 billion; and in 1980–81, $62 billion.[30] Documenting growth in the civil service is not so straightforward: Statistics Canada, the Treasury Board Secretariat, and the Public Service Commission regularly provide a head count of civil servants, but they differ among each other. The calculations by Statistics Canada include the RCMP and crown corporations, which those of the other two bodies do not. In addition, all three head counters have their own 'caveats.'[31] In recent years, the 'contract state' has classified consultants and contract people as outside the public sector, even though some do virtually all their work for government.

Still, however one may count, the federal public service grew and grew between the 1950s and the 1980s. A study prepared for the Royal Commission on the Economic Union and Development Prospects for Canada (Macdonald Commission) in 1985 concluded that 'the federal government did not grow merely incrementally, as growth in population alone would warrant, from 1960 to 1982 ... While total population in 1982 was 39 per cent higher than it had been in 1960, the total federal government employment had increased by almost 47 percent.'[32] Data reveal that growth in personnel was particularly strong between 1965 and 1975 (see Table 4.1).

Quite apart from size – or perhaps because of it – there were some dark clouds over the village. Leading politicians began to voice their criticism publicly about the work of their civil servants. Richard Crossman, a prominent minister in Harold Wilson's Labour government in Britain, led the charge from the political left, the traditional ally of the civil service. His concerns had more to do with what he felt was unresponsiveness than with management. In his widely read diaries, which began to

Table 4.1
Numbers of federal government employees, December, 1960–82

Year	General government[a] No.	% change	Government enterprises No.	% change	Total government No.	% change	% general government	% government enterprises
1960	205,360	–	131,118	–	336,478	–	61.0	39.0
1965	214,799	4.6	129,916	–.9	334,715	2.4	62.2	37.8
1970	254,993	13.1	123,906	–4.5	378,899	6.5	67.1	32.9
1975	328,580	34.4	132,046	6.5	460,626	24.9	71.3	28.7
1980	340,395	4.2	157,988	19.6	498,293	8.6	68.2	31.8
1982[b]	355,403	–	138,281	–	493,684	–	72.0	28.0

Source: As presented in Sutherland and Doern, *Bureaucracy in Canada: Control and Reforms*, 93. Statistics Canada, *Federal Government* Employment, cat. no. 72-044 (Ottawa: Statistics Canada, 1960–82).
a Excludes members of the Canadian armed forces and post office Christmas help.
b Per cent change is not calculated because it is a two-year period only.

appear in 1975, he claimed that 'whenever one relaxes one's guard the Civil Service in one's Department quietly asserts itself ... Just as the Cabinet Secretariat constantly transforms the actual proceedings of Cabinet into the form of the Cabinet minutes (i.e., it substitutes what we should have said if we had done as they wished for what we actually did say), so here in my Department the civil servants are always putting in what they think I should have said and not what I actually decided.'[33] Crossman opened a floodgate of criticism, and it has not abated. The criticism came as no surprise to the political right, particularly in the United States, which had long believed that the bureaucracy has been subverting its policy objectives all along.

Crossman's *Diaries of a Cabinet Minister* spoke of his exasperation with a bureaucratic machine that took on a life of its own, like an uncontrollable monster. The diaries gave rise to the popular BBC television series *Yes, Minister*, which attracted some nine million regular viewers in Britain and became the favourite program of the permanent secretaries. The series also gained a worldwide audience and became highly popular with some politicians and civil servants in Canada, the United States, and Australia. The not-so-subtle message was that public servants were running the country and that the Sir Humphreys of the bureaucratic world wielded considerable power. The series actually served to give credence to bureaucrat 'bashing.' A new breed of politicians who believed that non-elected officials had become too powerful in shaping policy began to surface: civil servants should implement policy decisions and manage government resources more efficiently. The new political leadership wanted to have partisan policy advisers on the public payroll and pollsters interacting with party strategists – to render obsolete the Sir Humphrey style of making policy.[34]

Canadian politicians from both the right and the left became critical of bureaucracy by the 1970s. The right-of-centre Progressive Conservative Party had long been suspicious of the public service, and its suspicions turned to public criticism after Joe Clark's government lost a confidence motion in Parliament in 1979 after only a few months in power. They lost the subsequent election, and Flora MacDonald, minister of external affairs in the short-lived government, went on the lecture circuit to denounce senior public servants, claiming that they employed clever ruses to push their own agendas and to circumvent cabinet and ministerial direction. She itemized what she termed the officials' entrapment devices for ministers, which included bogus options and delayed recommendations. Joe Clark himself became critical of the public service and spoke of misguided programs 'concocted by a small group of theorists' within the public service.[35]

That Progressive Conservatives would be critical of the public service surprised few people. It was, however, a different story to find leading members of the centre-left Liberal Party also doing so. The Liberal Party, which held office for some forty-six of the fifty years between 1930 and 1980, had a particularly close working relationship with the public service. They had together built Canada's welfare state, and by the 1970s some observers were noting an incestuous relationship between ruling Liberals and senior civil servants. It therefore surprised more than a few people when the deputy prime minister, Allan MacEachen, reported that if Liberals had learned anything during their brief stay in opposition (1979–80) it was that they would no longer rely so much on the advice of civil servants. Other senior Liberals joined in and publicly criticized the policy advisory and management capacities of public servants.[36]

Liberal ministers began to voice concern that they were no longer in charge. One minister in the Trudeau era spoke of his experience when he was first appointed to the cabinet: 'It's like I was suddenly landed on the top deck of an ocean liner and told that the ship was my responsibility. When I turned to the captain (i.e., deputy minister) I was told that he was appointed there by someone else and any decision to remove him would be made elsewhere ... When I asked for a change in the ship's course, the ship just kept on going on the same course.'[37] Another minister in the Trudeau government revealed that 'I found it very difficult to communicate, to seek out advice, when I needed it. I felt that the ritual of the paper work – the chain of command – made it virtually impossible to get the kind of information I needed when I needed it and I felt very helpless.'[38] Some ministers were also bemoaning their small role in the policy process, which seemed limited essentially to saying 'Yes' or 'No' to what their departments wanted. They insisted that saying 'No' was a negative power and so consequently were hesitant to exercise it. They wanted to be present when policy options were being considered and not be relegated to a policy role after the fact or when the die had already been cast.[39]

Life in the village was no longer simple. In Western societies, a general declining commitment to collective action was developing, along with increasing individualism and a sharp decline in deference to political authority. Robert Putnam coined the phrase 'bowling alone' – while more Americans were saying that they bowled, membership in bowling leagues had been declining rapidly.[40] This loss of 'social capital' created problems for a number of social institutions, and it reduced government's capacity to count on citizens' commitment to any organization larger than their own family.

The breathtaking speed of modern communications, especially television, has placed enormous pressure on government to make decisions quickly, for fear of appearing indecisive and not in control. This, precisely at a time when governments began to grow and decision making became increasingly complex. Newspapers were and remain in large measure local or territorial, but not so television. It, for example, gave its viewers a ringside seat during the Gulf War. TV's reach is global, it is increasingly critical, and it is widely accessible, even to the illiterate. Within minutes, it can zero in on any issue anywhere in the world and compare virtually any given situation in one country to a similar one in another. Above all, it has a capacity to intrude into the political arena and the operations of government and to inform the public quickly, visually, and with considerable impact if something is not working. The Vietnam War, as well as Watergate, had a profound impact on television journalism.

Political memoirs of former politicians reveal that many have given up any hope of the media reporting on their accomplishments objectively.[41] They may well have a point. George Bain, one of Canada's most respected 'postwar journalists,' wrote a book describing the new breed of journalists, who 'grew up in the heady 1960s ... and brought forward certain generational traits [including] ... a distrust of all things institutional, ... a general anti-everything prejudice founded on fond recollections of press clippings from their time as a generation of idealists.'[42] The media are quick to inform, but the information is much more often than not trivial and designed to be provocative. Jeffrey Simpson observes: 'Good news doesn't sell when it comes to government. Trash the government and headlines flow; praise it, however modestly, and get ignored.'[43] Anthony Westell, in his *The Inside Story: A Life in Journalism*, bemoans the 'adversarial and destructive' style of contemporary journalism, wishing that it would start 'from the principle of supporting democratic institutions.'[44] Although the media may well have empowered the electorate, they have done so often with limited regard for objectivity and for the finer points of public policy and the public policy process.

The information revolution has radically changed village life. Government's near-monopoly on the information that it generated used to strengthen its hand in its dealings with interest groups and the public. New communication technology and easier access to government information allow outsiders to develop positions on many issues and to challenge government policy. Outsiders are far better equipped to challenge the village elders than was the case forty years ago.

The rise of the global economy and global corporations holds major implications for national governments. Some traditional policy levers are no longer available to politicians, and others can no longer be as easily manipulated. Regional trade deals and the global economy have introduced 'straitjackets limiting the ability of government to intervene in the pursuit of social and economic goals.'[45] Global corporations meanwhile invariably denationalize enterprises and are particularly alert to government attempts to restrict the flow of capital or the location of economic activities.

Ironically, the government decision-making process began to slow down and became more complicated precisely when governments had to make decisions quickly and to deal with far more aggressive media. Pierre Trudeau reports in his memoirs that he set out shortly after becoming prime minister to strengthen 'the coherence of government [by ensuring] that all ministers be responsible for all decisions made by the government of which they are a part.'[46] There was of course a flip side to this objective. As Gordon Robertson explains: 'Ministers now, in many cases, have to give up some share of their authority and control to other ministers ... Speed of action is certainly less in the new system and ministers have less chance to appear in roles of clear and firm decision.'[47] Ministers in fact gave up authority not to cabinet but to the prime minister and central agencies[48] – a far cry from the world of the village.

It does not much matter whether or not politicians brought this new state of affairs on themselves. No doubt many of them believe that they have perhaps been 'lightning rods' for much that is wrong in the new order. National governments can no longer manoeuvre as they once could, not only as a result of globalization, but also because of the electorate's loss of confidence in their ability to intervene positively in the economy and because of a collapse of deference to political and administrative authority. One can appreciate why voters would come to regard career public servants as a sheltered lot, somewhat removed from probing and critical media, enjoying tenure, unhurried by election timetables, and rarely anxious to challenge the status quo. If the village could no longer protect politicians, the politicians in turn could see little reason to protect civil servants.[49] Many politicians came to the view that they or their close advisers should replace or at least work with some public servants.

Burning the Village: The 1980s

Britain again led the way: Prime Minister Margaret Thatcher not only articulated what was wrong with the status quo, she also pointed the way to a new model. She became convinced that government had become too cumbersome, too removed from the population, too rigid, too centralized, too hierarchical, and overly staffed.[50] If some politicians had also come to question the civil service but were hesitant to do something about it, Thatcher showed no such reluctance.

Thatcher's reforms have already been well documented.[51] Suffice to note that she turned to the private sector for inspiration. She sold or transferred government assets and enterprises, even traditional government activities, to the private sector. She insisted that private-sector management techniques be introduced to what she could not sell or transfer.

Thatcher embraced privatization with enthusiasm and took to selling assets on a 'grand scale.'[52] Within several years of coming to power, her government had sold British Aerospace, British Gas, British Steel, British Telecom, various public utilities, and one million public-housing units. She saw privatization as a sure route to lasting change. Spending cuts, as practised in the past, might result in bureaucracies spending less, but not necessarily in doing their work more efficiently. Privatization meant that bureaucrats could not reinstate the status quo by simply waiting out the political party in power. The new gospel was not lost on civil servants: it was now considered that there was no intrinsic value in what they were doing; private-sector managers were believed to have superior skills; and civil servants were no longer trusted to place the interest of the community before their own. Village life would never be the same.

Village life in Canada was also about to he transformed. The auditor general shook the political class when he wrote in 1976 that 'Parliament – and indeed the government – had lost or was close to losing effective control of the public purse.'[53] The warning had an impact. The message could not be more clear – there was something fundamentally wrong in government operations. It also enabled the Office of the Auditor General to expand its mandate considerably. The office would now carry out comprehensive and value-for-money audits, which would enable the auditor general to make some sweeping statements about the apparent inability of government to do many things right. One senior government official expressed the view in 1989 that 'the Auditor in the last ten years had moved light years beyond the role of auditor, towards a broad assessment of government management and decision making.'[54] The village now had a new, much more assertive enemy in its midst.

The auditor general's 1976 report led the federal government to establish a royal commission. The Treasury Board president, Robert Andras, wrote that 'Parliament, the Government and the citizenry were in a quandary' and that a thorough review of financial management and accountability was urgently required.[55] The Royal Commission on Financial Organization and Accountability (the Lambert Commission) had a mandate 'to ensure that financial management and control exercised at all levels ... meets the highest attainable standards (and) to establish effective accountability of deputy ministers ... to the Government and, where appropriate, to Parliament.'[56] The commission tabled its report in 1979, along with 165 recommendations.

The commission concluded that deputy ministers were largely deficient in management skills and that a sense of frugality in government operations was needed. It asserted that the serious malaise in management stemmed from an 'almost total breakdown in the chain of accountability.'[57] The commission identified ministerial responsibility as the culprit and urged that it be overhauled. It argued that the deputy minister should be formally designated chief administrative officer and be prepared to render an account of his or her department. It maintained that ministerial responsibility had to be reconciled with the complexity of modern government. A few of its recommendations were adopted, but the commission finally had very little impact. The reason: 'Many senior government officials felt that the commission even lacked a basic grasp of how parliamentary government works,' and many of its findings were dismissed out of hand.[58] But other developments would make life difficult for those in government, ranging from the tax-reform fiasco of 1981, through the introduction of new oversight bodies and access-to-information legislation, to the failed National Energy Program (NEP), launched in 1980.

Brian Mulroney would, as we saw above, borrow a page from Margaret

Thatcher in his attempt to reform government operations, although he never gave the matter the attention and priority that Thatcher did. But he went further than Thatcher in strengthening the ability of cabinet and ministers to shape policy. He established a chief of staff in each ministerial office, politically partisan and set at the assistant deputy minister level – a departure from both British and Canadian traditions. Government press releases describe the position as an 'official in the American style.' Mulroney felt that the initiative would assist his government 'to govern and to let managers manage.'[59] It is difficult to assess its success – again it depends on who is asking, who is answering, what the question is, and who the incumbent was.[60] We do know that Jean Chrétien abolished the position when he came to power in 1993. Still, again the message could not be clearer – the public service could not be trusted on matters of policy.

Conclusion: Changes Under Way

Over several decades, the Canadian civil service went from being a highly valued institution to one criticized by its traditional allies and suffering serious morale problems.[61] It had been esteemed for its ability to advise ministers, to shape policies, and to administer programs with a sense of frugality. It had a deep sense of community; the inhabitants not only knew each other well but also grasped intuitively who was responsible for what. Ministers knew that they held the power to decide and that they were not threatened by the work of their officials. In turn, deputy ministers would, as we saw, seek to serve their ministers well, offer advice even if it was not always welcomed, and instinctively eschew any public profile. Most were career officials who were both trusted policy advisers and administrators.

By the early 1970s village life was changing. The village was increasingly like an urban sprawl, and an element of distrust between politicians and civil servants had set in. Politicians felt that too much influence was in the hands of permanent officials. Trudeau, it will be recalled, attempted to strengthen the ability of his ministers to shape policy. Mulroney established an American-style senior-level, partisan position in ministerial offices to advise on policy.

There were other discontents. At the urging of the Glassco Commission, the government had scrapped a large number of central controls and simplified decision-making processes. The goal had been to let managers manage. Yet, ironically, from that day to this, the government has never stopped searching for ways to let managers manage. Indeed, every five years, almost like clockwork, the issue resurfaces. The government has tried everything, it seems. Yet there is a feeling that *plus ça change, plus c'est pareil* and that any reform will invariably fall far short of the mark.

Margaret Thatcher, more than any other Western leader, took a strong interest in government operations and didn't flinch from imposing ambitious reforms. She became a role model for other leaders who wanted to transform government operations. Yet current British Prime Minister Tony Blair has expressed his frustration with the country's civil service, suggesting that it has not changed much in the past fifty years.[62] In Canada, wave after wave of reforms from the 1960s to today has failed to produce one single effort that lived up to expectations. The auditor general summed up the widespread perception in Ottawa when he observed that all civil-service reforms tend to have a 'quiet death.'[63] And yet the various attempts at reform did, initially at least, offer hope that things could be improved. Could it be that we have misdiagnosed the patient?

PART TWO

Code Red,
1980s and 1990s

5

Diagnosing the Patient

In chapter 4, we saw that many politicians by the 1980s were giving up on the public service and on its traditional bargain with politicians. Given this state of affairs, how was the patient diagnosed? Better yet, who was the patient? How did the caregivers decide? Did they try to bring the patient back to life? Why were many politicians willing to break the traditional bargain that had served them so well over the years? What has actually changed?

Deciding What to Fix

As we saw above, there is plenty of evidence to suggest that public confidence in government institutions has dropped in many Western democracies. Belgium, Britain, Canada, Ireland, Italy, the Netherlands, Norway, Sweden, and the United States have all seen some reduction of trust in government.[1] Neil Nevitte maintains that, at least in Canada, this decline is part of a larger phenomenon – the decline of deference. But he adds that the loss in confidence is greater in political than in non-political institutions.[2]

Albert Hirshman, in his celebrated *Exit, Voice and Loyalty*, wrote in 1970 about the differences between the business world and government. He explained that in business 'the customer who, dissatisfied with the product of one firm, shifts to that of another, uses the market to defend his welfare and to improve his position. This is neat, tidy, impersonal, effective, and quiet. It easily lends itself to quantifying success and failure. With government, however, the "customer" uses "voice" to express dissatisfaction. Voice is, of course, much more messy than a quiet exit, since it can range "all the way from faint grumbling to violent protest; it implies articulation of one's critical opinions rather than a private secret vote in the anonymity of a supermarket; and finally, it is direct and straightforward rather than roundabout."[3] Public-opinion surveys now capture voice on a monthly basis, or even more frequently, if political parties desire it and are prepared to pay. The great majority of politicians react to the voice expressed in public-opinion surveys, and government operations are often in their direct line of attack as they seek to introduce corrective measures.

The voice heard towards the end of the twentieth century suggested that there was plenty wrong with government. We know that, as a last resort, citizens can only leave political parties or simply decide not to vote. There is evidence to suggest that this is in fact happening. Three students of Canadian politics recently concluded that 'Canadian party politics collapsed in the early 1990s' and add that 'gone are the days when all major parties agreed on the essence of all the major issues.'[4]

Canadians are far less deferential than they were thirty years ago and more 'self-reliant ... [and] therefore less inclined to follow established lines of authority.'[5] Canadians, no less than Americans and Europeans, now question the fountain of authority in many areas, and government is at the top of the list. Indeed, 'only about a quarter of Canadians believe that the government can be trusted to do the right thing all or most of the time [while] a generation ago the figure was closer to three quarters.'[6] Compared to the era described in chapter 4, Canada has witnessed a veritable collapse of deference, and it is hardly possible to overstate its impact on government operations.

A government-commissioned report warned in 1998 about 'the erosion of public confidence in governments and state institutions.'[7] A series of ongoing surveys also sponsored by the government and launched in 1994 pointed to disturbing trends. They reported pervasive dissatisfaction, hostility to government, and a desire for real change in government institutions. The surveys presented a shopping list of complaints about government. A majority of Canadians felt that the ethical standards of the federal government had slipped badly, that bureaucracy was inefficient and wasteful, that too many government programs did not work, and the list went on.[8] Other surveys revealed that 'most Canadians [held] federal politicians of all stripes in low regard.'[9] Politicians themselves now acknowledge the problem. Chuck Strahl, a widely respected opposition MP, observed in the House that 'Canadians simply do not hold members of parliament in very high esteem.'[10]

Thus there was by the mid-1990s a consensus that the country's political and administrative institutions were not working. The one consolation for Canadians was that they were not alone – the same phenomenon was evident in many other Western democracies. Yet recent comparative research shows that trust in political institutions declined more in Canada than elsewhere in the 1990s – from 61 per cent in the 1980s to 46 per cent in the 1990s – placing Canada at the low end among Western countries.[11]

When it came to assigning blame, there would be enough to go around. Some respondents argued that political and administrative institutions were frozen in time, unwilling or incapable of introducing substantive change. Some felt that modern technology had not only broken open the monopoly on policy advice but also provided a window on government operations to outsiders. Others argued that politicians and parties were to blame for abandoning substantial policy debates in favour of political posturing. They claimed that politics had become more concerned with producing staged events of no consequence than with promoting genuine policy debate. Others looked to the changing role of the media since Watergate to explain the decline in trust. Still others suggested that government had taken on too much responsibility and had become part of the problem, rather than the solution. In taking on so many responsibilities, governments had lost the ability to deliver on important issues. U.S. President Ronald Reagan observed, 'Government declared war on poverty and poverty won.'

Accordingly, there was no shortage of things to fix. The menu ranged from altering political institutions, through rethinking the role of parties, to lowering public expectations about government and reforming bureaucracy. Many Western democracies, however, would focus only on the last and set out to fix the bureaucracy. Again Canada was no exception.

This chapter looks at evolving popular perceptions of the civil service, especially in the media; at politicians' changing views of the role of career officials; at the emerging concept of responsive competence as a desideratum for top bureaucrats; and at management in the civil service.

Yes, Minister

The BBC television series *Yes, Minister* has a lot to answer for. It was a satire, but it had a profound impact on how the public service was perceived not just in Britain but in Canada and in other Anglo-American democracies. Sandford Borins writes that it became 'something of a cult program, exceedingly popular with a small following that is intensely interested in public affairs.'[12] In Britain, Margaret Thatcher had each episode videotaped, and she apparently subscribed to its caricature view of senior civil servants.[13]

The series painted a new portrait of the relationship between politicians and career officials. The portrait showed ministers as publicity-seeking dimwits and no match for the highly educated, unprincipled, and Machiavellian career officials. No matter the issue and however sensible the minister's position, Sir Humphrey, the senior official, would have a position at odds with the minister's, and he would invariably have his way. Sir Humphrey's views, however, were not rooted in an ideology that differed from the minister's or for that matter that stemmed from profound beliefs. Rather, he could always be counted on to favour the status quo and, more important, to do anything necessary to protect the interest of the department and the public service. Moreover, Sir Humphrey would not only shape all major policy decisions and run the department, but he would also manage political crises on behalf of his minister. No matter the issue, the minister in the end had to rely on Sir Humphrey's considerable political and bureaucratic skills simply to survive. The series brings to mind Harold Wilson's response when asked if he had ever regretted not becoming a permanent public servant in the Cabinet Office, where he served during the Second World War. 'Heavens no!,' he replied, 'I couldn't have stood the intrigues.'[14]

Thatcher's arrival in office in Britain in 1979 signalled a clean break from the past, not just in policy but also in political–bureaucratic relations. The *Yes, Minister* paradigm was about to come to an abrupt end, if we assume for a moment that it ever existed. The political impulse in Britain and later in the United States (Ronald Reagan) and in Canada (Brian Mulroney) was to roll back the state, to cut spending, and also, from time to time, to engage in bureaucracy 'bashing.' As one observer argued: 'In the Anglo-American democracies in particular, career public services were subject to an assault by politicians that was unprecedented in this century. Relations between politicians and the public service turned sour and public service morale plummeted.'[15] Politicians in power knew what they wanted, or at least they thought they did, and they saw no need to wait for advice from career officials. Indeed, if anything, they felt that career officials would try to steer them away from the policy agenda, given that rolling back the state would run counter to their own interests.

Politicians were no longer content to be amateurs in the policy process, as they were in the village life described in the previous chapter. They saw their role as much more than providing political legitimacy. Politicians elected to office in the 1980s had firm ideas on what needed to be done and were in no mood for compromise, supporting the status quo, or being told that what they wanted was not possible or that it should not be pursued. If they had to move into areas once reserved for public servants to ensure that their policy agenda was implemented, then so be it.

Politicians also came to office convinced that government operations were being mismanaged. This is not to suggest for a moment that they wanted to become administrators themselves or to have a stronger role in the day-to-day management of departments and agencies. What it does indicate, however, is that politicians believed that there was a great deal of waste in government operations and that reforms were urgently needed. Anglo-American governments were struggling with stubborn deficits and accumulated debt during the 1980s and 1990s. For politicians, the solution was not simply to roll back the state, but also to ensure that what was left in its hands would be better managed, and that depended on career officials, not on them.

Politicians thus assumed that if they could gain the upper hand in shaping policy and turn senior career officials into competent managers, then they would have gone a long way towards fixing government. This view underpinned major reforms throughout the 1980s and 1990s in the Anglo-American democracies. The efforts continued in this vein long after Thatcher, Reagan, and Mulroney left office.

The new village that politicians set out to build would inevitably redefine their relations with career officials and the work of the public service. Indeed, politicians began calling for a different breed of public servant. All the while, however, they avoided looking to their own institution or their own role, as they set out to fix government. Career officials, given their anonymity under ministerial responsibility, could not speak out, publicly at least. If they could have, they might well have argued that the civil service was not the problem. In fact, independent observers were increasingly expressing concern at the depth to which the reputations of both Houses of Parliament in Canada had fallen.[16]

Career officials could have made the case that all too often politicians lose sight of the fact that democratic institutions (including the civil service) are in the first instance organizations intended to foster democratic representation and accountability as an end in itself. They can never be merely means to promote other ends. The pervasiveness of bureaucracy in modern life has more to do with administration in a representative democracy than with simple efficiency. Bureaucracy is designed to administer the laws and policies set by elected politicians, and, as a result, authority delegated to career officials must be handled bureaucratically in order that public servants can accept direction.[17] It is for this reason that due process, fairness, and the keeping of records are all-important in government operations. Politicians can very quickly, as experience tells us, provide citizens a focus for their grievances.

These then are the realities of representative democracy, and they do not easily square with management reform, including the concept of empowerment and the objective of running government operations like a business. In Canada, the prime minister, Parliament, and the cabinet stand – or should stand – at the apex of political authority. Career officials may well have concluded, in private conversation, that it was not possible to reform the civil service and government operations while leaving political institutions virtually intact. They may well have been tempted to tell the political class, 'Heal thyself,' rather than trying to cure the public service. Politicians, however, were in no mood to hear this message, and public servants were in no position to voice the message publicly.

What Do the Politicians Want?

Michael Heseltine in Britain has summed up what politicians felt was wrong with the public service: 'Thinker-doers (were) in short supply. Thinker-advisers are the normal product of the system.'[18] Politicians saw senior career officials as non-partisan, detached, above the fray, concerned with the finer points of public policy and interdepartmental considerations, preoccupied with what their peers in other departments thought, capable of seeing all sides of any issue but, much more often than not, favouring the status quo. For this reason and for want of a better term, career officials who have made it to the top in Britain and Ottawa were labelled 'generalists.' They came from virtually any academic discipline and were expected to take on any policy issue in any department. They climbed an elaborate bureaucratic pyramid towards the top. They knew the difference between being loyal to the government and being politically partisan, and they learned how to avoid being caught in a politically partisan situation.

Pierre Trudeau got more than he bargained for when he overhauled the machinery of government in the late 1960s and early 1970s. He sought to strengthen central agencies and collective decision making in government because he and his advisers had concluded that senior officials in line departments had become too powerful. They ran departments, Trudeau felt, like personal fiefdoms and all too often left outsiders, including ministers, on the outside looking in. Trudeau was not alone in his thinking. Knowledgeable observers have argued that before the 1960s the federal government resembled a 'feudal state with rigid departmental boundaries and policy initiatives working their way up through semi-autonomous departmental fiefdoms.'[19] The solution was to promote conflicting interests within government. Hence the decision to strengthen central agencies, which would then be in a position to challenge the views of line departments. The Trudeau reforms placed a premium on countervailing views in making policy.

The Trudeau era had a tremendous impact on the future appointment of deputy ministers. No longer would they rise through the ranks of a single department to become its deputy minister. Career officials would now reach senior ranks by occupying several policy positions in both line departments and central agencies. Deputy ministers in the old school had an intimate knowledge of their sectors, their departments, and their policies, programs, operations, and personnel. Deputy ministers in the new school would be policy generalists capable of serving in senior positions virtually anywhere in government. Accordingly, through his reforms, Trudeau redefined the areas from which deputy ministers would be drawn. The result is that deputy ministers are no longer as familiar with the policies and administration of their departments as was the case before Trudeau's reforms.

Arthur Kroeger, a long-time federal public servant, contrasted the relationship between ministers and senior career officials in the pre-Trudeau period and today. He maintains that ministers used to have a high degree of autonomy within their portfolios, and cabinet discussions tended to take place only when a matter was ripe for decision. Policy development was largely the work of officials and, if necessary, of senior-level interdepartmental committees, which reconciled divergent interests. Fully developed proposals would go to the responsible minister, who, if the product met with his or her approval, would then take it to cabinet.

This brief description, Kroeger writes, could be taken to mean that officials pretty much ran the show and dominated decision making by ministers. This, he insisted, 'would be a serious misinterpretation. A key factor to be borne in mind is that the working relationship between ministers and their senior officials was much closer in the 1950s and 1960s than it is today.' While 'the commonest complaint of deputy ministers of my generation was the difficulty of getting time with our ministers – with bilateral meetings once a week being the best that most of us could manage – the normal practice in both Mr. St. Laurent's and Mr. Pearson's governments was for ministers and their deputies to meet at the beginning of every working day. Consequently, ministers could be kept fully informed about work that was in progress, and they were able to provide their officials with guidance on a regular basis. I have yet to meet anyone with first-hand experience of this period who is in any doubt that ministers such as Mitchell Sharp, Paul Martin Senior, C.M. Drury and Allan MacEachen were fully in charge of what happened in their departments.'[20] David Smith comments: 'The dominant cabinet figures (of the past more than the present) men such as Gardiner, Howe or Allan MacEachen – the regional lieutenants ... exploited an administrative structure that made them and their departments semi-sovereign powers.'[21]

A detailed study, 'Changing Profile of Federal Deputy Ministers, 1867 to 1988,' is very revealing. It reports that deputy ministers' prior experience in the department of appointment has declined to three years today from twelve in the early years of Confederation. In addition, deputy ministers now spend about four years at that rank and on average change departments once during that period. Unlike their predecessors, they no longer stay with and retire in their department: 'They can no longer head the same department for many years.'[22] Compared with other national public services, Canada's deputy ministers have less seniority in government on average than, for example, British permanent secretaries. Moreover, in Ottawa, recruitment of deputy ministers easily crosses the boundaries between departments, while countries such as France and Germany still choose the permanent head of the department from its senior ranks.[23]

Frank Swift, a former senior federal public servant, carried out a study of the background and work experience of deputy ministers. His conclusion reveals that 'experience in a central agency, most notably in the Privy Council Office, is now a virtual prerequisite for deputy-level appointments. Almost two out of three deputies have no previous experience in program management in a line department. Although there is evidence that more deputies have management experience outside of central agencies, this increase is more typically in policy and process management positions. Previous experience in the department ... is not usual for deputy minister appointments. It is considered less important to have experience in line departments delivering services to the public than central agency experience providing policy advice. In addition, most deputies have no federal public service experience in Canada outside the National Capital Region.'[24]

This situation affects the government and the public service. The 'have-policy' and the 'have-central-agency-experience' will-travel types have a different perspective from someone who has risen through the ranks of the department to become its deputy minister. For one thing, the former will be preoccupied with 'managing up' – that is, looking up to their ministers and to the centre of government, rather than down the organization, to establish priorities and a sense of direction. A federal task force recently argued that 'many senior public servants have made their careers because of their skills in managing up. They have been valued and promoted because they were adept at providing superiors with what they needed ... But if they [i.e., skills of managing up] are nourished in excess, to the exclusion of other important values, they can obscure the importance of managing down.'[25]

Yet it appears that some ministers, if they could, would happily turn back the clock to the old days, when senior officials came up through the ranks, where they had gained intimate knowledge of their sectors and of their departments' policies and programs. Managing up, it appears, has its limits, even for those whom it is designed to benefit. Roméo Leblanc, reflecting on his days as minister of fisheries and oceans, observed, 'I shared with many Ministers a somewhat jaundiced view of the idea that you can be a good ADM in anything, the moment you're transferred there by the system ... I still think that being able to talk with fishermen on the wharf or with farmers in their barns is important ... It is essential to have direct experience.'[26]

Yet the conventional thinking in the senior ranks of the Canadian public service was that thinker-doers were of the old school and thinker-advisers of the new school. It is difficult to determine what politicians wanted from the public service. They wanted strong policy advisers to guide them away from problems but they also wanted strong managers. However, as for policy, they felt that career officials took too much comfort in standing above the political fray. As a result, they were too detached and uncommitted to the government's policy agenda. As for management, the rhetoric of the politicians suggested that senior public servants lacked the management skills and the interest to run large government departments and agencies.

Responsive Competence

The traditional bargain between politicians and career officials has several elements. One suggests that officials advise, ministers decide, and then the officials implement the decision or do as they are told. If they should fail to do as they are instructed, then they are breaking the bargain. The theory is neat and tidy, and it makes the rules clear to both parties. Yet a widely held consensus emerged in the 1970s that many career officials in Canada's civil service were, willingly or not, breaking this part of the arrangement.

Politicians and career officials, as we saw above, had no difficulty working together in managing the war effort and in building the welfare state. The purpose was clear, and there was very little dispute about what was needed (i.e., government programs) and about the instruments to get the job done (i.e., government departments and agencies). It was a time when many policy issues could still be contained within a single government department. There is little disagreement when everybody knows which direction to push. In addition, the policies, the plans, and the programs were all prepared in relative secrecy by a small circle of politicians and senior career officials. It was also fairly easy for the latter to operate in the shade and give all the limelight to ministers. It was in brief a made-to-measure world, in which the traditional bargain flourished.

A theoretical challenge to the idea of a career public service as a condition for good government also began to emerge in the late 1970s in the Anglo-American democracies.[27] Public-choice theory and agency theory made the case that career officials promote their own self interest which could well be at odds with the wishes of elected representatives and those whom they represent. In addition, career officials, given their secure position, had more influence than politicians and could get their way in establishing government priorities. Agency theory suggests that career officials are 'agents' of the politicians, who are the 'principals.' The agents invariably have the upper hand because they have an information advantage in developing and implementing public policies. As one student of Canadian public administration explains, 'Public choice theory thus speaks to the limited capacity of politicians to direct the state apparatus; agency theory speaks to the limited capacity of politicians to hold their public administrators accountable.'[28]

Both theories, particularly public choice, became popular with politicians in the 1980s. Margaret Thatcher urged senior career officials in Britain to read the public-choice literature. David Stockman, one of Ronald Reagan's senior advisers, argued, 'Do you want to understand why government officials behave the way they do? All you need to know is that they are trying to maximize the budgets of their agencies. Do you want to understand what drives politicians? All you need to know is that they want to be re-elected. Do you want to understand legislation? Just see it as a sale of the coercive power of government to the highest bidder, like a cattle auction.'[29]

In Canada, some of Brian Mulroney's own senior policy advisers also selected public choice. My discussion with one such official revealed that the enthusiasm for public choice was based, however, more on its reported support of neoconservatism than on a deep understanding of the theory. Through their contacts with counterparts working with Reagan and Thatcher, some officials in Mulroney's office became sufficiently familiar with public choice to know that it labelled bureaucrats 'budget maximizers.'[30]

Public choice captured the right-of-centre political parties in the Anglo-American democracies in the 1980s, as Keynesian economics had seized government treasuries in the 1930s and 1940s. There were major differences, however. Keynesian economics did not have to confront entrenched programs and bureaucracies. Indeed, it had offered opportunities to those who wanted to expand the role of the state and their own programs. For another, Keynesian economics is much more prescriptive about what should be done, and how, than is public choice. Still, politicians used the theory to raise questions about career officials' policy making and to attack bureaucracy.

Policy making also became far more complex. Major policy issues would no longer fit neatly into a single department – a theme to which I return many times below. The need for co-ordination between government departments goes back to the 1940s in planning for the war effort.[31] However, by the 1970s, cross-cutting policy issues began to surface everywhere so that even traditional line departments such as Agriculture could no longer work in relative isolation from other departments or even other levels of government, and new policy measures, however modest, would by definition involve several departments and central agencies. The environment, trade, and human resources,

for example, would affect virtually every department. One senior official explained to me that 'the important issues now all cut across traditional departments and lines of authority. Ministers don't yet understand that, so public servants have to take up the slack to try to cope
with the changes.'[32] But this new situation would make it more difficult
for the civil service to produce firm, 'Yes' or 'No' policy advice in the
absence of clear political direction.

Stagflation, the energy crisis, and growing government debt did not
lend themselves to easy solutions. Political parties could not produce
policy prescriptions for major issues or even provide a meaningful context to guide politicians and career officials in establishing policy. It
would be extremely difficult for a handful of paid party employees and a
few volunteers preoccupied with scoring partisan political points to put
together a set of prepared and agreed-on policies for a party convention
to consider. Circumstances changed quickly, and even broad policy prescriptions could become outdated in short order.

However, politicians rarely accused career civil servants of being politically partisan. At least in Canada, any such accusations have never been
systematically sustained. Rather, politicians became convinced that
career officials had a much too narrow perspective on policy issues and
were unwilling to look at new and more creative solutions. One is
reminded of Hubert Humphrey's declaration in running for office, 'We
need a new, fresh, buoyant, forward-looking economics to replace the
tired, old economics telling us we can't do the things we want to do – the
things we have to do.'[33] Any opposition MP in Canada could easily make
a similar statement, and some would even see merit in it. In the absence
of both knowledge and the kind of discipline that political power
imposes, one can make virtually any kind of grandiose statement about a
better tomorrow – possible if only the right party had power and government officials could see the light. Many politicians, including ministers,
concluded that they had become overly dependent on career officials
and that their advice was not sufficiently creative. Moreover, many came
to believe that career officials would promote their departmental perspective, regardless of the party in power or the minister in charge. Some
politicians interpreted this to mean that officials would tell them that
there was really only one policy perspective that could possibly work *and*
win the support of other departments and other governments.

By the 1970s, many politicians came to the conclusion that career officials had gained too much influence on the policy agenda and in shaping policy solutions. They felt that 'bureaucratic politics' was replacing

'party politics' as the 'dominant theatre of decision in the modern state.'[34] Some argued that individuals wishing to influence public policy should no longer join political parties. Rather, they should learn the ways of the bureaucracy and work with relevant officials to shape new policy measures. Former Ontario premier Bob Rae reports that in private meetings Prime Minister Mulroney would, from time to time, say to him and other provincial premiers, 'This is a good idea, but they would not let me do it.' When asked who 'they' were, he would respond, 'the bureaucrats.'[35] In the 1950s, this would have been a sure sign that senior career officials were simply doing their job well. Thirty years later it was a sign that bureaucrats had too much influence.

How then do politicians and career officials differ on policy? There is plenty of evidence that career officials are pragmatists and centrist on most policy issues and that the civil service has a built-in conservatism.[36] Senior officials are often wont to offer their political masters 'a word of caution here before launching a new proposal.' As a rule, they prefer leaving things at rest until they are satisfied that the proposed changes are workable and that the political will exists to support changes and to stay the course. For senior departmental officials, political will means more than having their ministers support the proposal. Given that policy issues are no longer contained within a single department, the political-will test has become more demanding and more collective. In Canada at least, the prime minister is the key player in establishing a collective political will, notwithstanding Brian Mulroney's lament. Career officials have learned in climbing the hierarchical ladder that few ministers have the clout with the prime minister to carry a proposal without first going through an elaborate policy-making process.

Politicians define problems in terms of political advantage and the perceived impact on their regions, communities, and party. They also want policy decisions that meet popular demand. They can inject passion into a debate, and some can hold firm views on any given issue. Bureaucrats know full well that politicians come and go and have to make their mark in short order. Politicians want to see their ideas implemented fast and have little patience with bureaucratic requirements for fine tuning or leaving things at rest until satisfied that the proposed changes are workable. Ministers also expect their departmental officials to be on their side in getting their proposals approved.[37]

Yet ministers no longer want officials to be totally in charge of solutions. The Crossman diaries spoke to this issue: 'Very often the whole job is pre-cooked in the official committees to a point from which it is extremely difficult to reach any other conclusion than that already determined by officials in advance.'[38] This, however, is a relatively new concern (since the 1970s). In the days of the village described above, ministers expected officials to pre-cook policy solutions. In fact, they welcomed it and saw it as an important function of the senior civil servants. But things changed, and Crossman put his finger on a problem. A good number of ministers in Canada, whether Conservative or Liberal, have voiced similar criticism.[39]

Taking Care of Business?

'Empowerment' became one of the more popular buzz words in government in the Anglo-American democracies in the 1980s and 1990s. If politicians came to believe that career officials had too much influence over policy, they also worried that they did not have *enough* when it came to management. Worse, politicians suspected that senior officials had little interest in managing their departments. Increasingly, politicians actually talked about giving bureaucrats greater power to manage government departments and programs.

One student of public administration observes that 'the new public management that emerged during the 1980s in the four Westminster systems of Australia, Canada, New Zealand, and the United Kingdom clearly has entailed the acceptance of new paradigms for the administration of public affairs.' There were 'several common elements ... found across' the four countries.[40] One was a new emphasis on management. Another was a profound belief that private-sector management techniques were superior to public-sector techniques, that they could work in government, and, further, that they should be introduced to government operations as quickly as possible.

The vocabulary in government, if not government operations, was transformed during the 1980s and 1990s. It is safe to assume that career officials who served in the earlier village would have had difficulty identifying with it. Politicians and senior officials set out to change government operations into business units. 'Strategic plans' gave way to 'business plans,' and 'performance pay' would become a major element in compensation. The new vocabulary also served notice to career officials that their political masters had a new role model for them – the hard-nosed business manager. It was the first of many signs that some politicians wanted private-sector management practices to influence public servants.

According to Derek Rayner, one of Margaret Thatcher's key private-sector advisers on reforming government operations, 'the costs of administering the policies were regarded as the candle-ends of public expenditure' (i.e., minimal). He found in government operations an obsession with policy matters and a general hostility to management. The British civil service, he maintained, represents 'a huge slice of the Nation's best talents. It is ironic that, despite the talent, the quality of so much Whitehall management should be so low and that leadership has too often in the past fallen into the hands of those who know nothing of management and despise those who do.'[41]

The glamour of government work over the years in Canada, no less than in Britain, has been in policy, not in administration. Senior officials have been happy to live with elaborate administrative rules and regulations, so long as they were free to play a policy role. Some insiders assumed that functional units worried about rules for personnel, administration, and finances, while senior officials concentrated on politicians and policy issues. Some argued that in government (particularly in Britain and Canada) the managing of major departmental programs traditionally has been a job for 'junior personnel or *failed* administrative class people who are seen by the mandarins as not being able to make it to the top levels.'[42]

Before long, however, career officials understood the call by politicians to focus on management. The most senior officials began to stress, as never before, the need to strengthen management practices. In Britain, Robin Butler, secretary of the cabinet and permanent head of the Home Office, made management the central theme of his 1991 Redcliffe–Maud Memorial Lecture. He spoke about the road to 'better management in government' and the need for greater 'freedom for local managers,' and he compared the management of certain government units to a 'subsidiary of ICI.'[43] No secretary of the cabinet before the 1980s would have made better management and empowerment of local managers the underlying theme of a lecture. In Canada, Paul Tellier, secretary to the cabinet and clerk of the Privy Council, also made management the central theme in his 1990 John Carson Lecture and hardly touched on the traditional issues of public administration.[44] His lecture was essentially a report on the reform initiative Public Service 2000.

To introduce a new management culture to government operations, notwithstanding its strong ideological underpinning, is no small task. Taken at face value, the political rhetoric meant setting the civil service at its own throat. It involved a new vocabulary, a new way of thinking, and a proliferation of management techniques and procedures to force government operations to become more efficient, and it required public servants willing to make tough management decisions. Senior government officials would no longer be called administrators, principal officers, senior finance or personnel officers, or assistant directors. Now they were to be called managers, and if they could learn to work like their private-sector counterparts, then so much the better.[45] The change in vocabulary was a clear signal that career officials had to rethink everything. The message was that public servants could not be trusted to focus on managing government operations efficiently and politicians had no choice but to give *le mot d'ordre*.

Changing the vocabulary was the easy part. Changing habits anchored in years of tradition and in a firmly entrenched bureaucratic culture was another matter. Quite apart from having to rethink the myriad rules and other mechanisms designed to check administrative errors, both permanent government officials and politicians have long been mesmerized by the glamour of policy at the expense of innovative management. The challenge was to refocus the civil service so as to stress management rather than policy making.

Again, what was needed was a fundamental cultural change. Public Service 2000 (PS 2000), launched during the Mulroney years, sought to do this. PS 2000 produced a table to contrast the 'old culture' with the desired 'new culture' (see Table 5.1). The contrast between the two is striking and instructive. It probably came as a surprise for retired career officials of the golden era to discover that their culture was 'rigid' and gave rise to 'suspicious' and 'secretive' behaviour, which in turn served to 'stifle creativity,' which led them to 'communicate poorly.' Still, the message could not be clearer, coming as it did from the clerk of the Privy Council. The traditional values of public administration were not only dated, they were counterproductive. Career officials were told to ready themselves to bring business practices to government operations.

The PS 2000 Secretariat argued that the transition would require a change from a culture 'centred on prudence and probity, to one which recognizes the primacy of service to clients while accepting the need for reasonable prudence and probity.'[46] It put together more than 300 recommendations for 'delayering,' reducing central controls, reducing the number of job classifications from seventy-two to twenty-three, and making it easier to staff positions. A number of broad strategies would sup-

Table 5.1
Changing terms

Old culture	New culture
Controlling	Empowering
Rigid	Flexible
Suspicious	Trusting
Administrative	Managerial
Secret	Open
Power based	Task based
Input/process oriented	Results oriented
Preprogrammed and repetitive	Capable of purposeful action
Risk averse	Willing to take intelligent risks
Mandatory	Optional
Communicating poorly	Communicating well
Centralized	Decentralized
Uniform	Diverse
Stifling creativity	Encouraging innovation
Reactive	Proactive

Source: Public Service 2000 Secretariat, Ottawa.

port the change: decentralization of decision making; empowerment; trust and confidence in a non-partisan, objective, and professional public service; a reduction on controls on managers; more flexible organizational structures; upgrading the skills of government managers; and a stronger sense of service to the public. Departments were also encouraged to launch their own review exercises to identify 'useless' red tape and to 'delayer' management levels.[47]

Anglo-American politicians probably soon came to the view that they had diagnosed the patient correctly shortly after they came to power in the late 1970s and the 1980s. When she came to office, Thatcher ignored the claim in the briefing books that the 733,000-strong civil service was already stretched to the limit. The books argued that there was no fat in the system and that 'even modest' cuts would inhibit effective functioning.[48] The briefing books called for new positions. Not only did Thatcher reject this view, she announced a series of cuts early in her first mandate to reduce the civil service by nearly 15 per cent. By the time she left office in 1991, it had been cut by over 22 per cent, down to 569,000. She imposed the cuts by simply outlining targets. There was no performance indicator, no sophisticated strategy, or even a consideration of 'outputs.' Her focus was on input costs, pure and simple, and it 'worked.' Convinced that more could be done without reduction in services, she said that cuts could be absorbed through the increased efficiency resulting from private-sector management techniques. The Ministry of Defence, for example, reported that it would save 7,500 person-years by contracting out services such as cleaning and catering, while the diplomatic service reported projected cuts of 425 person-years by closing some overseas posts and by reducing the size of its largest missions.[49] In most instances, however, contracting out constitutes false savings, since the same people are employed doing the same things. They no longer appear as government employees, but governments still pay them, albeit on a contractual basis.

The government tried to determine the source of the cuts, to see if they were being realized through efficiency, contracting out, elimination of tasks, decrease in workload, general streamlining, decreased number of services, or a lower standard of service. It was quick to point out that a precise assessment was not possible, although it estimated that between 1980 and 1990 increased efficiency, general streamlining, and the dropping of functions accounted for 95,200 of the 169,900 positions eliminated. The remaining cuts came from contracting out (45,700) and privatization or hiving off (29,000).[50]

Brian Mulroney pledged to cut Canada's civil service by 15,000 person-years. On the advice of senior officials, he decided not to pursue the objective to the end. He declared victory after cutting about 10,000 positions, insisting that new circumstances had changed the government's agenda and added new responsibilities. Well over 1,000 of the positions shown as cut were in fact only transferred or devolved to provincial and territorial governments, Indian bands, and the private sector. In devolving the positions to other jurisdictions, Ottawa also transferred funds to pay their salaries.[51]

What senior officials later had to say about cuts in their institutions is interesting. British officials now reveal that they never believed that Thatcher's decision to shrink the civil service was foolhardy, despite their briefing books. Some actually agreed with Thatcher's decision, even though they acknowledge that, by all accounts, she simply took a number from the air. One official remarked: 'We worried very deeply about morale in the service. But we marched ahead, and looking back, it was probably the only way to proceed to cut back the size of the civil service to the extent we did.'[52] It was political will, not new private-sector management practices, that explains Thatcher's success. Still, the measures confirmed that career officials could no longer be trusted to manage on their own in a frugal fashion.

Senior Canadian officials report that they were looking to Thatcher in Britain and to Reagan in the United States in 1984 when Mulroney came to office and expected the Canadian public service to be cut by 15,000.[53] They were relieved when Mulroney decided to declare victory before achieving his objective.

Yet some ten years later the Chrétien government announced, during its program-review exercise, that it would cut 50,000 positions from the civil service. Although there was considerable creative accounting involved, Chrétien was able to announce that his government had met its objective.[54] There was no management or for that matter economic reason to believe that the Mulroney government could not also have achieved its objective.

Experience reveals that the most effective way to restrain public spending or growth in the civil service is to have a firm hand – hence, political will. Nevil Johnson argued that the imposing of firm spending limits is 'the only constraint analogous in its effects to the private business's needs to balance its books and secure a return on capital.'[55] As we see below, attempts by governments to devise output measurements in the budget process through value-for-money indicators of one kind or another to replace 'profit' have never lived up to expectations. This problem, however, has not prevented governments from launching one reform or another to force senior officials to become better managers and to determine if progress is being made.

Conclusion: Healing the Patient?

It is one thing to identify the patient and to prepare a diagnosis. It is quite another to bring the patient back to health. At least on the face of it, many politicians in government in the Anglo-American democracies knew what they wanted – senior officials should no longer preside baronially over policy domains, and they should learn to become competent managers. At the same time, many sought simultaneously to strengthen their own hand in shaping new policy initiatives and to enable career officials to become strong managers by looking to the business community for role models.

The analysis in this chapter necessitates at minimum a fresh look at the machinery of Canadian government and at the traditional relationship between cabinet ministers and career officials. Could the patient be healed without fundamentally altering how career officials work with politicians? What role would public servants actually play in policy making? How could politicians lessen their dependence on career officials in policy? Could public servants become managers like their private-sector counterparts? The rest of this book seeks to answer these questions.

6

Looking Elsewhere for Policy Advice

Anglo-American political leaders came to the conclusion that the civil service lacked the ability or the willingness to provide sound and unbiased policy advice, that it had its own agenda, and that they could never secure the kind of advice that they wanted to ensure that the public sector could or would actually change course.[1] For these reasons, they were no longer prepared to play by the old rules. The search was on for a new approach, one that would produce responsive rather than neutral competence. As far back as 1956, Herbert Kaufman had defined neutral competence as the 'ability [of career officials] to do the work of government expertly, and to do it according to explicit, objective standards rather than to personal or party or other obligations and loyalties.'[2] This model was no longer acceptable because it was considered insufficiently responsive to politicians and to public opinion. A number of politicians in Anglo-American democracies came to believe that neutral competence gave too much influence to career officials or drained away their commitment to their political and even policy objectives.

Politicians began to insist on responsive competence (see chapter 5, above) or at least on a proper blend of neutral and responsive competence. The academic literature suggested that career officials are not value-free in their behaviour and that their influence in making policy should not go unchecked.[3] Career officials were left to square this development with the basic values of their Whitehall-inspired institutions – an anonymous, neutral, and merit-based career service designed to promote detached, non-partisan, and objective policy advice. For some, these values would die hard, if at all. In Canada, as recently as 1996, a federal task force on values and ethics, chaired by a former deputy minister of justice and inspired by the work of Aaron Wildavsky, stressed the need for career officials to 'speak truth to power.'[4]

Just as some politicians were seeking to make policy advice more responsive to their views and their policy agenda, policy making became more complex. Think tanks and research institutes broke the monopoly that career officials held on the provision of advice.[5] Modern technology served to make information on virtually any public issue more accessible. Think tanks, lobbyists, consultants, and interest groups are now all able to obtain information quickly, and many can analyse it as well as anyone in government. As Patrick Weller argues, 'policy advice, once an effective monopoly of public servants, is now contestable and contested.'[6] Canadian career officials were also being challenged by other developments – the shift towards more collective policy making and the growing dominance of the prime minister and his office in that process; the pervasiveness of public-opinion polling to provide policy answers; the need to make policy on the run to accommodate 'news breaks' from more aggressive media; and policy overload and the interconnected nature of public policies.

A new model would emerge that would force career officials to look outside their departments to shape new policy measures. By choice or not, politicians would henceforth turn to several sources for policy advice, not just to their senior departmental officials. Career officials would no longer be allowed to offer policy advice by themselves. The process would now become 'porous' and involve many actors. This chapter introduces the new elements at play – new movements and stakeholders, public-opinion polls, think tanks, and electronic government – and then reviews the changes and their impact on the traditional bargain and on the ability of career officials to 'speak truth to power.'

New Movements and Stakeholders

Policy making under the traditional bargain 'hit a wall' in the latter part of the twentieth century. In chapter 5, we saw that governing politicians decided to carve out a new role for themselves in policy making, convinced that career officials had gained too much influence. There came a time in the 1970s and early 1980s when it seemed that, no matter what they did, government officials could not meet the policy expectations of their political masters. Some politicians (those of the *Yes, Minister* variety) doubted that career officials were policy neutral and believed them for the most part to be unresponsive to political direction. Others, however, insisted that the real problem was their passivity and their inability to bring sufficient enthusiasm and energy to developing and implementing innovative public policies.[7] In time, however, politicians would discover that they were dealing with a much larger problem. The traditional public policy process itself had lost some of its legitimacy.

Policies could no longer be struck in isolation inside government. The ability to arrive at a stable consensus over which problems to address, to secure an understanding with the relevant sectors of the public over actions to take, and to bring a 'horizontal perspective' to all issues of public policy became as important as the substance of the policy itself. The forces shaping this new policy environment were varied, as we saw in the previous chapter. Trust in politicians had been declining, bureaucracy bashing had taken a toll, and many citizens were better educated, more informed, and beginning to take an interest in the finer points of public policy.[8] They were no longer content to go to the polls every four years or so and then give government a free hand.

Marcel Massé, clerk of the Privy Council under Joe Clark's brief Conservative government and later a senior minister in Jean Chrétien's Liberal government, put it succinctly in 1993: 'The government sector can no longer impose its decisions without a fuller consent by the governed.' Government, he added, must now pay greater attention to 'partnerships' and 'accountability.'[9] Thus the hunt was on for new forms of citizen participation, such as public hearings and task forces made up of outside experts, and even for new ways of providing public services. All this would inevitably challenge established sources of policy advice. At minimum, these new channels would 'reshuffle' the process and its actors.[10] Arthur Kroeger has contrasted policy making today with that of fifty years ago: 'From the vantage point of the present, it is almost unimaginable that in the spring of 1956 Mr. St. Laurent's government pushed legislation authorizing the Trans-Canada Pipeline through Parliament in just six weeks – no public hearings, no environment assessment, no negotiations with Aboriginals, no federal–provincial conferences.'[11] Thus the challenge stemmed not only from the desire to promote 'horizontality' but also from the concern to engage the public somehow in the process.

Some citizens wanted to be involved. But many of them turned away from traditional means of participation – notably, established political parties. Instead, they opted for interest groups, social movements, or new political parties (such as the Reform Party and the Bloc Québé-cois). New interest surfaced in institutional mechanisms of direct democracy, such as referenda and citizen initiatives.

Citizens would come to accept that, apart from isolated instances (1972–74 and 1979–80), general elections had long supplanted the role of Parliament in making and breaking governments. Moreover, Parlia-ment's role had in turn been hijacked by disciplined political parties, which, on coming to power, would give way to the prime minister, his or her advisers, and a handful of senior cabinet ministers.

New movements also emerged, giving voice to dissatisfaction with the status quo and government policies and operations. A number of 'issue movements' came into their own in the 1970s: women's, peace, environ-ment, minority-language groups, Aboriginal rights, gay rights, and visi-ble minorities. Canada joined the United States by the early 1980s in becoming a 'rights oriented society.'[12] Many people who put forward claims under the Charter of Rights or on behalf of a movement were in no mood to negotiate or compromise. They wanted a straight answer to their grievances and government action, which if nothing else, nar-rowed the role of career bureaucrats in the policy process.[13] The move-ments would seek 'truth' in the courts whenever they could, rather than in the less clear-cut political–bureaucratic world. Canada's federal gov-ernment published a performance report on the Supreme Court in early 2002 and revealed that the court received 668 leave applications in 2001, up from 445 in 1991. The court attributes this change to an asser-tive population that is 'more willing to challenge the perceived wisdom of its leaders – often in court.'[14]

The new movements were able to attract both financial resources and members, and many of them have been able to carve out a presence in the public policy-making process. The environmental movement, in par-ticular, has gained a significant public profile, as well as credibility as an actor in the policy process. In time, most of the movements became bet-ter at staking out policy positions than were the organized political par-ties. As Robert A. Young reports, 'the Pulp and Paper Association has more capacity to do strategic analytical work than the Liberal and Pro-gressive Conservative parties combined.'[15]

Many of these movements have a credible research capacity. Some are particularly skilled at networking and at mounting effective campaigns in the media to promote their issues and viewpoints. More important, a good number have developed a well-honed capacity to identify and work with key career officials in their field of interest. Their success gave rise to further movements in the 1980s and 1990s, with goals ranging from safeguarding democracy (for example, Democracy Watch) to opposing globalization.

By the 1990s, government policy makers had accepted the fact that the policy environment had changed. If nothing else, the failure of the Meech Lake constitutional accord (1987–90) had shown that Canadians must be consulted for any major initiative to succeed. Meech Lake was hardly an isolated case: consider, among others, the National AIDS Strategy, the debate over U.S.–Canadian free trade, and the budget process.[16] Marcel Massé concluded: 'This means that those who traditionally simply made decisions will have to spend much more of their time explaining situations, setting out the various options and trade-offs, and persuading those involved, before proposed solutions become acceptable. A good part of the present unpopularity of both politicians and public servants is due to our insufficient adaptation to these new requirements of our jobs.' He saw a new role for career officials. 'In the post-modern government,' he explained, 'the task of understanding, consulting, explaining and persuading must be shared between politicians and bureaucrats.'[17] Career officials would have to engage in public dialogue with interested parties and lose some of their anonymity. This development would challenge their traditional bargain and their relationship with politicians. They would become actors on a stage traditionally reserved for politicians.

Massé was not alone in his view. Jocelyne Bourgon, shortly before being appointed clerk of the Privy Council by Jean Chrétien, wrote about 'developing a consensus ... Stakeholders [needed] to share an understanding of the issue and of the consequences of different choices.' She publicly applauded the work of senior career officials, including Arthur Kroeger, who established a consensus among interested parties 'on unemployment insurance (U.I.) reform'; Huguette Labelle, for 'achieving multi-stakeholder consensus on a vision statement for Transport Canada'; and Jean-Jacques Noreau, for 'achieving multi-stakeholder consensus on major agricultural reform.'[18] Bourgon's message would not be lost on young, ambitious career officials.

There has been no let-up in promoting the message. Consulting 'stakeholders' defined broadly, establishing new 'partnerships' and opening up government to citizens have become ongoing themes in the new annual reports by the Privy Council clerk to the prime minister on the public service, launched in 1992.[19] In addition, much has been said about new skills for the policy analyst. Senior officials have spoken about 'networking skills,' 'capacity for teamwork,' ability to 'reach out and build strategic alliances,' and a capacity to 'lead or follow the lead of others, depending on the needs or the time at hand.'[20]

The traditional bargain, however, does not allow such flexibility. The idea of the Privy Council clerk's annual report, tabled in Parliament by the prime minister, does not square with the traditional bargain. Some observers could argue that, in making public his or her views on the state of the public service, the clerk loses at least a tiny bit of anonymity.

Canada, however, is hardly alone in acknowledging the role of 'stakeholders' in policy making. The Organization for Economic Co-Operation and Development (OECD) produced a report, *Government of the Future*, based on the experience of its member countries. It states: 'Policymaking is influenced by a wide variety of players ranging from interest and lobby groups to think tanks and other policy entrepreneurs ... Increased participation by these groups reinforces the democratic process and helps government to better anticipate citizen desires.'[21]

It became fashionable in Ottawa in the mid-1980s to attach some kind of outside advisory group to most major government initiatives. The Mulroney government announced in September 1984 that Erik Nielsen would chair a task force to review existing programs, with a view to eliminating those that no longer served a purpose and consolidating others. The task force was assisted by an eleven-member private-sector advisory committee and set up nineteen study teams to review specific sectors. Some teams were led by career officials, but others, by private-sector people. All in all, 102 business people served on the teams, and 99 career officials.[22] This task force was not the Mulroney government's only effort to involve non-government people in major policy issues. It looked to non-government sources for advice, if not direct help, in the proposed Charlottetown Constitutional Accord, in its prosperity-planning exercise, in negotiating a free-trade agreement with the United States, in changing the unemployment insurance program, and the list goes on. The same can be said about the Chrétien government. Jean Chrétien went outside government for reviews of major policy areas such as health care, the environment, fisheries, and the knowledge economy. Two students of public policy concluded that 'consultation has become an expected feature of the public policy process in Canada in the 1990s.'[23] Until the early 1970s, career officials inside government would have done the job.

The new policy environment has also helped fragment authority, diffuse expertise, and create growing interdependence between state and society. Government departments and agencies no longer constitute the sole sources of knowledge and information, and career officials have had to become accustomed to giving their policy advice not only to ministers but to a whole range of other people.

This change has profoundly affected career officials, their traditional bargain, and their relationship with politicians. Career officials would now become legitimate policy actors outside government circles; they had no choice but to emerge from anonymity. Arthur Kroeger writes that deputy ministers now have 'a somewhat greater public role than they once did.' He explains why: 'In what is sometimes called the information age, the requirement to explain complicated programs, and to consult the public about proposed courses of action, is far in excess of what any minister could possibly manage.'[24] When citizens discovered that ministers do not shape all major policy decisions, they may well have concluded, as James Mallory did, that 'time is wasted in making representation to a member of Parliament or to the minister, when one could deal directly with the official concerned.'[25]

Public-Opinion Surveys

Public-opinion surveys entered Canadian politics in the 1960s as the Liberals started to import pollsters from the United States. Walter Gordon reveals in his memoirs how this began with some hesitation in the 1962 general election. Liberals used this 'relatively new technique,' as he describes it, for positioning their party in a favourable light before Canadians. But even at this early date, the surveys had an impact, albeit modest and limited to partisan politics, on the party's decision to pursue specific policies.[26] Focus groups have been added in more recent years, and governments have now 'become addicted to them.' Jeffrey Simpson maintains that 'very few major government policies are not tested in advance through focus groups, and very few, once announced, are not tested by focus groups for reaction.'[27]

Governments now spend a great deal of money to monitor public opinion, sometimes on a daily basis. Pollsters have become modern-day witch doctors, advising politicians on the national mood, on 'hot-button' issues, on policy prescriptions, on timing, and on the popularity of government policies and programs. Politicians have come to rely heavily on pollsters to help them get elected and, once in office, to remain in power. Public servants must now share their policy-advisory role with pollsters. Most politicians welcome *un deuxième son de cloche* from experts who have a better sense of what Canadians believe and who are less concerned about being seen as non-partisan. Indeed, prime ministers usually now count among their courtiers one or two favourite pollsters.

Public-opinion firms have flourished in Ottawa over the past twenty-five years, working on public-policy issues for government departments, lobbyists, and associations. The role of pollsters has also grown. They no longer simply conduct pollings on demand. They can initiate their own surveys on key issues or on the government's agenda and then sell their findings to government departments. They act as media pundits, commenting on policy issues and political events. They work as strategic advisers on public-policy issues to political parties, lobby firms, and large corporation.

Surveys have become the critical factor in governments' assessing priorities, deciding what is politically possible, and shaping new policy measures. The public is well aware of the fact that political parties and individual politicians make frequent use of polling surveys. What is less well known is the extensive use of such surveys by government departments. Gordon Robertson could write about his career (1941–79) as a senior public servant and make no reference to public-opinion surveys. Career officials have come to rely on such surveys and consider them vital to policy development and to managing emerging issues.

Officials know that they cannot go to their ministers or to the Prime Minister's Office without some polling data in hand to support their recommendations. They also realize that their political masters and their assistants will have their own such data but will be asking for polling figures produced for the department to double-check their own. But that is not all. Career officials also know that the more visible and influential interest groups are continually adding their own questions to periodic surveys or commissioning their own public-opinion studies so as to influence public policy and the government decision-making process.

A New Breed: Think Tanks, Research Institutes, Consultants, and Lobbyists

In public administration, as in other things, Canada imports many ideas from the United States. Think tanks and research institutes have long enjoyed a place in the public-policy process in Washington. Canada has made up for lost time since the 1970s.[28] Today, it has think tanks and research institutes covering virtually every area of public policy, and it seems that new ones are created almost monthly. In 1993, *Canadian Public Administration* devoted an entire issue to the work of think tanks and research institutes. The one major difference between the American and Canadian experiences is that Canada does not have research institutes or think tanks such as the Brookings or Heritage institutes in the United States that provide refuge to partisans while their parties are out of office.

Montreal's Institute for Research on Public Policy (IRPP) was established in 1972 with government funding and given a broad mandate to undertake research on public policy. Its mission is to 'improve public policy in Canada by promoting and contributing to a policy process that is more broadly based, informed and effective.'[29] The institute prides itself on being non-partisan and objective. Its role is to speak truth on major policy issues to whomever wants to listen. No sooner was IRPP set up than other such institutes followed to deal with several economic and social-policy fields and Canada's regions. These include the Canada West Foundation, the Fraser Institute, the North–South Institute, and the Private Planning Association, which became the C.D. Howe Research Institute (see Table 6.1).[30]

The 1980s and 1990s brought a plethora of new creations, including the Caledon Institute for Social Policy, the Canadian Centre for Policy Alternatives, the Canadian Centre for Arms Control and Disarmament, the Canadian Energy Research Institute, the Canadian Institute for Research on Regional Development, and Canadian Institutes of Health Research. Paul Martin's federal budget of December 2001 unveiled new funding for such groups, including a $10-million endowment for a research institute on minority–(official) language communities.[31] Canada may well have too much of a good thing. Indeed, some twenty years ago two political scientists expressed concern about an overload of papers and publications from such institutions.[32]

Research institutes perform various functions and roles. Leslie Pal maintains that they do not formally engage in 'making specific recommendations' so much as they stimulate debate, and he doubts that they have a 'discernible impact' on the policy process.[33] But Bruce Doern and Richard Phidd argue that, if nothing else, they do challenge the 'earlier bureaucratic monopoly of research and information.'[34] Some institutes, such as IRPP, make every effort to be non-partisan and, like career officials, provide a neutral perspective on policy issues.

It is difficult to determine the impact of such research bodies on the public-policy process. No major development in public policy is the

Table 6.1
Selected research institutes and think tanks.

Think tank	Date established	Location	1995 Revenue ($)	1995 Staff (FTEs)	2000 Revenue ($)	2000 Staff (FTEs)
Caledon Institute for Social Policy www.caledoninst.org	1992	Ottawa	550,000	3	1,126,953	4.2
Canada West Foundation http://www.cwf.ca	1973	Calgary	718,408	9	1,462,658	14
Canadian Centre for Philanthropy www.ccp.ca	1981	Toronto	1,573,000	16	2,641,701	30
Canadian Centre for Policy Alternatives www.policyalternatives.ca	1980	Ottawa	650,000	5	3,000,000	17
Canadian Council on Social Development (CCSD) www.ccsd.ca	1971	Ottawa	1,816,626	24	1,855,153	31
Canadian Policy Research Networks (CPRN) www.cprn.com	1994	Ottawa	2,024,613	4,5	2,802,630	24
Canadian Tax Foundation www.ctf.ca	1946	Toronto	3,745,000	23	5,000,000	28
C.D. Howe Institute www.cdhowe.org	1973	Toronto	1,875,471	16	1,853,222	17
Conference Board of Canada www.conferenceboard.ca	1954	Ottawa	22,995,000	190	26,109,000	210
Fraser Institute www.fraserinstitute.ca	1974	Vancouver	2,534,787	20	4,690,544	35
Institute for Research on Public Policy (IRPP) www.irpp.org	1972	Montreal	1,822,000	12	2,292,000	16.5
Institute on Governance www.iog.ca	1990	Ottawa	1,444,595	11.5	1,935,113	15
Public Policy Forum (PPF) www.forumpp.ca/	1987	Ottawa	1,000,416	10	2,688,657	21

Source: Based on data provided by Professor Evert Lindquist in correspondence with the author, Oct. 2002.

product of a single, linear progression of events and ideas. There are many rivulets of thought. Clearly, however, these institutes have become part of Canada's 'public policy architecture.'[35] Some observers suggest that their rise 'is a consequence, and yet another cause, of the decline of political parties as forces in Canadian politics.'[36]

Research institutes (and others) have made ambitious claims about their impact. Thomas D'Aquino, head of the Canadian Council of Chief Executives (CCCE), reports: 'Look at what we stand for and look at what all the governments, all the major parties have done and what they want to do. They have adopted the agendas we've been fighting for in the past two decades.'[37] Michael Walker of the Fraser Institute is no less boastful: 'The Fraser Institute has played a central role in most policy developments during the past decade and it is simply too onerous a task to specify.'[38] Apparently the C.D. Howe Institute helped convince Prime Minister Mulroney to pursue a free-trade agreement with the United States.[39] Much of the Canadian literature, however, suggests that most such groups provide little by way of deep, thorough analysis and research.[40]

The CCCE makes no pretence of promoting an objective policy agenda. Its purpose and its work are pro-business, and its approach is most akin to straightforward lobbying. Its objective is to apply pressure on government to incorporate a pro-business perspective in its policy agenda. There are other such groups, including the Fraser Institute, on the right of the political spectrum, and the Canadian Centre for Policy Alternatives, on the left. Neither claims to provide a neutral perspective.

There are groups, however, that are particularly responsive to the government of the day or have as their goal the promotion of networking between the private and the public sectors. The Ottawa-based Public Policy Forum (PPF), funded at least partly by the federal government, seeks to act as a 'trusted facilitator.' It maintains that its purpose is not to 'sit in judgement of what government does, but [to look] at how public policy is developed.'[41] David Zussman, its head, has close personal and political ties to Jean Chrétien, and the organization was particularly useful to Chrétien's government in reviewing certain sensitive policy issues.[42]

There are still other groups that act more as consultants than anything else. The Institute on Governance is a case in point. It is a non-profit organization that relies heavily on government contracts. It carries out a number of activities on behalf of government departments and agencies, including research contracts, professional development, conferences, workshops, and study tours.[43] There are now a number of groups in Ottawa heavily dependent on government funding and still others that are in fact part of the federal government. The Policy Research Initiative (PRI), for example, is a federal-government entity that brings together researchers from both inside and outside government to work on policy issues. It claims that its researchers come from 'over 30 federal departments and agencies, other governments, think tanks and universities.' PRI reports that it 'was launched by and remains a priority of the Clerk of the Privy Council.'[44] The group employs about 45 people and performs a number of tasks, including the 'sharing and use of policy research knowledge' and the building of a 'policy research community through networks, vehicles and venues.'[45]

The Chrétien government was the key player in the establishment of the Canadian Policy Research Networks (CPRN). It is Ottawa based and employs about twenty-five full-time people. One would be hard pressed to explain any substantial difference between PRI and CPRN, given that both are essentially networking policy groups. CPRN reports that during 1999 it received 'a long-term unrestricted grant of $9,000,000 from the Government of Canada.'[46] It also obtained project funding from seventeen federal departments and agencies. Its web page states that 'funding has been contributed by 61 departments or organizations, and 59 researchers from 16 universities have completed research contracts. This is what networking is all about.'[47] CPRN encourages government departments to look outside their own organizations for new ideas or research findings and academics to look to government departments to tailor or shape their research interests. In effect, it has received funding for taking networking in the public policy process to new heights. Judith Maxwell founded CPRN. She was a participant and presented a paper at the Aylmer conference that Jean Chrétien organized when in opposition to plan a platform for the 1993 election.[48]

One can assume that CPRN has taken networking to new heights only because it and the federal government saw a need for it. The number of institutes–think tanks always at the ready to influence Ottawa's policy process is an important development. Some of them fight for turf, much like government departments and agencies have done for years. A student of public administration observed: 'At the April 1998 conference organized by PPF (Public Policy Forum) and CPRN (Canadian Policy Research Networks) on behalf of PRI (Policy Research Initiative) although significant players such as C.D. Howe Institute were in attendance, others such as the Fraser Institute on the right of the political spectrum and the Caledon Institute and the Canadian Centre for Policy Alternatives on the left did not send representatives.'[49] The PRI adopted the PPF's formula for gaining visibility and support – organizing an annual gala dinner to honour individuals for their contributions to public policy.

Leaving aside some notable exceptions (such as the Fraser Institute), federal funding has played a major role in both launching and sustaining these institutions hovering around the Ottawa policy process. Indeed, without federal funding, a number would either not exist or would have to curtail their activities, including CPRN, the Institute on Governance, IRPP, the North–South Institute, and PPF.

Why did the federal government decide to do this, and what has been the impact? The IRPP was established in 1972 after a commissioned consultant's report concluded that there was insufficient multidisciplinary and policy-oriented research being conducted in Canada.[50] The previous decade was a particularly active one for the federal government. Ottawa launched major initiatives in virtually every sector, from health care to official languages. Federal thinking, as Les Pal has demonstrated in his *Interests of State*, was to create advocacy groups to promote the federal policy agenda.[51] That is, Ottawa had to generate a demand in communities or sectors in which it wanted to intervene. The best way to do this was to fund interest groups, associations, and research institutes in the designated areas. Federally funded research institutes are scarcely designed to promote reduced government involvement in their fields of research.

Particularly since the 1980s, Ottawa has sought greater policy capacity, more creativity, more horizontal thinking, and a longer-term perspective on major policies. Many career officials insist that they are much too caught up with the short term, with 'putting out fires,' to focus properly on the medium and the long term. There is a saying in government policy circles that the urgent always crowds out the important. Politicians in Canada and elsewhere became convinced that career officials lacked the creativity and ability to provide insightful policy advice. There is a long list of politicians in Britain and the United States – Edward Heath, Michael Heseltine, Richard Nixon, and Jimmy Carter, among others – who have argued that career civil servants had let them down on policy, had not been sufficiently creative. The political leadership, particularly in the 1980s, believed that bureaucracy had an 'inherent quality of inertia.'[52]

A senior Mulroney minister had this to say: 'The biggest letdown in government was the lack of creativity and clear thinking on the part of permanent officials. I imagined while in opposition that it was the Trudeau Cabinet that was stifling the public servants in their attempts to come forward with new ideas and new solutions. I was wrong ... Officials in departments will urge us to stick with the status quo and those in central agencies will simply give us twenty reasons why we can't pursue something.'[53] Another senior minister in Mulroney's cabinet explained: 'Every time I ask for something that is more than a few pages long or that breaks out of the narrow operating mode of the department, officials always tell me that they have to go to an outside consultant for the work. We have a pretty stale bunch in government.'[54]

Matters have not improved, it seems, with time. In 1995 the clerk of the Privy Council asked Ivan Fellegi, chief statistician, to chair a task force of senior officials to review the state of the government's policy capacity. The task force concluded that 'the most notable weaknesses at present relate to longer term strategic and horizontal issues. Resources are disproportionally consumed by short term demands. This is true both within departments and across governments.'[55] The task force offered several recommendations, all designed to strengthen policy capacity. It urged a much stronger emphasis on a 'horizontal and government-wide' perspective on policy and closer ties with the external policy-research community.[56] It was this task force that gave rise to the PRI.

Both politicians and career officials seemed to agree that they should look outside government and create a new policy-advisory capacity to strengthen policy making. Politicians hoped that this step would more readily challenge the status quo and be more creative. Career officials believed that it would make it easier to establish a consensus on policy prescriptions and enable their policy analysts to tap into the work of outside experts. As well, they would have someone to share the blame if policy proposals turned out not to be sufficiently creative.

The links to outside experts have taken place largely through research institutes, think tanks, consultants, and stakeholders. Politics thus enters the policy process much earlier than in the past, and career officials now share the policy-making space with a variety of actors. Indeed, the consent, if not the direct participation, of stakeholders is now required even at the data-gathering stage. It is no longer possible inside government to review policy issues without ensuring consent of the governed.[57] Many links have also been established between the executive and the research institutes and relevant stakeholders. The prime minister and his or her office can easily obtain the work of outside experts. Most research institutes and think tanks would consider it a measure of success if the prime minister and his or her entourage would be seen asking for their advice. The same can also be said about cabinet ministers and senior officials.

Career officials and the majority of outside policy experts live cheek by jowl. Career officials in effect manage the outside policy capacity and oversee its funding, monitor its work, and decide on its relevance. Consultants are hired by contract, and many of the research think tanks do not have an endowment fund to sponsor their work. They are dependent on government contracts and revenues, and career officials constitute the continuing link to them.

Parliament does not enjoy the same access to outside experts. It does not have the financial resources to grease an ongoing relationship. Outside experts want to influence the policy process and decision making and come quickly to terms with the fact that Parliament does not offer much opportunity on this front. Lobbyists, interest groups, and even research institutes try to sway the House of Commons only as a last resort, when it is clear that their attempts to influence the government have failed.[58]

The same is true about political parties. Some research institutes, consultants, and even lobbyists (career lobbyists, as opposed to those who sell access or who became lobbyists to take advantage of their close ties with the party in power) will purposely avoid being identified with a party. For many that would be the kiss of death. Because of their dependence on government funding for work and their ongoing relations with career officials, they avoid being tied to a party almost as much as do career officials. A long-term student of Canadian public administration observes: 'In contrast to other countries ... links between think tanks and political parties in Canada are relatively weak.'[59]

Career officials value anonymity, but many research institutes and think tanks do not – a public profile indicates success. According to Donald Abelson, 'There is a tendency among some journalists and scholars to equate media visibility with policy influence.'[60] Abelson looked to the media to determine 22 bodies' visibility. His rankings in descending order: the Conference Board, the C.D. Howe Institute, the Fraser Institute, the Canadian Tax Foundation, the National Council of Welfare, the Canadian Council on Social Development (CCSD), and the IRPP. At the bottom were the PPF (16th), the Caledon Institute (18th), and the CPRN (21st). Several top-ranked institutes operate outside Ottawa and enjoy considerable independence from government funding (C.D. Howe, Fraser, and the Canadian Tax Foundation), while those at the bottom are Ottawa-based and depend on government money (PPF and CPRN).

Gaining a media profile tells only part of the story. Ivan Fellegi asked senior civil servants to list policy research institutes that had helped them. The Conference Board, the CPRN, the CCSD, the Caledon Institute, and the C.D. Howe Institute topped the list. Abelson suggests that 'think tanks that have received little media attention have been actively involved in consulting government departments.'[61] Some institutes may well wish to avoid a high media profile and public controversy in order to have better access to career officials and the policy process.

What about impact on policy making and contributing research or policy designs and implementation strategies? The growing number of research institutes, think tanks, and contract policy workers has made the policy process more porous and more diffuse. Government now, in Marcel Massé's words, needs to 'explain,' to 'consult,' and to 'persuade stakeholders.' Therefore top-down command and control are difficult to sustain. Michael Howlett looked to four cases to assess if networks matter and if one could link networks to policy outcomes. His verdict: 'Networks do matter'; the 'same core sets of policy actors are involved in defining policy options, the common understanding of a policy problem and the solutions they develop from shared experience.' He also adds that it 'promotes incremental change.'[62]

To a senior career official of forty years ago, the current process might appear a kind of free-for-all, undisciplined process. Career officials, not just politicians, have now become key players in building consensus. In addition, consensus building often has more to do with identifying trade-offs and finding some common ground than with facts. As James A. Smith argues: 'All research begins to look like advocacy, all experts begin to look like hired guns, and all think tanks seem to use their institutional resources to advance a point of view.'[63] The federal government has made full use of its own resources to fuel selected research institutes and think tanks.

Consulting firms have grown in number and size over the past forty years. The yellow pages in the Ottawa telephone directory now contains hundreds of such firms in economics, program evaluation, and various aspects of public policy. Many of these employ former federal officials and perform tasks once performed by civil servants. A number of government departments now turn to consultant firms even to prepare cabinet and Treasury Board submissions – unthinkable forty years ago. These consultants do not have to live with the traditional bargain in their relations with politicians. They lack security of tenure and have an economic interest to promote. The next contract may well depend on how they perform on the current one, and so they may well want to present what they think the client wants to hear. They 'speak truth to power' at their peril and at a potential economic cost. Can consultants, keen to secure new contracts, say 'No' to power? One former senior official explained the importance of truth speakers. 'No one enjoys being a nay-sayer constantly pointing out difficulties. But when the difficulties are real, and important, you have no choice; to express unwarranted optimism, or to just keep quiet and let your minister discover the hard way that a pet idea won't work, is an abdication of what you're paid to do.'[64] Consultants do not have 'a minister'; they have clients. Career officials not only have ministers, they must live with the consequences of their policy advice.

There is another breed of consultant in Ottawa which, according to Jeffrey Simpson, has grown 'like Topsy in the last two decades' – lobbyists, or 'government relations experts.'[65] There were none thirty-five years ago; the Ottawa directory now lists forty-two lobbying firms – not including law firms whose 'hired guns' lobby on behalf of their clients. By one count, there are now 1,500 lobbyists in Ottawa. Some are highly paid and partisan and could not easily survive a change of power in Ottawa. However, their partisanship gains them access to ministers, and they are always ready to offer advice. They are hired to promote the interests of their corporate clients and paid to tell the truth about government policy – as their clients see it – to politicians.

Career officials insist that lobbyists have changed the nature of their work. Politicians can now turn to any number of paid lobbyists to get a second opinion on a policy issue. There are lobbyists available to argue any side of an issue. (A Tennessee school teacher was asked at a job interview: 'Is the world round or flat? His response: 'I can teach it either way.') There is even a pro-tobacco lobby. There is evidence that the work of lobbyists is having an impact in Ottawa. We know, for example, that one of them was instrumental in having the prime minister overturn the advice of career officials on the purchase of new corporate jets.[66]

The Ottawa lobby industry has created post-career employment for many public servants – a sea change in the culture of the public service and the operations of government. In recent years, many senior civil servants, including former deputy ministers and assistant deputy ministers, have joined lobbying firms, taking with them an intimate knowledge of how government works and who the key decision makers are. They also have an insider's knowledge of how to present a case and how to influence government policies and operations. They also know where to pitch a message to have maximum impact. Jeffrey Simpson goes to the heart of the matter: 'When surveyed, lobbyists and interest groups consistently placed members of Parliament at or near the bottom of their lists ... Lobbyists press the clients' case, if possible, to the Prime Minister's Office, then to senior ministers and top bureaucrats. They may make the rounds with MPs, but more as a courtesy or an insurance policy, because they understand that MPs have no power and only scattered influence.'[67]

Whatever their actual influence on policy, research institutes, think tanks, consultants, and lobbyists have made the government policy-making process much more porous. But they are not the only forces opening up the public-policy process.

E-Government and the Policy Process

The impact of e-government on government operations and provision of services is well documented.[68] Less obvious is its impact on policy development. E-government is already making vast quantities of information available to citizens, interest groups, think tanks, and research institutes and it should introduce a new dynamic to the policy-making process. A number of politicians and observers point to its enormous potential, suggesting that the information age will transform democracy.[69] British Prime Minister Tony Blair recently remarked on the potential for a 'second age of democracy.'[70] In Canada, the former leader of the Reform Party, Preston Manning, suggested that, because of the internet, 'We are building the Athens of the twenty-first century.'[71]

Governments have less control over who knows what and when, and the emerging networking model does not conform to the old command-and-control departmental model.[72] Boundaries within government, between departments, and between governments and outside groups and citizens are less clear than they were thirty years ago. The internet is opening up government everywhere to unprecedented scrutiny.[73] Mel Cappe, former clerk of the Privy Council, observed that 'e-government requires public servants without borders, people who can work effectively across departments, programs and other borders ... who see an issue in a broader, horizontal context.'[74] He had earlier written in his annual report: 'E-Government is not just electronic government. It is enabled government ... E-Government is about people: new skill sets, mindsets and leadership approaches. It will transform how public servants work, relate to each other, do business, and engage citizens and other partners.' As a result, government was 'moving away from a traditional model of public service based on hierarchical, directive management.'[75] A review of the impact of e-government sponsored by ten federal departments concluded: 'Many key decision-making processes within government remain beyond public scrutiny. By increasing the amount of available information on government, ICTs will result in new light being shed on these still-dark corners. As internal processes are uncovered, citizens will demand greater accountability from government, and greater participation in decision making.'[76]

New information systems are horizontal by design and capable of penetrating all sorts of 'boundaries' in government. Information now flows not only between departments but also between government and outsiders, tending to dissolve boundaries. This change makes it difficult to operate a hierarchical model. Nicolas Negroponte, director of MIT's Media Lab, argues that one simply cannot control cyberspace: 'It's uncontrollable. If someone tells you that you can, they are probably smoking pot.'[77] An observer of the Ottawa policy process writes that 'government officials are also starting to hook up to non-governmental chat sites and policy forum in sectors related to their responsibilities.'[78] They can do this anonymously and share policy positions with the outside world without having to clear it up the hierarchical ladder.

Many Canadians are embracing e-government with enthusiasm, and it is not a one-way street. The internet, unlike radio and television, allows people not only to hear and see, but also to be heard. In 1999, Canadians sent 12,000 e-mail messages to the federal government's web site, and in 2000, 30,000.[79] Ottawa pledged initially to put the full range of federal services on the internet by 2004 but later pushed the date back to 2005.

The government of Canada, by all accounts, welcomes the arrival of e-government. It was a theme of Prime Minister Chrétien's Speech from the Throne in 1999: 'The Government will become a model user of information technology and the Internet. By 2004, our goal is to be known around the world as the government most connected to its citizens, with Canadians able to access all government information and services at the time and place of their choosing.'[80] The speech did not speculate on the internet's impact beyond its allowing access to government services twenty-four hours a day, seven days a week.

Darin Barney writes that the internet may not in fact transform society's power structures and democracy.[81] He points out that 'the internet creates a sense of community between people, but in some ways this is a false sense because the people never meet. This contributes to a weakening of communal ties, including those to a democratic arena such as a riding or even a nation.'[82] Still, Lawrence Grossman maintains that new technologies are allowing citizens 'a seat of their own at the table of political power.' They 'make it possible for our political system to return to the roots of Western democracy as it was first practiced in the city states of ancient Greece.'[83] The *Economist* magazine, in a special survey on government and the internet, made the case that, because internet boundaries are now less clear within government and between government and citizens, e-government is raising expectations among citizens as to better levels of services and more input into the policy process, but it called for new efforts to ensure wider access to the internet.[84]

The jury is still out on whether new information technology will transform representative democracy, and history cannot be a teacher in this area. Certainly, however, the internet is empowering citizens and making them stakeholders in government policies and programs. As well, it is a two-way street that enables citizens to react and respond to emerging policy positions. If, as we are often told, 'information is society's great equalizer,' then the internet will reduce the influence of wealth on political participation and shaping public policies.[85] As Roger Gibbins observed in his 2000 presidential address to the Canadian Political Science Association, 'Change relating to information and communication technologies must have an impact; the only questions are where that impact is most likely to occur and what magnitude the effect will be.'[86]

E-government can also enable the government to seek the views, knowledge, and experience of citizens by making it easier for them to obtain public information, follow the political process, discuss and form groups on specific issues, and scrutinize government policies and operations. Government could conceivably consult citizens on a wide range of issues, from the allocation of financial resources to proposed legislation. The potential is there, but the reality may well be different. Treasury Board officials whom I consulted seem quite comfortable putting as many programs as possible on line to improve services and to provide better access to government information. However, they are quite uneasy about promoting 'e-democracy' or about using the internet as a means of consulting Canadians on such matters as resource allocation and proposed legislation. That territory, they insist, belongs to politicians, and only politicians can take the lead in this area.[87]

Yet interest groups, lobbyists, stakeholders with resources, research institutes, and think tanks already have access to decision makers, and now they can easily tap into government data and information to marshal better arguments to promote their particular interest.

Reforming the Machinery

Many politicians also looked inside government to strengthen their hold on the policy-making levers. They became convinced, as we saw above, that career officials were not value-free in their behaviour and that their neutral competence, while it had its advantages, also drained away their commitment to government objectives.

Pierre Trudeau introduced major reforms to the machinery of government to give ministers in cabinet a greater say in collective policy making process.[88] One Trudeau reform that has not received much attention was his instruction to ministers and their departments to put forward for his and cabinet consideration 'all possible solutions.'[89] The objective was to force career officials to be more creative, to review various possibilities, and to ensure that the best possible solution was identified. This was a significant change to the policy process. Previously, career officials were expected to sort out the problems and the contradictions inside their departments and then to seek the best possible solution for the consideration of their minister and, later, of the full cabinet. The message from Trudeau for career officials: there was more than one truth to every policy issue, and politicians wanted to review all of them before making a decision.

Career officials reacted somewhat dustily to this change. As we saw above, Gordon Robertson viewed many so-called solutions as straw men, put in to observe the rule but ready to be knocked down.[90] In time, politicians began to see the limits of this new approach and to realize that straw men were indeed being put up only to be quickly knocked down. They then began to look outside the public service for policy advice.

But there were also other changes. As we saw above, Brian Mulroney introduced 'chiefs of staff' in ministerial offices when he came to power. Margaret Thatcher used the rhetoric on the need for politicians to regain the upper hand in policy making, but it was Mulroney who sought to emulate the American model within a Westminster system.[91] Mulroney's decision had one purpose – to check permanent officials' influence on policy. The chief of staff was an assistant deputy minister and, according to government press releases, an 'official in the American style.' Although senior civil servants and outside observers argued that the move was incompatible with Canada's system, Mulroney pressed ahead.[92]

Mulroney was concerned that the machinery of government that he had inherited would resist change, particularly his Conservative policy proposals. Bureaucrats, one senior Mulroney adviser explained, 'should get back to their real job – to implement decisions and see to it that government operations run smoothly and leave policy to us.'[93] There is no doubt that many of Mulroney's key ministers and advisers were pushing him to go even further on this front. A senior minister commented: 'Something is basically wrong with our system of government. We are the only ones elected to make decisions. But we do like the British. We move into government offices with no support. Everything in these offices belongs to the permanent government. We are only visitors, barely trusted enough not to break the furniture. I prefer the American way. Politicians there move in with their own furniture [their own partisan advisers] and run the show for however long they are elected to office. Then they move out with their furniture to let the next crowd in. I have discussed this with the Prime Minister and so have many of my colleagues. But, you know, this kind of thinking so upsets the bureaucrats that he feels he cannot go much further than he has. Appointing chiefs of staff was seen in many quarters in the bureaucracy as a revolutionary act – no, an act of high treason.'[94]

All ministers had a chief of staff within days of Mulroney's coming to power. His transition team had put together a list of potential candidates for ministers to pick from as they were appointed. The chiefs of staff, however, had a mixed reception, often dependent on the quality of the incumbent. They introduced a new level between ministers and permanent officials, which gave rise to misunderstandings and complications. In some instances, the chief of staff acted as a mediator between the minister and permanent officials, screening advice going up to the minister and issuing policy directives going down to officials, much to the dismay and objection of deputy ministers. Many chiefs of staff took a dim view of the competence of permanent officials, who took an equally jaundiced view of them. The arrangement, one official said, 'has on the whole hardly been a happy or a successful one.'[95]

A former staff member in the Prime Minister's Office explains why the position was created. She writes that it 'was in large measure created to act as a check on bureaucratic power, to enable the government to do what it was elected to do.'[96] She makes it clear that chiefs of staff could 'offer policy advice over and above that provided by the department [and that] he or she could achieve this in part by soliciting opinions different from those held by the departmental advisers.' If the chief of staff had little expertise in the department's policy field, then the minister was encouraged to hire one or more additional 'senior policy advisers.' She adds that the chief of staff 'provided an interesting challenge to the deputy minister and the department in terms of policy development and control.'

Although the verdict on the experiment was mixed, it did affect the policy process. One student of government explains: 'While data gathering and basic analysis was still being done within most departments, in general those involved in policy work were much more cautious in how they cast their findings or how their findings were utilized within their departments. Alternatively, they simply called what they were doing something other than policy analysis.'[97]

Mulroney, like Thatcher, also expanded the scope for appointing outsiders to senior positions.[98] Although he was never able to attract as many new people as he had initially hoped to serve as deputy ministers, he did bring in a number of high-profile individuals, notably Stanley Hart at the Department of Finance. In addition, within twenty-four months of his assuming power, all deputy ministers who had survived the change of government or remained in government had new positions.

Mulroney was not the first prime minister to turn to appointments to make the civil service more responsive. When Trudeau appointed Michael Pitfield as clerk of the Privy Council and secretary to the cabinet in 1975, he sent out a clear signal that he valued responsive, more than neutral, competence and that he did not see the civil service as a self-governing body. Until the Pitfield appointment, there had been strong support among deputy ministers for the one among them chosen clerk and secretary. This was true for Arnold Heeney (1940–9), Norman Robertson (1949–52), Bob Bryce (1954–63), and Gordon Robertson (1963–75). They stood above their colleagues in qualifications and experience. In addition, Heeney and most of his successors up to Gordon Robertson saw the focus of their role and functions more properly tied to the cabinet than to the prime minister.

Pitfield, as clerk and secretary (1975–80 and 1980–2), would change the role. He and Trudeau had for many years been close friends. Trudeau appointed him at the age of thirty-seven, overlooking more senior public servants who had served for many years as deputy ministers both in line departments and in a central agency. Pitfield's experience in government had been largely in the Privy Council Office (PCO). The consensus is that Pitfield turned things upside down and, instead of representing the public service to the prime minister and cabinet, he represented the prime minister to the public service. No clerk since Pitfield, it seems, has been able to revert to the old model of the role. If Arnold Heeney successfully resisted Prime Minister William Lyon Mackenzie King's desire to make the secretary to the cabinet 'a kind of deputy minister,' or 'personal staff officer' to the prime minister, incumbents from Pitfield to today have not been as willing to resist the prime ministers' desires to make the position 'a kind of deputy minister' to him or her.'[99]

After Joe Clark came to power in 1979, he fired Pitfield as being 'too partisan.'[100] Colin Campbell writes that 'when Trudeau restored [Pitfield] to clerk-secretary after his return to power [in 1980], he confirmed definitively the politicization of Canada's top bureaucratic job.' Campbell adds that the fall and rise of Pitfield 'tipped the scales toward the conclusion that the Trudeau–Pitfield friendship has short-circuited the distance that previously existed between the prime minister and a clerk-secretary.'[101]

In his memoirs Gordon Robertson reports that when reviewing the list of possible successors in 1975, he wrote next to Pitfield's name, 'Too soon. Michael has not yet established the necessary credit and respect in the public service generally.' Robertson adds with obvious disappointment that Pitfield's appointment had become a contentious issue in the House of Commons and in the media. Opposition Leader Joe Clark asked the prime minister to make a statement 'outlining the principles to be followed in appointments to the senior public service ... and show whether the elevation of Michael Pitfield indicates a replacement of the merit system by the buddy system.'[102] The media also raised concerns over the politicization of the public service at the highest levels.[103]

Brian Mulroney also moved parts of the machinery of government outside the sphere of influence of career officials. Although he was careful during the 1984 election campaign not to commit his party to privatizing any crown corporations, there was a flurry of activity on this front within weeks of his being sworn in. He established a ministerial task force on privatization and later an Office of Privatization and Regulatory Affairs to manage the various activities associated with privatization and deregulation. The minister of industry declared after less than two months in office that the government would within a year sell all assets of the Canada Development Investment Company. The assets included large concerns, such as Canadair, de Havilland, Eldorado Nuclear, and Teleglobe. The minister of finance declared in his first budget that 'Crown Corporations with a commercial value but no ongoing public policy purpose will be sold.' The government also soon put some other corporations up for sale and dissolved a few that were either not active or in direct competition with other levels of government.[104]

Jean Chrétien, on taking power, abolished the post of chief of staff for ministers, although he was careful not to do so for his own office. He made the case that his government would value the work of public servants more than had Mulroney's. However, he continually sent out mixed signals on this issue. For example, in reference to the work of the Canadian armed forces in Afghanistan, he explained: 'They have to do their jobs. It's not a bunch of bureaucrats, these soldiers. They have to do their job. And after that, they report.'[105] The chief-of-staff post had introduced a new dynamism in Ottawa that lingers today. Executive assistants to Chrétien's ministers have not enjoyed the same salary levels as had chiefs of staff in Mulroney's government, but like their predecessors they challenged the policy views of career officials. My consultations with career officials in Ottawa suggest that relations between ministerial-exempt staff and career officials changed after Chrétien came to power, but only at the margins. Some executive assistants, much like some chiefs of staff, worked well with career officials, while others did not. Most tried to influence policy; some were successful, others, not.[106] Loretta J. O'Connor in 1991 outlined the major tasks and functions of a chief of staff. There is little in her description that does not apply to executive assistants in the Chrétien government. An executive assistant, like a chief of staff, is the senior political adviser to a minister, acts as director of operations and controller for his or her office, and ensures that ministerial directives are carried out within the department, so as to increase ministerial control and accountability.[107]

Trudeau's ministers had started to expand the role and size of their offices.[108] For example, Lloyd Axworthy, at Transport in the early 1980s, had 'a staff of about seventy-five,' we are told, 'to bend the operations of his department to his political will.' The seventy-five staff members included '31 seconded from government, 12 term civil service staff and

16 exempt staff' and amounted to 'two or three times' a minister's usual staff complement log. My recent consultations with senior officials at the Public Service Commission reveal that executive assistants are currently ranked at the level of Executive Category (EX) 2 or 3 – considerably higher than in the Trudeau years.[110]

Chrétien did overhaul the elaborate system of cabinet committees that Trudeau had expanded. He abolished several committees, insisting that the policy-making process had become too complex and cumbersome. He did not, however, overhaul central agencies and they remain much as they were when he assumed office. The one difference is that they no longer have to support the work of several cabinet committees. One can assume that they are kept busy focusing their efforts to support the prime minister and his advisers.

The Chrétien government showed increased willingness and capacity to look outside departments and agencies for policy advice. Paul Martin, for example, took great comfort and pride, as minister of finance, in making use of private-sector figures instead of relying exclusively on his officials to forecast budgetary revenues. In his budget speech of December 2001 he declared, 'As in the past, we have consulted some 19 private sector forecasters to obtain their best estimates of the economic outlook. Based on that survey, we then consulted with the chief economists of Canada's major chartered banks and then leading forecasting firms to discuss the most recent numbers and their implications for this budget's economic and fiscal projections.'[111]

Martin decided to turn to outside forecasters shortly after going to Finance. The huge discrepancy between the projections in the Mulroney government's last budget in April 1993 and the actual numbers in November had astounded him. He concluded that 'either the department had known the numbers to be wrong or it had got them wrong,' and he resolved never to let that happen to him. When he decided to go outside to audit Finance's numbers, officials there 'swallowed hard.' They told Martin's exempt staff that 'a public flogging would undermine the department's credibility both publicly and within the federal bureaucracy,' but 'Martin didn't relent.'[112] His decision served notice that career officials could no longer be trusted and that he would go elsewhere to get more reliable advice and not suffer the humiliation of previous finance ministers like Michael Wilson and Don Mazankowski. It also made the point that Finance officials would no longer do forecasting and offer budget advice by themselves.

Conclusion

Policy making began to 'leak' first under Trudeau from line departments to a process driven by interdepartmental and central-agency concerns, and it later moved from the government to associations and interest groups. Research institutes and think tanks gained access to information that would enable them to prepare policy positions and carry out research projects. Government brought in organizations and consultants under contract to work on policy issues. Lobbyists, e-government, and access-to-information legislation have pried open the policy process still further. Pollsters have become key actors, as public opinion is just as important as hard economic data – if not more so – in establishing 'truth.'

In response, politicians concluded that they needed more responsive competence, even at the expense of the traditional neutral variant. Ministerial offices and the Prime Minister's Office were expanded. Partisan advisers are now expected to work hand in glove with partisan lobbyists and pollsters to marshal arguments to challenge, if necessary, the policy positions prepared by departmental career officials.

Unlike the situation in the 1960s and earlier, policy proposals no longer bubble up from line departments. But even when they do, they need to be 'wrapped around' a consultative process of some sort to gain legitimacy. Outside advice has gained credibility at the expense of career officials.

Many politicians in government have told career officials to get things done, to emulate the private sector, and not to tinker with policy issues. From the early 1980s on, most politicians have made it clear, time and again, that they want doers and fixers in government, not thinkers, and that they and their partisan advisers would deal with policy.

These changes have had a profound impact on the civil service. The institutional self-confidence so evident under the traditional bargain up to the 1970s has been severely battered. Morale has plummeted. A former secretary to the Treasury Board and a highly respected career official, J.L. Manion, wrote that senior people were talking openly about a civil service 'in trouble, demoralized, losing confidence in its leaders and themselves, unsure of their roles and futures, overburdened with work, and chafing under perceived unfair criticism.'[113] Surveys comparing morale in the federal public service and in the private sector concluded that 'almost without exception, the private sector managers had a more positive view of the management practices in their organization than did their public sector counterparts, working at similar levels in their organization.' In addition, 'as one moves down the bureaucratic hierarchy, managers are less satisfied and less positive about managerial practices in their organization.'[114] Surveys at the departmental level were even more worrisome. A 1990 study on External Affairs reported that its advice was ignored and its staff made subject to public scorn, rebuke, and ridicule. Motivation had plunged, and morale was abysmal. The department was under siege from the outside and consumed by ferment from within.'[115] By the early 1990s, every large department could produce similar studies revealing serious morale problems. This situation has not changed, despite substantial increases in salary in the late 1990s. 'The problem,' one senior official at Treasury Board observed, 'has nothing to do with pay; it has everything to do with a lack of respect for career government officials.'[116]

Many career officials became uncertain about their policy work. The provision of fearless advice became difficult to sustain once a high degree of responsiveness was demanded. One could discern a tendency on the part of officials to recommend safe policy options and what 'politicians would wear.' They insist that no 'challenging' policy work is being carried out on 'big ticket programs' and that many of them are unwilling to 'say "No, Minister" or even "Be Careful, Minister."'[117] Some are reluctant to explain why things must be so, to provide objective, non-partisan advice, and to explain trade-offs for certain decisions. One former deputy minister wrote that 'loyalty itself is being redefined as obsequiousness and fawning. The honest public servant is in danger of being superseded by the courtier.'[118]

Career officials reveal that politicians want to see position papers that support their 'prejudices and that they do not have a favourable view of neutrality – or neutral competence – as they used to.' One official remarked at a seminar in Ottawa in the 1990s, 'I see advice going to ministers which is suppressing arguments because it is known that ministers will not want them, and that for me is the betrayal of the civil service.' This atmosphere is reflected in the philosophy: 'Don't tell me why I shouldn't do it, but how I can do it.'[119] One can get a sense of the sea change by contrasting the views of two deputy ministers. Al Johnson in 1961 insisted that 'frank talk' is paramount even if it may endanger a happy union between him (career official) and his political chief. He quoted Sir Warren Fisher: 'The preservation of integrity, fearlessness, and independent thought and utterance in their private communion with ministers of the experienced officials selected to fill up posts in the service is an essential principle of enlightened government.'[120] Contrast this with what George Anderson, a deputy minister in the Chrétien government, wrote in 1996: 'Overbearing advisers have a way of being cut down to size. The officials with most influence are those who are best attuned to the views and needs of ministers.'[121]

Many of today's politicians, it seems, want career officials to become competent managers like those in the private sector, and they want government operations run more efficiently. Politicians and their partisan advisers, we are told, can look after policy issues, but they need strong managers to operate government programs and deliver services. The next chapter looks at management in government.

7

Deputy Ministers and Management

When appearing before the House of Commons Standing Committee on External Affairs and International Trade, de Montigny Marchand, then under-secretary of state for external affairs, explained his lack of attention to 'paper trails.' He declared: 'I was running the war for External Affairs. I was in charge of the Gulf crisis. Twice a day, I was meeting with senior officials in meetings chaired by Mr. Tellier [clerk of the Privy Council].'[1] Marchand's point was that in attending to a crisis he had had little time to deal with less urgent matters. Crises, real, perceived or pending, are more common than is generally assumed – as the front pages of the *Globe and Mail*, the *National Post*, or *La Presse* will often attest. In any event, deputy ministers are extremely busy people, and there is never a shortage of things for them to do. Indeed, they must pick and choose among issues to focus on, and management matters rarely make the grade.

Arthur Kroeger, a former deputy minister in several departments, says: 'There are many different ways of being a deputy. You can be a general manager and try to have your hands as many things as possible and limit yourself to that, or you can, at the other extreme, pick one or two really big, difficult policy areas, say I'm going to do that, and then find ways to organize the work of the department so that it gets done without making too many claims on your time. As a deputy you have the ability to make that choice. And my preference was for that model of picking a few subjects.' He adds, 'General management, management with a capital M and management theory never interested me very much.'[2] Kroeger was not alone in this view. Gordon Robertson did not discuss management issues in his memoirs. He did, however, mention that administrative matters frequently left him insufficient time to deal with major policy issues.[3] Al Johnson, in his 1961 article, 'The Role of the Deputy Minister,' never once employed the word 'management.' He wrote: 'The role of the deputy minister is to make it possible for the minister and the cabinet to provide the best government of which they are capable – even better if either of them happens to be weak.'[4]

This is no small role, and it gives deputy ministers a relatively free hand to concentrate on issues that they deem most relevant to this end. Very few of them have a strong interest in general management, if only because it rarely, if ever, determines if a prime minister and cabinet can provide good government.[5] Good government is usually tied to policy, not to management practices. In addition, promotion most often comes from policy experience and rarely through management.

Yet governments and royal commissions since the 1960s have identified better management practices as a top priority. There has not been a government since John Diefenbaker's that has not pledged to let 'managers manage' and to strengthen management practices. Even more remarkable, they all unveil new management-reform measures and declare their commitment to move from a 'focus on rules to a focus on results' as if this were something new. Since the Glassco Commission tabled its findings in 1962, politicians have voiced this same message time and again. Yet we were recently told that 'value-for-money auditing, the creations of the Office of the Comptroller General, program evaluations and an alphabet soup of initiatives – PPBS, MBO, PEMS, IMAA – seemed not to have made any fundamental difference.'[6] This from the holder of an office that has for the past thirty years been urging program evaluation, creation of an Office of the Comptroller General, and letting managers manage.

The new public management (NPM), which came into fashion in Anglo-American countries some twenty years ago, held promise of real change. NPM looks to outcomes rather than to processes, distinguishes between customers, clients, and citizens, and encourages career officials to concentrate more on management than on policy. However, in Canada at least, NPM has not lived up to expectations.[7]

My purpose here is not to review management reforms since the 1960s or the impact of NPM. Rather, I look at deputy ministers and at their changing role as administrator, then general manager, and now administrator again. I explore the state of public-sector management in a Westminster-style system in terms of a model and a case study. I turn finally to deputy minister's accountability.

In chapter 2, I noted that Canada created the position of deputy minister in 1857 to ensure 'coordination' in each government department and to provide a permanent administrative head. The position has evolved a great deal of late and is now central to public administration. Deputy ministers have no counterpart in the private sector. They have to be comfortable in both the political and the administrative worlds, and they must be non-partisan. Placed at the top of the department-al hierarchy, they hold the key to better management practices. Are such modern management techniques as empowerment at odds with Westminster-style institutions? As many management reforms of the past forty years were inspired by similar measures first introduced in the pri-vate sector, how do the two sectors differ vis-à-vis management?

Deputy Ministers

Who Are They?

Jacques Bourgault and Stéphane Dion wrote in 1991: 'The deputy min-ister is one of the most important players in Canada's political system.'[8] This, even though most deputy ministers assiduously maintain a low pro-file. Who are these people? How did they rise to the top of the profes-sion?

Bourgault and Dion tracked the profile of federal deputy ministers over five periods, from Confederation to 1988. They found a highly edu-cated community that was mainly middle class and male, though recently opened up to women, with a lot of Ontarians, and by 1988 with a representative proportion of francophones. Most deputy ministers had risen through the public service and had little or no direct experi-ence in other work environments. The average number of years that they spent in the department before becoming a deputy had decreased steadily from twelve early in Confederation to three during the 1977–88 period. Deputy ministers no longer remain head of the same depart-ment for many years, and when their careers end they no longer retire as before. In more recent years their recruitment 'easily crosses the boundaries between departments,' unlike in other countries, such as France and Germany, where one in two administrative heads is recruited from within the department.[9]

A Privy Council study in 1981 revealed that 21 of the 35 deputy minis-ters had joined the federal service directly from university graduation or from a staff position. In addition, 28 of the 35 had had previous experi-ence in a central agency, such as the Privy Council Office, Finance, or the Treasury Board.[10] Frank Swift reported in 1993 that 'experience in a central agency, most notably the Privy Council Office, is now a virtual prerequisite for deputy-level appointment.' He added: 'Notwithstanding the increasing recognition of the importance of managerial performance and service to the public, almost two out of three deputies have no experience in program management; and most deputies have no federal experience outside the National Capital Region. Overall, deputies are primarily generalists, not specialists.'[11]

A review by Jacques Bourgault of deputy ministers in place in January 2002 reveals that his and Dion's findings of 1991 still hold. Central-agency experience remains *un droit de passage* for a potential deputy minister. However, deputy ministers now find that consultative and interdepartmental work takes up about 30 per cent of their time. Two of them estimate that they spend 75 to 95 per cent of their time on 'horizontal' management, defined broadly. They characterize horizontal management as 'fuzzy, nowhere and everywhere, but increasing significantly.' Their work seems more and more tied to 'networks' designed to get things done. One reports, 'Whether we want it or not, everything is now horizontal.' Many also report a larger legal component to their work, thanks to the Charter of Rights and the North American Free Trade Agreement. They also made numerous references to access-to-information legislation and its impact on their relations with their ministers and the clerk of the Privy Council.[12]

A New Buckle

The McCain Frozen Food empire operates fifty production facilities in thirteen countries. I asked Harrison McCain in April 2001: 'Which government do you enjoy working with the most and which one the least?' He answered: 'I think that you are asking the wrong question. A better question is at what level in a government do I enjoy working the most, because governments, by and large, all look the same to me. The answer to that question is the deputy-minister level.'[13] How very interesting, I replied, but I would have thought that you would prefer to work at the political level and with ministers. His reply was quick and to the point: 'Not on your life – half of the politicians I have worked with are buffoons and the other half do not stay in place long enough to see a deal through.' People such as Harrison McCain who are anxious to get things done quickly have learned to turn to deputy ministers to get results.

Deputy ministers, as Ted Hodgetts pointed out, occupy a 'curious half-way house.'[14] They are part of the permanent hierarchy of the public service, but they are also in a constitutional sense the alter ego of the minister. They are half in the political world and half in the public service, sandwiched between the neutral civil service and the partisan political ministers. It is, in the words of Al Johnson, a relationship that is 'full of paradoxes.'[15]

Deputy ministers serve ministers, but they are appointed by the prime minister – just one of many paradoxes. They must have a full appreciation of the dimensions in which the minister operates – elections; public opinion; question period, where a minister's career can be undone; and the media, where one lets down one's guard at one's peril. Political activities are the responsibility of the minister alone, and the minister alone is politically accountable for departmental activities. The deputy minister is prohibited by law and convention from becoming involved in partisan political activities and is barred from membership in the House of Commons.[16] Thus in theory two distinct 'spaces' exist – one reserved for politicians, the other for career officials. However, the deputy minister, to be successful, must be sensitive to politics and to all its requirements. At all times, however, he or she must guard against being perceived as being politically partisan. It is a fine line, and the Glassco Commission observed: 'It is no part of the job of public servants to substitute their own political judgement for that of their minister, but there is a need for them to recognize situations in which political guidance must be sought.'[17]

At the same time, deputy ministers must also operate in the world of administration, which is one of due process, interdepartmental consultations, red tape, evaluation reports, central-agency requirements, equal treatment, and probity and anonymity. They must strive to balance a sectoral or departmental perspective with the views of their political masters, which are often political and seldom sectoral. The report of a federal task force summed up the challenge: 'They must represent faithfully and effectively to their employees, the wishes, needs and choices of the government of the day so that these may be met or carried out. At the same time, they must represent, and be seen to represent, the values and contribution of public servants to ministers. The second is almost as important as the first, because it undermines morale and corrodes the values of public service if it is not seen to be performed.'[18]

The two realms judge the deputy minister's performance from vastly different perspectives. Policy communities and major client groups or stakeholders look to see if the deputy minister promotes the department's policy agenda and secures more funding for the department and its activities. The political world, meanwhile, has a short-term perspective and gives high marks for responsiveness to the government's political agenda, for flexibility, for making things happen and getting them done quickly and quietly.

The administrative world takes a longer perspective, applauds sound (read 'rational') policy and decision making, and favours a careful review of all issues before a proposal moves ahead. It is the deputy minister who must attempt to speak truth to power on behalf of the department. If the deputy is unable to stand his or her ground, then career officials down the line know that they too will not be able to do so. The deputy minister must also protect the department's long-term interests and is judged harshly by career officials if this is not done. A department's long-term interests do not always involve solid management practices but usually encompass expanding or at least protecting its turf, looking after its employees, making sure that its staff complement is maintained or increased, and being a major player in interdepartmental policy consultations.

In brief, deputy ministers operate in an environment 'where the rubber meets the road.' Because they straddle politics and administration, they are in an ideal position to get things done, to make things happen. One can easily appreciate why Harrison McCain would prefer to deal with them more than with anyone else in government. Deputy ministers not only know which lever to pull to make things happen, they can also speak with authority to both politicians and administrators.

This factor is important in the hierarchy-conscious world of government. Deputy ministers have easy access to other deputies, and they can and often do make use of this access to unblock departmental files. If, for example, the deputy minister of industry has taken a strong interest in a particular proposal that has run into difficulty with the Department of Environment, then he or she can pick up the phone or have lunch with his or her counterpart and they can together determine if the problem can be resolved and, if so, how. Officials down the line will probably find their own counterparts in other departments more rigid in presenting their perspectives, because they can only speak on behalf of their units. Ministers can, of course, pursue any matter with colleagues, but they are more likely to ask their deputy ministers to look into it. Ministers do not have the time, the background, and the requisite contacts in line departments and central agencies. No one in government is in a better position than a deputy minister to determine what is possible and what is not and how to bring another department or agency onside in order to move a proposal forward in the system.

This factor also explains why federal ministers attach more importance than do their provincial counterparts to their deputies' ability to influence the interdepartmental decision-making process.[19] My consultations with current and former federal ministers suggest that the 'ability to play the interdepartmental game,' as one former minister called it, ranks very high on, if not at the very top of, what ministers expect from their deputies. Politicians may stress better management during election campaigns, but, once appointed ministers, they expect their deputy ministers to help them get their proposals through the system and to avoid or manage departmental crises. In fact, when discussing expectations, federal ministers invariably point to their deputies' ability to influence the interdepartmental process, particularly at the Privy Council Office (PCO) and the Department of Finance.[20]

Perhaps because policy making is increasingly horizontal and interdepartmental, at least two tiers of deputy ministers have emerged. In discussions for this book with senior officials in the autumn of 2002, I heard many references to the five, six, or seven deputy ministers who really 'mattered' in Ottawa. I learned that some assistant deputy ministers – for example, at Finance or in a key economic portfolio – matter more than some deputy ministers. There always have been some deputy ministers who are more influential than others. Forty years ago, how-ever, some became part of the inner circle on the basis of their departments, so that the Privy Council clerk, the under-secretary at External Affairs, and the deputy at Finance were always members. Today things are different, and the under-secretary at Foreign Affairs is no longer automatically in the inner circle. Joining depends on other factors, such as relations with the prime minister or the clerk of the Privy Council – in other words, one's department has less effect on membership than in the past.

Most ministers know which deputy ministers have influence, and they lobby the prime minister and his or her office to get one of them for their own department, knowing that this can ease their favoured 'files' or projects through the consultative process. Having on staff one of the strong deputy ministers has become as important for ambitious ministers as the department to which they are appointed. As a result, having the right deputy minister has come to matter as much as having the right department to pursue an ambitious agenda.

General Lewis Mackenzie insists that ability to work the Ottawa system has now become a major factor for promotion, even within the military. 'Regrettably, the mastery of the Ottawa games became one of the criteria, if not the key criterion, for selection as the Chief of Defence Staff. This reinforced the opinion of field soldiers that senior field command was not the route to follow if one aspired to be CDS – a most unfortunate and uniquely Canadian development.'[21] Working well with the centre of government and other departments requires wide experience in the system, and one must learn 'to roll with the punches, learn to take things in stride, learn to be a bit detached and not too dogmatic about things.'[22]

Deputy ministers readily acknowledge that the nature of their jobs has changed in recent years and that today they are mainly negotiators and networkers. One keen observer writes: 'There is no precise job description for deputy ministers. It is a variable, multifaceted job, depending on political schedules, political crises and events arising from both outside and inside the organization.'[23] Henry Mintzberg and Jacques Bourgault reveal in *Managing Publicly* that deputy ministers now spend 'sixteen percent of their time dealing with crises and answering emergencies' – more than on managing human resources (i.e., 15 per cent). As well, 'they spend twenty percent of their time on strategic files that will move forward or change their organizations.'[24] The emphasis is now on networking, brokering, and problem solving in a fast-moving political context.[25] Deputy ministers 'will look for quick fixers and sound risk-takers who are capable of negotiating agreements that can be appreciated in terms of results and impact rather than in the usual vague terms.'[26]

Deputy ministers lead incredibly busy lives. A 1997 study of their workload tells us that on average they work eleven hours and twenty-eight minutes a day, or fifty-seven hours a week. As well, they spend on average one hour out of every three on interdepartmental issues. Typically they allocate nearly twice as much time to meetings with their peers as on matters involving their own ministers.[27] They are at the very centre of departmental activities and are always trying to accommodate 'the urgent,' the 'important,' and the 'unforeseen.' 'Planning,' the author argues, 'is always left wanting.'[28]

One deputy minister interviewed for this work reveals that he often receives over 100 telephone calls a day. The calls can be from the minister and his or her staff, senior departmental officials, his or her own staff, federal, provincial deputy ministers, central agencies (including the Prime Minister's Office, or PMO), media, heads of interest groups and associations, high-profile or important departmental clients, and the heads of crown corporations and government agencies. Deputy ministers cannot possibly return all calls, answer all e-mails, and pay close attention to all incoming correspondence. They must decide what is important, what to handle in their own office, and what to delegate down the line. They often decide on the spot, with little consultation. These decisions are important, however, at least for those phoning and writing. If the deputy minister takes an active interest, then one can assume a different handling of a file than if it is delegated down the line. In many ways deputy ministers, no less than ministers, act as 'gate-keepers' within the government.

How does a deputy minister decide which file to focus on and which to delegate? There is no set answer. It depends on the deputy and his or her interest, on departmental priorities, on the political circumstances, on whether the issue is already in the media or likely to be raised in question period. Thus there is no easy way to determine in advance which messages will receive responses. What we do know is that captains of industry (such as Harrison McCain), the clerk of the Privy Council, and the principal secretary to the prime minister will have their calls returned promptly. The deputy will also pay particular attention to messages regarding a political or bureaucratic crisis.

Although deputy ministers are appointed by the prime minister, they will, for obvious reasons, spend a great deal of time building a strong working relationship with their ministers. This is not to suggest that these relations are always solid, cordial, and productive. The majority of ministers and deputies do work well together, and most seek to maintain or improve relations. A minority of ministers, however, never learn to work with career officials, and they may pay a high price. Marcel Masse, a minister in the Mulroney cabinet, is a case in point: he had great difficulty establishing rapport with his deputies. The prime minister, his office, and the PCO all concluded that the problem was Masse, not the deputy ministers, and that Masse had limited influence on policy, including in the sectors for which he was responsible.

Usually, however, when relations turn sour, it is the deputy who pays the price. He or she quietly moves elsewhere, often first as senior adviser in the PCO and later to an embassy or to a low-profile agency. Deputy ministers, unlike ministers, do not get dumped in the glare of publicity, but some do get dumped. The exchange below between Senator John Stewart and John Edwards, head of the reform initiative PS 2000, is revealing.

SENATOR STEWART: What will happen to the deputy minister who goofs up?

JOHN EDWARDS: They ... quietly move on. .

SENATOR STEWART: How many deputy ministers have been fired in the last six years?

JOHN EDWARDS: The firing of deputy ministers happens in the same way as the firing of many vice-presidents in the private sector. It happens reasonably quietly. People get moved into early retirement or go off to other challenges in the private sector ...

SENATOR STEWART: Do you have a record?

JOHN EDWARDS: No, I certainly do not. The Clerk of the Privy Council may have, and I doubt that he would share it. These things are best done quietly as opposed to having a roaring battle in public.[29]

'Goofing up' can mean any number of things. If a deputy demonstrates a continuing apparent inability to work with ministers, then he or she is unlikely to remain as deputy for very long. But here too deputy ministers must learn to walk a fine line – they must 'make their ministers look good' but also must, for the prime minister, make sure that their 'ministers keep to the government's agenda.'[30] Long-serving and successful deputy ministers, however, know where to draw the line and when to ring the alarm bell and to whom. They will inform the clerk of the Privy Council, with whom they will work out a game plan to deal with 'a rogue minister.'[31] In fact, the clerk tells a new deputy minister that in the event of a major disagreement with the minister, the deputy should raise the matter with the clerk. A new minister receives similar advice: if there is a problem with a deputy minister, inform the clerk before raising the matter with the prime minister. Since the prime minister appoints deputy ministers, he or she can discuss responsibilities or concerns directly with the deputy.[32]

Successful deputy ministers can manage accident-prone ministers or even turn around an error-prone department. The prime minister and the clerk always keep a watchful eye on ministers and departments and will make changes if necessary. If a minister and deputy are associated with several problems highlighted in the media and raised in question period, then one of them will go. The firing of a minister (for example, Michel Dupuy) or the demotion to a more junior portfolio (for instance, Diane Marleau) will take place in full public view. A deputy minister will leave quietly (for example, John Edwards, from Corrections

Canada, over a report suggesting that department officials had mishandled an incident at the women's penitentiary in Kingston).[33]

Dealing with the prime minister's priorities, implementing the government's agenda, protecting the minister, networking with other deputies, the provincial governments, and the department's stakeholders, articulating and promoting the department's interests, as well as managing political crises can consume much of a deputy's work day of ten to twelve hours. These many functions have transformed the role into a kind of buckle linking the political realm, the relevant policy communities, and the key stakeholders to the permanent administration. Deputy ministers know that this role is how they can best leave their mark. Promoting the department's policy interests and expanding its scope and mandate are a tangible way to demonstrate success to politicians and administrators. There are not many other such clear standards of success available to them.

However, as deputy ministers deal with political forces from above and the demands of policy communities from outside, they have still other responsibilities. The PCO has produced a document outlining the 'duties and responsibilities of a deputy minister,'[34] which fall into three main categories: 'supporting the collective management responsibilities of the government; providing policy advice to the minister and the government and managing the internal operations of the department on behalf of the minister.'[35] Note: 'supporting the collective management' is first on the list, and 'managing the internal operations' is last.

From Administration to Management and Back Again

The deputy minister is responsible for managing most of the internal operations of the department. The Interpretation Act vests a minister's full governmental authority, with a few exceptions, in the deputy minister. The act aims to increase the minister's effectiveness by having someone act for him or her in areas related to departmental activities, consistent with the minister's individual and collective responsibilities.[36] In addition, each departmental act generally includes a standard declaration that the governor-in-council may appoint a deputy minister and explicitly delegate power to him or her for the independent exercise of his or her authority in specified areas, not just in administrative issues, but also, in some instances, in managing programs. This is particularly the case in departments that have regulatory functions in such areas as customs, excise, and immigration. In addition, since 1967, the Treasury

Board and the Public Service Commission have been able to delegate specific management authority to deputy ministers. As Ted Hodgetts writes: 'In the sense that this authority does not flow from or depend upon the minister, but may be devolved directly on the deputy by the two central management agencies, an important formal alteration in the conventional minister-to-deputy minister relationship has occurred.'[37] But while the authority gives deputy ministers a certain independence from their ministers, it is never absolute. All deputy ministers, regardless of the department, must abide by the requirements outlined in the Financial Administration Act, the Official Languages Act, the Public Service Employment Act, and so on.[38] Thus, despite some delegation of authority, red tape, administrative processes, and audits in government are in place to ensure proper exercise of this authority.

There was a time, however, when career officials saw a great deal of merit in red tape and due process and said so publicly. As Al Johnson saw things in 1961: 'The Civil Service Commission may be slow and meticulous in the recruitment of staff, but this is because parliament rightly insists upon every citizen having an equal right to try for a job. Appropriation and allotment controls may impose on field workers certain delays, but parliamentary control over expenditures is much more important than these minor inconveniences. The same applies to controls over individual expenditures: these must be reported in the Public Accounts in order that parliament might review them, and a good deal of 'book-work' is justified in making this possible.'[39] Government 'supervisors' had no profit motive to encourage them to streamline work – simplify performance standards and the rest – and nor should they.[40] No deputy minister would make such a statement today. They and other senior career officials have generally accepted the new public management (NPM), or at least its rhetoric, and the virtues of business management. Most now speak about becoming task-oriented achievers and look to clients for guidance rather than to institutions and historically derived processes and identities.[41] Many have publicly called for the dead hand of bureaucracy to give way to what they regard as an invigorating management concept inspired by the private sector.[42] By the 1990s virtually every department was using the word 'business' and related phrases in virtually every planning document.

It seems that everything the government did could be restated from a business perspective. Peter Harder, secretary to the Treasury Board and comptroller general, explained how the government had turned around its difficult fiscal position in the mid-1990s: 'We did what all good businesses do when they first see the signs of trouble. We focused on the costs of inputs.' But that was not enough, because 'it did not lead to a rethinking of our business and business processes.'[43] Ralph Heintzman, a senior career official, suggests that things are now out of hand: 'Without blushing or even without a second thought, we now talk about our "customers" or "clients" in a way that would not have occurred to public servants three or four decades ago. And this is just the tip of the iceberg.' He adds: 'Sometimes the results of this attempt to reinvent the public sector into the private sector are quite bizarre. I recently visited a well-meaning colleague who proudly presented to me the organizational renewal efforts of a high-priced foreign consultant that consisted in, among other things, the translation of all terms of public administration and parliamentary democracy into private sector equivalents, including the reinvention of members of Parliament as the shareholders of the corporation and Cabinet as the Board of Directors.' In the early 1990s, with the new public-management approach in vogue, a deputy minister had waxed 'expansively about what he believed to be the renewal and transformation of his own department. "This is really serious stuff," he exclaimed proudly. "It's just like the private sector."'[44]

While politicians and the more senior career officials sought better management, insisting that red tape and the old bureaucratic culture were crippling performance, they would soon discover that the old culture had staying power. Career officials with a management bent have to learn on the job, since they have no access to role models. Don Yeomans, a former deputy minister known for his interest in management issues, observed: 'I never did learn about being a Public Service manager.' As he was climbing the bureaucratic ladder, he found little guidance in management. He often found himself asking, 'How would George Davidson deal with that or how would Bob Bryce? ... Davidson was a terrible manager but a highly skilled negotiator and diplomat and weaver through the bureaucracy ... Bryce, he was just too busy.'[45]

Just as NPM was hitting its stride, Gordon Osbaldeston, a former clerk of the Privy Council, published a government-sponsored study on accountability. He reviewed the three formal duties and responsibilities of the deputy minister and called for greater attention to policy advice and the deputy's relationship with the minister as adviser and confidant. He reported that deputy ministers still spent much of their time assisting the minister and steering departmental initiatives through consultation and negotiations inside and outside government – and that is how it should be.[46] Osbaldeston was, if anything, uneasy about management responsibilities, in terms of both accountability and performance, and noted confusion about the respective roles of ministers and deputy ministers.[47]

Osbaldeston was simply reporting the obvious. There are signs everywhere that policy still rules in Ottawa and that management still appears to be for functional specialists or technicians. The objectives are to satisfy the central agencies, play by the rules to avoid undue scrutiny by the Office of the Auditor General, and keep administrative problems or mistakes from surfacing in question period and the media. If one plays by the old rules and culture, administrative foul-ups are less likely. Opposition parties and the media will rarely, if ever, comment on good management practices, and they will not waste valuable time on issues that will gain them no credit. This atmosphere does not encourage empowerment and risk taking – key elements of the business-management model. Both are needed if front-line workers are to take charge and solve problems and not have to rely on red tape and detailed direction from above. A well-known student of management, D. Quinn Mills, notes: 'Risk taking is necessary to innovation and successful change. But risk taking involves the chance of error. A strong organization learns to profit from errors; a weak one tries at all costs to avoid them.'[48]

There is also de facto a striking separation between policy and administration or at least between policy making and operational responsibilities in Ottawa.[49] Policy proposals and major initiatives are presented to central agencies and cabinet committees in very broad terms and hardly consider management or administrative issues. According to Frank Swift, a former senior official, 'Most of the critique of departmental proposals to Cabinet has come from central agencies primarily concerned with strategic and expenditure considerations. Operational considerations such as design and quality of delivery systems or their sensitivity to regional differences have received much less attention.' He adds: 'Typically, operational managers have had little opportunity or authority to influence the design of a departmental initiative or to allow flexibility in implementation.'[50]

It would clearly take a strong wrench of the wheel to move many career officials away from the comfortable and predictable world of administration to a new, untried business model. Asking them to 'let the managers manage' and follow the business-management approach is also like asking them to transform the administration of government without tackling its theoretical basis. It seems that few have taken the time to inquire whether such a model is compatible with the traditional doctrine of ministerial accountability. Fewer still have wondered whether a new accountability framework is necessary, and no one has called for changes to the work of various oversight bodies, ranging from the auditor general to the commissioner of official languages. In brief, the new management culture was to be imposed on the existing political-administrative structure as is, warts and all. The goal was to shift to a business-management model, 'empower' front-line workers and their managers, and at the same time have error-free government. D. Quinn Mills's management theory suggests that the objective was to create both 'strong' and 'weak' organizations at the same time.

When errors have surfaced, the political–administrative structure has quickly reverted to its old ways and culture. The media are also now much more aware of how government works, and, as we saw above, they have also learned to use access-to-information legislation to find out what has gone wrong in government. There are plenty of such examples. In a front-page article on 15 February 1997, for example, the *Globe and Mail* reported an excess of empowerment. Officials in the Department of Health had come up with a scheme to turn their $500,000 travel budget into $630,000 worth of travel. They had been granted the budget after they had been asked to carry out an ambitious computer project to redesign income-security programs. They prepaid the entire travel budget to American Express to enable it to invest the fund to buy more air tickets. No one benefited personally, and the only intention had been to stretch the department's travel budget. It meant, however, spending for services to be delivered at a later date, and this certainly did not square with standard federal accounting practices. Auditors argued that the 'cheque issuing provided an opportunity for misuse and was not prudent.' The *Globe and Mail* saw the incident 'as a reminder that where public money is concerned, there is value in safeguards, watchdogs, and even red tape.'[51]

Alasdair Roberts, in his review of the PS 2000 reforms, writes about a 'control lobby.' Controversies involving public servants purportedly 'running amok' captured media attention. One involved the Canada Communications group, which Roberts describes as 'a child of the PS 2000 exercise.' The group had received Special Operating Agency status and a mandate to 'be more businesslike' and 'entrepreneurial.' It soon became the target of complaints from competing businesses. Five industry associations presented a brief to the government, and so David Dingwall, the minister responsible, asked for an outside audit. Elements of the media, including the *Citizen*, the *Financial Post*, and the *Globe and*

Mail, screamed about 'abuse of governmental power.'[52] Even government MPs started to voice their concerns, with one suggesting that the group was 'scaring the hell out of private business.'[53]

Things took a turn for the worse when it was revealed that the group had accepted $2.5 million from the Department of Industry for work that it had not completed. The department's aim, it appears, was to 'park' part of its appropriation in the group's revolving fund. The media had a field day, with a front-page story in the *Citizen* suggesting that the incident 'might have been predictable when a public institution was ordered to operate like a private business.'[54] Dingwall was urged in question period to punish the public servants responsible. The head of the agency was removed, and a few months later the government declared its intention to sell off the agency.[55]

Public servants operate in a highly politicized atmosphere. Government managers do not enjoy the same kind of privacy or private space that their private-sector counterparts do. Any decision can become the subject of a public debate, a question in Parliament, or a ten-second clip on the television news. The managers who decided, for example, to replace windows at the Department of External Affairs never expected that their action would receive intense media coverage, give rise to questions in Parliament, and move the minister of government services to declare that the decision was 'stupid' and that he 'wanted a full explanation,' since he had never been made aware of the file.[56]

Ten years after the introduction of PS 2000 and nearly twenty years after NPM first surfaced, Human Resources Development (HRDC) found itself mired in a full-blown political crisis. Senior officials became concerned in 1998 that one program was not performing as well as they had hoped, and so they launched an internal audit. The results began to emerge in mid-1999 and triggered a political firestorm that dominated the media for several months. The crisis, according to a former senior official at HRDC, became a 'significant preoccupation for the Prime Minister [and] dominated the entire department and its minister.'[57] The matter gave rise to 800 questions to the minister in question period, 17,000 pages of information on the department's website, 100,000 pages of material released to the media under Access to Information, numerous reviews and task forces, and a special examination by the auditor general.[58] The crisis ended with the release of the auditor general's review in October of the next year.

The media and the opposition had pounced on the 34-page internal audit to declare that there was a 'billion dollar boondoggle' at HRDC involving the Transitional Jobs Fund. The document in question was not a financial audit but a 'paper review' to establish the extent of documentation on file in a random sample of projects sponsored under the program. Paper work on some projects was incomplete (for example, lacking cash-flow forecasts and a description of activities to be financed), and that there was little follow-up on some projects that had been approved.

The minister in a media scrum declared that 'there is sloppy administration and that we need to do a better job of ensuring that our files are complete.'[59] That night the item got top billing on the TV news, with reports of stunning revelations about government mismanagement.[60] The next day the print media got into the act led by the *Globe and Mail*'s front-page story headlined 'Bureaucrats Mismanaged $3 Billion,' *La Presse*'s 'Un momunental fouillis administratif,' and the *Vancouver Sun*'s 'Sloppy Records Keep Public from Knowing If $1 Billion in Federal Grants Wrongly Spent.'[61] The *Globe* suggested that the minister, Jane Stewart, was not to blame because she was not in charge when the grants were awarded, but that the then–deputy minister, Mel Cappe, should accept some of the responsibility. The *Globe* noted, however, that Cappe had since become clerk of the Privy Council and now 'heads the entire Civil Service.'

Opposition MPs the next day called on Stewart to resign, citing the doctrine of ministerial responsibility. Soon others got into the act. The federal information commissioner declared publicly that 'the file management system within the government has collapsed and continues to collapse.'[62] The media began to ask questions about 'who knew what, where and when, and whose head should roll (of the Watergate variety)' and questioned the neutrality of the public service. Career officials were asked to testify before the House of Commons Standing Committee about what, how, and why things had gone wrong. They also appeared in the media, losing their traditional anonymity in order to answer questions and to report on new measures to strengthen the department's grants and contributions.[63] When Mel Cappe agreed to answer the committee's questions about his old department, some observers remarked that 'the days of the faceless public servant entrenched in the Westminster system are over.'[64]

The Transitional Jobs Fund (TJF) was born in the aftermath of cuts to the unemployment-insurance program in 1995–96. The TJF, it was believed, would make the cuts more acceptable to MPs representing regions with high unemployment. The HRDC's minister, Doug Young, directed his officials to consult MPs in implementing the program – if only, he argued, because each MP knew the needs of his or her community. The role of MPs in TJF was to be advisory, given that they were not asked to approve or veto projects. Still, local HRDC officials were told to work directly with their MPs, which would open the door to the MPs possibly influencing the decision-making process. A number of community groups subsequently became confused over the role of MPs, and the auditor general observed that 'written recommendations from the member of Parliament for the area as one of the inputs for the project approval process ... confuses traditional accountability relationships.'[65] The approach allowed MPs to enter the realm traditionally occupied by career officials, and it left little room for Woodrow Wilson's politics–administration dichotomy.

The controversy lingered on for months in Parliament and the media. Jane Stewart's year in hell saw the media cast her in an extremely negative light almost daily. The *Globe and Mail* reported on its front page on 2 August 2000 that she was 'expected to be named Canada's ambassador to the Netherlands ... because of the controversy surrounding the way officials in her department administered a job grants program.'[66] The media, including the *Globe*, were always quick to add, however, that the criticism directed at her was unfair because it was Pierre Pettigrew who had been minister when the grants were handed out.

The controversy ended only when the auditor general's office reported that the audit of the one- or three-billion dollar 'boondoggle' had centred on 459 projects selected at random from 10,000 projects, that the total amount of money involved in the 459 projects was about $200 million, that less than a dozen of the projects were 'problematic,' and that there was hardly any missing money.[67] Jane Stewart tabled a detailed report to the Standing Committee on Human Resources Development on the department's 16,971 active files on grants and contributions. The total value of these files amount to $1.58 billion, and, of this amount, the only outstanding debt to the government was $65,000.[68]

The media quickly lost interest in the story. Meanwhile, so did opposition parties, and both paid precious little attention to the actual facts as they were being made public. But the first impressions have taken root, and to this day one still hears references to the $1-billion boondoggle at HRDC.

HRDC and central agencies have been left to sort out the lessons to be learned from this incident. For its part, the government cancelled the Canada Jobs Fund and reallocated $50 million to improve the management skills of HRDC employees. This served as an accusation, implying that career officials did not have the basic skills to document an application and to follow up on a file.

The crisis also led the government to 'rebureaucratize the government' by imposing new processes and controls on its programs. A former deputy minister of the department maintains that the crisis sent a message to career officials that they were to forget about empowerment and showing flexibility to local needs. He wrote: 'The only way to keep out of trouble is to do things by the book, and here is a new much thicker book to replace the one you've been using.' He added that the message to ministers was equally clear: 'Make sure your department doesn't do anything that could result in you becoming the next Jane Stewart.'[69] The government decided henceforth to vet all audits of departments before publicly releasing them to ensure that they 'are well-managed from a public relations point of view.'[70]

Front-line officials came to terms with the fact that, while MPs would wish to promote their projects with considerable enthusiasm and encourage civil servants to be less bureaucratic and to expedite the approval process, they would not be around to lend a helping hand should a controversy erupt. Indeed, some MPs became highly critical in the media of the civil service for 'mismanaging' public funds. Prime Minister Chrétien also pointed the finger at front-line workers: 'There is some explanation, perhaps, from the fact there is some devolution of decision making in the regions.'[71] The media, the auditor general, and MPs focused exclusively on program inputs – a fact not lost on career officials operating on the front line. These lessons carry far more weight for career officials than any number of task-force reports on bringing private-sector practices to government and any amount of literature on the advantages of the new public management.

Little wonder that the new management model soon came up against a widespread culture of disbelief in the civil service. The culture acts as a psychological defence against proposals or initiatives that threaten the stability of public servants' belief systems and their work. Thus many of them dismiss out of hand new management concepts, especially those imported from the private sector. They view them as self-serving promises for politicians seeking election. The solution for many career officials was to batten down the hatches and wait out the descent of the private sector and the passing storm. Experience told them that this too would pass and life would eventually return to normal. Career officials also believed that politicians, more than anyone else, did not want to 'rock the boat' and risk administrative foul-ups because of new management practices. They remained convinced that ministers would continue to look to their senior bureaucrats, not as managers in the private-sector mould, but as a kind of fire brigade to help them extinguish political 'fires' and the inevitable crises.

Why then did deputy ministers not tell politicians and the exponents of the various management reforms that the approach would not work, or not work well, if only because empowerment and risk-taking meant a greater chance of error? Because there could well be a high political price to pay? Given that the issue goes to the heart of public administration, why did senior officials not speak truth to power? Politicians were in no mood to hear that government departments could not be better managed. The focus was on generating savings in government operations through better management practices and on avoiding too many hard political decisions on government programs. One can also assume that few politicians understood the full political implications of introducing private-sector management practices to government operations. One former senior public servant insists that 'ministers were not told the truth because the senior public service did not believe for an instant in New Public Management reform measures.' He added, 'PS 2000 was mostly hot air.'[72]

However, unlike the situation in Britain, where Margaret Thatcher took a strong interest in public-service reforms and in fact was the main architect of several of them, in Canada it was career officials, not politicians, who pushed the reforms.[73] As we have seen above, senior officials felt the sting of bureaucracy bashing and agreed that the private sector was better managed than the public sector. Politicians, the media, business executives, and public-opinion surveys all told them so. A survey of 1,202 Ottawa-based career officials in 1996, for example, revealed that 77 per cent of them thought that 'the public viewed them ... as lazy and uncaring.'[74] Even former officials said that the private sector was better. Paul Tellier, former clerk of the Privy Council, made it clear only a few years after he left government that he believed that business-management practices were superior to those that he found in government.[75]

If public servants embraced a new management model, it would, if nothing else, send out a signal to politicians and the public that they were trying to improve government operations down the line. In any event, what could possibly be wrong with reducing red tape and making it easier for front-line managers to get the job done and improve relations with clients? Taking on a private-sector vocabulary and business-management techniques became, in the words of a senior official, 'an act of self-defence, a rhetorical strategy to shape up the self-esteem and prestige of the public sector. At a time when the self-confidence of the public sector was faltering and the prestige of the private sector was roaring, it was an act of legitimate self-defence for the public sector to appropriate to itself the language and model of its more prestigious rival. By discovering for ourselves that we too had customers or clients, public servants were initially making a bid for respectability in the eyes of the world, and even in their own eyes.'[76] The need for respectability and for boosting morale among public servants was apparent even to the most casual observer. The clerk of the Privy Council in her annual reports to the prime minister expressed concerns in the mid-1990s that the civil service was confronting a major morale problem. The secretary of the Treasury Board publicly acknowledged in 1999 that 'public servants were losing confidence in what they thought public service was about and most were feeling undervalued and underpaid.'[77] Some media pundits began to take notice of the problem when a senior official quit in 1997 at least partly because 'the political level does not accord public servants the respect or recognition they deserve.'[78]

Borrowing the vocabulary and management practices from a private sector soaring in prestige and confidence does not change the obvious fact that managing government operations in a parliamentary democracy and running a business are two vastly different things. Private-sector managers work in private, with a few unambiguous goals – make a profit and capture a high share of the market. Public-sector managers work publicly and must accommodate many conflicting goals.

Senior career officials must now manage their operations in a much more public environment than was the case some thirty years ago. Access-to-information legislation, the media, MPs involving themselves in decision making, and the need to accommodate stakeholders are all making the world of civil servants public. In addition, career officials no longer dominate program administration away from public scrutiny.

Two Cultures

Looking Up, Looking Down

In *Bureaucracy: What Government Agencies Do and Why They Do It,* James Q. Wilson employs a four-part classification system – production, procedural, craft, and coping – for measuring outputs and observing work in government departments and agencies:

- first, machine or *production* organizations (controllable on the basis of outputs and processes readily observable)
- second, *procedural* organizations (not controllable on the basis of outputs and processes readily observable)
- third, *craft* organizations (controllable on the basis of outputs and processes not readily observable)
- fourth, *coping* organizations (not controllable on the basis of outputs and processes not readily observable).

In the case of the first, he reports, the tasks are simple, stable, and specialized. Consequently, they are often centralized and formal – for example the processing of tax returns and government printing bureaux. The second category (procedural organizations) includes peacetime armed forces; the third (craft organizations) includes audit services and inspection and enforcement services; and the fourth (professional organizations) includes central-government consulting services and some policy and advisory units.[79]

Wilson sees the work of government departments and agencies as varied and complex. He maintains that government departments can and do have their own distinct organizational culture.

But this does not tell the complete story, and it may not tell the most important story, at least in Canada. There is growing evidence that the federal public service has two groups that view the world from different perspectives and that two broad organizational cultures are at work. One looks up and in, and it is concerned primarily with the policy process, ministers, central agencies, question period, and the senior public service. The other looks down and out – to citizens, clients, programs, program delivery, levels of services, and the managing of staff and financial resources. The *Discussion Paper on the Task Force on Values and Ethics in the Public Service* (1996) pointed to the differences between 'managing up' and 'managing down' and argued that managing up has as its focus 'ministers and their needs or purposes' and constitutes 'an essential element of our democratic system of government.' But 'it has its side effects. One of them is a preoccupation with managing up ... [which] ... obscures the importance of managing down.' The problem is that 'many senior public servants have made their careers because of their skills in managing up. They have been valued and promoted because they were adept at providing superiors with what they needed, in a timely fashion.'[80]

I have been invited over the years to make presentations to departmental executive committees (chaired by deputy ministers) and to management committees (chaired by a senior line manager or by senior regional managers). The difference in perspective is striking. I can do no better than to quote a senior federal official who saw an 'Ottawa-based culture ... [and] the culture of the federal public service outside Ottawa. And the relationship between them is often a dialogue of the deaf.'[81] Another career official with both policy and program experience explains that policy-oriented people 'are concerned with policy, process and ministers' and 'looking up for decisions,' while program people are 'concerned with program and program delivery. The first is more tentative when it comes to taking action and making decisions. The second is much less concerned with this aspect. They are preoccupied with their programs, their staff, their clients and how to make ends meet. They are used to making decisions on the spot.'[82] Round tables involving senior officials are also revealing. The Public Policy Forum (PPF) reports that discussions with managers in Ottawa suggest that 'the current culture emphasizes a must have now, must be perfect attitude. Participants asserted that individuals at all levels of the organization are frustrated with the stress caused by relatively insignificant issues ... Today's executives feel inundated by process, the prevalent micro-management, and the need for a committee to make decisions.' Discussions with regional executives, however, brought a different perspective. The PPF reports: 'Regional executives felt they had more autonomy and authority over their immediate work environment than did their counterparts in the National Capital Region. This circumstance was attributed mainly to their further proximity from deputy ministers and ministers.' [83] Front-line managers grouped deputy ministers and ministers together.

Many in the managing-up group will happily launch new task forces and produce reports to promote empowerment, reduce red tape, and strengthen services to the public. Most of the managing-downers regard these efforts as essentially 'paper exercises,' convinced that red tape is, in any event, created by politicians working hand in hand with the managing-up group. They will insist that they have for years been trying to improve service delivery and express puzzlement over why the first group only recently discovered its importance. They also view the debate about clients, customers, and citizens as empty. One senior field official with Corrections Canada explains that he and his colleagues 'long ago sorted the whole client business. We have more than one client and we have had to deal with this every day. We have people in prison, people on parole, people who successfully completed parole conditions and we have Canadians. Nothing more needs to be said.'[84]

Some observers have even discerned a general fault line separating senior and policy-oriented officials from program managers and front-line workers.[85] I say more below about accountability at the deputy minister level. But program managers and front-line workers find themselves accountable to a variety of people, including immediate supervisors, clients, and Canadians generally. Senior and policy-oriented officials, in contrast, tend to look up to the political and policy process for accountability. The 1996 task force on values and ethics saw a fault line: 'Our dialogue with public servants revealed to us a certain divide between levels in the public service, perhaps especially where public service values are concerned. Many at the middle and lower levels of the public service to whom we spoke or from whom we heard do not feel well connected to the senior levels, and they are not sure whether they necessarily share the same values as those at higher levels.' Its report added that one 'source of this fault line appears to be the confusion about accountability, and the tension between customer accountability and political accountability. Those closest to the front lines of accountability feel their primary accountability to citizen/customers while those farther up may feel primary accountability to citizen voters and taxpayers, as mediated by the political process.'[86]

Notwithstanding distinct departmental histories and cultures, managing up and managing down differ substantially, probably more than do types of managing in production, procedural, craft, and coping organizations. Program managers and front-line workers in departments such as Corrections, Industry, and Revenue have more in common with one another than with their own senior departmental management and policy people. Two distinct strata of career officials are emerging within the public service – those who prefer or are asked to manage up and are preoccupied with the policy process, and those who are preoccupied or have to deal with program implementation and look down to the front-line workers providing services to Canadians.

Speaking Politics to Science

Management of the natural and physical sciences should transcend the managing-up and -down cultures. Managing scientists should embrace two fundamental democratic values: trust and legitimacy. Indeed, if science is not managed properly and if trust and legitimacy are not firmly established, it can give rise to crises in resource conservation and public health. In public health, scientific findings can have life-or-death consequences (for example, tainted blood products), and in resource conservation, they can determine the continuing viability of an economic sector (such as the fishery). There are a number of important management issues in the sciences, but our concern here is with scientists' ability to present their findings unfiltered and untampered within the decision-making process – to speak scientific truth to political power. Political power can do what it wishes with scientific advice, because it is directly accountable to the public and has to live with the political consequences of its decisions. But senior bureaucrats should not tamper with scientific findings to make them more palatable to their superiors or to make the findings say what they do not say.

Politics, public administration, and science have always lived in uneasy cohabitation. John Fraser, when minister in the Department of Fisheries and Oceans (DFO), overruled his department's inspectors and ordered that canned tuna declared unfit for human consumption be released for sale. Word leaked to the media and to opposition parties, and Fraser's decision came under attack in question period. A few days later, Fraser resigned.[87] He had decided to disregard advice from departmental scientists so as to protect jobs in a slow-growth area of the country and ended up paying the ultimate political price.

Science workers are different from most other government officials. They have higher-than-average qualifications and credentials, tend to see themselves as largely autonomous in their work, and value intrinsic and professional recognition. They accept adjudication of their work by their peers, but less readily from organizational authority. Their work, quite apart from the time required for adequate peer review, can be long, tedious, and unpredictable and can take months, even years, to generate acceptable results.[88] A public–private round table entitled 'The Credibility and Acceptability of Science Advice for Decision-making in Government' concluded that all this 'cannot be accomplished in time for Question Period' or for the immediate political or bureaucratic agenda of the minister and the department.[89]

The round table took place in response to a barrage of negative media coverage in the 1990s which suggested that bureaucratic politics threatened scientific integrity in government. The assault followed when a number of federal scientists announced their concern that their 'scientific findings' were 'filtered or distorted by management for political reasons.'[90] Some scientists even decided to leave government over this issue.[91] They insisted that an apparent inability to get science right in government was exacerbating public cynicism about government.

DFO's Jeffrey Hutchings, described as 'one of Canada's leading biologists,' co-wrote a peer-reviewed article in the *Canadian Journal of Fisheries and Aquatic Sciences* in 1997 which said that DFO 'manufactured consensus among its staff, misused scientific studies, and deliberately ignored the warnings of independent scientists when their research agenda conflicted with the agenda of the day.'[92] Ransom Myers, who left DFO for Killam Chair of Ocean Studies at Dalhousie University, told the media that DFO 'routinely suppresses papers it doesn't like.'[93] Specifically, the scientists accused the department of developing 'optimistic stock surveys' for Atlantic cod, 'despite evidence that the research was wrong.' Further, it was, they said, unwilling to share the data with other DFO scientists and then 'ordered concerned scientists within the department to keep quiet.' Myers told the media that 'in terms of the amount of twisting of information and manipulation, the actual truth is much worse (than the article in the learned journal suggested), and they're still covering it up.'[94]

Myers and others were objecting to politics moving in below the deputy-minister level. Ministers are free to make political decisions, they maintained, but career officials should not manipulate scientific findings to assist them. A clear line should separate what is political from what is not, and the political and partisan should not filter down below the deputy minister. Give ministers the scientific goods, they argued, and then let the chips fall where they may, and one must hope that ministers will make the right decisions. Some scientists suggested, to this end, grouping science workers together in an arm's-length organization that reports directly to a minister and mentioned the Office of the Auditor General or Statistics Canada as possible models.[95] Their goal would be to remove scientists' work from bureaucratic filtering by having them report directly to the minister. DFO's deputy minister, Bill Rowatt, disagreed with them and wrote to Arthur Carty, president of the National Research Council, which helps fund the journal: 'These are not scientific papers. They are tabloid journalism. I am appalled at the unprofessional and unsubstantiated nature of their attacks on DFO, its scientists and its managers.'[96]

Scientists in other departments also voiced criticism over how they and their findings were being managed. Michèle Bill-Edwards reported that she left Health Canada in 1996 because 'senior non-medical bureaucrats continued to make ill-informed decisions and the experts were bullied into silence.'[97] Scientists in departments such as Environment and at Parks Canada also went public with similar claims. One reported: 'I've seen the mandarins not only suppress scientific material, but make policy decisions and then suggest that the scientific material buttresses their policy. Time after time, science is completely contrary to political decisions made at the top of the agency.'[98] Michael Prince offered a diagnosis of the problem: 'There's a trade-off between giving [scientific] advice and surviving in the bureaucracy because sometimes your advice is unpalatable to your superiors, and the more you persist in giving the truth, the more you jeopardize your own survival within the organisation.'[99] When the scientists went public, they lost their anonymity and took on an explicitly political role in their efforts to 'delegitimatize' the government decision-making process.[100]

A report from the Treasury Board Secretariat published in September 1997 – *Getting Science Right in the Public Sector* – sought to shed light on the controversy from the government's perspective and to deal with the 'barrage' of media criticism. By its own count, the secretariat reported over '80 articles' in 'all major Canadian newspapers.'[101] Its report argued that it is now 'widely accepted in the social sciences, and to a lesser degree in the natural sciences, that just as there can be no objective search for truth neither does an objective truth exist.' Yet 'when scientists come to the conclusion that they are unable to speak truth to power, there are some possible explanations. The first is that their input truly has not reached top decision makers. The second is that it has, but the impact of their contributions has not been properly communicated.' The document quoted from the 1997 paper by Hutchings and his colleagues: 'The perceived need for scientific consensus and an *official* position has seriously limited the effectiveness of government-based research to contribute effectively to policy decisions' and 'towards an understanding of the collapse of Atlantic cod.'[102]

The secretariat's report added that scientists appeared 'more comfortable with traditional public administrative values than they do with the market-driven NPM.'[103] The document noted tension between the pursuit of scientific knowledge and a 'result-driven' and 'client-friendly' approach (i.e., private-sector firms that are being asked to pay some of the cost), both closely identified with the new public management. Some health officials spoke about this tension and reported that the government's cost-recovery measures had forged a new relationship with industry. They insisted that the public is no longer the client and that private firms, because they are footing part of the bill, now feel free to make client-type demands on government scientists. One scientist explained: 'If you accept the Queen's shilling, you have to dance the Queen's tune.'[104] Stuart Smith, chair (1982–7) of the National Round Table on Environment and the Economy, weighed into the debate with the observation that those 'who fund science will always try to influence the results.'[105]

At the root of the controversy lies the fact that managers and scientists have 'two languages, two cultures, and a sea of myths' and different 'accountability requirements.'[106] Senior managers insist that they have to take into account different considerations as they formulate advice to ministers. They point out that they never have the luxury of just concentrating on one point of view, one perspective, however convincing, in moving advice forward. Scientists such as Hutchings may resent the 'perceived need for scientific consensus and an *official* position,' but that, they claim, is the reality of making policy and decisions. Deputy ministers, including those at DFO, Environment, and Health, may point out that they are accountable for *all* the operations of their departments, including units concerned only with research and generating scientific advice, and ultimately for the validity of advice to ministers and for the interdepartmental policy-making process.[107]

Introducing a 'result-driven' and 'client-friendly approach' also changes the landscape for science workers in government. They too no longer dominate their field within government. They have to share it with people who are preoccupied with managing up and with protecting the political interests of their ministers and their departments, the concerns of other departments, and private-sector firms that are asked to pay some of the costs. It may well have been easy in the past for scientists to occupy a relatively clear space in a government department, from which they could generate data, produce objective conclusions, and then march their findings unencumbered up to the deputy minister and the minister, but this is much less possible today.

Deputy Ministers and Accountability

Deputy ministers are not only extremely busy, they must constantly keep an eye on a multitude of oversight bodies and accountability requirements. The *International Encyclopedia of Public Policy and Administration* defines accountability as a 'relationship in which an individual or agency is held to answer for performance that involves some delegation of authority to act.'[108] By definition then, accountability suggests some measure or appraisal of performance and an obligation to answer to a person or a group.

The above begs the questions: to whom is a deputy minister accountable, and how does one measure his or her performance? We know that in theory at least deputy ministers are not accountable to the public. The doctrine of ministerial responsibility makes the minister responsible for everything done in the department and means that career officials have no constitutional responsibility or responsibility distinct from the government of the day. The doctrine also suggests that deputy ministers are not legally accountable to Parliament and, even in the case of the Public Accounts Committee, report only to Parliament on behalf of the minister. Thus this much is clear: deputy ministers are not accountable to the public or to Parliament. This, however, is where clarity ends.

Deputy ministers, as we saw above, have the following duties and responsibilities: to support the collective management of the government, to provide policy advice to the minister and to manage the internal operations of the department on behalf of the minister. This suggests that deputy ministers have an accountability relationship with:

- the prime minister, who appoints them and can remove them. One can assume that they will put the prime minister at the very top of their list
- the clerk of the Privy Council and secretary to the cabinet and (for the past twelve years or so, or since PS 2000) head of the public service (all one person). Deputy ministers emphasize this relationship: the clerk's advice probably helped get them their job, and the clerk prepares the annual performance review of deputy ministers
- the minister, who is consulted in the deputy minister's annual performance review
- the Treasury Board and the Financial Administration Act
- the Public Service Commission and the Public Service Employment Act

The PCO maintains that the accountability of deputy ministers 'cannot be exercised without reference to the responsibility of ministers to Parliament.' It is also linked to the 'triangular relationship between Prime Minister, minister and deputy minister,' which 'defies precise dissection.'[109]

Deputy ministers must also contend with oversight bodies, all with a specific mandate to police government administration including the access to Information Commissioner, the ADRG (Conflict of Interest), the Commissioner of Official Languages, the Human Rights Commission, the Office of the Auditor General, the Privacy Commissioner, the Public Service Staff Relations Board, and parliamentary committees. One could add the media.

The accountability regime and the management environment illustrate the vast differences between the public and the private sectors. In the private sector, accountability is straightforward. A line runs unencumbered from employee to supervisor to manager to vice-president to chief executive officer to board of directors to shareholders. Performance expectations are equally straightforward – to outperform the projections of financial analysts and investors, to capture a larger share of the market, to produce a higher return on investment, and so on. The chief executive officer knows to whom he or she is accountable and how performance will be determined.

Now consider the deputy minister. Apart from ministerial responsibility, the lines of accountability are not clear nor are performance measurements, despite extensive literature that shows how difficult it is to evaluate performance in government.[110] How do you measure the value of a defence program or a diplomatic initiative, let alone the role of the deputy minister in charge? How can government departments and agencies know if they are doing a good job? How can Parliament possibly decide whether departments and deputy ministers are doing a good job? How can one possibly isolate the deputy minister's contribution in a government-wide initiative?

Program evaluation and performance reviews have been, at best, problematic since their introduction to Ottawa in the 1970s. The record of program evaluation has been dismal. In 1992–93 Ottawa spent $28.5 million on 168 internal and external program evaluations. Only 1 per cent resulted in program termination, 9 per cent in reform, and 20 per cent in modification.[111]

The concept's biggest supporter, the auditor general, tabled a report in 2001: 'We expected that by then [2001] most managers would be trying to manage for results and that many would have good systems in place. We found some progress in a few areas, but managing for results was clearly not yet the norm in the departments we audited ... The main problem is less a technical than a cultural problem. Public servants are not inclined to produce information that could embarrass their ministers. The accountability battery never gets charged up.'[112]

Departments have learned to cope with program evaluations and a stream of outside consultants. Deputy ministers find evaluation of little assistance,[113] and departments still regard it mostly as a kind of 'gotcha' tool for the auditor general and the Treasury Board Secretariat. The auditor general acknowledged in his annual report that 'it is too often as though departmental managers are saying – if central agencies want us to provide financial and program information and measurements of our efficiency and effectiveness, we will of course provide them. But we don't see that information as being at all relevant to the day-to-day job we are being asked to do. So, providing it is a tiresome task, we will perform it in a desultory manner.'[114] Many managers regard evaluation as a means to generate information for someone outside the department, including the media, to come back and point out where they have failed. As Doug Hartle once observed: 'It is a strange dog that willingly carries the stick with which it is beaten.'[115]

What about performance evaluation of deputy ministers? Sadly, progress here is not much better. Performance, it seems, is in the eye of the beholder. I continue to marvel at how reputations are made, or at times lost, and at how senior officials become deputy ministers. For any deputy minister there will be six senior officials who will claim that that person should never have been appointed. Another six will approve the appointment. There are simply no clear-cut criteria of competence. I doubt if such benchmarks could ever be identified. There are simply too many variables, too many factors at play. More important, the work of the public service is by nature increasingly collective, which makes it difficult for individuals to shine (on a strictly objective basis) over others.

Other governments have been no better at assessing senior career officials. The American, British, and German governments, among others, have struggled to introduce a performance-pay management system with, by their own admission, limited success.[116]

Stovepipe management – when deputy ministers could simply run their own departments – applies less today, and the implications for performance evaluations are obvious. Career officials still operate in hierarchical units, but their work increasingly depends on other government units. The sheer expansion of government has added potential overlaps and clashes to policy and management. There is hardly a single problem today that could fit neatly into one policy niche or a single government unit. This factor helps explain the rise of interdepartmental and intergovernmental committees and of advisory groups. As we saw above, departmental mandates have been pushed outward, often blurring lines of responsibility and hence of accountability for senior officials. The number of 'coordination,' 'liaison,' or 'integration' units has mushroomed. Comparing government telephone directories starting from the early 1960s and going up to the 1990s is revealing. In the early years, there were no units within departments called 'liaison' and 'coordination.' The late 1960s and the 1970s saw the creation of co-ordination or liaison units to monitor and participate in interdepartmental consultations. By 1987 the Department of Industry alone had twenty-five units devoted to a co-ordination, evaluation, liaison policy, or to a combination of them.[117] By 1995, it had thirty-five. By 2002, notwithstanding program review, it had thirty-three. Nor does this figure include units containing the words 'planning' or 'economic analysis,' of which there are several. However, because of the 1993 government reorganization, Industry is now much larger, encompassing more activities than it did in 1987.

It was a great deal easier to speak truth to political power when one could talk from the perspective of a single policy niche or a relatively self-contained government unit. Now one must speak from an interdepartmental consensus. In turn, it was also easier to tell the truth to managers when they ran their relatively autonomous shops with a minimum of oversight.

The PCO produced a document to assist deputy ministers in preparing performance assessments. The performance of deputy ministers was to include *at least* one commitment related to public service–wide priorities: recruitment, retention, and learning; e-government; strengthening policy advice; and official languages. Possible 'performance measures' include:

- on recruitment and retention: more employees, particularly from visible minorities and the disabled, and more acceptance of diversity
- on e-government: effective links and partnerships with other levels of government and with the private and voluntary sectors, both in Canada and abroad.
- on strengthening policy advice: expanding the roles of citizens, of other stakeholders, and of academics in the policy process and establishing links and partnerships with the private and voluntary sectors and with other organizations key to good policy advice.
- on official languages: on-line information and services of equal quality in both official languages.[118]

These potential measurements of performance are not only difficult to quantify and to link directly to the deputy minister, they also provide a great deal of flexibility in determining success – hence performance often depends on the eye of the beholder.[119]

Deputy ministers have also complained of insufficient feedback on performance.[120] Their evaluations or appraisals, as well as those of senior career officials, are 'qualitative' and 'personal in nature and place particular emphasis on management style.'[121] This factor and others allow them to take limited interest in 'general management' and, as Arthur Kroeger explained, to pick 'one or two really big difficult policy issues' to work on.

Conclusion: Brave New Breed

Aaron Wildavsky may well have had deputy ministers in mind when he wrote that 'the most senior bureaucracy now is only for the brave.'[122] The demands of the jobs have increased substantially in recent years as issues invariably transcend departmental mandates.

As well, deputy ministers have been confronting a work environment analogous to a perfect storm. They might as well be working in a glass house, given access-to-information legislation, several oversight bodies policing their work, and more aggressive media. The media now focus much more on critical scrutiny and revelations of improper behaviour than on providing official reports of current events. The *National Post* ran a front-page story in its business section on the 'bank memo controversy' and took Kevin Lynch, deputy minister at Finance, to task for denying that he had discussed bank mergers with a senior private-sector executive. The article claims that what was said at the meeting 'appears to be as rife with backpeddling, obfuscation and semantic hairsplitting as anything seen north of Arkansas in recent times.'[123] The same paper had another story on 26 January 2001 with the headline 'Cabinet Secrets Stolen from Bureaucrat's Car.' It revealed that the 'bureaucrat' in question was Wayne Wouters, deputy minister at DFO, whose car was broken into by thieves. The newspaper got the story through an access-to-information request and described the incident as 'the most serious of at least eight security mishaps.'[124]

As deputy ministers became more visible, usually not by choice but by circumstances, captains of industry and others began to knock on their doors to get things done quietly and quickly. They discovered that deputy ministers were in by far the best position within government to move a file forward, given increasingly interdepartmental decision making.

Deputy ministers have stood in the direct line of fire from politicians making claims that bureaucrats have too much power. Bureaucrat bashing has had an impact in Ottawa, as elsewhere. Many senior public servants began to lose confidence in their institutions, if not in themselves. Well aware of the criticism in the media and in learned journals, particularly from the public-choice school, they began to doubt their policy advisory role. In some cases, they simply looked up to politicians and said, 'Okay, now you drive.' Many senior career officials have decided to step aside and to let politicians and their partisan advisers define the policy agenda. Gordon Osbaldeston, clerk of the Privy Council, 'insisted' when preparing briefing material for the 1984 transition in power on a 'strict separation of background briefing from advice or, stated differently, the separation of administration from politics.'[125] It is also extremely difficult, if not impossible, to assess the performances of deputy ministers from any objective perspective.

But once in power, ministers quickly discover that they need their deputy ministers to navigate the policy process, and they become highly dependent on them for advice. Things are never as simple in government as they appear to be from the outside or from the back benches. The policy process, question period, the media, and interest groups all pose daunting challenges, and ministers soon learn to rely on their deputy ministers, if only to ensure their political survival. Deputy ministers, well aware of the criticism that bureaucrats have too much influence, have made efforts to be responsive to the prime minister and ministers. They have performed a variety of tasks, including lending a hand to put out political fires and managing negative media stories. In doing this, however, they have lost some of their anonymity, as in the 'billion-dollar boondoggle' at HDRC.

But their efforts to 'manage up' created a new set of problems. As we saw above, the Task Force on Values and Ethics wrote in 1996 about a fault line growing between senior departmental officials and policy advisers on the one hand and front-line managers and workers on the other. The controversy over the work of scientists also suggests a split between senior managers and scientists. In brief, deputy ministers discovered that they were caught between a rock and a hard place.

But that is not all. Senior career officials also came under sustained criticism for their apparent lack of interest in management issues. A consensus emerged in Canada, as it did in other Anglo-American democracies, that senior bureaucrats were extremely poor managers. Michael Sabia, who left a senior position in the 1990s to join the private sector, reports that he and colleagues faced derision in the private sector: 'They saw us as stumble-bum bureaucrats.'[126]

The solution? – to emulate the private sector and introduce business-management practices to government operations. Since the days of PS 2000 (early 1990s), if not earlier, there have been sustained efforts to make management in the public sector look like management in the private sector. But nothing much has changed. NPM has had to come to terms with the fact that there are important differences between the public and the private sectors and that these relate less to what is done in both sectors than to the conditions under which tasks have to be performed.[127] We now talk about management, not administration, and about empowerment, not red tape transforming public administration into something like the private sector. But we learn that 'human resources management in the public service has changed little in 30 years despite continued dissatisfaction, many studies, and repeated efforts at reform ... The federal government needs almost four times as many human resources management professionals per employee as the private sector.'[128]

At the same time, the traditional world of deputy ministers has changed beyond recognition. They now focus not on their department so much as on the government's collective policy and management processes. They are not nearly so familiar with departmental policies, programs, and administrative units. The Bourgault survey revealed that consultative and interdepartmental work takes up a large chunk of their time and that they describe horizontal management as 'fuzzy, nowhere and everywhere, but increasing significantly.'

Introducing the business-management model did change some things in government, not for the better. Greed may well have accompanied the model into government. Senior government officials are still looked after at the end of their careers, but they no longer go quietly into retirement. They now have opportunities to earn money – as consultants or lobbyists and on special government contracts. Indeed, high-level experience in government has become a valuable qualification in the private sector, particularly with lobby firms, associations of various kinds, and government-relations offices in large national or multinational firms.[129] Post-employment guidelines are less demanding for senior career officials than for ministers.[130]

In chapter 1, we saw that the traditional bargain provided them with a stable career, relatively good pay, and the promise of a generous pension – security allowed them to focus on the collective good. Notwith-standing cuts during the program review (c. 1995–97), they still enjoy stable employment and indexed pensions. In addition, we now look to the private sector to establish salary levels for government managers. There was a time when the clerk of the Privy Council, the secretary to the Treasury Board, and the chair of the Public Service Commission would get together and discuss compensation levels; then the clerk would meet with the prime minister and they would agree to new salary levels. Today, an Advisory Committee on Senior Level Retention and Compensation is chaired by a senior private-sector executive. Although the committee reports that the pay of senior government officials is lower than that of senior private-sector executives, compensation levels in business help determine the pay of government executives.[131] In addition, while comparing pay is relatively simple, it is not at all clear how one can compare the work of a senior official in the public and the private sectors.

Career officials in government now receive base and performance pay. The advisory committee called for more attention 'to identifying and managing marginal or poor performers. There is little more de-moralizing and detrimental to superior performance than ignoring situations where performance is weak or inadequate.'[132] It offered little by way of advice or solutions. Senior public servants, however, used up the entire $25-million budget allocated in 2001 to reward them for strong performance. The chair of the advisory committee observed that the committee 'will refrain from recommending further increases to the at risk pay program until the government shows a commitment to ensur-ing the program does not reward poor performers.'[133]

Perhaps because government operations are much more transparent now or because the public service today is much larger, we read more about wrongdoings. The literature indicates that 'a new breed of public servant has emerged with an ethos less oriented to public interest and frugality than towards career advancement and making a mark through bold plans and expenditures.'[134] The press also tells us when career offi-cials spend far too much time travelling, or receive a golden handshake only to return to the same work on contract ('double dipping'), or even commit outright fraud. The Public Service Commission reports: 'Public perceptions of the ethical standards of public servants are currently at their lowest point in seven years ... Many other professions were rated higher. For a Public Service striving for an exemplary reputation for integrity, these findings are troubling.'[135]

Introducing a business vocabulary does not change the simple, obvious, but powerful facts that public servants operate in a political context and that their activities have political implications. It is ministers, not career officials, who insist on error-free government, because they operate in a partisan political theatre, where even minor administrative miscues are fair game to opposition MPs. Ministers, far more than career officials, want departments to present the least possible target for attack and to avoid controversy. The next chapter explores the world of partisan politics and how it relates to public administration.

PART THREE

Reconfiguring the Pieces

8

Parliamentarians, Ministers, and Public Servants

The worlds of politics and bureaucracy are so different that one wonders how the two could possibly learn to work with one another. Politics is, by definition, bottom-up, with all voters having one vote. Its boundaries are defined by geography, by a constituency with community and regional interests to promote. All politicians, particularly in Canada, view things through regional or territorial lenses and look to the democratic process for guidance and a verdict on their performance. This is a world shaped by images and by ten- or fifteen-second linear bursts of bombast on television or in question period. As many have observed, in politics perception is reality. Impatience rules – to an outsider, things appear far easier to fix than they do from within government departments. A long-term perspective in politics is four years, yet its practitioners must always remain in tune with the voters, who may not appreciate why solutions are not always at hand or being implemented.

Government bureaucracy, in contrast, has until recently worked top-down and transmits decisions and directives from higher to lower ranks. It consists of skilled policy analysts and administrators, and its boundaries are defined by hierarchy, not by geography. Its perspective is sectoral (for example, agriculture and energy) and horizontal (i.e., seeking policy coherence for operations). It is a very patient realm, which values consensus and considers itself the permanent custodian of society's problems.

The prime minister and the cabinet are expected somehow to bring politics and bureaucracy together, and, in conjunction with Parliament, to express the public will and to establish the broad duties of the civil service.

The purpose of this chapter is to consider the forces that shape politics and bureaucracy. It reviews how one succeeds in each field and how they have learned to work with one another. It looks at recent developments and their impact on the workings of Parliament, government, and the public service. It seeks to answer a number of questions. How does Parliament relate to the government and to the public service? How do ministers work with career officials? How are policies struck? How do ministers and career officials deal with Parliament's accountability requirements?

This chapter seeks to answer these questions by examining a career in politics – more specifically, in the House of Commons. It considers how people get to Parliament in the first place, what being there involves, the crucial business of voting supply in the House, and becoming a minister, and at tapping into the expertise of civil servants, who are *always* there.

Getting There

As we saw above, most Canadians now hold federal politicians of all parties in low regard. Nearly two-thirds believe that MPs misuse their office to secure personal benefits, and many MPs themselves often lament the fact that they no longer command respect in society.[1] Why then would someone want to become an MP? The question is all the more perplexing, given that there is never a shortage of candidates – 2,155 in the 1993 election and 1,808 in 2000.

We do know how one becomes an MP. David Docherty writes that the quest for office begins at the local level, where most potential candidates first seek the blessing of the constituency association.[2] Leaving aside some relatively modest efforts by political parties (for instance, the Liberal Party) to reserve some ridings for women and visible minorities, local associations have a free hand in picking candidates. Prime Minister Chrétien stated at one point that he would protect sitting MPs from single-issue groups (such as the 'right to life') from storming a nominating convention to have someone sympathetic to their cause secure the nomination by signing up a large number of new members. He has also on occasion hand-picked a candidate for a specific riding (for example, Stéphane Dion, Marcel Massé, and Pierre Pettigrew) and simply asked the riding to accommodate his wish. But party leaders very rarely do this, even Chrétien.

Any candidate can sign new members and stand at the local nominating convention. Benoit Serré, a northern Ontario MP, readily admits that he was never able to secure the association's support but won the nomination by recruiting some 2,000 new party members.[3] Thus the association and local residents have a large say in selecting the party's candidate.

In Britain, in contrast, a party's national office can strongly influence the selection of candidates. Mitchell Sharp recently spoke about this major difference: 'Most important of all, as I can testify from my personal experience is this – [in Canada] the local party members, not the headquarters of the party, will decide who will be the candidates at the next election.'[4]

Once nominated, candidates must quickly learn party discipline and toe the party line on policy issues. The leader's office tells them that their views can be interpreted as their party's and if they are too provocative or controversial they can come to the media's attention – never a good thing. They could embarrass the party leader, place him or her on the defensive, and hurt the party's chances at election time. But they also get a helping hand. They receive briefing books containing tips on running an election campaign and talking points for selling their party's electoral platform. One Liberal candidate comments: 'When I ran for the nomination it was just myself and one or two others. Now we have a whole team with the national party providing us with all the materials we need. I don't have to spend any time organizing, which would be inefficient. I go into the office, the canvassing chair has materials ready and has organized the riding into areas of electoral importance.'[5]

Local candidates do not have much say in putting together their party's electoral platform. Pollsters, advertising and marketing specialists, close associates of the party leader, and a handful of senior party activists, all working closely with the leader, produce the national platform and retain a central role in the campaign organization and running of the national campaign. This is true even of the governing Liberals, notwithstanding a strong caucus and cabinet ministers from which to draw ideas. Reg Whitaker explains: 'Neither Cabinet ministers nor the grass roots matter as much as they once did. National campaigns are poll and media-driven as never before.' He adds: 'Mr. Chrétien came to the top with no policy agenda whatever, other than becoming prime minister.'[6] Another commentator goes further: 'The strategic plan of the new Liberal government, in short, looks very much like that of the Conservatives when they assumed office in 1984.'[7]

Party platforms are notoriously vague and all encompassing, and few of them can ever be accused of underpromising. They establish little in the way of distinct policy. Their goal is to avoid antagonizing voters by being too specific about policies and plans. In Canada, parties hoping to form the federal government have to be particularly sensitive to the regional factor. A *faux pas* or an oversight about a region or how a particular policy or program would or would not apply there can very quickly erupt into a major crisis there and greatly reduce the chances of party candidates. For example, the Liberal platform in 2000 promised to cut taxes, increase spending in research and development, provide high-speed, broadband internet access to Canadians no matter where they lived, and invest in cultural programs, education, childhood development, health care, Aboriginal development, the environment, public-transit infrastructure, rural development, and so on. The platform had nothing to say about spending cuts. The NDP's proposed spending plan was more ambitious and covered more ground (health care, job creation, post-secondary education, removal of the GST on books and magazines, new anti-poverty programs). The party was a little more forthcoming on spending cuts – it proposed to abolish the Senate and redirect some economic-development spending to regions and communities with the greatest need. It never explained, however, how it would get the provinces to agree to abolish the Senate. The Canadian Alliance Party proposed some new spending in health care, the environment, and security but pledged to cut taxes and 'bring an end to boondoggle spending.' It hinted that it would put an end to the regional-development agencies and sell the 20 per cent federal stake in Petro-Canada.[8]

Platforms are an essential element of the ritual of campaigns. But they hardly determine the outcome. They are usually so vague that they do not generate heated debate or score many political points.

Party leaders appear increasingly to be the only substantial candidates in the election race. The national media focus on them rather than on selected candidates, even those enjoying a high profile in their regions. Journalists buy seats on their chartered aircraft and follow them everywhere. The media and, by extension, the public focus on the clash of party leaders. The leaders debate on national television, in both English and French. How a leader does there can affect – or be perceived to do so – the campaign if not the election itself.[9] It is now widely accepted in the literature that 'debates are more about accidents and mistakes than about enlightenment on the capabilities of candidates to govern.'[10] When Brian Mulroney told John Turner in the 1984 campaign, 'You had an option, sir' – referring to Turner's decision after taking office to proceed with Pierre Trudeau's patronage appointments – or, when Turner told Mulroney in 1988 that he was standing up for Canada in debating the free-trade agreement, the exchanges left party handlers scrambling to minimize political damage. A widely read study of the 1988 campaign suggests that 'had the debates not happened, there is every indication that the Conservatives would have coasted home to victory.'[11] Chrétien's handlers, in contrast, were relieved after the 1993, 1997, and 2000 debates that he did not fare as badly as some had feared.

Parties' objective at election time is to 'sell' their leaders rather than their ideas or their policies. A study by leading students of election campaigns observes that 'Canadian elections, in common with elections in other Westminster-style systems, as well as with presidential elections in the United Stares, inevitably turn on the question of who – which individual – shall form the government.'[12] It adds, for example, that the Liberal surge during the 1988 campaign 'reflected John Turner's rehabilitation.'[13] A senior official in the PMO argues that national 'trends,' and to some extent regional ones as well, decide who 'wins a riding and who does not.' The local candidate 'is not much of a factor anymore and he should not feel too badly if he loses.'[14] If the leader secures a majority it is generally assumed that the party is in his or her debt, not the other way round. When Chrétien scolded Liberal MP Carolyn Bennett in a caucus meeting for criticizing the lack of women promoted in the cabinet shuffle of January 2002, he told her, 'You were elected because of me, Madame.'[15] When a government MP challenged him in caucus on his decision to compel MPs to vote the government line as a matter of confidence on compensation for victims of hepatitis C, he shot back, 'Why don't you resign your seat and run in a by-election.' We are informed that 'the caucus fell silent.'[16]

Party leaders, with the help of spin doctors, pollsters, and advisers, run the national campaign, and they keep a watchful eye on the media and try as best they can to control campaign developments. History has shown that a sure recipe to win power is to hug the political centre. Even the Canadian Alliance, a populist party, came to terms with this requirement in the 2000 campaign. Reg Whitaker explains: 'Distinctive policies that set the Alliance apart from its competitors, including the Progressive Conservatives, were quickly dropped on the advice of Alliance advertising advisors. Delegates to the party's founding convention had enthusiastically adopted a flat tax ... Focus groups showed there were perception problems with a flat tax and it was unceremoniously dropped from the party platform.' He adds that, because of Liberal campaign tactics, 'there was furtive backpeddling even on the Alliance's commitment to direct democracy.'[17]

It is no sin against Canadian democracy if all parties decide to converge on the political centre. But when they do, voters must look to other matters in deciding how to vote. Some may choose to abstain, and there is evidence that this is in fact happening, given a decline in voter turnout in recent years and weaker loyalty to parties. But electors who still wish to vote usually look to the credibility and competence of party leaders.

Voter perception, often shaped by the media, help establish leaders' credibility and competence. Campaign mistakes widely reported on television news also influence perception. Stockwell Day experienced this at first hand in the 2000 campaign when he forgot that Lake Erie was part of the Great Lakes, as did Kim Campbell in 1993, when she declared that the unemployment rate would probably not drop below 10 per cent before the turn of the century. This pessimistic statement sounded the starting gun of the campaign and dogged her party's campaign to the end. Similarly, it was she alone, not other party candidates, who was left to explain and later apologize for her party's television ad highlighting Jean Chrétien's partial facial paralysis. The incident was replayed on the news for several days, seriously damaging Tory chances. The Canadian Alliance saw its advantage on health care during the 2000 campaign turned on its head when Jason Kenny, formerly Stockwell Day's key campaign strategist, opened up the issue of two-tier medical care with some 'poorly chosen words' on television.[18]

Local candidates are often at the mercy of their leader's performance and of the party's spin doctors and pollsters. Modern campaigns are such that leaders try to pave the way to success by scoring political points in the national media and by avoiding political gaffes. Decades ago, things were different. Leaders played a major role, but regional ministers (such as Jimmy Gardiner, Ernest Lapointe, Allan MacEachen, and Chubby Power) or local party bosses were also crucial. Today, the local candidate is expected to campaign hard, to keep his or her name out of the limelight, to avoid getting the party in trouble, and to leave the campaign decisions to the professionals in Ottawa – who, they are told, are always in a better position to see regional trade-offs, understand the national interest, and protect the party leader. Harold D. Clarke and his colleagues write that candidates have no choice but to 'organize around leaders rather than political principles and ideologies and expect the leader to work out the multitude of compromises required for the party to enjoy electoral success.'[19] This process is a sign of things to come if his or her party should form the government. The party's lack of firm political principles and ideologies and of a clear understanding of what it wants to accomplish also affects the work of career officials. It also means that policy making, to the extent that takes place at the political level, centres around leaders.

How do candidates prepare to serve in Parliament? Docherty reports that many 'follow conventional patterns of party participation, first entering as a party member, serving on the executive, moving to a senior position locally, and eventually running as a candidate.' A good number prepare for office by following the activities of the House of Commons.[20] R.K. Carty and L. Erickson, however, describe a 'career structure' of 'amateurism.' That is, MPs lack prior experience, and some (about half) had weak links to their party before being nominated.[21] Any relevant experience tended to be at the local level – some 20 per cent of candidates had served on municipal council or the local school board.[22] Thus MPs are indeed political 'amateurs,' particularly at the national level. Their preoccupations, concerns, and mindset are often local.

This is clear from the particularly high turnover of MPs in general elections. Both David Docherty and C.E.S. Franks stressed the impact of this high turnover on the work of the House. Docherty observes that 'the lack of long-serving members is problematic and viewed as detrimental for a number of reasons ... Simply put, it is difficult for both government backbenchers and opposition members to keep Cabinet accountable when they lack the experience and parliamentary savvy of members of the executive.'[23] Franks compares British and Canadian experience. 'The average Canadian member of Parliament is a newcomer who is likely to leave before he has served ten years and is most unlikely to serve for fifteen years. The average British member has been in the house for at least ten years, and is very likely to serve for at least fifteen years ... This comparison of parliamentary experience of MPs and of time in office of prime ministers shows there is a very different relationship of power between the two bodies in Britain and Canada. In Canada, a strong, solidly entrenched prime minister faces an insecure and transient House of Commons; in Britain, an insecure and transient prime minister faces a strong and solidly entrenched House.'[24]

A good number of aspiring and even some sitting MPs in Canada regard their lack of national political experience as a plus. American politics has influenced in Canada, and just as many U.S. presidential and congressional candidates have since the 1970s 'run against Washington,' some Canadian MPs take considerable pride in bashing Ottawa. This is obviously the case for Bloc Québécois candidates, but it is also true of the Canadian Alliance and even some Liberal backbenchers.[25]

Being There

There are a number of points about the Westminster parliamentary system that American influence may obscure. First, the Canadian Parliament's influence may have declined in recent years, but it has never had power equal to that of the U.S. Congress. There was never a golden era in Britain when Parliament actually had power, and there was never a sustained period when Parliament dominated the crown. Ministers, as we saw in chapter 2, came to dominate Parliament with Parliament's full blessing. Subsequently, the prime minister and a handful of advisers came to dominate policy and decision making, presumably with the cabinet's acquiescence, if not its blessing.[26] Parliament in Canada has not kept pace with changes in the executive and with the growth of departments and agencies. It has not refined its instruments of scrutiny, control, and criticism of the executive and its capacity to make suggestions, to voice opinions, and to speak on behalf of Canadians. Parliament has lost its ability to express and redress popular grievances – it has now become the focus of these grievances.

Second, the role of Canada's Parliament is not to legislate, but to criticize and to hold the government to account. It is the executive that prepares legislative proposals, not Parliament. Third, cabinet needs to dominate the House of Commons in order to get its legislation through. Fourth, it is not a contradiction to say that the House needs both a strong government and a strong opposition. Fifth, a degree of party discipline is necessary for the House to function properly. Many students of government have quoted Edmund Burke's famous message to the electors of Bristol, 'Your representative owes you not his industry only, but his judgement.' They have overlooked, however, Ernest Bevin's more down-to-earth message at Brighton, 'An MP cannot hawk his conscience around to every issue that turns up.'[27] Coherent policy development, a sense of accountability, and voters' capacity to make an informed decision at election time require party discipline.

Many newly elected MPs arrive in Ottawa uncertain about their role, the role of the House, and its relation to government. They may not fully appreciate that the role of government is to govern and that of the Commons is to subject political power to certain controls, to provide legitimacy to government action and activities, and to hold the executive to account.[28] They see that government and public servants run policies and programs, and they want to participate. After all, they can argue that they were elected by Canadians to look after their interests. They are invited to attend what one MP called 'rookie school,' where they are briefed on the role of Parliament. Short briefings can provide a broad review of how things work and outline new office arrangements, but they can never be a substitute for actual experience. MPs may be uncertain about their proper role in making policy and decisions but they do understand that one of their most important objectives is to get re-elected and to promote their party's interests.

The government party in the Commons has a different relation between MPs and political power from that of opposition MPs and power. A government party with a majority mandate has its hands on all the levers of power to decide, to appoint, to finance, and to produce legislation.

The difference is this: some government MPs have access to power, while the rest have access only to levers of influence. Neither of these is available to opposition MPs. Something like one in five government MPs will ministers, about twenty will be parliamentary secretaries, twenty will chair a committee, one will be Speaker, and another government whip. All in all, some seventy or more government MPs hold a position of power or influence. The rest enjoy a privileged position in Parliament because they are members of the government caucus, where they hear about legislative proposals before they are introduced into Parliament. More important, they have weekly opportunities to challenge the prime minister and ministers in private and to voice opinions about government policies or operations. Government MPs reveal that some of these caucus sessions can be quite stormy and that strongly worded criticism directed at individual ministers is frequent. C.E.S. Franks observed pointedly: 'An MP on the government side has a good chance of holding a position of power; those left out have a good prospect of achieving a position of power someday, and backbenchers have more direct contact with cabinet. Nor should the prospects of future rewards be neglected.'[29]

The prospect of future rewards also strengthens the hand of the prime minister. Although some MPs are quite happy not to be in cabinet, they are very much in the minority. One minister suggested that 'at least 90 per cent of the government caucus, if not more, would welcome an opportunity to sit in cabinet. For the great majority of us, that is why we run for Parliament.'[30] Someone elected MP has to make a run at the party nomination and then for several weeks of political campaigning knock on doors, speak to local service clubs, and attend all-party meetings. Chances are that an individual who successfully navigates this obstacle course is highly motivated and ambitious. He or she will probably want a seat at the cabinet table. But that is not all. MPs know full well that the prime minister appoints viceroys, senators, judges, ambassadors, and members of boards, task forces, and commissions. That power of appointment constitutes an indispensable tool to ensure party discipline, and maintaining the confidence of the House is a sine qua non for governing.

Prime ministers emphasize party discipline and do not easily tolerate dissent, no matter what they may have said when in opposition. For instance, Docherty points out that Brian Mulroney rejected the recommendations of the McGrath Committee 'that dealt with confidence' and that Chrétien 'did not follow through on the Red Book' commitment to treat gun control as a matter of conscience. MPs are expected to be 'guided by longstanding notions of party solidarity and, with few exceptions, defy the logic and function of discipline in the day-to-day workings of the Commons at their own expense.'[31]

Opposition MPs are also expected to embrace their party's policies, to vote with the party on legislation, and to fall in line behind the leader. Opposition leaders can always hold out the promise of appointment if they ever achieve power. In addition, they can remove some MPs from relatively high-profile 'shadow-cabinet' positions. MPs know that internal dissension can hinder their party's chances in the next election.

Yet opposition MPs have a much freer hand in speaking out on policy issues and government operations than do government MPs, provided that they do not harm their party's image.[32] The goal is very often to humiliate the government and to gain a profile in the media. Again, so long as one does not embarrass his or her leader, everything seems to be fair game. John Nunziata, a former MP and a member of the so-called rat pack of four Liberal members who always taunted the Mulroney government in question period, explains: 'We were carefree and at times careless. We were a hot commodity.' He reported that fellow rat-pack member Brian Tobin 'repeatedly rehearsed ripping up a report in private before performing it publicly during question period. The line was going to be "it's not worth the paper it's printed on," and Brian practised tearing it in half and in half again and throwing these bits of paper up into the air; that was the TV clip.'[33]

Docherty's research, however, reveals that opposition MPs spend more time on policy development and legislative work than do government MPs. First, there are more government than opposition MPs, and the latter have to assume more policy work. Second, government MPs have access to far more resources. For most MPs, he concludes, policy work is 'not a strategic activity. Members invest a good portion of their working time on such work, but not necessarily for self-interested reasons.'[34]

Policy work does not give MPs much of a media profile, and so they do not see it as helping in the next election. The image of Tobin ripping up a report is worth many hours of policy work behind the scenes.

The prime minister, his advisers, and senior ministers would much sooner see government MPs leave serious policy work to them. It is their turf. They regard policy not only as complex but as filled with potential regional, interdepartmental, and political pitfalls. Unless one can connect all the dots and ensure that the finer points of policy requirements are met, a crisis may well be in the making. Government MPs have access to resources, but with limits, particularly vis-à-vis expertise in departments. Public servants are uneasy about sharing their policy work with MPs, even when their ministers ask them to do so. MPs may run off with information prematurely to score political points, and information may be misinterpreted outside. There are also no rewards for career officials engaging MPs in policy work.

The risks are even greater in regard to opposition MPs. Career officials know that their ministers would not like their officials to share policy work before it becomes public. The adversarial nature of politics affects the public service, even though officials assiduously distance themselves from politics. C.E.S. Franks does not mince words: 'In the question of the formation of policy and legislation ... the member of parliament (i.e., both government and opposition) is virtually excluded from the process ... There are two separate worlds in Ottawa: the public world of parliament and the media; and the private world of the public service, cabinet, central agencies, and their contacts with interest groups.' He adds that 'senior public servants in Canada tend to relegate MPs to the periphery of the policy-making world more so than those in Italy, Germany, the United States, or the United Kingdom.'[35]

Government MPs 'sing' from the policy 'hymn book' given to them by the government. Opposition MPs use the book provided by the party's last electoral platform, particularly for issues that have grabbed the media's attention or that will enable them to score political points. Opposition MPs have precious little research capacity for policy work. Caucus research bureaux have limited staff, and much of their work centres on question period and working with the party leader on a variety of issues.

The result is that policy work produced outside the private Ottawa world is weak. Without the benefit of the expertise available in-house, inside government, or in the multitude of policy institutes and centres sponsored by government, and in the absence of clear political ideology to guide them, opposition parties are left to manufacture proposals that will embarrass the government. They could of course collect and sift through material from independent think tanks to produce policy options and to test them against government policies, but this too requires expertise and resources. In any event, political parties have few incentives to do this, preferring to apply resources to scoring political points or promoting MPs in their constituencies. In addition, opposition parties can put forward policy positions with little regard for their consequences. Their first objective is to win political office. The Liberals' commitment while in opposition in the early 1990s to kill the goods and services tax (GST) is a case in point. As opposition leader, Jean Chrétien asked three MPs to look for alternatives to the GST. Unable to come up with an alternative, they urged Chrétien not 'to make rash GST promises.' However, few in the Liberal caucus agreed, and 'the promise was made anyway.' Once in power starting in 1993, however, the Liberals had no alternatives, and the 'resulting flip flop' hurt the new government's credibility.[36]

The lives of those in power contrast sharply with those who do not, in terms not just of perks, status, and power to appoint and to make decisions, but of being able to see the merits of an idea. In opposition, the Liberals made a firm commitment to appoint an independent ethics counsellor. Once in power, however, they voted down a motion to 'appoint an independent Ethics Counsellor.' A senior Liberal minister explained that 'after we formed the government we got the explanation that it was not the proper way to do it. That's why the Ethics Counsellor reports to the Prime Minister.' A newly elected Liberal MP, Stephen Owen, explained his vote: 'I didn't come here to ... oppose the government. If I wanted to come here and oppose the government, I would have joined the Canadian Alliance.'[37] A week before the vote, Owen had voiced concerns about the counsellor's apparent lack of independence.

The message is clear: toeing the party line and accepting party discipline are more important than an MP's stance on virtually any issue.

It appears that many MPs are able to see the light on policy only in government, particularly in Cabinet. Brian Tobin, as a member of Chrétien's program review committee in the mid-1990s, went 'after the deficit with missionary zeal.'[38] One senior official reports that 'Tobin in opposition when the Mulroney government was trying to introduce spending cuts was a far cry from Tobin as a member of the cabinet committee on program review. It was like night and day.'[39] Tobin told his colleagues, 'I've become the right-wing fiscal conservative of this government.' He also reported that his conversion took place on a trip to Japan, which impressed on him Canada's vulnerability to the 'whims of foreign lenders.'[40] Some officials whom I consulted scoffed at this observation, saying that, if Tobin could add, he would have known much earlier about Ottawa's serious fiscal difficulties. They argued that it was simply convenient for him to oppose spending cuts when Mulroney was in government but to change his tune when Chrétien was in power.

Doug Young, while an opposition MP, launched a high-profile campaign to fight the Mulroney government's plan to reduce Via Rail services in Atlantic Canada and to introduce cuts to the Unemployment Insurance (UI) program. He urged New Brunswickers to help him stop the government dead in its tracks, on the grounds that both measures would hurt the provincial economy.[41] He even offered to organize public hearings to enable all New Brunswickers to demonstrate their opposition to the plans. Now, fast forward to Chrétien's first mandate, where that same Mr Young turned all his energy to fiscal concerns. He took to the program-review exercise with gusto and promoted a policy to sell the country's air navigation system, privatize CN Rail, reduce still further subsidies to Via Rail, and do away completely with freight rate subsidies for Atlantic manufacturers.[42] Moreover, he came out in favour of substantial cuts to UI. What explains his remarkable about-face? One can only assume that it was not political ideology or sound policy work. Rather, it was the pursuit of political power and a recognition of the reality of public policy once he was in power.

MPs who run for Parliament to serve and promote the interest of their constituencies are more likely to say that their expectations were met than are those who ran to contribute to policy development. Both government and bureaucracy expect MPs to look after their constituencies, and most members are happy to oblige because of simple demand, the desire for re-election, and the capacity to produce results. Docherty shows that community service was 'the strongest motivating factor in many MPs' initial decision to seek office. Over half of all members of the 34th Parliament ranked serving the constituency as the most important factor in their decision to run nationally.' He adds that, unlike policy work, working on behalf of one's constituency is 'passively encouraged by the Commons preference rule.'[43]

Government MPs will usually harbour any political capital they have to promote their constituency, province, and region. First, a regional caucus encourages them to look at government policies and programs from a regional or territorial perspective. Second, an MP's efforts on behalf of his or her constituency take place away from the media, are usually non-threatening, and are often one-on-one (an MP and the relevant minister or career official). The prime minister and cabinet never feel threatened or even challenged by an MP working on behalf of the constituency. They see it as an important part of an MP's work. When Prime Minister Chrétien was taken to task for intervening before a crown corporation on behalf of a business in his constituency (i.e., the so-called Shawinigate scandal), or when he secured public funds to build a water fountain in the riding, he responded by saying that he was simply doing his work as an MP.[44] Docherty sums up the situation, 'Members of Parliament who come to Ottawa with expectations that involve local service are more likely to find satisfaction in their career than members who expect to engage in detailed policy development and legislation. It should not be surprising that many members of Parliament soon begin to engage in constituency-related activities that have little impact on the legislature or its folkways.'[45] To do this, however, they must move in on program administration and career officials.

If a minister cannot respond positively to a request from a government MP, he or she can always blame the 'bureaucrats.' It is not uncommon for a minister to tell a government backbencher that he or she would like to help but that the bureaucrats are unwilling to 'move the file forward.' The official meanwhile cannot cry 'Foul' and tell the MP that it is the minister who is to blame or that government policy – not bureaucratic preference – is responsible. A former MP has shown me his correspondence with the prime minister and ministers complaining about certain bureaucrats' insensitivity to his concerns. Former ministers have also provided me with written exchanges with their deputy ministers designed to encourage their departments to brief MPs on their activities. It would not be appropriate for me to reveal the identity of the authors, but the material is very instructive.

One former government backbencher complained to the prime minister on behalf, he claimed, of several of his colleagues (all of them government MPs) about an assistant deputy minister, particularly about his insensitivity to MPs' views. The letter was sweeping and general, identified no specific charges or problems, and asked for removal of the bureaucrat. The author insisted that his letter should not be interpreted 'strictly in terms of partisan political consideration' and claimed that the official regarded all MPs as 'unnecessary evils.' What MPs wanted, he wrote, was 'someone who can communicate effectively with us.'[46] The relevant minister decided not to intervene on behalf of the official. The prime minister never responded, although four months later changes occurred with senior personnel in the department, including that of the deputy minister and later the assistant deputy. It was not at all clear that the letter provoked the changes.

A former minister handed me copies of correspondence with the deputy minister on 'MP involvement' in departmental activities. The minister and his exempt staff wrote to the deputy to encourage the '*involvement* of MPs in the decision-making process.' The deputy minister and senior officials responded by acknowledging that the minister had 'on many occasions expressed the wish that MPs be kept fully *informed* of departmental activities.' One side spoke of involvement, the other of information. The minister and his staff wanted an all-encompassing process, while officials strongly recommended a 'pilot briefing basis.' The minister and his staff saw no difficulty in quick action. The deputy minister and senior officials brought up a number of unresolved issues, including fear of raising MPs' expectations influencing programs; the problem of 'truly confidential or privileged information,' whose 'operational premise is that information placed before MPs becomes public information; and the question of whether to treat opposition MPs the same way.[47] The matter was never resolved, and the issue came to an end when the minister was moved. Still, involving MPs in program administration is often debated in the corridors of power. It ranks very high on the list of grievances of MPs who insist that it can help restore public trust and confidence in government.[48]

Not all ministers, of course, are happy to see MPs involved in their departmental decision making – probably many would not want that to happen. Most regard the government caucus or one-on-one discussions as the best method of involvement. That arrangement leaves the minister in control and short-circuits an elaborate process that could take on a life of its own. It does not open up new channels of communication between politicians and career officials. It also avoids treating all MPs (government and opposition) the same way.

Career officials intuitively shy away from bringing MPs into their department's decision making. They see a clear dividing line between ministers' roles and MPs', either collective or individual. They also regard Parliament as separate from them, with a different purpose and a different role.

MPs play four roles in relation to the civil service. Collectively they assign or confirm departmental mandates and authorize financial and human resources; individually they query officials regarding their activities and act as a watchdog/ombudsman on behalf of constituents or the general public.

Acts of Parliament define the authority and broad responsibilities of departments and agencies. Career officials cannot function without reference to them, including their departmental acts and the Financial Administration Act. In addition, Parliament alone gives legislative approval to bills. Parliament, under the 'power of the purse,' approves the government's plans for expenditures and revenues. The government cannot raise or spend public funds except under the statutory authorization of Parliament. Parliament has the right to question, to probe, and to expose via question period, examination of public accounts, the media, and parliamentary committees. MPs can also turn to the work of parliamentary agents, especially that of the auditor general, the information commissioner, and the language commissioner, for assistance in holding the government to account. Opposition MPs have opposition days to enable them to focus on specific issues of concern to them, and all MPs are free to pursue any matter with the government on behalf of their constituents.[49]

Career officials are well aware of this situation. They also know that there is a great deal of difference between form and substance and that form often takes precedence over substance. Most of them are careful not to point the finger at politicians for this state of affairs. Indeed, most insist that there is not a single reason for the situation. They may cite a multitude of factors, from the size of government, through the complex nature of policy making, to the changing role of the media.

Parliament still expects public-service managers to implement and uphold the letter and spirit of the laws that it has passed. But even a cursory look at legislation over the past forty years or so reveals that it consists of broad, complex, documents of little direct interest or concern to civil-service managers in their day-to-day work. The auditor general explains why: legislation sets out 'the objectives for programs, often in general – not operational terms.'[50]

Parliament's legislative agenda is always very crowded. Government departments and agencies know that they cannot easily go back to Parliament to clarify a point or to remedy some legislative deficiencies. They draft proposed legislation in very broad terms to provide maximum flexibility in implementation. The Department of Industry Act illustrates this point. It reads that the 'Minister shall exercise the power ... in a manner that will ... focus on small and medium-sized enterprises and the development and enhancement of entrepreneurial talent ... initiate, recommend, coordinate, direct, promote, and implement programs and projects in relation to regional economic development in Ontario and Quebec.' The act states that 'the Minister may make loans to any person ... make grants and contributions to any person ... acquire, exercise, assign or sell a stock option or other financial or similar instrument.' As well, 'the Governor in Council may, on the recommendation of the Minister and the Minister of Finance, make regulations relating to loans.'[51]

The Industry Act is typical of departmental legislation. Mandates are now not only broad but also broadly stated, and the finer points of program guidelines are moved over to regulations. In all my conversations with career officials during the past fourteen years, I have rarely heard them refer to departmental legislation as hindering day-to-day work, and they readily acknowledge that broad legislation provides considerable flexibility and advantages to program managers, who are always looking for greater freedom to manage their operations. Given that socio-economic circumstances are constantly in a state of flux and the fact that Parliament can scarcely cope with the existing workload and requirements that it must accommodate each year, one can easily appreciate why the government would not wish to outline its policy and program objectives in clear operational terms. But the flexibility comes at a cost – lack of clarity creates ambivalence in accountability and uncertain boundaries in the programs within which public servants must operate.

The Business of Supply

The concept that the crown requests public funding and Parliament grants supply is central to the system of raising revenue and spending public funds. The BNA (Constitution) Act of 1867 created a Consolidated Revenue Fund and gave the House, not the Senate, the preeminent role in public finances. The business of supply hinges on three fundamental points: the executive must have some assurance that its requests for funds be dealt with by certain fixed dates if it is to continue providing services to Canadians; Parliament must have a reasonable opportunity to examine proposed expenditures; and failure to grant supply by not approving the estimates is an established means for demonstrating non-confidence.

The business of supply and its three basic principles seem straightforward and simple to grasp. Yet when MPs and informed observers want to show that the parliamentary system is in a serious state of disrepair, they invariably point to supply. As far back as 1962, W.F. Dawson wrote in his influential *Procedure in the Canadian House of Commons* that 'there is no part of procedure in the Canadian House of Commons which is so universally acknowledged to be inadequate to modern needs as the control of the House over public expenditure.'[52]

A series of measures, including special committees, was launched in 1963 to overhaul the business of supply. The efforts came to a close in 1968, when the House adopted the report of a special procedural committee and agreed to substantial changes to supply. The committee concluded that 'among the most time consuming, repetitive and archaic procedures inherited by the Canadian Parliament are those relating to the business of supply.'[53] The new standing orders adopted in December 1968 introduced several changes. First, debate on estimates moved from the House (Committee of Supply) to standing committees. The Committee of Supply, however, was the House meeting under another name and under relaxed rules. The House could now focus on other matters, including the government's legislative agenda. Second, the changes also give the government a firm financial calendar. All estimates are to be referred to standing committees on or before 1 March and are to be back to the House by 31 May. When committees do not report by then, they are deemed to have done so. Third, under the old system, opposition parties used filibusters to extract concessions from the government. Twenty-five days were labelled 'allotted days,' during which two motions could be tabled as motions of non-confidence in the government, and the allotted days now became 'supply' or 'opposition days.' Opposition parties could now criticize the government's overall economic policies in the House and before the press gallery.

There have been further adjustments since 1968, but the broad outline remains intact. The more recent changes have, for example, reduced the number of allotted days from twenty-five to twenty; in the

early 1970s changes to the estimates allowed spending plans to correspond to broad program objectives; and in 1981–82 the estimates were
overhauled (divided in three parts) to provide more background information. Before 1968, MPs could focus on administrative details or
inputs (numbers of civil servants, their salaries, travel expenses, and so
on) and urge spending cuts in these areas. They could easily grasp salary and travel budgets and compare the operation of one administrative
unit to another. Still, this process came under heavy criticism because it
tended to focus political debate on administrative issues rather than on
policy or program objectives.

There is now wide agreement, however, that, the 1968 changes have
made things worse. It is extremely difficult to find anyone, other than
perhaps some ministers, satisfied with the current arrangement. Scholars have argued that 'from all sides the view is the same: the review of
the Estimates is often meaningless' or that MPs have 'been relegated to
a role in the financial process of government that is very marginal.'[54] In
1993 the chairs of all standing committees tabled a report: 'As a result of
the 1968 decision to transfer estimates from Committee of the Whole to
Standing Committees, Canadian MPs in a majority Parliament have
effectively lost the power to reduce government expenditures. Members
are therefore making the very rational calculation that there is no point
devoting time and effort to an exercise over which they can have no
influence.'[55] Herb Gray, a veteran MP who served before 1968, observed, as government House leader under Chrétien, that 'the Estimates are complex and difficult to analyse and are, for constitutional
reasons, difficult to change. In addition, their consideration is subject to
a rigorous timetable. As a result, the examination of the Main Estimates
has become rather cursory and there has been no focus for parliamentary debate on government spending before its spending priorities are
actually set.'[56] Robert Giroux, former deputy minister of public works
and government services and secretary to the Treasury Board, reports
that, in all his appearances before a House standing committee, he
could remember only 'once when actually a question was asked on the
document we called Part III of the estimates.' He added that he would
always, while briefing ministers, say, 'don't worry about all that information, you will not get a question on that. We know what to expect and
that is what will enable the opposition to score political points.'[57]

Career officials are hardly any more positive about the estimates process. John L. Manion insists that the 1968 changes altered Parliament's
relationships with the government and with career officials. He argues

that only the government obtained long-term benefits. Parliament could no longer delay supply indefinitely and apply pressure to lower spending plans because of a fixed calendar for approval. Manion reveals that opposition parties accepted the changes in return for some funding to support activities in their constituency offices and in Ottawa.

But, Manion argues, this advantage came at a tremendous cost, since it 'caused Parliament to lose its main function, i.e., holding the Government to account.' In a report to the Office of the Auditor General, Manion explained: 'The new procedures produced significant advantages for the government, principally a fixed supply calendar, greater freedom to advance its legislative program and some reduction of the potential for opposition harassment offered by the Old Supply process. By 1991 (opposition MPs) were complaining that ministers had reduced attendance at committees to a minimum, often restricting their input to a pro forma opening statement at the commencement of the review of the estimates, then have their officials handle all but policy questions. This practice has continued and reflects an erosion of the principle of ministerial responsibility, while exposing officials to the sometimes hostile treatment of frustrated MPs.' He adds, 'Within the new committees, there was seldom much interest in expenditures – except to demand more for their constituencies and ferret out information for political purposes. Committee proceedings are generally of little interest to the media, are not televised, and many members have lost interest.'[58]

Career officials report that they have sought to do their part in improving the estimates process by providing more and better information to Parliament. Today, the estimates involve thousands and thousands of pages of detailed information.[59] They are tabled in three parts over a four-week period. Part I provides an overview of federal spending and summarizes key elements of the main estimates. Part II presents a detailed listing of the resources required by individual departments and agencies for the next fiscal year (parts I and II of the 2002–3 estimates contain 338 pages). Part III outlines individual expenditure plans for each department and agency, but not for crown corporations. For 2001–2 there were 87 reports. That for Agriculture and Agri-Food Canada, for example, contained 67 pages. Part III also provides for a report on departmental performance (DPR). It is designed to report on 'the government's commitments ... to improve accountability for results.' For the period ending 21 March 2001, twenty-one departments submitted a DPR. Agriculture and Agri-Food Canada's DPR contained 81 pages. But that is not all. The Treasury Board president also regularly tables documents such as *Results for Canadians: A Management Framework for the Government of Canada* to further explain financial-management practices. The president of the Treasury Board also regularly tables expenditure plans for crown corporations on behalf of the ministers who preside over them.[60] Finally, the government annually tables thousands of pages of information under the rubric of public accounts.

MPs now complain that they are inundated with information, data, and documents. When the estimates under the present format were introduced in the early 1980s, they had to be hauled into the House on heavily laden carts, much to the amusement of MPs.[61] There is considerable evidence to suggest that MPs do not read the material. The ones whom I met tell me that they do not, and career officials have expressed frustration that they have answered questions in standing committees simply by *reading* sections of part III.[62]

Quite apart from the estimates documents, there is also a constant stream of program evaluations made available to MPs, but most are inconclusive and rarely understood by the non-specialist. MPs, like any amateur, could understand the elements of a straight line-item budget, such as the number of civil servants required to run a program. The information was concrete and easily grasped. Bob Bryce, former clerk of the Privy Council and deputy minister of finance, was sceptical about the new, 'elaborate systems of goal-setting and the evaluation of efficiency and effectiveness in many fields where these defy measurement.'[63] If these evaluations, as it is claimed, were designed to assist Parliament to hold the government to account, they have failed where it matters the most: – in helping those whom they were intended to help – MPs. Most of the mountain of information that the government sends to Parliament every year is simply ignored. A former secretary to the Treasury Board suggests that even ministers no longer understand the process. He writes: 'The annual Estimates cycle is the engine of a frantic annual process which has been so impossibly burdensome that Ministers and Parliament alike have effectively given up.'[64] The answer that a government MP gave to my question – Do you believe that civil servants speak truth to power when they appear before your committee? – is telling: 'They speak volumes, not necessarily truth.'[65] An MP cannot properly interpret results without detailed information on staffing, budgets, geographical location of spending patterns – information that they no longer receive.[66] The territory today is a great deal murkier than it was before the 1968 changes. Thirty-five years ago the estimates process held valuable advantages for MPs. The information was accessible and easy to grasp, given its focus on input costs.

Making It There

Robert Thibault, clerk-treasurer of Argyle, a small community in rural Nova Scotia, was elected to Parliament in 2000, and Jean Chrétien immediately appointed him to cabinet. Leaving his first cabinet meeting, he told journalists: 'I finally know what paradigm shift means.'[67] Overnight Thibault became not only a member of the cabinet but also the minister responsible for the Atlantic Canada Opportunities Agency, which had a $400-million annual budget and a staff of over 300.

On the first day on the job, a minister meets his deputy minister who hands over several thick briefing books. These introduce departmental policies, program objectives, key staff, and issues and challenges. The minister immediately becomes responsible for everything done in the department, past and present, and everything may be the object of parliamentary scrutiny. He or she is accountable to Parliament and to the public. The minister can hire staff to manage the office, to deal with the media, to advise on policy, to look after political interests, and to deal with the party. Limousine and chauffeur are always at the ready to whisk him or her away to another meeting.

Ministers attend weekly cabinet meetings and obviously have easier access to the prime minister and the Prime Minister's Office (PMO) than do backbenchers. Ministers can also turn to career officials, outside consultants, and central-agency officials for advice. Unlike backbenchers, they are in a position to bargain with cabinet colleagues to secure projects for their constituencies. For most ministers, it is a dream come true, and they do not easily part with that dream. Few ministers quit on the basis of ideology or policy differences with the prime minister. It is rare indeed to see a minister resign over a policy issue or because of 'solidarity problems' – unable or unwilling to agree with colleagues or with 'the Prime Minister in particular.' The last minister to resign for reasons of solidarity was Lucien Bouchard (1990), and he did so over national unity. Over 40 per cent of ministers who have ever left cabinet did so to accept a political appointment offered by the prime minister.'[68]

Not all ministers are created equal, and it is very difficult to make general observations about their relations with Parliament and career officials. Long-serving MPs are invariably more comfortable as ministers than are newly elected ones. Some ministers learn quickly to work well with their officials, while others never do. Some are able to focus on a handful of priority issues, while others are not. Some are sure-footed with the media, and others are not. Some can 'deliver' files or projects on behalf of the prime minister or their departments, but others cannot.

What then makes a minister successful? In Canada at least, longevity in power is its own reward. There are very few who make it to cabinet at the federal level for having strongly identified with a political ideology or a policy position. That is not the Canadian way. Cabinet ministers may well hold strong views on language and on regional issues but rarely from an ideological or policy perspective. One former deputy minister summed it up well: 'My experience as often as not was that the minister had no view on policy.'[69] In the absence of clear policy principles, the minister's objective is to survive, to protect his or her political interest and that of the government. When he shuffled his cabinet in January 2002, Jean Chrétien observed that 'it is a privilege to be a minister. It isn't a long-term contract.'[70] Most ministers see cabinet in terms not of ideology or clear policy positions, but rather of ambition and survival.

If political survival is the key to success in Canadian politics, how then does one survive? The first year of ministers' tenure consists of on-the-job training. They find out what they can do and try to stick to that area.[71] Not only is there no training available or any advance test of suitability, but no job description outlines what to do and how to do it. Apart from getting elected on the winning side and the prime minister's favour, a minister needs only a security check. A teacher, a small-town lawyer, an entrepreneur, a medical doctor, or a town clerk can join the cabinet and find himself or herself in charge of a large, sprawling department.

Some ministers are anxious to leave an imprint on their department, but many are content to just let it continue to run. They will not challenge the department to do things differently – which is fine by its officials. These ministers hope to gain a positive media profile, to stay out of political trouble, and to try to secure new initiatives for their constituency or their province. They can be successful, at least in the eyes of their riding and province, simply by staying on and taking care of the people who elected them. In Ottawa, they may well be viewed as parochial, but back home they will be seen as being able to look after their constituency and region. If they can secure an appointment to a government board for a long-standing party member or get new funding, however modest, for a high-profile initiative in their region, their constituents will see them as having influence in Ottawa. As well, although it is the prime minister who appoints senators, there is nothing to stop a minister from taking the credit for an appointment. If a minister can secure a comfortable share of patronage appointments, he or she may well remain loyal to the prime minister, whatever difficult policy issues may surface.

What matters to ministers who decide simply to linger on is that they retain a seat in cabinet or are able to win that prized possession again and hold on to it. The key to success thus is straightforward: stay out of trouble with the media, and handle question period with dexterity. The prime minister and no one else decides if ministers are successful or not. He is the boss.[72] One long-serving deputy minister (more than ten years) observed, 'You have no idea what kind of power the prime minister holds over ministers. He has in his hands the minister's car, his chauffeur, his office, his job, his ego, and so on. I have been in the public service for nearly thirty years in the Privy Council Office and line departments, and I can tell you that the grovel count in the great majority of ministers has always been quite high and, if anything, it keeps getting higher as the years go by.'[73]

Those who choose to linger on, or who, for any number of reasons, are forced to linger on can still be very busy and give the appearance, at least to those outside government, that they are making a difference. There is never a shortage of things for them to do. They must spend time in their constituencies and province. They have to attend to party matters, attend caucus, prepare for question period, and be accessible for media interviews. They also have House duties, including attending to committee matters. They must meet regularly with their senior departmental officials. There are also always any number of reasons to travel to different parts of Canada on behalf of the party or the department. Powerful or not, ministers always have specific projects to promote or some government funding to secure for one reason or another. If the funding requirement is modest and can come from within the department, so much the better. If the relevant program is in another department, then the minister and his or her office will have to lobby or negotiate to secure the project or the funding. This too takes time.

Ministers, regardless of portfolio, put in extremely long hours, especially when Parliament is sitting. There is hardly an open spot in any ministerial agenda. Nor do their agendas chronicle all that ministers do in the course of a week. There are always last-minute meetings to be arranged, telephone calls to return (often in the evenings), correspondence to deal with, documents to read, and so on. As two students of politics wrote over twenty-five years ago, politicians 'miss meals, neglect children, and lose sleep for politics. For them, politics is a central, vibrant and continuing preoccupation. Formal statements of purpose cannot adequately account for their involvement.'[74]

A former clerk of the Privy Council and secretary to the cabinet, Gordon Osbaldeston, once issued a warning to ministers that 'having many roles, you will be under constant and unremitting pressure to allocate some of your time to this or that worthy endeavour, [Ministers] must establish priorities and the time frame within which they want to accomplish them and allocate their time accordingly. If they don't do this, and do it well, they will be lost.'[75] He added that ministers work between seventy and eighty hours a week but that 'surveys indicate that they often have only three hours a week to spend with their Deputy Ministers.'[76] Being busy and having an impact are two very different things.

Not all ministers, however, are happy just to linger on. Some want to challenge the status quo, and sometimes all ministers have to deal with powerful forces (such as program review) that push departments to change course. Others work hand in hand with their officials to promote departmental interests, to secure new funding from the prime minister, and to persuade the minister of finance to support new initiatives. Still others may be tempted to overhaul departmental policies and programs because they want to see a change of course.

The key to success for these energetic, ambitious ministers is gaining the support of the prime minister, his or her advisers, and central agencies and establishing a strong working relationship with senior departmental officials. Otherwise there is not much hope for success. Indeed, any ministers who set out alone to overhaul departmental policies will be identified as rogue ministers by the PMO and the PCO. If that happens, the minister will be reeled in. Departmental officials will then take their cue from the clerk of the Privy Council, and although they will give an appearance of support, their efforts will actually be modest. New ministers have the career officials who served their predecessors and as a rule do not intervene in promotions within their departments.

If, however, the minister has the prime minister's support, then departmental officials give their best effort. They consult outside groups, engage the interdepartmental policy process, work with central agencies, and provide the minister with all the support needed to pilot proposed measures through the decision-making process. The goal is to get the measures through the policy process, and career officials achieve the required consensus among departments.

All ministers know that the House of Commons helps determine success, in the eyes of the prime minister, colleagues, government caucus, the media, and ultimately Canadians. As we saw above, for many ministers, the Commons means question period. Very few ministers encounter problems in a standing committee. To start with, they do not spend much time there, because government MPs constitute a majority and the media hardly pay any attention to work there. Apart from question period, many ministers ignore the work of the Commons and MPs often speak to a near-empty House.

Question period, however, is a different matter. Senior officials monitor it very carefully and often turn on a television to watch it. They know that it is a forum for the opposition, which hopes to put ministers on the defensive, to identify policy or administrative miscues, and to grab media attention. There is always the risk that the department could be caught in political cross-fire.

Some ministers perform well in question period and actually enjoy the cut and thrust of political gamesmanship (examples are Allen Mac-Eachen in Trudeau's cabinet, Bernard Valcourt in Mulroney's, and Paul Martin in Chrétien's). But the majority regard question period as an ordeal. Harold Wilson, a former British prime minister, reported in his memoirs that he had known ministers to be physically sick in anticipation of question period. Yet British ministers, unlike their Canadian counterparts, see questions in writing at least forty-eight hours before they must answer them.

Many in the media and the public see question period as the best, if not the only, means for the Commons to hold the government to account. If ever the government meets the opposition on a level playing field, it is there. If opposition parties are ever able to draw attention to a ministerial error, an administrative shortcoming, or a flaw in government policy, it is probably then. Ministers can try to evade questions, but they must not mislead Parliament. They must anticipate questions and always stand at the ready with a reply.

Ministers can count on the support of their departmental officials as they prepare for question period. No one, least of all deputy ministers, wants to see an administrative shortcoming showcased. They may take comfort in the knowledge that it is the minister who must face the music, but they realize that shortcomings reflect more on how deputy ministers run their departments than on the minister. Deputy ministers and other senior officials see no contradiction in supporting their ministers and giving them as much ammunition as possible, while at the same time considering themselves non-partisan. Their long experience in government has taught them to know intuitively when to support a minister responsible for the department and when to back away if the minister is looking for partisan support.

Deputy ministers, however, must constantly perform a balancing act between empowering managers and front-line workers and avoiding administrative shortcomings. Peters and Waterman maintain that strong businesses have 'simultaneous loose–tight properties.'[77] That is, the board of directors and chief executive officers are very firm about what they expect their managers to achieve but are loose about how they go about achieving it. Despite firm goals, managers are relatively free to identify the means to achieve them. In government, we see the opposite. The prime minister and senior cabinet ministers are fairly loose about goals except for top government priorities, but in tight about means. They want tight operations to ensure error-free government or at least to minimize the chances of error, because they constantly face question period and the media. In the event of trouble, they also expect career officials to come to their rescue with arguments or whatever else they may need. This is one more reason why it is not possible to make government operations look and act like the private sector. These worlds are by nature different and operate under vastly different circumstances and rules.

Always There: Tapping into the Civil Service

The PCO published a document in 1990 on the role and responsibilities of career officials in relation to politicians. It states that it is the responsibility 'of individual public servants to provide advice and information to Ministers, to carry out faithfully the directions given by Ministers, and in so doing to serve the people of Canada. Public servants are accountable to their superiors and ultimately to their Minister for the proper and competent execution of their duties.' Responsibility for providing information 'to Parliament and its committees rests with ministers.'[78]

These quotations suggest that relations between civil servants and politicians have hardly changed since 1867. A number of other factors suggest a degree of stability in relations between the two groups. The basic departmental structure remains essentially intact, the merit principle still applies in staffing, and the bulk of the civil service remains largely non-partisan. The doctrine of ministerial responsibility may have faded in recent years, but it still applies. Most deputy ministers are still 'lifers.' The civil service continues to be the chief nursery of senior bureaucrats, since the great majority of deputy ministers and assistant deputy ministers come from within its ranks.

But beneath the surface things have changed, the most significant being a loss in confidence. One can also detect subtle but major shifts in relations between politicians and career officials. The latter are less assertive in their dealings with politicians, notably ministers, than was the case twenty, thirty, or forty years ago. There are signs everywhere that senior officials have started to accept the criticism of the late 1970s and early 1980s – that they held too much influence over both policy and government operations. We saw in an earlier chapter that they decided in the 1984 transition of power to hand over the policy steering wheel to the incoming government with the implicit message, 'Now you drive.'

There is also evidence that career officials are less assertive on the operations side. The presence of ministerial exempt staff is more tolerated in government operations than it was twenty-five years ago. Access-to-information legislation and the media have made government operations and programs more sensitive to politics and political direction. Exempt staff want to get to the bottom of any potential news story so as to brief the minister and possibly the PMO on its development and political implications. Going up through the traditional bureaucratic channels to the deputy minister and then to the minister and the PMO will no longer do – that takes time, and the media won't wait. Many officials have no objection to exempt staff members being present in government operations because they agree that matters that have become issues of partisan controversy are not appropriate for formal briefings and they welcome any opportunity to isolate themselves from the partisan political process. In any event, in many instances it is better for them to have exempt staffers brief the PMO than to do it themselves.

Notwithstanding their desire to avoid political controversies and to be anonymous, career officials have become more visible since the early 1980s. The *Globe and Mail,* the *National Post,* and the *Ottawa Citizen* all have staff members who report on major civil-service appointments and promotions. The clerk of the Privy Council and secretary to the cabinet now appears in public at least once a year to table his or her report on the state of the public service. The growing emphasis on consultation and partnerships in developing and implementing government programs also compels career officials to negotiate directly with interest groups and all types of 'stakeholders.' Paul Thomas maintains that 'these trends have not brought us to the point where public servants are recognizable household names, but they are better known ... and interested members of the public are better able today to identify the occupants of important positions within the bureaucracy and may even feel confident in attributing certain policy perspectives to such individuals.'[79]

The PCO rarely publishes 'How to' documents. But it decided to do so to assist career officials in *Crisis Management* – the title of a publication. That book declares that 'a crisis is a crisis when the media, Parliament and/or credible or powerful interest groups identify it as a crisis.' Someone *outside* the civil service decides that a crisis exists – speaking truth to power turned on its head. Although each crisis is different, the media and interest groups react with 'predictable sameness.' They want to blame someone and ask, 'When will the party at fault be fired [and] when did the organization discover the problem?' The publication tells career officials that the usual arguments, for 'being silent must be resisted, such as the need to assemble more facts.' They should 'take the initiative, make news.' It adds, 'Do not hesitate to admit that you do not have all the answers,' because 'a crisis is *not* the time to defend policies on the basis of a superior record or outstanding performance in the past.'[80] If nothing else, crisis management has forced career officials to shed some of their anonymity.

Crisis management has also produced a chain reaction that has repercussions throughout government. Decisions are sucked to the top, and senior officials at central agencies and deputy ministers deal with issues perhaps better left to bureaucrats down the line. Whenever confronted by a real or potential crisis, the prime minister and ministers want it in a safe pair of hands – known to ministers and their partisan advisers and always located at the top of the organization. There is hardly a day that goes by without a major file, an important controversy, or a potential crisis lurking somewhere in a government department or agency about which people at the centre know but on which the opposition parties and the media have yet to focus. Safe hands that can put things back on track are invaluable.

What about policy development? There are three routes: policies defined by the party in power; policies defined by the prime minister and a

handful of advisers, including some senior ministers; and policy proposals that bubble up from departments.

Career officials are not present when political parties set out to define
policies and their electoral platforms. As we saw above, policies are
defined and packaged by a handful of advisers working with the leader.
Once in power, a prime minister will turn to ministers and officials to
implement the party's policies. Career officials are quite good at doing
what they are told to do, and the Liberal Red Book of 1993 is a case in
point. Career officials kept a checklist of things to do flowing from those
commitments and on implementation.

The problem, however, is that the civil service is rarely told clearly
what to do.[81] Even the Red Book exercise – one time when politicians
came to office with a list of things to do – had its limits. The purpose of
the Red Book was to draw attention away from the negative press coverage over Jean Chrétien's alleged inability to articulate a vision for the
country, to present new ideas, and to dispel the charge often heard in
the early 1990s that he was 'yesterday's man.'[82] Before Kim Campbell's
débâcle in mid-campaign, public-opinion surveys reported that Chrétien was found lacking on several fronts and that the media were por-
traying him as 'idea-less Jean Chrétien.' He and his advisers set out to
deal head on with this charge and concluded that the Red Book would
be the solution. It would draw attention to a series of campaign commitments and thereby suggest that Chrétien could indeed generate new
ideas.[83]

Quite apart from its true purpose, the Red Book had more success
before Chrétien came to office than after. Once the party was in power,
the book lost at least some of its relevance. Finance Minister Paul Martin
instructed his departmental officials time and again to ignore it. Martin
is quoted as telling his senior Finance officials, 'Don't tell me what's in
the Red Book ... I wrote the goddamn thing. And I know that a lot of it is
crap ... the Goddamn thing [was] thrown together quickly in the last
three weeks of July. Things hadn't been properly thought through.'[84] In
any event, the government reneged on a number of commitments –
both large and small – including the pledge to renegotiate NAFTA, to
introduce daycare, to replace the GST, to strengthen the Department
of the Environment, and to cut spending on outside consultants by
$620 million annually, beginning in fiscal year 1995–96.[85]

Once firmly in power, a prime minister and his or her court of advisers usually introduce new measures to fit emerging economic circumstances (hence the program-review exercise) or to pursue measures of

strong interest to them – for example, Chrétien and the Millennium Scholarship Foundation, Mulroney and the Canada–U.S. Free Trade Agreement, and Trudeau and constitutional patriation and the National Energy Program.[86] When a prime minister decides that an issue or an initiative should be pursued, the role of career officials is clear: deliver the goods. They clear 'roadblocks,' deal with constraint, and ensure that measures are implemented as envisaged. In some ways, then, they become accomplices to the prime minister and his senior advisers.

The great majority of new policy measures, however, bubble up from departments, and they are shaped differently from those defined from the top down. The bulk of policy proposals no longer come from a single department. As we saw above, not only they are interdepartmental by design, but they also reflect the requirement to consult interested parties outside government.

Proposals that enter the elaborate federal policy process from a department policy process usually emerge at the other end changed dramatically. One of Chrétien's policy advisers explained why the prime minister decided to ignore the policy process when he introduced the $2.5-billion Millennium Scholarship Fund, described as the government's most significant millennium project: 'If we had respected the process, the idea would never have come out at the other end the way we wanted it. Intergovernmental affairs would have argued that the matter was provincial, not federal. Human Resources Department would have argued that the idea was in its jurisdiction, while Heritage Canada would have made a similar claim. The prime minister asked one of us to call Paul (Martin, minister of Finance) and his deputy minister to let them know what we were doing. In that way he got what he wanted.'[87]

Exasperation with the policy-making process has pushed prime ministers – the only people with the clout to do so – to make policies by announcements. That is, the prime minister simply delivers a major speech to unveil a new policy (for example, Chrétien and the Kyoto Protocol) and then lets the policy process pick up the pieces. The process then follows the announcement. Canadians now recognize the power of the prime minister, and they will make every effort to harness it. For example, a group of concerned citizens from northern New Brunswick held a press conference to reveal that they had asked to meet the prime minister to ask that a stretch of road in their community be upgraded. A meeting with the provincial minister or, for that matter, the federal minister of transport would not do.[88] If residents in a small rural community know where political power lies, so do MPs. They know that the prime minister can, at the stroke of a pen, or with a simple 'Yes,' make things happen. When this does not occur, then the process is porous and shared, and in such an atmosphere policy actors, including ministers, have influence, not power. Jean Chrétien left no doubt on this point when he observed: 'The Prime Minister is the Prime Minister and he has the cabinet to advise him. At the end of the day, it is the Prime Minister who says, "yes" or "no."'[89]

Prime ministers know better than anyone else the price to pay for having one's ideas go through the standard policy process. In many instances, an idea is reduced to the lowest common denominator among varying positions. The boldness found in initial policy proposals has been watered down, and decisions may well result from a need to arrive at an agreement. It may be described as a process of mutual co-optation. The department initiating the proposal has to put a fair bit of water in its wine to secure agreement. Consulted departments need to show that their presence in the process had some impact. Outside advisory groups also want to see their influence if they are to give the final measure a sense of legitimacy among interested parties. Ministers are not present in this elaborate process. They are briefed from time to time, and the PCO monitors proposals very closely as they are defined, if only to brief the prime minister.

Career officials must look not only to ministers but also to Parliament as they go about their work. The PCO published a document in 1990 to assist public servants in managing their relations with Parliament. It states that career officials appearing before parliamentary committees 'are expected to answer all questions.' However, 'additional considerations come to bear in the case of public servants since they appear *on behalf of the Minister.*' Career officials do not have a 'higher obligation to Parliament.' Matters of policy and political controversy are reserved 'more or less exclusively for Ministers,' otherwise senior officials would invariably be drawn into 'controversy, destroy their permanent utility to the system and indeed undermine the authority and responsibility of their Ministers.' The document outlines a series of *guidelines* for career officials and insists that they should not 'defend policy ... [and] answers should be limited to explanations.'[90]

Senior officials know that in their dealings with Parliament and MPs they must always stay inside a line 'drawn in the sand' that is visible to them, if not to others. They can explain certain programs and policies, but they can never do so as an accountability exercise. One career official explained: 'When you appear before a parliamentary committee, you always do so on behalf of your minister. You act like a lawyer before the court in that a lawyer is there on behalf of his client. Well, it is the same for us. I always assume that I appear before a Standing Committee on behalf of my minister. Some MPs understand this, but many do not. There are MPs looking to score political points against your minister through you. You have to be on guard against this and against MPs trying to draw you out into a political debate. Sometimes it is a bit of game and you need to know how to play it.'[91] The appearance of public servants before standing committees is not without risk, for they can embroil their minister in a political controversy. They understand the adversarial nature of Parliament, and they go to great lengths to prepare. Some hire outside consultants to coach them.

Opposition MPs do not hesitate to push career officials as far as they can if they sense a political controversy in the making. Some can be outright rude. Standing committees provide them their one opportunity to get back at insensitive and inaccessible bureaucrats. One assistant deputy minister had to deal 'with hostile questions' and 'felt harassed' in the autumn of 2001.[92] One former senior deputy minister called backbenchers a 'bunch of charmless primitives.'[93]

Most career officials consider MPs to be actual or at least potential adversaries. Peter Dobell, founding director of the Parliamentary Centre, writes that 'within the public service, Parliament is seen, and at times referred to, as a minor process obstacle.'[94] Civil servants seek to tell standing committees as little as possible, to protect the department, and to provide as much flexibility as possible in the days ahead. Officials offer stick to the specific question, provide a short, to-the-point answer, and volunteer nothing else. Unless MPs have enough information to pursue the issue, then the matter will never be fully explored. They ask obvious questions and receive obvious answers. More substantive issues go unattended. This, according to an official who works with MPs and standing committees, 'happens a great deal more than is generally assumed.'[95]

Robin Butler, secretary to the cabinet in Britain during the 1990s, told an inquiry that 'half an answer' by a civil servant could be accurate in reply to parliamentary questions and that at times it is necessary to give an 'incomplete' answer, which falls short of the whole truth.' He explained that 'government activity is more like playing poker than it is like playing chess.'[96] Robert Armstrong, his predecessor during the Thatcher years, spoke of having to be at times 'economical with the truth.' In Canada, no less than in Britain, civil servants do not volunteer information on delicate matters. They ensure that their answers are brief, factual, and appear to have addressed the question fully. They also make sure that the answer, if challenged, can be proven to be accurate.[97]

Career officials go to some lengths to protect ministers, to avoid embarrassment, and to promote an error-free culture. To avoid mistakes and embarrassment takes precedence over being frank, and over speaking honestly about shortcomings in policies, programs, and government operations and how to remedy them. Access-to-information legislation and more aggressive media make it more difficult for senior career officials to protect their ministers and to avoid embarrassment. However, the fact that the policy- and decision-making process is now porous, interdepartmental, and consultative makes it easier for career officials to sidestep or defuse awkward developments within their departments.

Conclusion

Although recent developments have served to broaden their policy and program realm, senior career officials in Canada are less confident today than was the case forty years ago. The reasons for this change are varied. Because of more insistent media and laws on access to information, ministerial staffers are able to roam through departmental hierarchies to secure answers quickly. In addition, Canadian career officials, like public servants in other Anglo-American democracies, appear to have accepted the argument that bureaucrats had too much power. The decision by the clerk of the Privy Council to hand over control of policy to the incoming government in 1984 speaks volumes.

The majority of policy proposals now emerge from an interdepartmental consultative process. Most new policy proposals must receive the blessing of stakeholders and several advisory or consultative groups. Thus senior officials must share their departmental policy space. This, and the fact that partisan ministerial assistants can stroll through departmental offices in search of answers, may well help explain why a public service–wide survey in 1999 revealed cynicism towards the senior bureaucracy.[98]

Institutional myths survive long after they have lost their power. The business of supply is central to the parliamentary system, and the standard belief is that Parliament scrutinizes the government's spending plans and holds it to account for its actual spending. Parliament receives thousands of pages of information during the estimates process, but no one still harbours any illusion that the House has the capacity to grasp, review, criticize, or even support the government's spending plans.

Question period provides good theatre, but little else. Television has transformed the exercise by placing a premium on ten-second clips that can grab the attention of news editors. Charges and accusations fly across the floor, but neither the minister nor career officials ever seem to pay for mistakes. That serves to strengthen the perception that accountability is missing. Yet a culture of error avoidance permeates government operations and inhibits officials from being forthright about any shortcomings. Ministers are quite happy to see decisions sucked to the top of the organization to minimize the chances of administrative miscues.

This situation, we are told, is a result of Parliament and its requirements. Yet MPs readily criticize the failings of their own institution. It is not uncommon, for example, to hear an MP describe Parliament as 'a totally dysfunctional institution.'[99] The Ottawa-based publication *Parliamentary Government* published in 1995 a collection of comments and observations from MPs on the workings of the Commons. The following observation is typical: 'I've found being an MP in Parliament and Parliament itself more irrelevant than I thought.'[100]

If institutional myths have lost their meaning, how then do political, policy, and administrative actors cope, and what actually governs their relations? The next chapter seeks to answer these questions.

9

Reshaping the Bargain

The world of politics and public service in Canada has changed dramatically since it first took form. At Confederation, Canada had little bureaucracy. Today there is a large bureaucracy with several federal departments and agencies bigger than large Canadian towns. Many people believe that the bureaucracy has become too powerful; others suspect that it is often ineffective; still others insist that it is misunderstood.

In the early part of the twentieth century, much of government business consisted of dispensing patronage. Today, the role of government extends to virtually every aspect of economic and social policies. Thirty years ago, career officials were able to advise ministers in relative secrecy. Today, access-to-information legislation, less deferential and more aggressive media, and e-government have opened up policy- and decision-making processes. Thirty years ago, hierarchy shaped policy making, which was guided by deputy ministers who had an intimate knowledge of their departments, having come up through their ranks. Today, policy is no longer the product of a single department working with its minister to secure cabinet approval. Policy making is now much more an interdepartmental affair, with outside groups brought in to inform new measures and to legitimize the policy process. In addition, public servants have become policy actors outside of government circles.

Forty years ago, members of the House of Commons informed the prime minister and cabinet how their regions, provinces, and constituencies felt about government priorities and policies. Today, public-opinion surveys are quicker and more accurate. Forty years ago, the House of Commons and politicians commanded some respect and credibility. Today, they themselves are reporting that Parliament is losing relevance and politicians rank at the bottom of the professions in which

Canadians trust. Some MPs now speak openly about their institution being in crisis.

It is unclear if there ever was a golden era for Canadian political parties. However, we do know that they once had strong, visible regional spokespersons who helped shape their party's political and policy agenda. Today, parties do not work on long-term policy agendas, instead turning to public-opinion surveys to learn what Canadians want and what 'sells' politically.[1] We also know that the foot soldiers of political parties (local candidates) are less important now in winning elections than was the case forty years ago. Today, television advertising, pollsters and spin doctors are the key ingredients, not foot soldiers, and they not only require a substantial amount of money, they have a weak link to the party.

Forty years ago, the public service was still relatively small. Though not well paid, public servants were true career officials, shared a profound belief that they were serving a collective national purpose, and could look forward to a decent pension so did not need to pay close attention to their material self-interest. They also understood the need for rules and red tape. There was a village-life atmosphere to working in government, and departments had a well-developed organizational memory against which to test new ideas. The emphasis was on controlling input costs, and a sense of frugality was deeply ingrained. Twenty years ago, traditional public-service values became regarded as outdated, and public servants stood accused of many and, at times, contradictory things. Today, many Canadians seek to make public administration behave like business and strive to empower managers without tackling the theoretical base of public management. Yet the sense of frugality – once a defining characteristic of the public service and in government operations – is no longer evident.

Today's public servants no longer remember what village life was like. In fact, they now live in several villages. Interdepartmental consultation has become a village of its own, guided by complex diplomacy and providing scope for officials to represent the interests of their departments and to sort things out across committee tables. One may well ask how a national purpose can possibly emerge from this web of conflicting interests, interdepartmental diplomacy, and constant consultations with outside stakeholders. This village is populated by policy specialists whose promotion is rapid, and virtually all of the work is carried out in Ottawa. The inhabitants know intuitively that they must avoid embarrassing their ministers or being too controversial, for fear of blotting their copy-books and, by ricochet, losing the chance for promotion. This realm looks to the prime minister, the Prime Minister's Office (PMO), the Privy Council Office (PCO), and some ministers and deputy ministers for guidance and for a sense of how they are performing.

There is another complicated and diverse network-type village peopled by program managers and front-line workers. Promotion in this village is slow, and much of its work is carried out away from Ottawa – in local tax offices, prisons, and laboratories. Its inhabitants tend to look to their clients, to citizens, and to their program objectives for a sense of how they are performing. Most spend their entire careers in the same department and retire in traditional fashion, and their services are rarely sought after by anyone once they leave government. They are public servants in the traditional sense, and because they spend much, if not all, of their career with the same department, they gain an intimate knowledge of its programs and clientele. This village is in reality a network spread out across the country, connected loosely by shared values and administrative constraints defined in Ottawa.

Above these two villages is yet another, populated by deputy ministers, with, at its core, the most important deputy ministers. Forty years ago, deputy ministers were concerned primarily with their own departments and identified strongly with them. One former deputy minister reports that when he was first appointed in the early 1970s he would not have recognized one third of his counterparts had he come across them on the street.[2] Today, deputy ministers spend nearly as much time with one another reconciling the interdepartmental process as they do with senior departmental managers. The club has regular breakfast, luncheon, and retreat meetings. Members identify strongly with the club, and each may well serve over time as deputy minister in three or four departments. Loyalty is as much to the club, if not more so, than to their departments. As with most clubs, members are expected to remain loyal.

Deputy ministers have become as much a part of the centre of government and the interdepartmental process as they are administrative heads of their departments. As we saw above, they are now selected for their knowledge of how the system works rather than for their sectoral expertise or for their knowledge of a department and its policy history. They constitute a separate community from other career civil servants, not least because of a sharp difference in perks. They have access to a chauffeured departmental automobile with their own distinct licence plates. They also enjoy a special pension plan not available to others, which can pay up to 90 per cent of their salary based on their six best salary years; the plan is also indexed and tied to the country's inflation rate. I once asked a former clerk of the Privy Council why deputy ministers have been given a much more generous pension plan than other career civil servants. She replied that it was because they are no longer as secure in their job as they once were or as other career officials still are. In effect, the generous pension plan is a form of danger pay. Yet lucrative post-employment opportunities have become available with lobbying firms, with the private sector, and consulting for governments at home or abroad.

One hundred years ago, most ministers got involved in the details of the day, down to the acceptance of a tender for the installation of a pump. Forty years ago, ministers tended to forge a strong partnership with their deputy ministers and together prepared policy proposals for cabinet's consideration. Senior officials in line departments would provide the knowledge and expertise and outline policy and program prescriptions to their ministers, who would take them to cabinet or to Treasury Board to debate their merits with their colleagues. We learn, for example, that Alvin Hamilton was able to secure cabinet approval for the Roads to Resource program in the 1960s only on the basis of an oral presentation to full cabinet. There was never a memorandum to cabinet, and the only official document was the cabinet's record of decision.[3] The prime minister and cabinet could accept proposed solutions, give them political legitimacy, and then try to convince Canadians.

Forty years ago, ministers and public servants had few oversight bodies auditing and reporting on their work. The Office of the Auditor General carried out financial audits to ensure that departmental financial reporting was in order, and the Public Service Commission ensured application of the merit principle. Today, there are several oversight bodies, including the access-to-information commissioner, the privacy commissioner, the official-languages commissioner, and the Public Service Commission.

Forty years ago, one could easily discern separate and distinct realms for the public and private sectors. One need only read what former deputy ministers, such as Al Johnson and Gordon Robertson, wrote to see that they had no desire to emulate the private sector. Today, the public sector tries to emulate the private sector in most things. The Treasury Board Secretariat, for example, now defines its programs along 'business lines' and its planning process as 'business plans.'[4] Departments and their policy processes were also more self-contained back then.

Where does the traditional bargain between politicians and career officials fit in today? I reported in chapter 1 that public servants exchanged overt partisanship and some political rights in return for permanent careers, anonymity, and merit selection. They could then offer advice to ministers without fear or favour. Politicians gave up the ability to appoint or dismiss public servants and to change their working conditions at will in exchange for civil servants' guaranteeing non-partisan obedience and professional competence.

The purpose of this chapter is to assess whether the traditional bargain can still hold and to determine what has happened to the notion of space, which has shaped Canada's machinery of government. The chapter reviews recent developments against the backdrop of the traditional requirements of our political and administrative institutions. There are a number of practitioners, observers, and students of Canadian public administration who believe that the traditional bargain still remains the best. They argue that changes over the past forty years do not detract from the normative theory – ministers, not career officials, should have the final say, because they bear final accountability to Parliament and the public. They believe that the responsibility of career officials should remain the same: to advise ministers, to outline fully the options and constraints that they face, and, when ministers decide, to make the best of the decisions. They also make the case that the bulk of the reforms have either been misguided or amounted to little, being impossible to implement or sustain over time. Reformers should give up the never-ending search for alternatives and return to the traditional model.

But is this possible? Can politicians and public servants 'go home again'? This chapter answers these questions in the first two sections and then picks through the pieces of a bargain undone.

A Public Service in Flux

The challenges that a country's political and administrative institutions must cope with today are vastly different from those of forty, sixty, or one hundred years ago. But what about the traditional bargain? Have the changes rendered it obsolete, and can we go back to the way things were?

An important difference between then and now is the expansion of government operations. Growth and government overload have been well documented. James Douglas writes: 'Modern democratic governments are overwhelmed by the load of responsibilities they are called upon ... to shoulder.'[5] There is a sense of urgency at the highest levels in government. For a prime minister to promote an agenda for change, he or she must pick a handful of major policy issues and put aside most of the rest for the system to cope with.[6] Unforeseen issues will surface in the form of actual or potential political crises, which require the attention of key officials.

Cuts in programs and operations could reduce the size of government and thus reduce the overload problem. The program review in the mid-1990s did eliminate or transfer 50,000 positions from the federal public service. But this was a special initiative dealing with what was perceived as a crisis. In early January 1995, the *Wall Street Journal* described the Canadian dollar as a 'basket case.' It ran an editorial called 'Bankrupt Canada?' and declared that 'Mexico isn't the only U.S. neighbour flirting with the financial abyss.' It argued that 'if dramatic action isn't taken in the next month's federal budget, it's not inconceivable that Canada could hit the debt wall and have to call in the International Monetary Fund to stabilize its falling currency.'[7] The editorial shook ministers hesitant to accept spending cuts. David Dodge, deputy minister at Finance, labelled the editorial a 'seminal event' in the preparation of the 1995 budget. Line departments were instructed to produce significant spending cuts, and the program review resulted in $29 billion in cuts.[8] Events and new spending commitments since then reveal that the program review was indeed a 'one-off' event. In addition, its impact was felt mostly at the program level, where some programs were cut; others were restructured into arm's-length organizations (for example, air-traffic controllers and Navcan, which operation removed spending and person-years from the government's books); and still others – a majority – saw their budgets reduced.

The effect on deputy ministers and central agencies, however, was modest. There is plenty of evidence that deputy ministers and interdepartmental consultation emerged much better off than did program managers and front-line workers. We know, for example, that central agencies were not cut to the same extent as line departments.[9] More important, the program review is proof that government could never be reduced to the size that it had under the traditional bargain. For this to happen would require the election of a majority government clearly committed to a sharp right turn and capable of a tremendous wrench of the wheel. The requirements of modern democracy and the pervasive and tenacious nature of the welfare state are such that we simply cannot turn back the clock.

This is not only a Canadian reality. Governments throughout the Western world have not been able to cut spending and programs as much as they promised. Thatcher, Reagan, and Mulroney all tried, but the overall size of government did not decline much during the 1980s in their countries.[10]

Canada's federal government could follow the lead of Britain, Australia, and New Zealand and restructure its operations. These countries have essentially created or tried to create two public services – one to manage ongoing programs and deliver services, and the other to provide policy advice and support.[11] However, this model has had only limited effect on the overall size of government.

Ministers will also remain few in number compared to career officials. They will not be able to rely on direct, face-to-face control to the extent that predecessors could even forty years ago. Probably less than 1 per cent of government decisions go before or are reviewed by ministers. We know, for example, that the Immigration Department alone receives on average 40,000 'status requests' a year from inquiring MPs and that very few of these requests actually make it to the minister's 'in' basket.[12] Ministerial direction and control now involve less and less ministers issuing orders and are more and more a matter of indirect influence, broad policy directions, and 'climate setting.' The days have long gone when government was small, when the pay clerk knew everyone in the department, when the Ottawa-based public service was like a small village, when the PMO and the PCO could occupy just a few offices in the East Block of the Parliament Buildings, and when ministers, at least strong ones, ran their departments with a firm hand.

Modern bureaucracy in Canada dates back to the Murray Report (c. 1917) and to the aftermath of the Second World War, when the 'Ottawa men' set out to build Canada's welfare state. They tackled problems directly, simply, successfully, and with limited interdepartmental and outside consultation. There were no lobbyists, and there were no electronic media keeping a close watch. One need only to read Bob Bryce, Escott Reid, and Gordon Robertson to see that the public service had an entrepreneurial spirit and was bounding with confidence. It had its own space and knew well the boundaries that defined it. Those who found the boundaries too restrictive ran for elected office (for example, C.M. Drury, Lester Pearson, and Mitchell Sharp). As they met with success, Canadians and their politicians demanded more. Thus the public service grew, and elaborate processes were introduced to manage government operations. In turn, it became more change-resistant, less confident in its abilities, and prone to useless or failed reform measures.[13] By the time career officials made it to the top ranks in the 1980s, the civil service had become an institution under siege, accused by some of being too powerful and anti-democratic and by others of being ineffective and wasteful.

There are also some things over which the public service has no control. Access-to-information legislation is now firmly part of the government landscape. One could make the case that there are times when hiding behind secrecy is in the interests of good government. I know of no empirical evidence that claims that the legislation makes for better government or that it has strengthened the bonds between government and citizens. Access to information certainly inhibits public servants from committing frank advice to paper for fear of embarrassing their ministers or compromising their political neutrality. As the work of the public service becomes less and less committed to paper, its organizational memory is sure to suffer. Advice given to ministers may well lack a historical perspective, and documents going to ministers may be less frank and fearless than they should be. Access to information will probably remain, however, if only because of increasing calls for greater transparency, in the form of information disclosure, to make government more responsive.

The media will never allow the government, let alone the public service, to dictate their role. The media now use the legislation to secure information about how government works, to learn about emerging policy issues, and, according to John Crosbie, 'to ferret out snippets of information with which to embarrass political leaders and to titillate the public.' One can hardly expect the media to support any suggestion to do away with the legislation. The media also demand instant information and do not much care whether it comes from politicians or career officials. There is a saying current in government that ministers can be in only one place at a time, but the media can be all over the place.[14]

E-government is also not about to disappear. Ottawa prides itself on being at its 'leading edge.' An international consulting firm ranked Canada at the top of twenty-two countries in promoting government on-line programming.[15] But e-government poses serious challenges for the traditional bureaucratic model. Two students of public administration go to the heart of the matter: 'Can (career) officials be in any sense anonymous and faceless when every one of them has an e-mail address listed on their departmental internet home page?'[16] A senior federal official elaborates: 'A teenager with earrings working on the departmen-

tal internet site can decide to answer a question from a citizen, deciding
that there is no need to bother senior officials up the line. The answer
could have important political or policy implications. Moreover, with a
simple click, a citizen can ask the same question to several departments.
How is the government able to coordinate responses? How is the government to control how questions are handled and who decides on the
front line if the questions have political or policy contents? We are about
to discover that technology always does more than what is intended.'[17]
Technology is also redefining the notion of departmental space and
how it can be directed and controlled.

The information society has heightened the interrelation of policy
issues. As we already saw, most policy issues now cut across departments
and governments. As issues became more complex and interconnected,
it became apparent that no single department had all the policy tools
and program instruments required to bring about a solution. The result
is that each department comes to the interdepartmental table with only
part of the answer in hand, unable on its own to impose a solution.

Policy issues no longer respect boundaries. And, as policy making in
government becomes more 'horizontal,' more actors are drawn into the
process. The more actors, the more likely it is that the status quo or policy development by *petits pas* will prevail. However, the presence of more
actors also 'thickens' accountability: information can be distorted, and
there can be disunity of command and administrative inertia. Accordingly, it becomes extremely difficult to hold someone or even a government unit responsible for poor analysis, lack of action, problems not
solved, or lack of creativity.[18] Blame avoidance becomes easier in this
environment. How are we to determine, for example, when an unsatis-
factory result has stemmed from lack of creativity? Better yet, how could
we possibly know who was responsible for lack of creativity even if we
could establish that this had been the problem? How, for example,
could we hold to account an interdepartmental committee of twenty-
five officials representing twelve departments and agencies? If the centre of government and the relevant deputy minister decide that a particular policy unit within a department did not produce the right product
and the right conclusion, then it will quietly install new capacities and
new leaders. But what are they to do when the package is the product of
twelve or twenty units from several departments working in a collaborative effort?

There are now many policy actors with a vested interest in the thickening of government. Stakeholders have a place at the government

table looking at data and proposals and shaping new measures. One can hardly imagine that they would want to give up their place at the table in the interest of more streamlined operations and clearer accountability. Research institutes, consultants, and lobbyists draw funding or contracts from a thicker government, and they too are unlikely to turn against it. Ministers can now turn to several sources for advice rather than having to rely exclusively on career officials, and thickening government is one way to avoid the 'Yes, Minister' syndrome. It also enables ministers to point to others, including other levels of government, to explain their lack of action in a specific field.

Career officials, meanwhile, see new positions being created to manage the interdepartmental and consultative process. Tables 9.1 and 9.2 reveal recent growth in the executive community (EX), which, together with its feeder groups (levels just below the EX category), constitute the main body managing interdepartmental and consultative processes. Notwithstanding cuts resulting from the program review, the feeder group actually gained over 1,300 members between 1991 and 2001. The EX category, meanwhile, dropped from 3,730 in 1995 (the year the program review was launched) to 3,517 in 2001, down 213. However, the community has begun to grow again, starting in 1999, and by 2002 it was bigger than in 1995, or prior to the program review.

Government needs to bring a horizontal perspective to most issues of public policy and to the vested interests of a host of actors – politicians, career officials, outside stakeholders, and hired hands. This powerful brew will scarcely allow any turning back of the clock.

An Apolitical Civil Service?

The traditional bargain requires an apolitical and institutionalized civil service. During the past thirty years or so many politicians have turned to various means to reassert their authority, because they came to the view that the public service was not sufficiently responsive to their wishes. The PMO has been considerably strengthened, as have ministerial offices. In addition, ministers have sought assistance from sources outside government, such as consultants, pollsters, and lobbyists, to assist them in their work, including their departmental responsibilities.

Officials working in ministerial offices, unlike career officials, are not politically neutral. In many instances, both political assistants and career officials may well provide the same advice to ministers. There will, however, often be a political slant to the work of a ministerial assistant in draft-

Table 9.1
Numbers of EXs, 1995–2001

Year	Numbers of EXs
1995	3,730
1996	3,396
1997	3,011
1998	3,201
1999	3,419
2000	3,293
2001	3,517
2002	3,890

Source: Public Service Commission, 14 Dec. 2001
and 23 Oct. 2002.

Table 9.2
Numbers in principal feeder groups for EXs, 1991 and 2001

Classification	1991	2001
PM 6	1,439	1,434
AS 7	800	860
ES 7	166	279
ES 6	501	1,045
CO 3	754	854
FS 2	679	783
FI 4	247	297
PE 6	118	270
IS 6	132	235
AS 8	3	88
Total	4,839	6,145

Source: Public Service Commission, 14 Dec. 2001.
Note: These ten classifications provided 70 per cent of new EXs.

ing a speech or a letter or in commenting on a policy proposal. The career official is expected to refrain from such a bias because his or her position is, by definition, politically neutral. Accordingly, instead of doing away with the apolitical civil service, politicians simply worked around it to secure responsive competence from wherever they could get it.

Many politicians naturally want the civil service to be an accomplice in promoting a political and policy agenda. There is, of course, a thin line between what is policy and what is political. There is nothing new here. What is new is that governments now expect career officials to be policy actors not just inside but also outside government circles. As we saw above, the policy process now involves other departments, other governments, research institutes and consultants, and stakeholders.

Given the new consultative process, career officials have little choice but to become representatives of the government in policy matters. Their role is not just to explain government policy. The process is dynamic, and they are expected to voice their views as proposals take shape. This was fine so long as the process was limited to government circles and ministers had sufficient time to meet interested outside parties – which were few in number even as recently as forty years ago – to explain and sell their proposals. It would now be extremely difficult for career officials to participate with non-government actors, in the policy process as neutral observers unwilling to support a policy position.

As career officials assume a more visible role, they also lose more of their anonymity. They lost some particularly during the 1980s and 1990s. They now frequently appear before House of Commons standing committees, and an increasing number now discuss their work in the media. The clerk of the Privy Council each year reports to Parliament on the state of the public service. These views may not be partisan or particularly profound and newsworthy, but they are political by definition, for they take clear positions on the health and needs of a national institution. Shortly after being appointed clerk in 2002, Alex Himelfarb declared at a symposium that 'we will have Human Resources reform, we will have health reform and we will have an innovation agenda and we will have a skills and learning agenda and we will reach out to Aboriginal people and poor people and we will make sure every kid has a good start in life.'[19] Forty years ago such a speech would properly have been left to politicians: one can hardly imagine predecessors Robert Bryce (1954–63) or Gordon Robertson (1963–75) giving a similar talk despite their strong roles. It would be impossible to give a full account of the Trudeau period without reviewing the work of Michael Pitfield (1975–9, 1980–2) or of the Mulroney era without Paul Tellier (1985–92). The clerk is no longer a political eunuch or a faceless bureaucrat – that era is long gone.

The shift to results-based management and the establishment of service standards pushes accountability, albeit with limited success, down to those directly responsible for meeting performance targets and service standards. This shift not only makes career officials more visible, it also renders them potentially answerable to more authorities and interests.[20] How can one 'let managers manage' without striking a new bargain between politicians and career officials and defining a new space to enable managers to manage? There is every indication that this paradox will continue. There are few voices suggesting dropping the notion of letting managers manage and going back to pre-Glassco practices. In fact, one hears quite the opposite. Government officials still want to make administration of the public sector resemble that of the private sector. The desire is always there, but the required changes are never introduced, albeit for valid reasons.

For career officials to return to greater anonymity would mean declaring the civil service off limits to the media, moving the policy process back inside government, abandoning private-sector management techniques, and admitting the impossibility of measuring the performance of many government programs. There is no appetite anywhere for this.

The civil service has also lost some of its other earlier characteristics. The organization is now in a muddle. There are traditional line departments, operating agencies within these departments, large departments recently transformed into agencies, and new arm's-length foundations or organizations. There is also now a much greater tendency to contract out for services and to hire consultants for policy work.

There are models – agencies, foundations, and collaborative arrangements – that do enjoy greater autonomy and operate differently from traditional departments. The Canada Customs and Revenue Agency, the Canadian Food Inspection Agency, and Parks Canada are separate federal agencies with their own chief executive officers who report to a minister and have more autonomy than a traditional line department. They do not have departments' centrally prescribed administrative, financial, and human resources rules. For example, their separate employer status exempts them from the workings of the Public Service Commission, particularly the application of the merit principle. Has Ottawa created a two-tier public service, with one tier more pure than the other, less subject to political pressure to make partisan political appointments, and downplaying the merit principle? Has it created two distinct types of career officials and hence two different organizational spaces – one that has to play by the rules of the Public Service Commission and the other not?

There are also new organizations to which the government has delegated full discretionary authority for planning, management of program design, and delivery of services. Their corporate boards of directors operate within a very broad strategic framework. Examples include the Canada Foundation for Innovation (with an endowment of $3.15 billion), the Canada Millennium Scholarship Foundation ($2.5 billion), and Genome Canada ($300 million). These foundations are part of neither the private nor the public sector. The head of the Innovation Foundation, David Strangway, insists that this body is 'a non-governmental organization.'[21] He is right, given that the foundations do not operate even at arm's length from the government, since the government and Parliament have no authority to direct, control, hold to account, or impose sanctions on them, nor does any minister. Yet they are also not part of the private sector because they are not subjected to market forces. In brief, they are self-governing entities spending public funds somehow accountable to no one in particular other than to themselves. Finally, the federal government has entered into special collaborative arrangements with the provinces, and with the private and the voluntary sectors, sharing both program authority and risk.

This all constitutes a significant departure from the past. Traditionally, the government has delivered its services through departments and agencies under a unified public service, all subject to ministerial accountability. The government could establish a crown corporation and assign it a mandate to pursue a fairly specific public-policy objective and distinctive accountability requirements. The new situation affects both the public service and accountability. For the public service, there is a danger that career officials will work in a series of unconnected organizations with little in the way of staff transferability or shared values and traditions. This in turn could well compromise the concept of a unified public service. Several public services could emerge, each with its own pay structure, recruitment system, and expenditure controls. What will be the glue that will hold all these organizations together?

Also disturbing, the new agencies have been more expensive than was at first envisaged. In fact, they cost more than the traditional departments that they replaced. Three of them had to go back to the Treasury Board for new money to stay in business. In addition, a recent national survey revealed that 'client satisfaction' with the Canada Customs and Revenue Agency dropped over a two-year period while it went up in the case of a large traditional department – Human Resources Development Canada.[22] If they cost more to operate and if citizen's satisfaction has declined, what is the point of these agencies? Still, the government will not disband them and return to the traditional departmental model unless they become a continuing political liability. And no doubt the search will continue for new models to make government operations look more like the private sector.

But even traditional departments no longer operate as they did in pre-Glassco days. The shift away from line-item to program budgeting has made them less parsimonious and less concerned with input costs. Forty years ago, a typical government department operated with a deputy minister, four assistant deputy ministers, and some fifteen to twenty directors general. Today, the same department has perhaps one deputy minister, one to three associate deputy ministers, two or three senior assistant deputy ministers, several assistant deputy ministers, several more associate assistant deputy ministers, and still more directors and directors general. One department alone now has seventeen assistant deputy ministers. Yet the past decade has seen program review and massive government restructuring, both designed to streamline operations. The 1993 restructuring reduced the number of departments from thirty-two to twenty-three by reshaping eight departments, providing new mandates to three others, and merging or breaking up fifteen more.[23] Prime Minister Kim Campbell declared that the move represented a major step 'toward providing Canadians with leaner, more accessible and more efficient government to meet the challenges facing Canada.'[24] Some eighty assistant-deputy-minister positions were eliminated.[25] The program review scrapped about 50,000 positions and produced over $30 billion in spending cuts.[26]

It is hardly possible to overstate the difference between pre-and post-Glassco days. Formerly, the government had program administrators – not managers – and controlling input costs was important. There were, for example, controls in place to ensure that parliamentary appropriations were not overspent. A comptroller had to pre-audit all spending to make sure that funds were available to cover salaries, travel expenses, and programs.

In post-Glassco days, administrators became managers, and many centrally prescribed controls were reduced or eliminated. Management was perceived to be a skill quite independent of the subject matter being managed and managers could be transferred to completely different economic or social programs. If managers had the skills and access to the necessary data, they could, it was thought, run anything. Budgets were now to be developed and presented on a program rather than on a line-item basis. Departments presented cartloads of information to the Treasury Board, which had great difficulty trying to sort out what it all meant.

Newly minted managers quickly discovered a range of survival techniques that the program-budgeting approach allowed. The first was to secure and retain slack in the budget. With central agencies incapable of properly analysing program data, it became fairly easy to pad the budget. Given current efforts to make program evaluation work, one can only imagine what it must have been like when program budgeting began to take shape. Since the people actually running the programs and government operations were the only ones with the relevant information, they were the only ones controlling program allocation. It became extremely difficult, if not impossible, for outsiders to find the 'slack.'[27] Budget cuts had to be introduced by fiat, more often than not through across-the-board spending cuts, so that most departments were treated the same way regardless of their position on the government's priority list or of how well their operations were being managed. Program budgeting haunts us still. Even the program review of the mid-1990s for the most part used across-the-board cuts.[28]

A fundamental component of the traditional bargain is the merit principle. Indeed, this principle provided the battle line for reformers early in the last century as they set out to modernize the public service and transform it into a professional, non-partisan institution. To this day, it remains one of the most enduring themes in public administration.

Frederick C. Mosher writes about the merit principle in terms of 'consideration and judgement.' He explains, 'A judge considers an argument on its merits; a scientist considers a proposition on its merits; an employing officer considers a prospective employee on his or her merits. In both usages merits have to do with considerations of intrinsic, relevant value or truth.'[29] However, the government of Canada has never defined the merit principle in law. It is a concept that may suggest 'truth,' but its application has been sufficiently flexible to accommodate new objectives or new truths whenever the need arose.

The merit principle has been sufficiently flexible in recent years to satisfy government objectives in promoting gender equality, linguistic requirements, and the hiring of persons with disabilities, Aboriginals, and members of visible minorities. The stated goal, in terms of hiring the most competent individual, took a back seat. The Employment Equity Act does not set quotas. However, it does refer to 'numerical goals' to be achieved through 'reasonable progress.' Aboriginals, for instance, receive priority status for positions that directly concern them. Accordingly, appointing the most competent individual from an open competition is less important than other objectives. It is also clear that the merit principle is now used as a check against ministers forcing their deputies to make partisan appointments while providing sufficient flexibility for the government to introduce a variety of affirmative-action programs. A former senior deputy minister, the chair of the Public Service Commission, Huguette Labelle, said as much when she recently made the case that the 'Public Service Commission was created in 1918 to snuff out patronage and ensure people were hired on the basis of their experience. It was the beginning of a formal merit system.'[30]

Yet the application of the merit principle has not prevented the government from allowing partisan ministerial assistants to enter the public service on a priority status. Specifically, section 39 of Canada's Public Service Employment Act provides for the priority appointment to a permanent public-service position of a candidate with three years of service as a partisan political assistant. No such provision exists in Australia or Britain. Ministerial assistants can be (and many have been over the years) appointed to a position without competition, if they meet established qualifications for the position.

One senior official with the Public Service Commission reports that the practice began in earnest during the Trudeau years.[31] Nor did it change when ministerial assistants began to occupy more senior level positions during the Mulroney years (for example, chiefs of staff were ranked at the assistant deputy ministers). Today, executive assistants in ministerial offices are classified at the senior executive 2 or 3 levels (just below assistant deputy ministers) for the purpose of priority appointments to the Public Service Commission.

Someone appointed on a priority basis at a junior level will be exposed to public-service values before he or she occupies an executive position. However, it is different for someone who was hired in part for his or her ties to the party in power and who sits in a minister's office one day, looking after the partisan interests of the minister, but the next day occupies a senior position in the public service, expected to have lost all partisan interests overnight. Pierre Tremblay, former executive assistant to Public Works Minister Alfonso Gagliano, was accused by the auditor general of having an 'appalling disregard' for rules and regulations in approving government advertising contracts as director general in the department.[32]

The ability of partisan political advisers to enter the public service and the lack of clarity vis-à-vis the merit principle further muddle the space traditionally occupied by public servants. It is difficult to imagine that an adviser who has served as chief of staff or executive assistant to a minister for three years and established strong ties with other ministers and their staff can overnight jettison partisan political interests and fully embrace the professional and non-partisan values of the public service. One can assume that Alfonso Gagliano felt that having his for-mer executive assistant as director general, responsible for government advertising contracts, would better serve his party's political interests than installing a career public servant who had come up through the ranks. One questions whether former executive assistants can enter the public service and declare, like a former senior official, 'It is a matter of perfect indifference to me which (political party) is in power.'[33]

Françoise Ducros resigned as director of communications for Prime Minister Chrétien after her reference to U.S. President George W. Bush as a 'moron' had dominated the media for several days. She declared in her letter of resignation that her plans were to 're-enter the public service.' The prime minister wrote to Ducros to acknowledge her desire to 're-integrate into the public service a few weeks earlier than anticipated.'[34] On the day of her resignation, the *Globe and Mail* described her in an editorial as 'fiercely partisan.'[35] Yet no one in the media or in the Public Service Commission asked how someone so 'fiercely partisan' and occupying such a high-profile, politically partisan position could become a non-partisan, professional public servant. It appears that the dividing line has become so muddied that few people even ask such questions.

Nonetheless, career officials maintain that the merit principle is the 'line in the sand' separating things political from things administrative. It even impinges on the doctrine of ministerial responsibility. As we saw above, ministers are individually accountable to Parliament for the management of their departments, except vis-à-vis human resources, notably staffing. The Financial Administration Act (section 7) explains that 'personnel management in the public service of Canada, including the determination of the terms and conditions of employment of persons employed therein' and 'the organization of the public service of Canada or any portion thereof, and the determination and control of establishment therein,' is the responsibility of a committee of ministers – the Treasury Board. Accordingly, a committee of ministers, not individual ministers, deals with such matters as classification, compensation, and employment equity. In addition, ministers collectively or individually are left out of staffing, because the law gives authority to make appointments to the Public Service Commission, which, for staffing, is under the control of Parliament, not of ministers.

What is new is that the public service has in certain areas become self-governing, not only for promotions but also in such areas as classification, which affects pay and compensation. The message to 'let managers manage' has forced the Treasury Board and its secretariat to decentralize some authority to line departments and agencies. Deputy ministers, for example, have received considerable decision-making authority in managing financial and human resources, including classification. It has left the Treasury Board and its secretariat uncertain about their role as guardian of the public purse. They have sought to promote a tentative 'softer' approach in their relations with departments and agencies in their desire to embrace a more modern business-management model and to provide more decision-making authority to line departments and agencies. They have attempted to do this by having fewer *policies* and by processing fewer transactions from departments, and they have succeeded. In 1983, the Treasury Board issued 6,000 decisions.[36] In 1987, the number had dropped to 3,500.[37] By 1997 it had fallen still further, to 1,100.[38] Today, it is less than 1,000.[39] Fewer Treasury Board decisions means that decisions are pushed down to departments. There are fewer government-wide controls on financial and human resources, and the Treasury Board has vacated an important part of its traditional mandate.

'Classification creep' is not new. However, it is much more prevalent of late (see Tables 9.1 and 9.2). In addition, a variety of new positions have emerged at senior levels – notably, associate assistant deputy minister, associate deputy minister, and senior associate deputy minister. 'Associate' positions became relatively common some thirty years ago, during the Trudeau era, and at first they were limited to associate deputy ministers. The role was to complement the work of a deputy minister who may have had strong skills in policy but not in management. Today, there are nineteen associate deputy ministers, as well as three deputy secretaries in the PCO who are classified at that level. In addition, there are eighteen associate assistant deputy ministers.[40] Central-agency officials were not able to tell me the total number of associate directors general or associate directors. A second position at the level of associate deputy minister (i.e., senior associate deputy minister) has been created in recent months.

One can only imagine what Max Weber would make of this development.[41] He sought to define in specific terms how a bureaucratic organization should function. He insisted that officials should be organized in a clearly defined hierarchy of offices; that each office should have a clearly, legally defined sphere of competence; that work in the office can constitute a career; and that officials are subject to strict and systematic descriptions and controls in the conduct of their office. Weber saw distinct roles and responsibilities not only for government departments, but also for each position, so that the incumbents would understand clearly what was expected of them and then be held to account for their activities. Weber's bureaucracy was designed to operate on the basis of office hierarchy, with clear lines of authority and subordination. Hierarchy and technical skills are important for a host of reasons. Defining the necessary technical skills not only ensures an efficient organization but also insulates it from 'dilution by influences from outside and corruption from within the organization.'[42] Hierarchy provides clear lines of authority, through which commands can be transmitted, and allows 'calculability of results' for those in positions of authority.[43] Moreover, a hierarchical division of responsibility and authority ensures that the higher office does not take over the work of the lower and also gives the 'governed' a clear line for appealing 'the decision of a lower office to the corresponding superior authority.'[44] Creating new 'associate positions' muddles the distinct spaces Weber envisaged for every box in departmental organizational charts.

If one wanted to document a lack of management coherence, consistency, and discipline in government, one would need to look no further than a Treasury Board initiative of 1989. The secretariat announced with considerable fanfare that it had launched a new initiative to 'cut executive-level jobs in a bid to improve morale and operations.' It expressed concern that the executive category had grown to 2,562 members and argued that 'if you take a whole layer out of the management pyramid, then the managers below automatically gain greater control over their operations.'[45] Twelve years later the secretariat made no mention of this line of thinking as new management and new associate positions emerged in every department and as the executive category grew by over 1,200 members.

Few people, if any, in either central agencies or line departments would deny that classification creep has affected human-resources management. It has benefited mostly Ottawa-based officials and those concerned with policy and the interdepartmental policy process, not program managers and front-line workers.

I put the following question to two deputy ministers and one associate deputy in February–March 2002: how does one explain classification creep? They all argued that it was the price to pay to keep competent people in place. Although the classification system is designed to assess positions, not individuals, it is relatively easy for an incumbent to rationalize his or her qualification to a new classification. As one official observed, the 'personnel system has been transformed into a personal system.' He argued that the government-wide wage freeze imposed during the mid-1990s forced deputy ministers to find other ways to award pay increases to the more senior officials, and reclassification was the only way to do so. He added: 'We did what we had to do to manage the organization, and reclassifying some senior positions was the price to pay to keep things going and to get things done.'[46] The job-classification system seems to be in disarray. For example, the government announced in May 2002 that it was scrapping its ten-year, $100-million effort to establish a 'universal classification' system.[47] Job classifications are now viewed as a minor administrative requirement that departments can easily get around by hiring the right consultant to do the necessary paperwork.

Officials down the line, while acknowledging that reclassification does provide pay increases, point out that it is a great deal easier for a deputy minister to agree to a reclassification than to deny it. The deputy minister can no longer blame the Treasury Board for turning down a reclassification request, given that authority now lies in his or her own hands. No market discipline influences the decision, and there is little advantage in saying 'No.' But there are plenty of reasons for saying 'Yes' – not least, having happy senior officials. Deputy ministers are incredibly busy, and they would much sooner spend their energy and efforts on other, more pressing and difficult issues. Saying 'Yes' means that someone else will look after the paperwork – probably an outside consultant – and a happier management team will result; saying 'No' could mean an unhappy senior manager and possibly a need to initiate staffing action if the disgruntled official decides to go elsewhere. Both deputy ministers and senior officials down the line told me that, everything considered, reclassifying senior positions does not cost the treasury a lot of money. But when I asked about total cost, no one seemed to know. When I asked if classification creep was not a way for the senior bureaucracy to ignore the wishes of ministers in their decision to impose spending restraint resulting from the program review, no one seemed to want to answer the question.

This is a major departure from a parsimonious public service and a Treasury Board closely watching departmental operations and spending. It is a great deal easier for deputy ministers to let things slip by under program budgeting than it was under line-item budgeting. They need to worry only about performance evaluation, but this begs the question: can one evaluate the performance of a deputy minister based on the number of positions reclassified in the department? The Treasury Board cannot reinstate firm controls over such matters as job classification: government operations today are much more complex, and virtually everyone in and out of government has embraced 'empowerment' and 'letting managers manage.' The public service cannot go home again. But how to hold the government – a large and complex machine, where a variety of discretionary decisions take place at all levels – to account? This is where Parliament comes in.

Parliament: What's an MP to Do?

Home for Parliament is probably not what many Canadians, including some MPs themselves, believe it to be, and properly defining the role of Parliament could well constitute a useful contribution in itself. A Westminster-style parliamentary system involves party government and responsible government. Responsible government means that cabinet takes charge of the government's legislative program and holds all prerogative powers and that ministers have authority over the bureaucracy. Parliament does not, cannot, and should not govern. Rather, its central purpose is to legislate and to hold the government to account.

That said, it is not true that Parliament has no power or influence. It clearly occupies a central place in the country's political life. As R. MacGregor Dawson once observed, the House of Commons 'can speak, as no body in the democracy can pretend to speak for the people ... It serves as the people's forum and the highest political tribunal.'[48] It is the country's great debating chamber and the only national institution with direct political ties to all communities. It enables communities to organize themselves behind a political voice, and, once elected, that voice has the right to be heard in Parliament, however unwelcome it might be to other communities or to other voices. In Canada, communities are free to elect even people dedicated to breaking up the country, and they can make full use of the Commons to promote their message. The House also plays a role in creating an alternative government by having in its ranks and on the opposition benches leaders and their parties ready to assume power. And Parliament also provides the personnel for cabinet – a not-inconsequential role. It enables the formation of a government from the majority party or a coalition of parties.

The House of Commons also possesses effective tools. It can bring down the government – of course, an extremely powerful instrument, which the U.S. Congress lacks. Though rarely used, it is sometimes, as Joe Clark's government discovered to its dismay in 1979.

It is political parties, not individual MPs, that hold this power. As we saw above in chapter 2, the shift of power from MPs occurred with the rise of political parties and party government. Early students of Parliament, including John Stuart Mill, could not have predicted how the role of parties would in turn shape the role of Parliament. Party discipline and solidarity are now such that it is a national event when an MP votes against his or her party or openly challenges the leader. If the member should continue to defy the wishes of party and leader, then his or her political future will very likely be compromised.[49]

Parliament can approve mandates for the government and its spending plans, and it has the right to probe and to expose questionable activities. Parliament, in John Stuart Mill's words, has the authority to 'watch and control government, to throw the light of publicity on its acts; to compel a full exposition and justification of all of them that anyone considers questionable, to censure them if found condemnable.'[50] For this reason, if for no other, the government does not share power with the opposition. The Canadian constitution states (sections 53 and 54) that taxing and spending bills must originate with the government (i.e., cabinet ministers) and the Commons, so no opposition member can introduce money bills. Jennifer Smith puts it very well: 'This division, seemingly so innocuous, makes the institution adversarial. It is always a matter of government versus opposition.'[51] She adds: 'Early experience in the practice of responsible government quickly highlighted the utility of disciplined political parties in the search for reliable legislative majorities. It is much easier to form and maintain majority support on the basis of a disciplined, loyal cohort as opposed to a coalition of individuals who fancy themselves to be independent ... What is at stake is governing power – in that sense responsibility is a zero-sum game in which the winner, the government, takes all. Thus the incentive to form the one-party governing majority in the legislature is overwhelming.'[52]

Again, nothing new here. The fundamental principles underpinning the work of the House of Commons are as old as Canada. But things are not really so simple, and some things have changed. If nothing else, there is now a widely held consensus that Parliament's prestige and influence are diminishing.

C.E.S. Franks argues that the decline of Parliament can be viewed from two perspectives: actual measures that indicate its decline and the growing complexity of modern politics and government, which has made it much more difficult for Parliament to perform its role.[53] The first wound is largely self-inflicted, and the second includes forces that are beyond its immediate control.

Ample evidence suggests a substantial decline in the quality of parliamentary debates and in their significance to Canadians and to the government.[54] The prime minister and ministers increasingly make major announcements outside the House. Interest groups or special gatherings of one kind or another provide an ideal backdrop and also guarantee favourable reactions on the national evening news. Representatives of opposition parties are often not in attendance to add a negative spin. Contrast this with the Commons, where opposition parties can react immediately and point to flaws, real or contrived.

Parliament – no one else – decided to let television cameras in the House to record its deliberations, and it is hardly possible to overstate their impact. They have brought the House – notably question period – into Canadian homes but also pushed much of the rest of Commons work to the sidelines, at least as far as coverage is concerned. Franks reports that from 1993 to 1995 major Canadian newspapers carried only fifty-four articles of any sort about committee proceedings. He explains: 'Considering that in an average year there will be more than 500 committee hearings, this does not suggest adequate coverage or public discussion ... indicating a lack of interest in most committees.'[55]

Question period has become the only show in town. It is now both contrived and overly confrontational. But TV clips are effective and can be politically explosive. Indeed, some ministers who have lost their seats in cabinet claim that it was question period more than anything else that 'did them in.'[56] In politics, perception, not substance, is everything.

Question period seems to be a powerful means by which the opposition can hold the government to account – for some Canadians, probably the only means. Parliamentarians and the media may well agree with Canadians generally that what really matters is question period. No sooner is it over than the Commons empties. On a typical day, the presence of members immediately drops from perhaps 280 to about 25. Similarly, the press gallery and the public galleries are often packed for question period, then quickly empty once it is over.[57] Debates proceed, but it seems that no one is listening. The media and Canadians also ignore much of the work of committees.

Committees do meet, and they do review proposed legislation and departmental spending plans. But it seems that few MPs are happy with their work. One reports: 'I have found – and I say this in a non-partisan way – that if the government has its mind set that this is the direction they're going to take, it borders on being useless to be on the committee. It's just an absolute waste of time.'[58] James Gillies and Jean Pigott, two highly respected observers, write that 'while it is quite true that since the reform of Parliament in 1968 and 1969 all legislation must go to a parliamentary committee, no committee can change the intent of legislation and only the most naive believe that parliamentary committees, when they are considering legislation, will ever change or modify the legislation against the express desire of the government.'[59] According to C.E.S. Franks, 'The appearance of success by a committee may occur because the committee's report reflects the government's intentions so clearly that any claim that the committee is influencing government policy is illusory.'[60]

Success for committees, it seems, is the ability to shape or influence policy. This explains why they attach a great deal of importance and much of their limited resources to producing special reports or studies. Some of their reports have enjoyed a high public profile and forced the government to act or to respond to their suggestions and recommendations. MPs, the media, lobby groups, and many Canadians equate power and influence with the ability to shape new policy, not with the ability to hold the government to account. Bill Graham, chair of the foreign affairs committee before he was appointed minister of foreign affairs by Jean Chrétien, explained why the committee had decided to produce a report and hold public hearings on Canadian–U.S. integration. 'Ultimately the purpose of the parliamentary committee report is to put it in the House and have the government give a response to it. It forces the government to come down and say this is our policy on that.'[61] It looks as if the House is trying to be a major actor in the policy-making realm traditionally occupied by the government, albeit with limited success.

A recent survey of leading private and government executives is quite revealing. It concludes that backbench MPs are 'almost irrelevant.'[62] Only 7 per cent of senior officials and only 12 per cent of private-sector executives surveyed felt that MPs had influence (Table 9.3). The respondents were also asked to compare the influence of players today as against five years ago. There is a consensus that the 'influence of the Prime Minister's Office, cabinet ministers and their political staff, and deputy ministers is increasing, while the influence of the Members of the House of Commons ... and less senior public servants is perceived to be declining.'[63]

Table 9.3
Influences on decision making, by position, 2000

	Private sector (%)	Public sector (%)
Cabinet ministers	63	81
Prime Minister's Office	60	76
Deputy ministers or equivalent	52	80
Cabinet committees	41	50
Assistant deputy minister or equivalent	37	57
Members of the House of Commons	12	7
Directors or equivalent	12	11
Parliamentary committee	12	11
Other levels within the public service	7	5

* The question put was: 'How would you assess the current extent of influence over federal government decision making of the following?' This question was put to corporate executives responsible for government relations in Canada's top 800 corporations, to corporate members of the Public Policy Forum, and to 513 senior government officials in the positions of deputy minister, associate deputy minister, and agency executive director. The survey was produced by Public Policy Forum, October 2000.

Backbench MPs may want access to policy-making levers or to influence new policy measures, but the government will invariably guard such access with great care and will even hesitate to use parliamentary committees to shape public opinion. Interest and research groups seem more trustworthy because they are not always on the lookout for ways to embarrass the government. As Jonathan Malloy explains, 'The main reason that parliamentary committees may not be well-suited for policy-making is the high level of partisanship found in the modern Westminster system, and it is ironic that partisanship is even more prevalent in the Canadian than in the British House of Commons.'[64] Thus, given the 'influence' criterion, it is very difficult for committees to succeed in their work. History, however, does not record a time when Parliament or its committees had their hand on the policy-making levers. Accordingly, Parliament cannot go back to this golden era because it never existed.

But what about the capacity of the House of Commons to hold the government to account and to scrutinize its proposed activities? Here it falls far short of the mark. On this issue, there was a time when it had a much greater capacity to do so.

It is necessary here to recall a few points that I made earlier. Issues today are far more complex and interwoven than they were forty years ago. For this reason, and because parliamentary time has become a precious commodity in Ottawa, the government has abandoned detailed legislation in favour of very broadly stated laws that say precious little about what will be done. A good part of the legislative power that once belonged to Parliament is pushed down to the government, which makes detailed regulations. When Parliament reviews and scrutinizes proposed legislation, it is in fact looking at broadly stated intentions that do not invite detailed reviews, because bills are now drafted with clauses enabling regulation rather than defining activities. Fifty years ago, legislation established in fairly clear terms how a government program would operate and defined boundaries within which career officials would operate and make decisions. Today, this is no longer the case.

Parliament is no match for the government. MPs have to consider a multitude of issues, departmental spending plans, and a variety of proposed legislative measures, but they have limited resources. Their committees have only a few staff members who are junior in rank and preoccupied more with logistics than with substance. The staff is supplied from the permanent establishment of the clerk of the House, which usually assigns four generalists to each committee – clerk, junior clerk, committee assistant, and committee secretary.[65] There is no reclassification creep here. Committees can also draw on the research branch of the Library of Parliament. But staff members have to cope with a variety of requests from both Houses of Parliament dealing with every area of government activity. They do not have easy access to departmental briefings and data and are not invited to participate in interdepartmental consultations, which are off limits not only to MPs but also to their staff and to the non-partisan research staff of the Library of Parliament.

The standing committee structure still attempts to break things down by department, while the government now seeks to deal with major issues from a horizontal perspective, while Parliament and its committees, for the most part, still consider issues from a departmental perspective. A serious review of proposed departmental plans would permit MPs to poke their noses in more than one department, which the committee structure does not easily allow.[66]

The departmental structure, as J.E. Hodgetts explains in his widely read *The Canadian Public Service: A Physiology of Government*, provided a coherent basis for organizing government activities. As we saw above in chapter 2, Hodgetts argued that a 'coherent description of programme allocation can best be achieved by adopting broad functional categories for the basic responsibilities of government.' He listed several such categories, and he traced the evolution of departments through these lenses. Departments, even as recently as thirty years ago, had fairly clear mandates and a distinct turf to protect. In addition, the public-administration literature applauded these well-defined mandates. Luther Gulick had a simple machinery-of-government test or question to guide policy makers: 'little bleeding.'[67] Although departments were hardly ever water-tight and self-contained, they could go about their work with limited concern about the work of their counterparts. They protected their turf because they occupied a fairly well articulated space. Today, departments 'bleed' profusely and government policies and programs are increasingly linked together. Indeed, as we saw above, the ability to network and to work horizontally is now widely applauded by senior career officials, including the clerk of the Privy Council and secretary to the cabinet. The government simply cannot go back to an earlier era, and the implications for holding ministers and departments accountable are far-reaching.

The Power of the Purse

In Britain the basis of the growth of parliamentary power in relation to the monarch was Parliament's power of the purse, exercised through the voting of supply. In theory, voting supply remains an invaluable instrument to enable the House to scrutinize government plans. There was a time when the Commons did make effective use of the estimates process to review government plans in detail and to establish guidelines to hold the government accountable. This is much less the case today in Britain and Canada. We saw above that restructuring of the estimates curtailed the capacity of the House of Commons in Canada to ask specific questions about the rationale for increasing individual salaries, enlarging departmental organizations, raising operating costs, or expanding program spending. Information accompanying the estimates is now complex, voluminous – and, in the eyes of many, convoluted – and it not easily accessible to MPs or their staff.

Departmental officials do appear before standing committees, yet discussion there centres on the information provided by them in the estimates. One deputy minister explains candidly that the estimates process reminds him 'of Brezhnev and the old Soviet Union. Workers pretended to work and the Government pretended to pay them. We pretend to provide full information to Parliament and MPs pretend to hold us accountable.'[68] Even if the information provided was clear and concise, scrutinizing proposed departmental plans and holding the departments to account are difficult. We saw earlier that there is a high turnover of MPs at election time in Canada. Inexperienced MPs with limited access to expert staff face long-serving officials who are well versed in the ways of government and who have ready access to expertise and the elaborate interdepartmental consultative process.

When the government submits details to the House to accompany the estimates, it casts them in terms of program evaluation. But it seems that program evaluation is always a work in progress, for both long-established departments and new agencies. For example, the Canadian Food Inspection Agency was created on 1 April 1997, bringing together nineteen programs and 4,500 staff members from four departments. Some programs had been in place for a long time, including the Canadian Agricultural Products Act and Meat Inspection Act. The agency tabled a 'Corporate Business Plan' in Parliament in early 1998. The document provided an overview 'of the performance management framework, including objectives, strategies and expected results.' But it added that 'because the performance management framework, including measurement and reporting systems, is not yet fully implemented, only limited information to assess performance against the Corporate Business Plan [is available].' It reports that 'the agency needs to find effective ways to inform Parliament and the public about how well it is carrying out its inspection responsibilities.'[69] In its annual report for 2000–01, the agency's head wrote: 'We concur with the Auditor General's finding that further improvements are required to the performance information in this Annual Report ... We acknowledge the work still to be undertaken by the Agency to achieve a more fully developed performance report.'[70] Program evaluation, it seems, has never penetrated the bureaucracy.

Other developments have undermined Parliament's ability to oversee the government's spending plans. Under the banner of new public management, several new tools have empowered career officials in their relations with Parliament. Departments now can carry forward budget surpluses, which allows officials to develop a more managerial relationship with Parliament. These surpluses, however, disappear in a sea of information that departments submit to Parliament every year in parts I, II, and III of the estimates and in other reports.

Whatever the reason, MPs, including those on the Public Accounts Committee, take little interest in such reports and rarely discuss in detail the performance of a department and its programs. In any event, committees do not have the resources to pore over documents for MPs and to investigate performances.

There is another, perhaps deeper, problem at play here. MPs are interested in issues that have a political content. Cartloads of information on program evaluation and performance are beside the point. For MPs, accountability is about politics and responsiveness. Performance measurement meanwhile seeks to de-emphasize politics in a highly political environment.

MPs are always on the lookout to score political points. Career officials know this probably better than anyone. Their primary loyalty is to the government, and this is much more obvious in Canada than it is, for example, in the United States. Career officials regard MPs as real or potential adversaries to be helped as little as possible. They see every reason in keeping as quiet as possible about any real or potentially politically sensitive issue.[71] As this study explains, this can mean anything and everything.

Senior officials wish to avoid providing targets to the opposition. Failures in administration and inability to reach performance targets could offer the opposition inviting opportunities to score political points and embarrass the government. Performance measures – if they could ever work properly in the public sector – could help administrators make better decisions in non-political areas, but they can provide ammunition to the opposition. The challenge is to identify non-political areas in the public sector. It is difficult to imagine many, however, so long as they can be raised in question period.

There is one accountability mechanism that the government can hardly control – question period. Many observers see it as the only such instrument that works. The nature of question period, as we have seen, illuminates the mistake-avoiding culture of the bureaucracy and its deeply ingrained notion that it must avoid embarrassing ministers and catching the government off guard.

Much is expected of question period. It is the centrepiece of parliamentary life. It provides good political theatre. It gives the opposition rare opportunities to expose scandals and the impact of misguided policies. If opposition MPs can uncover enough scandals and wrongdoings, Canadians may vote the government out of office in the next election. Question period, under the watchful eye of the television camera, now resembles a permanent election campaign. It does serve as an effective safeguard against all kinds of abuse. All career officials and ministers have or should have it in the back of their minds when they face a controversial decision. Still, it is inadequate as the main instrument of accountability. Parliament is too weak and lacking in expertise and resources, and government is now too big and takes too many administrative decisions, for question period to provide proper scrutiny.

While it may be difficult in government to define and measure success, politicians have no difficulty in establishing failure: the prime minister intervening for a constituent with the head of a crown corporation; a minister exerting pressure on a deputy minister to award a consulting contract to a friend or a political ally; an internal audit that suggests misspending of public funds; or windows on a government building prematurely replaced. The media, access-to-information legislation, and leaks provide the grist for the mill of opposition parties. Forty years ago, the government used central controls to prevent inefficiency and waste. Today, central controls have been reduced, and inefficiencies are ferreted out by audits, access to information, the media, and question period. The headline of the *Ottawa Citizen* on 16 November 2002 read in bold letters, 'HRDC's $16 M computer bungle.'[72] Such banners are now all too common. Accountability seems little more than a quest for sleaze and embarrassing administrative miscues. The media and access-to-information legislation fuel the search, and question period is 'an ideal' venue to expose it. One can reveal sleaze by pointing to tangible wrongdoings and by identifying who did what. In this sense, it is distinctive since both the wrongdoings and the individuals responsible can be identified. The recurring headlines about waste and inefficiency point to the irrelevance of evaluation reports. Input costs remain central to accountability in government, and no one can still claim that the moral authority of the civil service is based on its ability to be parsimonious.

Still, the House of Commons has full control of most of its own processes and procedures. There are other things, however, over which it has little control. We have seen that democratic institutions in the Western world – and the Canadian Parliament is no exception – have fallen into some degree of disrepute. The environment in which Parliament has to operate has also changed. The focus of public opinion, as expressed through public-opinion surveys, has empowered Canadians, as recent attempts to amend the constitution have shown. Citizens have less need to rely on MPs to voice their concerns and in the late 1980s and early 1990s most MPs were simply bystanders with limited influence when Canadians pondered whether or not to amend their constitution. Voters decided that they could not depend on their MPs to promote their views: if a majority of MPs had had their way, the Charlottetown Accord would be part of the constitution today.

The business community now operates in a global market, and parts of it can in theory at least 'vote with their feet.' To business, accountability means something vastly different today from what it did forty years ago. Business people can now look to several forums, not just to the House of Commons, to promote their interests. We saw above that alegiance to parties has declined, while powerful movements for the environment, women's issues, Aboriginal issues, and so on, have emerged. Forty years ago perhaps the House of Commons (and the provincial legislatures) could hold everyone and everything in government to account, but this is no longer the case and probably never could be again.

What then is the proper role of an MP, and what can he or she do? There was a time when if a person wanted to have a hand in governing the country he or she might become an MP and eventually rise to minister. This is less obviously so today. Parliament now has to compete with a private sector that has fewer rules and regulations, with think tanks and research institutes, and with lobbying firms that have lucrative contracts to influence public policy. Think tanks and lobby groups are free to probe and to question government departments and in effect to hold them to account. Because they do not have partisan political views, they seem to many to be legitimate policy actors. One has only to scan daily newspapers to see that representatives of think tanks or research centres get invitations to comment on public-policy issues, not MPs.

MPs themselves have become increasingly uncertain about their own role. Some look to the United States and see no reason why they cannot have the kind of direct influence that members of Congress have. There, representatives and senators are not simply mouthpieces for party leaders. They speak their minds, represent their constituents, and vote with their conscience on legislation. The difference, of course, is that Congress is not a parliament.

Other Canadian MPs have sought to influence public policy by participating, like other interested observers, in public hearings. Sometimes, however, they have been shut out from this process. Liberal MP Carolyn Bennett asked to appear before the Romanow Commission on the future of health care, but she was turned down. A medical doctor by training, Dr Bennett held a town hall–type meeting in her Toronto riding to gather views from her constituents to present to the commission. But the commission informed her that it did not have sufficient time to allow rank-and-file elected representatives to make presentations at the public hearings. Some opposition MPs quickly jumped to her defence. For example, Keith Martin, an Alliance MP and also a medical doctor, labelled the decision 'ridiculous.'[73]

MPs are also ill-equipped to compete in the new public-policy environment. They had a difficult enough time holding the government to account when policy and decision making flowed up vertically and when departmental estimates were presented in a simple and accessible fashion. Matters, as this study demonstrates, are vastly different today.

Jonathan Malloy recently reviewed how technology is changing the relationship between MPs and public servants. He reports that civil servants are able to communicate with each other much more quickly now and that citizens have more opportunities than ever to communicate their views to their governments. He adds that many of the recent efforts in implementing new communication technologies have been designed to improve the relationship between public servants and citizens. Little, however, has been said about the role of legislators, even though, as he points out, their 'ombudsman function is a fundamental and distinctive characteristic of Canadian politics.'[74] Malloy reports that communications between Canadians and their MPs are much more frequent today than forty years ago (as MPs play an ombudsman role), but that MPs and public servants do not communicate with each other as often as one may assume. He quotes MPs, who suggest that 'most departments go into a panic when they find you're a member ... They want you out, to go through the Minister's Office.' One MP observed simply, 'When an MP contacts a public servant immediately red flags go up unless you've got a pretty secure employee.'[75]

MPs have three comparative advantages: question period is particularly useful to the opposition benches, the capacity to obtain projects for their ridings is available particularly to the government side, and MPs can act as a kind of ombudsman for constituents. This last ability can strengthen an MP's chances for re-election. David Docherty quotes one MP: 'Helping people will not get me re-elected. But not doing it will sure get me defeated.'[76] In addition, promoting the interest of his or her constituency will avoid conflict with the party leader, the party, and cabinet ministers. Yet, in their attempts to tilt government programs towards their constituencies, they are stepping into administration and public servants' turf. Yet MPs operate in an institution and in a public-policy environment that leave them little else to do. Government has become too big and too horizontal, and the information flowing from it to Parliament is too complex to enable them to hold government to account, as was possible eighty or forty years ago. Robert Stanfield describes the dilemma: 'There is, I believe, only one choice. We can accept the loss of parliamentary re-sponsible government or we must accept a limited role for our federal government.'[77] Canada has tried another approach since Stanfield wrote these words in 1978 – it tried cheating to get around basic rules, precedents, and other requirements governing national political and administrative institutions. There have been many instances when politicians and career officials decided to cheat rather than to deliver their side of the bargain.

A Bargain Undone

A political storm erupted in Parliament around Defence Minister Art Eggleton during the Afghanistan war in 2002. He told the prime minister and the House of Commons that any questions regarding the treatment of prisoners was purely hypothetical because Canadian troops had taken no prisoners. At the same time, newspapers carried photos depicting the capture of prisoners by soldiers from Canada's Joint Task Force (JTF). A few days later, Eggleton informed the prime minister and then the House that Canadian troops had indeed taken prisoners, whom they had turned over to the Americans.

Immediately, opposition parties called for Eggleton's resignation on the grounds that he had misled Parliament. The issue dominated question period for several days, and the media ran a number of front-page stories on the matter. At the urging of the Canadian Alliance, the matter was turned over to the House of Commons Standing Committee on Procedure and House Affairs. The issue boiled down to who knew what and when, and the search was on to find out when career officials briefed Eggleton on the matter. The committee determined that Eggleton did not inform the prime minister or the Commons until eight days after he was first informed that Canadian forces had captured suspected Al-Qaeda members and handed them over to U.S. authorities. The House committee's report stated that Eggleton had made a mistake but that he had not intentionally misled the Commons. Predictably, the Liberal majority on the committee supported the report's conclusion, while the opposition parties denounced it.[78]

The controversy suggests that when a mistake becomes public, some career officials no longer hesitate to abandon their anonymity and come forward with their version of events. That is, so long as the problem remains within the government and under control, senior officials will make every effort to protect their ministers. Once it is in the public domain, it is a different story. In this case, senior bureaucrats made it clear that they had properly briefed their minister within twenty-four hours of the prisoners' capture. They went further and revealed that it took Eggleton more than one briefing to understand the situation. One official explained publicly, 'If I can put it in sort of visual language, there was a click after the minister was briefed three times.'[79]

The media ran a number of stories asking why military officers refused to 'take heat' for their political bosses?[80] Doug Bland, head of a defence-management program at Queen's University, was pleased: 'Canadians ought to be enormously proud of the integrity and forthrightness of their military officers.'[81] This harks back to the Somalia inquiry, held several years earlier. A Somalia teenager was tortured and killed while in the custody of Canadian soldiers. Defence Minister Kim Campbell reported that she had never been properly briefed on the matter, that there were charges of doctored military documents, and that departmental officials had made attempts to cover up the controversy. Senior military officers meanwhile were not permitted to present their version of events, and there was a 'feeling in the uniformed ranks after the Somalia inquiry that some senior officers had let the side down.'[82] The new lesson was that if charges of incompetence surfaced, they would fall on whomever was responsible, even the minister.

But this sharing of responsibility is not a one-way street. Ministers are also no longer prepared always to play by the traditional bargain. They have always preferred to assume responsibility for popular or successful initiatives, while being less enthusiastic about mistakes or failures.[83] John Manley, as minister of foreign affairs, sought to put considerable distance between himself and departmental officials after a Russian diplomat was involved in a fatal accident in Ottawa while intoxicated. In February 2001, Manley made it clear that career officials could have handled the whole affair better and that they were not as forthcoming in briefing him as they should have been about their handling of the diplomat's previous two drunk-driving charges in Canada.[84]

A heated political controversy erupted when it was discovered in October 2001 that Health Canada had purchased $1.5 million worth of anthrax drug from a Toronto firm, Apothex, thereby violating Canadian drug patent laws. Bayer Canada holds the patent. When Bayer heard about the purchase, it complained that Health Canada had violated the laws of its own government. Health Minister Allan Rock made it clear that departmental officials, not he, made the decision to purchase the drug. The *National Post* reported: 'Facing a public relations disaster, advisors to Allan Rock ... and other senior government officials said the department will blame junior workers for purchasing one million generic Cipro tablets.'[85] Sure enough, a few days later departmental 'sources' told the media that a 'junior procurement official' had made the decision, and they were not sure 'whether it was a conscious decision to go around the Patent Act, or an ignorance about the provision of the Patent Act, or a panic in the situation.'[86] Health Canada subsequently also purchased Cipro from Bayer, and, when the media lost interest in the story, the controversy died down.

It would be wrong to assume that only Liberal ministers blame career officials when things go wrong. One has to think back only to the Al-Mashat affair, which occurred under Mulroney. Although such cases do not occur daily, and some ministers (such as Jane Stewart at HRDC) are still prepared to play by the old rules, these are not by any means isolated cases.

Such cases have a number of elements in common. First, there is the negative spin. Second, the story invariably stays on the front pages of newspapers for several days and dominates question period for at least as long. Third, some career officials lose their anonymity. Indeed, because of access-to-information, the name of the officials is easy to ascertain. For example, officials at Industry Canada, in a memorandum on the fallout from the Cipro case, reported that the case was hurting Canada's investment climate. The *Globe and Mail* noted that 'the senior official whose name is on one key document as author Andrei Subzenko says the memo was a draft written by junior officials.'[87]

Not all senior officials still play by the traditional bargain. Michael Pitfield, a top-ranking career official in 1968, decided to take on a partisan role behind the scenes to support Pierre Trudeau's leadership campaign. Trudeau later named him clerk of the Privy Council and secretary to the cabinet. The appointment changed the public service, sending a powerful message to career officials down the line and serving notice that some politicians and senior officials were no longer prepared to adhere strictly to the bargain. If the prime minister and the country's top public servant could cheat on the arrangement, then what would stop others from doing the same?[88]

Retired public officials are increasingly speaking out on how things were when they served in government. For example, Fred Bennett, director of financial and economic analysis in the Industry Department, gave a media interview shortly after he retired; he claimed that senior officials would order analysts to bury questions or criticisms about whether the department should be supporting certain cases. He stated: 'Once it was perceived that the minister wanted something, then there was extreme pressure on everyone down the line not just to do it but to make it look like it should be done. They didn't want any documentation that would contradict their decision.'[89]

Emphasis on management and the introduction of new public management (NPM) have also given rise to new opportunities to cheat on the traditional model. NPM separates policy and management. Busy ministers now find it easier to ignore management issues unless they grab headlines. As a result, the public service has become more self-governing, particularly in such areas as human-resources management. The government may decide to impose a wage freeze for several years because it faces a particularly difficult fiscal situation, as occurred in 1995, when it decided to launch a program review. As we saw above, a number of senior officials simply reclassified their positions.

NPM has also shifted the traditional bargain, giving officials greater managerial space in exchange for their rendering clearer accountability for results. The bargain and ministerial responsibility do not easily square with this new approach. The prime minister and ministers still want error-free administration, and blame-avoidance still dominates thinking in departments. Ministers still prefer to talk about program goals in broad and shifting ways to avoid establishing targets for the opposition. Civil servants counter that soft performance targets are either meaningless or easily achievable.[90]

Recent years have seen charges of 'bureaucratic patronage' hurled at government managers. One MP contrasted 'political' with 'bureaucratic' patronage. 'Political patronage provides public accountability, ensuring that appointed people who share a vision with the elected government keep bureaucrats with too much inertia on their toes ... This frustration is exacerbated by the hidden patronage in government that far exceeds the transparent, accountable political patronage.'[91] Stéphane Dion, an academic turned politician, writes that 'since competency and merit are often subjective criteria, difficult to establish and verify, public servants take advantage of this fact to quietly establish their own network of contacts and patronage. It is also felt that, in the upper echelons of public administration, where officials are called upon to advise governments on major policy directions, the definition of competence is even more subjective, and leaves much room for value judgements.'[92] When the clerk of the Privy Council announced in the summer of 2001 plans to overhaul management of human resources he soon discovered that the media, political circles, and rank-and-file government employees worried about bureaucratic as much as about political patronage.[93]

The lack of objective measures for the merit principle gives managers a free hand to hire pretty well whomever they wish. Merit lies now in the eye of the beholder, and managers who look in the mirror usually like what they see. If senior officials see more merit in policy skills than in management skills, then officials perceived to have policy skills will be promoted more easily, notwithstanding the rhetoric about management and the private-sector model. Senior managers can now hire more easily or promote whomever they wish, despite stated government priorities. Who is to know, how is one to know the difference, and, if one ever did know, what could be done about it?

The traditional bargain implied a *ménage à deux* between ministers and career officials.[94] The model has evolved and now there is a *ménage à trois, ou quatre ou cinq*. The PMO and ministerial offices have been considerably strengthened. Research institutes, some think tanks, and consultants have become relevant policy actors, at least on some issues, with some consultants performing essentially the same role as permanent officials. Lobby firms and pollsters enable the prime minister and ministers to test new ideas and also the advice coming from career public servants. As Chris Hood argues, given the arrival of new actors, career officials see 'possibilities for bypassing games, as a form of cheating ... while politicians and some other civil servants may see it as a perfectly legitimate counter to cheating in the form of subtle disloyalty by top public servants in the ménage à deux minister–permanent head structure.'[95]

Interdepartmental consultation affects every policy issue except the prime minister's own and permits cheating all round. Ministers can tell the government caucus that they would like to promote bold measures but that the process will not allow them to do so. Career officials can deal with pointed questions more readily, insisting that they can push their minister's perspective only so far. An example: by one count, sixteen federal departments and over forty-five programs deal with children.[96] Given these numbers, a minister in one of the departments wishing to influence the government's agenda on children may well conclude that getting to the bottom of a question is a lot like trying to grab smoke.

Canada poses special challenges and also opportunities for cheating, given a dominant political party, such as the Liberals – the 'government party,' as Reg Whitaker describes it.[97] Long association makes some ministers and officials comfortable with each other. For career officials, getting close to the governing party is not as risky for their careers and promotion prospects as it is when parties are highly competitive and governments change frequently. Similarly, the prime minister and some of the stronger ministers, given their length of service, can become as settled in the decision-making process as are career officials. What is political and what is administrative can also become fuzzy. For example, in early 2000, the Canadian Alliance proposed to introduce a 17 per cent single-rate income tax. Political staffers in the office of the minister of finance asked the department to 'develop an argumentation why a flat tax is a bad idea and will benefit the wealthy not middle and low income people.'[98] The directive was not about a neutral, detached estimation of the merits of a single income-tax rate. It asked career officials not to speak truth to power but rather to provide a preordained response and ammunition for the Liberals to use against opponents.

Public accountability in the traditional sense has been lost in a bewildering assortment of quasi-public or quasi-private agencies or foundations. The funds provided to several foundations identified above enable the government to reduce its annual surplus by transferring money to them at the end of the fiscal year. Thus the money is regarded as spent in the last weeks of a fiscal year rather than when the money is actually handed out to groups, businesses, or individuals.[99] The government thereby circumvents basic rules of Parliament, which require it to ask the House annually for supply for non-statutory spending.

It seems impossible to return to the traditional bargain between politicians and career officials. That arrangement held many advantages, enabling ministers and officials to work together and Parliament to hold ministers and departments to account. With modern government, a vastly different public-policy environment, an increasingly horizontal policy- and decision-making process, a less deferential population, globalization, and a relatively small, open economy, there can no longer be distinct realms of political and administrative power. National political and administrative institutions have become more flexible in recent years through cheating, if nothing else. They no longer occupy distinct worlds, to the extent that they once did. What now? The next chapter seeks to answer the question.

10

Redefining Accountability

Canada's national government uses hierarchically defined lines of command and control designed to address policy issues and to deliver programs and services through compartmentalized administrative structures. Everything comes together at the political level at the top in ministerial offices, cabinet and in the Prime Minister's Office (PMO). Central agencies meanwhile provide the link between the civil service and politicians as well as support and advice to the prime minister, cabinet, and its committees.

The notion of establishing what we today term *space* and *boundaries* to define responsibilities was evident everywhere as Canada's national political and administrative institutions took form. Ministerial responsibility, hierarchical organization, departmentalization, division of labour, specialization, division of responsibility, the merit principle, specific responsibilities assigned in the form of job descriptions, and federal–provincial responsibilities defined by the constitution all set out boundaries. Boundaries serve many purposes. They determine who has legitimate access to certain decision arenas. They control departmental mandates and define who is responsible for what. They enable those at senior levels to exercise control and to hold subordinates to account for their decisions and activities. Ministers and officials are accountable only for outcomes or processes that they can control, which necessitates a clearly defined space in which they can operate.[1] In brief, institutional structure matters because it provides specific roles to policy actors.

The first part of this book describes how the early architects of Canada's political and administrative institutions looked mostly to British experience. Part II shows how various forces have been chipping away at these formulations. We have now reached the point where it is no longer possible to isolate and control public-policy issues within clearly delimited boundaries – most public issues no longer fit within a single government let alone a single department. Administration is increasingly being muddied by forces that include business-management culture, the growth and expanded mandates of oversight bodies, and deputy ministers' responsibilities for managing in a new political and policy-making environment. Many changes have been subtle, and elements may resemble what existed some thirty years ago. However, as a group they create new realities in the public service and in its relation to the political level. Meanwhile, there has been very little effort to review the role of members of the House of Commons and ministers in this brave new world. Debate about MPs' proper role has seemingly responded to Pierre Trudeau's observation that 'MPs are nobodies fifty yards away from Parliament Hill.' Some people, including MPs, insist that they are now nobodies even on the Parliament Hill.[2]

Drawing boundaries establishes space or territory within which people can operate but also offers a visualizable rendering of how things work. Removing them negates that understanding, and, as O.C. McSuite writes, without boundaries in public administration, we 'end up with a big conceptual mess.'[3] This is true particularly if the institutions do not develop a new frame of reference and new boundaries. This chapter reviews briefly how government has removed boundaries. It then explores limits and options. I hope thereby to launch a debate on the state of Canada's national political and administrative institutions. It finally anticipates the new configuration that will limit politics, government, and citizens.

Removing Boundaries

A Brief Review

Boundaries in Canadian politics and public administration have in recent years been assaulted from many directions. That is, the spaces that politicians and public servants once occupied either have been opened up to outsiders or have become shared territory. Twenty federal departments were directly involved recently in planning new measures to promote development in Canada's north. The process took nearly two years to run its course and involved extensive consultations with stakeholders and a number of consultants' reports. This is typical of how Ottawa now handles major policy issues.[4] It also shows why the one individual with the power to do something about this complex process – the prime minister – would decide simply to ignore it whenever he or she decides to pursue an important policy goal. When the issue is not on his or her radar screen, the process works just fine from his or her perspective, because it ensures that things run on their tracks and reduces the chances of creating a political problem for the government.

Access-to-information legislation has shed light on what was once a private realm that ministers and career officials occupied in a village-like atmosphere. E-government is opening up governance by enabling citizens to access information more readily and also promotes two-way communication between officials and citizens. Ministers, in their attempts to make the machinery of government more responsive, have enlarged their offices and upgraded the status of their partisan staff. But that is not all. Partisan staffers, as we saw above, may enter the public service in senior management positions on a priority basis after working three years in a ministerial office. They then become senior executives, expected in theory to embrace instantly the values of a professional, non-partisan public service. I asked officials with the Public Service Commission how many ministerial exempt staff members have joined the public service over the past ten or twenty years, but they told me that this information has not been compiled.

New public management (NPM) is also breaking down boundaries that once served to guard the traditional bargain between politicians and career officials. Several time-tested administrative principles underpin the traditional bargain: merit, permanence, and anonymity. Merit has been adjusted in recent years to accommodate political objectives so as to pursue various affirmative-action measures. Although permanence does not apply to the army of consultants now inhabiting Ottawa, they provide policy advice and perform functions similar to those of career officials. Mandarins, most notably deputy ministers, are today shedding their anonymity and becoming public figures in their own right. But even career officials down the line have become active participants in the elaborate public consultative process and thereby abandoned their anonymity.

The notion of empowering clients is also breaking down traditional boundaries that separate agents and providers inside government from consumers of public services outside. As Andrew Stark writes, NPM is designed to 'fuse the roles of provider and payer,' which invariably breaks down boundaries.[5] In increasing the role and voice of customers in service delivery, governments are converting citizens into clients, who presumably have clout vis-à-vis standards of service and quality.[6] But that is not all. Committees of citizens or clients may now make recommendations to ministers on specific projects, and some have been delegated full authority to make program and spending decisions.[7] In the case of the Canadian Foundation for Innovation (CFI), ministers and career officials have simply turned over all policy and decision making to committees of stakeholders. There are other similar examples.

MPs have also given up some of their traditional space. In the past, government and the House of Commons were quite good at measuring input in terms of administrative and program costs. They understood this world well: it was clear, accessible, and enabled MPs to compare departmental spending plans. Now, government and the House are not nearly as good at measuring output or evaluating programs or even the actual performance of career officials. As James March and Johan Olsen write, 'in government, whether a particular program, strategy, or practice has favorable outcomes is frequently unclear, even after the fact.'[8] If Parliament can no longer hold the government to account through the budget and estimates process, then a great deal of accountability disappears. Parliament's role since its very beginning has been to provide oversight in taxation and spending. As David E. Smith observes, 'Even though the executive initiates and determines the priorities of expenditure, its control and supervision are pre-eminently in the task of the legislature.' However, 'it is evident ... that in practice the executive ... violates that pure theory of legislative control of finances.'[9]

Agents of Parliament such as the auditor general have sought to break out of the traditional boundaries to establish new space for themselves, but not necessarily at the urging of Parliament. Indeed, they now appear to function as free agents accountable to no one. The Office of the Auditor General once had a distinct mission, with clear boundaries defining its role and responsibility. It was staffed by accountants, and its purpose was to assist the audit committee of the House. Its mandate was to report to that committee the results of its investigations of financial probity and compliance with appropriation authority.[10] Today, nearly 60 per cent of its office budget goes to what Sharon Sutherland calls 'qualitative' or 'soft reviews' that 'bear little apparent relationship to efficiency or economy in use of funds, human resources or material.'[11] Neither the office nor the media bother to explain that qualitative or soft reviews can never be as certain or as conclusive as financial audits. But such exercises enable the office to contribute to policy debates and to participate in the making of public policy. In addition, the office now often informs the media first of its findings, not Parliament. It has created its own space to carry out its work and views Parliament as just another consumer of its reports. But when a new space is created, existing ones must adjust.

The privacy commissioner held a press conference in June 2002 to announce a Charter challenge to the RCMP's video-surveillance activities in Kelowna, British Columbia. He was doing so, he explained, after being unable to persuade the solicitor general to 'exercise his responsibility and instruct the RCMP to take down the camera.'[12] His press release made no reference to consulting Parliament in initiating this action. He did report, however, that he had consulted a former justice of the Supreme Court, who, 'prior to his retirement, wrote many of the Supreme Court's most important decisions on privacy rights.'[13]

Agents of Parliament can claim to occupy a distinct, relatively self-contained space. John Reid, the information commissioner, admitted as much when he revealed that his annual reports are all but ignored by MPs 'who are more concerned with exposing political scandals.' He explained that MPs 'don't take me to task' and that he has never been grilled. He added: 'I would expect that they would want to go through my expenditures, my activities with a fine tooth comb.'[14] The chief human-rights commissioner called for new measures to 'ensure that there is direct input from MPs and senators on the level of resources and type of work we should do.'[15]

Career officials point to the courts as yet another factor that has reshaped their work over the past twenty or thirty years. A senior official at Fisheries and Oceans (DFO) reports that twenty-five years ago civil servants rarely thought about the courts as they went about their work. Today, he maintains, the courts are never far from people's mind when planning departmental activities. He explains, 'When you launch a new activity or unveil an important decision, you should always make provision for a court injunction to stop the department from moving forward.'[16] He adds: 'In 1979 there were three lawyers handling DFO legal issues. Today [i.e., May 2002], there are twenty-six lawyers handling our cases. That in itself tells you what has happened inside government.'[17] Another senior line-department official reports that he and his staff are very careful about putting things down on paper for fear that the information will be employed against the department in a future court case.[18] Civil servants in the Department of Justice confirm this development. One senior official there reveals that, despite the program review of the mid-1990s, the number of lawyers in the department responsible for 'litigation' and 'litigation avoidance' has 'more than doubled over the past ten years.'[19]

The courts have been drawn even into management issues. A senior manager with Corrections Canada reports that both employees and their unions now turn to the courts about issues that thirty years ago were quietly handled internally. It has never been easy to deal with non-performers in government. It is still more difficult today, as employees and their union representatives go to court if management initiates any action to remove anyone for non-performance. Again, senior officials at Justice reveal that the number of lawyers working on behalf of the employer in personnel-related cases has increased substantially in recent years.[20]

My consultations with career officials revealed that many government managers have simply given up trying to terminate employees on the basis of non-performance, fearing that they will have to defend their action in court. Data from the Treasury Board Secretariat appear to confirm this. In 1999–2000, 4,228 public servants were 'separated' from their employer. Some 3,289 employees either resigned or retired from the public service, but only 29 were released. In 2000–01, the total number went up slightly, to 4,270, but the number 'released' dropped to 16.[21] How this squares with the introduction of private-sector management practices has never been explained. In any event, the courts represent a new space for government managers – one that they do not know well and cannot control. They also represent one more reason why government managers can never be as free to manage as their private-sector counterparts.

Even senior public servants have turned to the courts to challenge the government or their own employer. The Supreme Court ruled that the government had to release parts of documents classified as cabinet secrets to its own lawyers who were suing the Treasury Board for a pay increase. The material in question explained why government lawyers in Vancouver were excluded from salary increases given to their Toronto-based colleagues.[22] One can easily appreciate why Canadians and even public servants could be drawn to the courts to resolve public policy issues. The courts occupy a distinct space, and they are able to strike clear decisions without reference to the porous consultative process.[23] It is a luxury that a multitude of other policy and administrative actors do not enjoy.

The Consequences

We saw in the preceding chapter that we cannot go home again. Although there is room to clarify 'space' and 'boundaries' (eliminating a number of associate positions in central agencies and line departments would be a start), it is clear that the world of village life – of the traditional bargain, of departments operating in relative isolation and successfully protecting their policy turf, of the administrator or policy specialist working away from the scrutiny of the media and unencumbered by access-to-information legislation – now belongs to the history books.

Still, this new world does not easily square with responsible government in a parliamentary system, which invariably exhibits direction control of both vertical authority and accountability. Because of the growing complexity of making policy and decisions, the 'true locus of government activity' has shifted from institutions and departments that were formal and visible (and thus occupying a distinct 'space') to those that 'are diffuse and obscure.'[24] It has moved from a traditional model of government, which rested on clearly defined offices and unbroken chains of command, to a new model that encourages career officials to step outside hierarchical constraints in search of partnerships with other departments, other governments, the private sector, stakeholders, and research institutes.[25] A horizontal perspective has always been present in cabinet and at the most senior levels of the public service. But now the work of middle-level managers has horizontal components. Political and administrative institutions, however, have been adjusted only at the margins, and there are now agencies and officials that occupy no clearly defined place on the vertical line of accountability of Westminster-style government. These include some public–private partnerships and outside policy actors, especially research centres, pollsters, lobbyists, and consultants.

How to find new boundaries and establish new spaces? As we saw above, few individuals in government still retain the power to create their own space. As for the rest, they have influence, not power. Holding influence accountable is more difficult than holding political power accountable, because it is less tangible.

Deputy ministers have probably been able to secure management space. As politicians, senior public servants, and private-sector lobby groups accepted the business-management model, deputy ministers gained new leeway to manage departmental operations. Many central controls have evaporated and senior administrators – now read 'managers' – have considerable authority to reallocate money within established spending limits, to reclassify positions, and to hire staff. Tom Kent reports that 'one of the toughest battles' that he fought with the Treasury Board when he was deputy minister at Manpower and Immigration in 1966 was to obtain more senior classification levels 'for some senior officials.'[26] Today, deputy ministers have no such battles to fight, because they effectively hold classification authority for their departments. They also have more say in staffing positions, as the Public Service Commission has delegated such authority to departments as it sought to accommodate or empower departmental managers. But this development means that one person gains space at the expense of someone else. The Association of Professional Executives in the Public Service (APEX) insists that the Public Service Commission 'has lost its independence and become part of bureaucracy which has chipped away at the ability to safeguard merit ... They have drifted into the tent that they are supposed to be keeping an eye on.'[27]

We saw in chapter 7 that deputy ministers have constantly to deal with an overcrowded policy agenda and real or potential political crises, so that management issues very often take a back seat. In addition, agents of Parliament, the courts, and access-to-information legislation have played havoc with departmental management. The business model has never been able to determine whether or not a deputy minister is a solid manager. Just as indicators of management success are difficult to establish in government, so are markers of failure. As a result, a deputy minister can approve a series of reclassifications, and few people will ask if it was a wise decision. In any event, how could one possibly know that the positions needed reclassification? There is no method to determine if the decision was wise.

The business-management model, as we saw above, overlooked the fact that removal of relatively firm, centrally prescribed controls undermines the one overarching constraint that compares to the private-business requirement to balance the books and secure a return on capital.[28] Thus, although management may have opened up in government, no mechanism exists to assess managers' performances. Government has ended up with the worst of both worlds – a vacuous management space. There is neither the brutal discipline of the marketplace to sort out non-performers nor the kind of control that outside guardians once exercised to act as a check against administrative abuses. We know about 'classification creep.' But what about other, less visible problems such as excessive travel in the age of frequent-flyer miles and free nights for frequent stays at selected hotel chains? Government may well have received more than it bargained for when it decided that management performance could actually be measured objectively – that is, apolitically. As one student of public administration points out, 'on the basis of this exalted, and fundamentally flawed assumption ... it is claimed that Parliament, or, more precisely the House of Commons can base their assessments on technical reports.'[29]

The business-management model has served senior public servants well, and there is no reason for them to turn their backs on it. An advisory committee largely from the private sector helps determine their salaries. Their pensions are more generous than ever, and they have many opportunities for employment after they retire. The porous consultative process itself has spawned a multitude of high-paying jobs in industry associations, lobbying firms, and consultancy. Networking skills – which are a function more of whom you know than of technical knowledge or sectoral expertise – are now in strong demand around Ottawa and come easy for anyone who has been a deputy minister. Such skills are essential for the upper echelon of the public service.

In the absence of a market mechanism to assess performance and management success, ministers are responsible for ensuring proper administrative and financial controls and procedures. Ministers, however, have limited interest in management issues or in apolitical assessments. In the tradition of the politics/administration dichotomy they have been told that it is best to leave management to career officials.

What ministers want in the age of access-to-information legislation and around-the-clock television news is error-free administration. They wish to avoid blatant administrative miscues that reach, for example, the front page of the *Globe and Mail* or a television news clip. Consider the following scenarios: several senior positions reclassified in a department, several unnecessary trips to Europe by a senior official in one year, or an official with twenty subordinates when ten could easily do. These do not qualify as errors that can embarrass a minister, but they are costly to taxpayers, and the introduction of the business-management model to government made no provision for controlling such developments in a non-competitive environ-ment. The result is that large and complex government departments and agencies now can determine administrative inputs and produce more needs for administrative, human, and financial resources without possessing a clear capacity to determine if these demands are truly needed. MPs may, or at least should, have an interest in administrative and financial matters. But, as this study shows, it is an area not readily accessible to them. This makes the case once more that in government 'every reform creates a new problem.'[30]

When a prime minister and his or her advisers want a clear space, they simply move everything out of reach of ministers, central agencies, departments, and career public servants, as happened when Jean Chrétien created several foundations. Crown corporations have been part of the machinery of government for some time, but these foundations are beyond Parliament's reach. The government is reverting to foundations, arm's-length agencies, and the like more often and to deal with activities traditionally housed in departments (for example, management of national parks and tax collection). It is nothing short of creating a distinct space to pursue relatively clear objectives. Traditional departments, because space is now difficult to create or maintain, attempt, as best they can, to expand their space to deliver what their ministers want and to promote their own interests. This trend is rendering the bureaucratic model and departmental structures obsolete. The original model divided policies, functions, and work into chunks or compartments and then held ministers, departments, and individuals accountable for the different pieces.[31] But here, too, every reform creates a new problem. The new model may well have given rise to self-steering organizational networks that government can no longer steer and Parliament can no longer hold to account.[32]

Removing boundaries has also made it difficult, if not impossible, to establish the true size of government.[33] Ottawa now has a multitude of think tanks, consultants, and former public servants on contract, and all are on the federal payroll in one form or another. How does one draw boundaries between the public service and private consultants when both are paid to do the same job, in some instances at the same time and even in the same office?[34] It is not at all clear how basic public-service values such as merit fit in this new model.

The model has also given rise to 'thicker government' – more management layers, more networks, more processes, more shared positions. Political direction and control are more difficult, except for a prime minister who can take charge of a handful of files. Information can get distorted on the way up as it goes through various layers and networks, and political guidance can get lost on the way down.[35] Ministers prefer a deputy minister who has intimate knowledge of the system, can work well with the centre of government, and has the ability to get proposals through the consultative decision-making process over one with sectoral expertise or who knows intimately the department, its policies, and its history. The thickening of government has reduced accountability more than any shortcomings in the doctrine of ministerial responsibility.

Limits and Options

Looking for Solutions: There Are Limits

In our search for prescriptions we must remember that in a number of instances institutional solutions to institutional problems do not exist. Some problems may not be problems at all – we may simply be looking at developments from a different perspective and a different time. Despite our concern about the state of Canadian democracy, we should never forget that some of the early architects of Canada's national political and administrative institutions held deep 'suspicions, even hostility,' towards democracy.[36] This explains why they saw little need for elaborate checks and balances.[37]

Today, Canadians and many of their political leaders are deeply suspicious of, even hostile to, anything and everything that they see as undemocratic and non-transparent. Yet we are still working with the same institutions. Democratic institutions by definition cannot always operate in a neat and tight fashion, and we can hardly define a solution that is all-encompassing, acceptable to all citizens, timeless, and able to resolve political conflicts, and easily and quickly sort out the inherent contradictions in public policies.

The country's political culture and Canadians' expectations of their institutions are still taking shape in an emerging political and policy-making environment. How else can one explain the fact that Canadians want at the same time decisive government and participatory policy making? Governance is about gaining political power, maintaining it, and holding it to account for its policies and decisions – hardly a neat and tight affair. Making policy and decisions in government is inherently political and involves bargaining and compromise. We simply do not have the knowledge to create a government system that can easily reconcile the struggles for political power and eliminate the need for bargaining and compromise. There is also none in sight.

With this caveat in mind, this study makes a number of observations designed to assist Parliament and government in an increasingly horizontal environment that can no longer define policy and decisions as clearly as they once did. Our purpose is to begin the discussions, not to end them. Our search for solutions will be slow, and we will probably revert to trying 'this and that' to see what works, what does not, and what holds promise. What is important is to launch the debate, even though it is not at all clear where it will take us. 'Governing without space' is a new phenomenon, and it will take time to develop new roles, establish standards, and promote a new domain of accountability.

That said, we can already make a number of general observations. First, the introduction of the business-management model to government operations has been a failure. The reasons: the two sectors are vastly different; the business model needs the market to determine performance, and no substitute is possible; it requires some autonomous decision-making space to operate; and in government administrative matters can quickly become highly partisan political issues. Second, rethinking the notion of space and its application to the machinery of government offers prospects to tighten political and administrative institutions and to make them more accountable and more responsive to Canadians. Third, yet another public-service reform measure is pointless. Past reform efforts have been built on fantasies rather than on theories, and one can readily appreciate the words of a mid-level public servant, 'O Lord, deliver us from further conceptualization and lead us not into new approaches.'[38] Fourth, the study suggests that we have been looking at the wrong end of the problem. Our focus should be on political actors and move from there to career officials, rather than the other way around, as experts have been doing for forty years. Fifth, we should make every effort to protect the non-partisan nature of the public service. This is one of the few constraints remaining on the power of the prime minister and his advisers, and we need, if anything, to strengthen it. Finally, we should identify ways to bring back the parsimonious culture within the public service and government operations that began to wither away some thirty years ago. It was that culture, as much as any other factor, that gave the public service credibility and standing with Canadians, and demonstrated its ability to put aside self-interest to promote the public interest.

There is no need to abandon the doctrine of ministerial responsibility. The doctrine is not what ails institutions, and doing away with it would accomplish very little. It would not strengthen the hand of political actors in their relations with career officials, increase accountability, improve policy making or government operations, or make government more responsive to Canadians. The doctrine involves a minister's duty to Parliament to account for the work of his or her department or agency and does not mean that he or she must take the blame for every mistake or bad decision made by a career official. The doctrine holds career officials responsible for their activities, although they are not directly accountable to Parliament. Thus there is no need to muddy further the space that ministers now occupy in Parliament or to give public servants access or force them to become participants in a space that is not only political and highly visible but also highly partisan. We note once again that partisanship is more prevalent in the Canadian than in the British House of Commons. The doctrine remains sufficiently flexible to accommodate new requirements and even a redefinition of space in the machinery of government. For example, it still works for crown corporations.

Many commentators who are calling for the doctrine to be jettisoned may not fully understand its application. Nicholas d'Ombrain explains: 'The confusion between a minister's conventional responsibility and his or her accountability for the exercise of power needs to be clarified. Ministers are required to answer to Parliament ... for all activities of the state, subject only to the requirements of the law and the rules of natural justice. This applies to all activities of the state, including those held at arm's length from ministers. The basis of this requirement is the basis of parliamentary democracy, namely that Parliament is entitled to know how the power of the state, which it has assigned, is being used.'[39] This is what the doctrine means and nothing more. It does not mean that ministers are accountable for the exercise of power assigned to others. It is now accepted that it is unreasonable to hold a minister personally responsible for the errors of administrative subordinates and that career officials can and should answer to parliamentary committees for administrative matters, but not for policy or politically controversial issues.

To abandon the doctrine would, as has often been argued, force senior administrators to defend themselves in a political arena and possibly compromise their political impartiality even further and hence their tenure in office.[40] Little would be gained, and a great deal could be lost to good government, should public servants lose still more anonymity. In any case, it is difficult to imagine how public servants could be directly accountable to Parliament without creating a corresponding space or a positive authority for them. Our system vests departmental powers, duties, and functions in ministers, not in departments and agencies, through statute. Britain did for a time (c. the 1850s) vest powers in boards and agencies but gave up the practice because it was difficult to hold them to account.

Nick d'Ombrain has also defined 'responsibility,' 'accountability,' and 'answerability.' First, 'Responsibility refers to the constitutional relation-

ship of ministers to the House of Commons; and, secondly, to the assignment and exercise of the powers of the state by elected and non-elected
officials.' Second, 'Accountability refers to the way in which office-holders, elected and non-elected, explain the actions taken through the use
of powers conferred on them by Parliament or delegated to them by
ministers or other office-holders.' Third, 'Answerability refers to the
relationship of ministers to the House of Commons when providing
information about the actions taken by non-elected office-holders in
whom Parliament has vested the powers necessary for such actions;
and, secondly, to the way in which departmental officials, in particular
deputy ministers, support the accountability of ministers principally
through appearances before parliamentary committees.'[41]

These definitions provide clarification about the application of the
doctrine of ministerial responsibility, which is sorely needed in the light
of recent developments and comments about its continued usefulness.[42]
There have recently been suggestions that Canada should import the
concept of 'accounting officer' long established in Britain. Jean Chrétien probably had that in mind when he announced on 11 June 2002
that he was asking the president of the Treasury Board to bring forward
'new measures ... to provide for more explicit accounting by deputy
ministers for the affairs of their departments.'[43]

Introducing the concept poses no difficulty, provided that accounting
officers operate within the broad framework of ministerial accountability to Parliament for the policies and actions of their departments. Ministers must be present in Parliament to answer questions relating to
their own powers and to powers assigned to arm's-length bodies that
report through them to Parliament. More specifically, 'Ministers should
always accept responsibility for the exercise of their own powers
(accountability), and will undertake to provide as much information as
possible about the use of powers assigned to others (answerability) and
where appropriate will take remedial action within the minister's
authority in the event of abuse or error. Everything else is a matter of
convention and practice.'[44] Failure to ensure that accounting officers
operate under this framework may push career officials into a highly
charged, politically partisan arena and turn them into political actors.
A recurring theme of this book is that seemingly unimportant administrative matters can erupt into a high-profile political controversy. If
public servants are held directly accountable for a political controversy,
they will wish to defend themselves, which could easily give rise to con-

flicts between them and ministers. The implications for a professional, non-partisan public service are obvious. In any event, if officials were proven wrong, who would impose sanctions on them – Parliament or the minister?

The accounting-officer concept holds promise in that it can create an administrative space for career officials while respecting the doctrine of ministerial accountability. Appointing such an officer (presumably the deputy minister or head of agency) in every department and agency would introduce a personal responsibility for the propriety and regularity of public finances. That officer would be given a specific space from which he or she could take action if the minister should propose a course of action counter to propriety, regularity, and even economy, efficiency, and effectiveness in public spending. If the minister insisted on the course of action, the accounting officer could ask for a written instruction from the minister before implementing the decision; if the minister gave such written instruction, the officer should in all cases immediately inform the clerk of the Privy Council and the secretary of the Treasury Board and, in cases involving propriety and regularity of public finances, the House of Commons, through the Public Accounts Committee. However, accounting officers should refuse to entertain questions from parliamentary committees that deal with the conduct of individuals and with efforts to allocate individual criticism or blame. Ministerial responsibility would still apply, and ministers would still be able to have their way provided that, if necessary, they were prepared to give instructions in writing.[45]

Nothing in the past has prevented deputy ministers from requesting their ministers to put in writing instructions when propriety is in question, but there has never been formal recognition of such a responsibility. Such recognition might well have strengthened the hand of the deputy minister at Public Works and Government Services. His minister and the office of the prime minister directed career officials to give advertising contracts to Groupeaction in 1996 and 1997 without respecting the requirements of the Financial Administration Act. The auditor general, after reviewing the contracts, declared that senior public servants had 'broken just about every rule in the book.'[46] They awarded contracts worth $6 million without seeking competitive contracts and proper follow-up to ensure that the work had been carried out. The *Globe and Mail* reported that 'numerous sources in Ottawa and Montreal [said] that the advertising system fell apart because the traditional boundaries between politicians, the bureaucracy and the private sector became blurred.'[47] An accounting officer would enable deputy ministers to establish a boundary between politics and administration.

Some Prescriptions

I put the following question to all deputy ministers whom I consulted for this study: how do we begin to fix what is ailing Canadian democracy? Responses varied, but several pointed to problems with political parties. One deputy minister claimed that parties have become largely irrelevant to the policy process, and another remarked that they would be surprised to discover that the public service is in fact particularly good at doing what it is told to do. Election campaigns, however, often produce 'meaningless generalities' and provide little policy direction, and parties 'now have little original policy content to them.'[48] Another deputy minister maintained that while the public service is quite good at doing what it is told to do, parties are not very good at saying what they want. [49]

The fact that the Liberals have held power for over thirty of the past forty years hardly helps matters. The party has become more of a conveyor belt for the prime minister to communicate decisions to party members than a major player in the policy process. Parties have lost some of their ability to influence public opinion.[50] They have policy positions only on issues that are useful to them in forging a majority consensus As for the rest, they will rely on their leader and modern electoral techniques. The goal, as we saw above, is less one of clarifying a policy position than of packaging and selling the leader and of discrediting the other parties and their leaders.

Canadians need to consider how best to strengthen the policy capacity of their parties. The issue is much too important to leave to party leaders and their advisers. Parties could set up foundations with their own in-house research capacities and ability to promote party policy objectives. If the public policy process is to involve many actors and be porous, the country's key political institutions and actors need to participate knowledgeably and voice informed views and policy positions. If taxpayers can support research institutes and think tanks, then some of this funding could enhance the policy-research capacity of political parties.

The role of the member of the House of Commons is another good place to strengthen institutions. Despite all the concerns about the democratic deficit, Canadians' apparent disillusionment with government, and their increasing disengagement from the political process, precious little research has examined the role of MPs. Ottawa has over the past thirty years sponsored numerous research institutes and think tanks, which have produced many studies and reports covering virtually every issue of public policy and many aspects of governance, but, for the most part, ignored the backbench.

It seems that everyone hesitates to trespass on the space occupied by MPs. I reported above, for example, that officials of the Treasury Board Secretariat have spent time and resources making e-government a reality but fear promoting e-democracy because they concluded that this territory belongs to politicians, who must take the lead. Meanwhile, members of the Commons have, as we saw earlier, limited resources to launch new measures that may serve to strengthen e-democracy and they are left on the outside looking in as everyone around them adjusts to new information technologies. In practice, government controls the public purse and willingly supports any number of usually non-partisan research institutes, centres, think tanks, and consultants, but not the House of Commons. When one considers that the government has a substantial budget available for consultants, research institutes, and think tanks (in the billions, according to a Treasury Board Secretariat official, though he could not provide a specific figure), while Parliament has very little, one can also easily appreciate why research groups therefore have limited interest in the role of a member of Parliament.

Yet fundamental questions need addressing. Gone are the days when policy issues were simple and an MP could argue for or against a proposal simply on the basis of his or her knowledge and expertise. The 'distinguished local amateur' can no longer cope with complex public policy and the machinery of government. Being an MP is now a full-time job. Yet the member has lost prestige in both the constituency and in Ottawa and is no longer on top of things, compared to when government was smaller and the policy process more simple.[51]

It appears that Canadians and indeed MPs themselves are no longer clear about the space that MPs should occupy. Many MPs see the consultative policy process operate, and they want to participate. Politics is about power, and there is a U.S.-inspired view that all elected representatives should have access to some of it and that they have more right to participate than anyone else. But a Westminster-style system means 'government in and with, but not by, parliament.'[52] Parliament does, or should, create an alternative to the government through the opposition, but it is not part of the government.

The proper role of MPs traditionally has centred around the following: reviewing and approving legislation, authorizing financial and human resources, representing constituents in the Commons and to government, and acting as watchdogs on government. We can ask whether the support is sufficient for them to perform these roles as legislators and as watchdogs.

Parliament needs a stronger capacity to review, improve, or repair legislation and to review regulations. Unless this is done, the task of making laws may pass to judges, who will be called on to reconcile them with the Charter or other legislation. The Charter provides an opportunity to test legislation and existing policy and to evaluate new policy initiatives against a higher law.[53] Parliament and even ministers may discover to their dismay that what they got in legislation is not what they wanted.[54]

Some of the non-partisan personnel now in government should be reallocated to parliamentary committees on a permanent basis to work with MPs to review in detail proposed legislation. Contacts between ministers and mid-level career officials in departments are no longer as easy and as frequent as they once were because ministers simply no longer have the time and because there are many layers now separating them. Contacts between elected representatives and technical experts are valuable for testing the application of proposed legislation before it becomes law. This contact could take place not just inside government but also in Parliament, given close relations between MPs, committees, and the non-partisan research staff in the Library of Parliament. In a major speech on the 'democratic deficit,' Paul Martin explained: 'Government officials propose and draft legislation from the perspective of those responsible for its administration and implementation. Members of Parliament review and adopt legislation from the perspective of constituents who will be affected by these laws. A well functioning system must balance both perspectives with the bias to the latter. I can think of no piece of legislation that would not benefit from active debate and scrutiny by members of Parliament.'[55]

We need to reconsider the roles of MPs in making government more accessible, in responding to specific complaints, and in lobbying for constituents. Canadians should be asking whether constituency representation reflects today's complex and information-rich society. Given the scope and size of government, does that concept square with the notion of equal treatment, so crucial in the public sector? Governments have been trying for two decades or so to strengthen their service-delivery capacity and to make programs more flexible and responsive, albeit with uncertain success. The saying 'Government is now too big to make decisions' is simplistic, but it does ring true to some and helps explain the growth of the lobbying industry. Horizontal government has not only slowed decision making but also made it much more complex. One can easily understand why MPs would want access to government programs for their constituencies and constituents. Every time an MP takes a position on a controversial issue, he or she makes enemies as well as friends. But when he or she helps constituents or brings home government largesse, then there are only friends being made.

Jean Chrétien, in defending his efforts to secure federal funding for a fountain for his riding and his intervention on behalf of a constituent before a crown corporation argued that he was simply doing 'his work as an MP.' In June 2002, he went further: 'In our system of government, one of the most important responsibilities of Members of Parliament is to represent the interest of their constituents,' and he added that 'that responsibility is not extinguished by virtue of being appointed to the Ministry.'[56] John Manley's web site reports on his accomplishments for his constituency, including arranging for the transfer of a stretch of highway to the local government. If Manley, as deputy prime minister representing an Ottawa constituency, involved himself to ensure this transfer, one can only imagine what MPs from other regions must think they have to do to move government. Dealing with constituents' grievances and 'bringing home the bacon,' particularly if one sits on the government side, claim the largest part of MPs' time.

But what does this actually mean? What is the proper 'work of an MP'? Should MPs lobby ministers or the prime minister and career officials to push and pull projects or government spending towards their constituencies? If so, how can opposition MPs compete with government MPs? Better yet, how are opposition MPs to compete with ministers? Where does the notion of equality – a fundamental value of Canadian democracy – fit? What guidelines, if any, should be in place for MPs to lobby public servants on behalf of their constituencies? Is it realistic to assume that career officials will give all MPs 'equal treatment' as they lobby for their ridings, given that the prime minister and deputy prime minister can have far greater impact on their careers than an opposition MP? What if you are the prime minister? Why is it that ministers may no longer promote the private interests of any individual corporation or non-governmental organization, including a constituent, directly with a crown corporation, but many do so with departments and agencies? These are important questions, but many people assume that they know the answers, prefer not to ask, or actually believe that they are not important.

A New Configuration?

Politics without Boundaries

We need to guard against tilting the policy- and decision-making processes to favour the organized, the articulate, and the powerful in society. A horizontal policy process accessible to networks of stakeholders, lobbyists, think tanks, and research institutes ensures that the strong, the organized, those with resources, and the vocal will be heard. But what about the weak and the unorganized? Again, a defining value of the public service in Anglo-American democracies has been the ability to promote a sense of equity and fairness. It is not at all clear how these core values can continue to apply in an open government where powerful stakeholders help shape new measures and make program decisions.

A new hierarchy, one based on influence rather than on power or authority (leaving aside a handful of policy actors, notably the prime minister), appears to be taking shape. Influence is available to those who can marshal the resources and expertise to participate in consultative processes. The new hierarchy of influence may function well for some time, but it may create a new class of haves and have nots. People unable to participate may well decide, in Albert Hirschman's words, to 'exit from the democratic process,' since influencing it seems impossible.[57] Why bother to vote, they may ask? Why try to influence public policies and program implementation between elections if you lack the resources to do so or access to the process that generates proposals?

Clearer space for public servants to perform their tasks and the traditional values of public administration provided for accessibility, openness, fairness, impartiality, and legitimacy and promoted frugality in government operations. The shift to a more managerialist focus and the effort to make career officials more responsive to politicians and outside forces on policy have moved government operations away from delivering programs uniformly. Many observers have also in recent years confused responsiveness to clients or consumers with political accountability. As a result, government operations and programs have opened up to accommodate different circumstances and client groups and have created a patchwork of government measures that apply unevenly across

Canada. Again, this has served to place added pressure on MPs to 'deliver the goods' for their constituencies.

Many people assumed that they could hold everyone and everything to account by measuring civil-service performance in all things in an objective and apolitical manner. That was wrong. A former secretary to the Treasury Board observed: 'There has been little performance measurement on performance measurement.' He added: 'Many of the best public service managers do not use performance management; indeed, they do not like it ... Although performance management has been linked to performance measurements and to reduced expenditure, the connection is not always clear.'[58] Performance measurement hardly replaces the notion of space in holding government operations accountable. Looking to it in all things to establish new boundaries will never provide the complete answer.[59]

How then does politics connect with the new public-policy environment? How can politicians influence the process? How can the new environment be made more accountable? It is one thing to conclude that program evaluation has limits and that the traditional department can no longer produce the right policy mix and achieve meaningful ministerial direction, control, and accountability.[60] It is quite another to prescribe solutions.

Our common language about conduct and performance was defined when government was small, when either a major part of the work of departments was performed directly by ministers or they were able to keep a close watch on it. Public servants had a very limited role in policy formation, their ministers knew them by name, and their responsibilities and duties were imposed on them by law.[61] Because Parliament felt confident in its control of the executive and in its ability to hold it accountable through the spending estimates and other means, it willingly delegated powers to ministers and accepted the concept that public servants were accountable through ministers and that they should enjoy anonymity. This arrangement enabled the creation of ministerial departments, described as one of the most important nineteenth-century 'inventions' in British governmental machinery – an invention that Canada happily adopted.[62] The result divided government activities into functions and defined organizational boundaries. Everything came together at the top in cabinet. The more important decisions went to full cabinet, and ministers assumed a collective responsibility. Parliament then voted funds, allocated them to departments and to specific ends, and then carefully monitored spending to ensure that it was spent wisely.

The broad outline of Canada's accountability regime has remained pretty well intact over the years. But everything else has changed. Precious few issues now fit neatly into departmental moulds. As a result, with exceptions noted above, the machinery of government no longer provides clear space to policy actors and to individual public servants to assume policy and program responsibilities. And responsibility is the crux of the problem that needs to be addressed.

Institutions consist of individuals. Senior public servants acting together in a department guided by a minister and a deputy minister and by policy and program objectives can provide a sense of responsibility and 'ownership' to employees down the line about what needs to be done and how. Hierarchical organizations are useful: inspired by the military model, they encourage central planning, discipline, and accountability. In addition, employees have some authority and rules of behaviour designed to prevent chaos, and these provide the basis to blame someone when things go wrong and when the rules are not followed. The new policy environment groups together numerous departments, agencies, and stakeholders to pursue shared objectives in both policy formulation and in program delivery. The individual public servant meanwhile is lost in the crowd. For those wishing to avoid responsibility, the system works fine. For those who do not and who wish to perform tasks and assess how they are doing, the system does not work well.

Hierarchies have been decoupled, and there is plenty of evidence of this. They have given way to hierarchies of documents (strategic, corporate, and business plans), centres of influence (lobbyists, think tanks, research institutes), oversight bodies and processes (access-to-information legislation, commissioner of official languages, Office of the Auditor General), and centres of political power (the prime minister, his or her office, and the Department of Finance and its minister). Thus the porous, consultative, interdepartmental, and intergovernmental policy process has become more important to ministers than their own departmental policy or management issues, particularly for controversial issues.

The thickening of government urgently necessitates removing layers and simplifying, if not eliminating, parts of the porous policy-making process. Growth has been substantial, but mostly by stealth. Rolling it back will not be easy – it will require a Thatcher-like will. There are always plenty of voices within the elaborate policy networks asking for more resources and, conversely, precious few suggesting that growth should be stopped, let alone reversed.

Margaret Thatcher and Canada's program review of the mid-1990s have taught us how to introduce cuts in management layers and streamline government. Leaving matters to the system and to the policy-network community will not work. There is need for a distinct but temporary space – a task force to do the job. All non-elected policy actors both inside and outside government must try to show that their contribution both is important and requires public funds. Organizations have mattered and will continue to matter in promoting accountability because, as we saw above, almost all statutory powers belong to ministers. But 'governing without space' requires a focus on specific tasks, on projects, and on federal participation in collaborative arrangements in order to move policy proposals forward. A considerable amount of time will need to be spent clarifying the chain of accountability: Which department is in the lead? What are the incentives to co-operate and to define goals and needs? What is at stake now is not only how to control the bureaucracy democratically but also how to control an elaborate, porous, non-hierarchical policy process democratically. The no-man's-land that has separated the political from the bureaucratic has expanded considerably and now is home to many people including partisan advisers, consultants, lobbyists, and even public servants. Thus accountability can no longer centre around a single form of accountability and follow a consistent pattern.

The Americans have designed a pluralist political system, with multiple centres of power acting as checks on each other. It seems that Canada is in the process of adapting its political system to a pluralist system, with multiple centres of influence rather than of power. The multiple centres of influence may be quite good at creating a consensus on policy and programs. However, the process is not without problems. Beyond a certain level of complexity, nobody can sort out who is responsible and accountable for what. The model also provides numerous opportunities for blame avoidance.

Politicians for the most part are frustrated because they are no longer certain of their role and standing in society or of their power and influence inside government. Most public servants are frustrated because they are less able to use their knowledge and skills in their work or to see the impact of their work. If public-opinion surveys are to be believed, citizens are frustrated because they view government as remote, inaccessible, and unresponsive. There are also signs that they are turning away or withdrawing from political life. It appears that only those who draw direct material benefits from the new policy environment – consultants, lobbyists, other hangers-on in Ottawa, and various stakeholders – are happy with the new arrangement. After all, they now participate in a world that was once reserved for politicians and public servants, and they now have a greater opportunity to influence government and to benefit directly from it.

We may well have reached the point where ac-countability – in the sense of retrospectively blaming individuals or even departments for problems – is no longer possible or fair. This shift will require major adjustments, if not a new way of the thinking, from politicians, media, career officials, and Canadians. They will need to accept the idea that individuals in government, including ministers and public servants, should be accountable – for personal probity, for respecting established rules and processes, and for their contributions to policy- and decision-making processes.[63] Because public policies and even many programs are now the product of many hands, we now need to think in terms of co-accountability or shared accountability. As Marsh and Olsen argue: 'Organized interests are accountable to policy makers even as policy makers are accountable to organized interests. Policy makers are accountable to bureaucrats, even as bureaucrats are accountable to policy-makers.'[64]

Anyone setting out to develop prescriptions on responsibility and accountability in the public sector must begin by looking at the interests of the various policy actors. Politicians, public servants, consultants, stakeholders, departments, and agencies all act in their own interests. This is not to suggest that they are motivated only by self-interest. As Anthony Downs pointed out over thirty years ago, they accept certain constraints imposed by widely shared ethical values.[65] Still, understanding their interests, broadly defined, can guide people in enclosing responsibility, if no longer space, in the machinery of government.

Enclosing responsibility and interest can never be as straightforward a matter as enclosing space. Co-accountability holds some promise of preserving a degree of responsibility and accountability. A traditional bureaucracy makes policy top-down, establishes consensus by enforcing acquiescence to higher authority, and ensures smooth operations by insisting on respect for authority, rules, and traditions. A system of co-accountability needs to establish who does what and to develop a new common language and concepts. It also requires both vertical and horizontal accountability. It retains some elements of traditional accountability and creates new ones, such as pooled budgets and cutting across departments to determine how a comprehensive program agenda was supported. It means having a capacity within institutions to dissect collaborative arrangements so as to determine the government's commitment to them, which departments are involved, what their role is, and how to know if they are living up to their end of the bargain. Government must be able to identify specific tasks and responsibilities in every collaborative arrangement so that administrative units, if not individual public servants, have a role and responsibility.

Co-accountability may well require a different machinery of government, which makes interests and responsibilities more apparent. A regime of co-accountability needs to first decide what institution should hold whom accountable. Parliament can hold the executive accountable, but it cannot do so for broader relationships. For example, it can hold the Department of Indian Affairs and Northern Development and its minister accountable, but it cannot do the same vis-à-vis Indian chiefs, even though they may spend a sizeable part of the department's budget. Governing by proxy poses yet other challenges for Parliament and ministers.

Governing without space is far more complex than governing through a vertical axis where the line of command is the same as the line of responsibility. Increasingly, government will need to adjust accountability codes and requirements. Policy networks agreeing to define new measures must accept a share of responsibility, and the more explicit this responsibility, the better for making politicians accountable for what is accomplished.[66]

Ministers with departmental responsibilities have the resources to oversee the consultative, porous policy process. Their participation takes various forms: they are – or should be – the only people able to give approval to efforts to define new policy measures. They should ensure that the process is all-inclusive and not limited to stakeholders with resources. Only they should present new funding requests. They should approve federal government participation in all new policy packages, and they should be answerable to Parliament for all questions relating to government participation in collaborative arrangements. They cannot be accountable for the entire spectrum of arrangements, but they should be for their own department and agencies. This is where the government should offer political direction and where Parliament should insist on political accountability.

If politicians and career officials cannot go home again, as we saw in chapter 9, then they need a new home, a different but meaningful world for them to operate in certain situations. Political institutions need to recognize what government officials have recognized for some time: one space can no longer solve any number of problems. When a major problem arises or the government wishes to address priority issues (for example, dealing with 11 September 2001, science matters, developments in Aboriginal communities, major cuts in the budget), senior government officials should gather up the problem and relevant officials into a new, temporary space to deal with the issue. The new space should be headed by a deputy minister–level official reporting directly to a minister, who should report to the House of Commons on its establishment, progress, and conclusion. In brief, the new space, consisting essentially of disposable policy units, should never operate beneath Parliament's radar screen.

This approach would have the added benefit of defining space for policy analysts inside government. Governments have gone to great lengths in recent years, with uncertain results, to create distinct space for program managers and their staff. Policy specialists meanwhile have been left on their own and on the defensive, accused, as we saw above, of being uncreative and unresponsive to the government's views and priorities. Creating a new space to deal with major policy issues would enable the government to bring together policy specialists from different departments and agencies. This approach has been adopted from time to time in the past, but the space created has not been sufficiently frequent, formal, visible, and accountable to Parliament.

What Parliament, particularly members of the House of Commons, requires is access to knowledge and expertise to probe, to ask tough questions, and to offer alternatives. It also needs not only its own centre of influence but, unlike other policy actors inside or outside government, the capacity to hold the executive to account both for its policies and for its administration. The 'distinguished local amateur' needs more than a good brief to be able to perform his or her role, and I say more about this below.

A rookie MP is often unable to ask the right question or to present constituents' complaints so that the prime minister and ministers can ask the public service to respond. That same MP may have even greater difficulty grasping material relating to the government's spending estimates and what it actually means. Yet it is equally difficult to understand why the Privy Council Office and the Department of Finance, both with virtually no program responsibilities, together employ about 1,600 public servants, many of whom are there to provide non-partisan policy advice to the prime minister and the minister of finance, respectively, while all the members of both Houses of Parliament can draw on only eighty non-partisan policy advisers to hold all of the executive to account. The Department of Finance alone has 541 full-time equivalents on staff working under the 'policies and advice' category.[67]

The solution to the concentration of power in the hands of a few in the executive is not to define governing instruments for Parliament. Rather, it is to develop a strong professional advisory capacity in political parties and in Parliament and, if necessary, a weaker one in the executive. I am always amazed at how policy advisory units in central agencies and departments or in policy-research networks tied to the executive can grow by stealth, while such a capacity in Parliament is held in check. Reducing this capacity in the executive and increasing it in Parliament would in itself be a positive development. It would create a new, distinct, non-partisan policy advisory capacity in Parliament and make the existing policy dimension in the executive smaller and clearer by ensuring that officials have more meaningful work.

Parliament's role in holding to account a porous policy-making process requires the means to probe. It should be able to determine if the process provides a voice for the powerless as well as for the powerful. It should have the opportunity to influence policy outcomes and to be aware of which departments proposed what and of how the arrangements were struck, their costs, and their likely impact. Parliamentary committees could be restructured to correspond to broad policy areas rather than to government departments. However structured, they should have access to resources to equip members to hold the porous policy process to account, to ensure that the information submitted to Parliament is reliable, and, precisely because the policy process is shared, to assess the total cost of the government's participation and its contribution to the initiatives. Committees will wish to determine, for example, how much 'new' money, as opposed to 'reprofiled' departmental funds, will support a new program and compare that support to commitments made by all partners. Finally, they will want to determine whether the consultative process allowed all interested parties to contribute to the process.

To hold a policy process accountable is only part of the story. The House of Commons has not done a very good job of reviewing the government's spending plans and then holding it to account for how it spends allocated resources. As we saw above, bureaucrats too easily accepted the notion that quantitative measurement could be objective and value free and somehow replicate market discipline for evaluating government programs and operations. In doing so, they have dismissed qualitative assessments and proper review of input costs. Some programs and operations can be measured, and evaluation efforts should concentrate on these, but some of the things that government does cannot be measured, including the quality of judicial decision making, the provision of policy advice, and the management of foreign affairs.

The House of Commons needs not only the tools to help its members review overall spending plans and input costs of specific programs and operations but also a process to review in detail individual spending plans or pooled budgets. The Commons, not the government, should decide in what format it wishes to receive expenditure estimates. The House, and no one else, has the responsibility to review spending estimates, which remains one of its most important duties. If MPs prefer line-item budgeting, then so be it. If they want a format to compare the travel budget for department X versus department Y, so be it. If they decide to pick at random the spending plans of three departments or three large programs for intensive study by a newly constituted Committee of the Whole and leave the rest to the following year, then so be it. One cannot help but think that somehow the House of Commons has been led to believe that the only performance information and measurements that matter are those that reveal program outputs and outcomes in relation to goals and performance standards. Information about inputs, such as financial resources and staff, is not only a legitimate evaluation tool but is both inexpensive to provide and easily accessible to parliamentarians.[68] It is also information for which MPs have been asking.[69] One could assume that the 'gun registry fiasco,' which became public in December 2002 and saw projected expenditures go from $2 million to about $800 million, could have been avoided or dealt with earlier if MPs had received administrative input costs annually and if the Department of Justice had been asked to focus on such costs in reporting to Parliament.[70] The recent establishment of a new Government Operations and Estimates Committee holds promise for review of such spending issues, and it will be interesting to see if it has access to the requisite resources and expertise.[71]

The House of Commons would find it extremely difficult today to determine the total administrative overhead cost of the government. I asked senior central-agency officials if such a figure was available, but no one, it seems, has the answer. Forty years ago, one could easily secure the answer because of line-item budgeting. As recently as fifteen years ago, the Treasury Board Secretariat had some data on the total administrative cost of government, as the PS 2000 exercise revealed. The government's expenditure plan provides for personnel, transportation and communications, information, professional and special services, and rental costs, but it is very difficult to secure total amounts by departments and agencies and for the government. The spending estimates for 2002–03 provide $37 billion for operating and capital spending. But central-agency officials made it clear to me that it was like comparing apples and oranges to attempt to break down operating and capital spending. Line-item budgeting entailed no such difficulty, and MPs could quite easily secure answers on spending for such items as salaries and travel.[72]

There is plenty of evidence, as I show above, that management-avoidance culture is commonplace in the public service. Still, civil servants have a special responsibility to manage the financial resources provided by Canadians. There is also evidence, as we saw above, that ministers and MPs have little interest in administration unless a scandal is brewing. They may well have accepted the notion that administration is the preserve of public servants, not of politicians. If this is so, then it is a mistake. Indeed, the need to oversee the spending of public monies is what initially gave life to Parliament in England.

Presumably because Parliament is not asking them, a number of important questions go unanswered. For example, in 1989 the Treasury Board launched a management-delayering exercise in order, it argued, 'to improve morale in managerial ranks.' Why then have departments since the mid-1990s been building new layers by adding 'associates' to many senior executive positions? Why, for example, does the chair of the Public Service Commission attend the weekly breakfast meeting of deputy ministers chaired by the clerk of the Privy Council while other agents of Parliament do not? How do the government and the public service deal with non-performers? How could government waste untold millions and millions of dollars on a new job-classification system that was scrapped before it was even introduced?[73] To be sure, these are uncomfortable questions for public servants, but they need to be asked and answered. The literature would suggest that such questions were never far from the surface until thirty years ago. Canadians, for obvious reasons, stand a better chance of knowing the answers if Parliament rather than the government asks them.

Parliament should consider establishing an Office of Public Administrators to serve a new House of Commons standing committee on public administration. The committee could ask the above questions and many other similar ones. It could also explore whether it is possible to draw a line to separate policy from administration, what decisions ministers can delegate to public servants, and what the proper role of MPs is in program delivery.

Although there would be no guarantees, I would hope that the establishment of a House committee on public administration would encourage a more objective, less partisan discussion of administration and performance. The committee should review the role of parliamentary agencies and matters relating to the quality and standards of administration. In some instances, space needs to be better defined in order to be brought under the control of the House. Parliamentary agents operate in their own space, as they see fit. The new Commons committee should hold these agents to account for their activities.[74] For example, no one has explained why the Office of the Auditor General has yet to be subjected to a comprehensive audit, although it is the office that aggressively promoted its application throughout government.

The Commons committee should, for example, also reconsider the role that the Office of the Auditor General has been able to carve out for itself since the late 1970s. Financial-compliance audits, as conducted by the auditor general for the Public Accounts Committee, constitute a valuable function of accountability. They are important because they are based on generally accepted accounting principles and practices that are clear and objective and can be applied to government financial transactions. Problems arise, however, when these audit functions are extended to questions of policy and program effectiveness. At this point they 'enter the realm of applied social science with all its limitations in regard to objectivity,' even though they may be produced under the authority of the auditor general. Pronouncements from the auditor general on general policy and program effectiveness are 'all too often interpreted by the opposition, the press and attentive publics to have the same claim to professional "objectivity" as financial compliance audits.'[75]

A Commons committee on public administration could establish the expectations and requirements of program evaluation and thus create a political space overseeing its development. The committee would do reviews where program evaluation has a greater chance of success, determine how it could help Parliament to hold the government to account, and ask officials to concentrate their efforts in these areas. The committee could also explore a Public Service Code with ground rules for relations between public servants and ministers and between public servants and parliamentary committees.

The committee could explore ways to address one of Parliament's main challenges: how to deal not just with a powerful executive, but also with elaborate, sophisticated policy networks possessing the technical expertise to act as centres of influence shaping public policy and even program decisions. It is difficult for MPs to understand, let alone break into, these processes and systems, but they must be given the resources to do so. For its part, the government should continue to adjust a porous policy-making process. It should refine its own capacity to give the process political direction and control, to make it more democratic, to manage various centres of influence, to identify and isolate their interests, and to define an overarching perspective that speaks to Canada's public interest.

Simply establishing such a committee in itself is also not the complete answer. The House has a Public Accounts Committee, and its members have full authority to guide the work of the Office of the Auditor General and to request a comprehensive audit on its operations. It is difficult to see the committee directing or even guiding the auditor general. We should no longer hesitate to ask fundamental questions about the interest, skills, experience, and even motivation of MPs to engage in a more objective, less partisan discussion of the work of the executive.

As I reported above, students of Parliament have noted the high turnover of MPs in general elections and its impact on the work of the Commons, particularly in keeping the government accountable. It is worth repeating the views of C.E.S. Franks: 'In Canada, a strong, solidly entrenched prime minister faces an insecure and transient House of Commons; in Britain, an insecure and transient prime minister faces a strong and solidly entrenched House.'[76] Institutions matter, and observers and participants can identify many options to improve the working of Parliament and its committees. But they also must develop means to strengthen the capacity of politicians to participate in the new policy-making process and to recognize that the days of the 'local distinguished amateur' are history.

There is still a widely held assumption that all Canadians need to do is to elect an MP and the MP will have what it takes to make a contribution. The assumption is wrong. Strengthening the policy and research capacity of Parliament and political parties will help, but again this will not be enough. We must increase MPs' ability to participate, to ask the right questions, to interpret research, and to understand the policy process and government operations. If Canadians could find the resources for a learning centre for senior executives (the Canadian Centre for Management Development has an annual budget of $25 million), they should be able to create one for MPs. Given the complexity of government, their lack of training and experience in this area, and the time required to be kept fully informed of developments back home, MPs have a greater need to learn than do senior public servants, who are usually well educated and have years of experience in government.

We saw above that a retired senior deputy minister described backbenchers as 'charmless primitives,' and I described the differences between the political and the bureaucratic worlds. Sending MPs to Ottawa in the hope that somehow they will grasp how policies are struck, bills drafted, financial resources allocated, and decisions made and then be able to marshal the right questions and arguments to hold the government, with all its resources, to account on substantial policy and administrative issues is no longer a leap of faith. It is now hopelessly dated. Failure to recognize this while establishing a Commons committee on public administration would run the risk of creating yet another agent of Parliament operating freely in its own space and accountable to no one.

The consultative policy process described in this study is fed by a network of influences, lobbyists, and consultants and by a management cadre that 'looks up' and is for the most part Ottawa-based and elitist. The further the ordinary citizen, community, or region has to go, in both physical and psychological terms, to find a listening post in government, the more likely participation will be an exercise in frustration or protest.[77] If even for this reason alone, politicians should become the crucial link to all Canadians in the new policy environment. They are the only people with the legitimacy to guard against a policy process accessible only to policy elites and those with the resources to retain hired hands to see, understand, and influence new policy measures. MPs hold a comparative edge over all other policy actors – political legitimacy and the capacity to give voice to the concerns of average Canadians and to ensure that policy elites do not exert too much influence over the policy process.[78] If they are not provided with the tools and knowledge to act as a check on behalf of ordinary Canadians, policy making may remain the fiefdom of a relatively small circle of policy elites and those with the resources to hire expertise to promote their interests.

A Public Service without Boundaries

The public service has a responsibility to perform with integrity five distinct tasks: to analyse policy issues, to formulate policy under political direction, to implement policy, to deliver services to the public, and to manage resources.[79] This study suggests that the civil service is doing very well in formulating policy under political direction and in managing the policy process, but less so in the other areas.

The public service has been left on its own to redefine its role and purpose and to answer the question: what do we want our career officials to be? It has not been very successful in this exercise, despite numerous attempts. To an outsider, the public service appears to be an institution obsessed with itself, launching new reform measures constantly, but always with modest success. As this study has pointed out, Canada is moving away from Max Weber's classic model, in which the individual bureaucrat is not allowed to 'squirm out of the apparatus in which he was harnessed ... He is chained to his activity by his entire material and ideal existence.'[80] Governing without space now allows public servants to 'squirm out of the apparatus' because there are different harnesses available, most of them are porous, and one is no longer adequate on its own.

The loss of space, as we saw above, has not only shifted boundaries between those inside and those outside government, but also within government itself. It is one thing to stress a horizontal perspective in policy making, but quite another to make it work. The departmental structure still exists, and policy officials will, as the old saying goes, often stand where they sit. Their objective is to influence the policy process as much as they can from their departmental perspective. But to do so, they must be prepared to compromise. The centre of government oversees the process, and it will identify 'high flyers,' or officials who can forcefully articulate a point of view and influence the process. Ambitious departmental officials know this full well.

Horizontal policies, by definition, can produce elusive goals. Achieving consensus can become an end in itself. It invariably requires compromise, which rarely produces clarity of purpose. Lack of clarity in goals can give rise to conflicts in implementation and make it still more difficult to assess government programs.

When you turn over policy making and decisions not only to a process that is interdepartmental within government (something that has been part of government for some time, though it is now much more prevalent and important) but also to external consultations that now serve to drive policy development (something more recent) rather than to a minister working with the relevant line department bringing forward proposals to cabinet, you also redefine the relationship between government and Canadians. Influence is divided and dispersed, and public servants manage the bargaining and accommodation processes. However, citizens who are not engaged or represented by stakeholders in the processes may well come to view the public service as slow and unresponsive to their views and individual public servants as incapable of acting responsibly. As we saw above, they may also conclude that the process is only for organized stakeholders or the well-off.

Career officials meanwhile are caught between a rock and a hard place. They must ensure that the elaborate consultative and interdepartmental policy process is respected while searching for a consensus and dealing with instant opinion-forming fed by the media, which leads some citizens to expect problems to be solved immediately. It may well explain the perception that government policy is often in a muddle until the prime minister gets involved and provides firm leadership. This is one case where perception is reality. One can assume that the Kyoto Protocol would have been handled very differently if Prime Minister Chrétien had not decided to take charge.

The public service must monitor very carefully developments in the PMO, which means that it must now manage two distinct policy processes simultaneously. First, there is policy by announcements, when the prime minister announces a policy (for example, Kyoto and the scholarship fund) and then public servants scramble to put the policy and administrative pieces together to ensure some degree of success. Second, policy emerges through the elaborate, porous process described in this book.

The public service, as we saw above, has been unable to redefine or even modernize its operations. Today, for example, people who were close to PS 2000 state that the exercise was 'mostly hot air.'[81] Its main architect, Paul Tellier, now laments its failure and blames the 'bureaucracy.' PS 2000 was only one of many attempts by the public service to reinvent itself. There are signs that the latest initiative – the effort to modernize human-resources management unveiled by Chrétien on 3 April 2002 – is taking on water and will not deliver what was promised.[82] Yet reform attempts, including *La relève*, PS 2000, and the Task Force on Human Resources, were mostly self-inflicted; unlike the case in Britain, it was not the prime minister or ministers who insisted on them. The fact that they never lived up to expectations is hardly the fault of ministers. The prime minister and ministers always have important issues such as health care, fiscal problems, the war on terrorism, and the latest scandal to deal with that invariably overshadow public-service reform.

But, at least in Canada, ministers have accepted the notion that such reform is the proper business of career officials. One former practitioner points to public servants in two central agencies as one reason for its lack of success. 'The efforts at reform did not achieve very much, principally because the central agencies responsible for management (the Treasury Board Secretariat and the Public Service Commission) did not foresee that their roles could be strengthened through reform and mandate changes, rather than weakened.'[83]

This book, and it is hardly alone, reports on an erosion of the pride and reputation of the public service. To be a public servant is less prestigious today than it was a couple of decades ago, and there is much to suggest that citizens' trust in public employees is low.[84] We also know that morale problems have plagued the public service in recent years and still do.[85] A report produced by the Public Service Commission in September 2001 on recruitment and retention in the public service is revealing. It states that new recruits ranked the ability 'to use their knowledge, skills and abilities' first among several reasons for accepting a position. Yet, once in the public service, 27 per cent indicated that they were planning to leave 'within five years.' The number-one reason for wishing to quit was to find 'work where they could better use their skills and where their efforts would have an impact,' and the third was to 'see the impact of their work.'[86]

The survey revealed that retention was an issue not only with recently hired employees. Job satisfaction among executives and equivalents varied according to their place in the hierarchy. Job satisfaction was highest for the more senior executives (EX-5, just below associate deputy minister), but progressively decreased and was lowest for EX-1 or equivalents.[87] About 40 per cent of executives reported that they were planning to leave government within five years. The majority planned to retire within that period, but others (10 to 13 per cent) intended to pursue a new career. The most prevalent reasons for wishing to leave were 'to earn more money (74 per cent); to see the impact of their work (60 per cent) and to better use their skills and abilities (59 per cent); to receive recognition for good work (58 per cent).' Less common reasons included 'opportunities for training (17 per cent)' and 'problems with supervisors (14 per cent).'[88]

New recruits and senior executives have common frustrations: the apparent inability to 'use their knowledge, skills and abilities' and to see 'the impact of their work.' These frustrations have a great deal to do with space, with not having sufficient room to employ one's skills and then being able to see the impact of one's work.

The public service is also changing. In 1990, some 60 per cent of federal civil servants were blue-collar workers. Today, some 60 per cent are knowledge workers.[89] Computers and machines are assuming more routine work. However, managing a horizontal and highly consultative policy process is labour intensive, or appears to be. It is time-consuming, keeps public servants busy attending meetings, and invariably leads to charges of bureaucratic red tape. Meetings beget other meetings. In addition, providing policy input by bits and pieces and creating a consensus can well frustrate the human desire for personal recognition. All workers need their own space to perform their craft, to see their accomplishments take form, and to assess their performance. Again, all workers, but especially knowledge workers, need space to have job satisfaction. The 2001 survey is revealing for several reasons, but one stands out. New recruits ranked the scope to 'use their knowledge, skills and abilities' as the number-one reason for joining the public service – and 27 per cent ranked it again at the top of the list, with their desire to 'see the impact of their work' as third, as reasons why they were planning to leave government within five years. There is not only the matter of attracting and retaining knowledge workers, but also the difficulties in motivating them to perform on shared territory. The fact that senior executives also identify their inability to use their skills and to see the impact of their work as reasons for leaving government shows how widespread the problem is.

Career officials can no longer quietly operate away from political debate and citizens' scrutiny. They must now share the policy advisory space with many other actors, as policy making and even program delivery now involve consultations and consensus. Departmental space should give way to broader, more open and participatory, but also more competitive space. Leaders of the public service will need to guard against overstaffing. It is far more difficult to assess human-resources requirements for a porous, consultative policy process than for a relatively self-contained government program. The tendency will be to add staff to deal with or counter other centres of influence both inside and outside government. The risk, however, is that knowledge workers will not have enough meaningful work and be left 'busy turning a crank not attached to anything.'[90]

The new policy processes mean a loss of influence for the public service. Rather than having policy and program decisions in their hands, as under the traditional bargain in the village, they share it either with stakeholders, outside experts, and groups of citizens, or with the prime minister and his or her close advisers. Public servants now spend a great deal of time trying to blend and harmonize different perspectives and influences. In doing so, they are increasingly called on to create new advisory boards, to organize consultations with interest groups, and to deal with the media – in brief, 'to network.' At the same time, they are still expected to provide error-free administration and to avoid embarrassments to their ministers. This will not change unless question period is abolished and politicians' competition for political power in the television age is overhauled. But this is unlikely.

Why would someone wish to join the public service? Think tanks, polling firms, and consulting firms in Ottawa offer attractive employment without the requirements of access-to-information legislation or the need to keep one's minister out of political hot water. The prospects of applying skills to resolving policy issues are much greater in policy centres outside government than inside, because the work space there is clearer. Creating temporary policy space for career public servants to deal with priority issues holds promise, because it is as close as one can get to establishing a clear space for competent and motivated policy analysts to apply their knowledge and skills and see the impact of their work.

Looking to Canadians

Ultimately, however, it is Canadians themselves who must make their political and administrative institutions work better and impose requirements for how the political and policy spaces now emerging should operate. The rise of a better-educated, more individualistic society combined with the emergence of strong interest groups, research institutes, new information technology, and more aggressive media has had a profound impact on political parties, government, and Parliament. Canadian institutions remain intact because they have adapted to change. That is the genius of the Westminster model. Canadians need to make this genius work again and to revise their understanding of how responsible government can be made to work in contemporary society. Change is not likely from those who are in power today and their associates. Rather, it will come from politically engaged citizens who belong to parties, who may decide to run for election, and who have reached the conclusion that reforming institutions is important and that they need to play their part. Canadians should ponder the words of Gordon Robertson, former clerk of the Privy Council: 'The concentration of power is greater than in any other government with a federal cabinet system.' He added: 'With the lack of checks and balances, the prime minister in Canada is perhaps the most unchecked head of government among the democracies.'[91] The Senate cries out for reform not only to ensure that the regional perspective is heard and debated in Ottawa, but also to strengthen the capacity of Parliament to hold the executive to account. History tells us, however, that the push for Senate reform must come from citizens to have any chance of success.

Democracies require the accountability of citizens. Yet as Paul Thomas points out, 'many citizens lack knowledge of the basic features of the Canadian political system.' He asks a provocative but insightful question: do Canadians have 'the right stuff to meet minimum requirements of democracy, such as to cast a relatively well informed vote once every four years and to hold political and administration officials accountable between elections?'[92] We are informed that only 20 per cent of Canadians have ever written to their MP, one in twenty voters do not know who the prime minister is, and most do not know the name of their MP.[93]

Still, there is no need to put the hammer to institutions or to emulate the American system of government in the hope that we can start over again. The flaws in Canada's system of governance – the decline of parties, the apparent inability of the public service to define precise goals and measure performance, the tendency to define loose mandates for government departments and agencies, and the emphasis that both politicians and senior public servants place on deflecting potential crises – are a function of developments in Canadian society and Canadian politics, not in the failure of the parliamentary system or of the Westminster model to adjust.

The expansion of government, combined with the growing belief among Canadians that politicians and public servants should no longer be trusted to occupy the policy and administrative space exclusively and in relative secrecy, explains both the changes that have taken place and also the challenges at hand. Although the solution is not a hammer, there is also little point in trying to reapply the traditional boundaries of public administration. Think tanks and research centres should look beyond their stakeholders and engage Canadians in a debate on how to strengthen political and administrative institutions.

We can never lose sight of the fact that government programs are ultimately the product of what politicians desire and, accordingly, should 'depend on the accountability of ministers, not on the measurement of bureaucrats because many government programs are designed to meet multiple objectives to satisfy such things as fairness and regional balance criteria.'[94] We should also never forget that the House of Commons is the only legitimate national political institution with direct political ties to all communities and a mandate to debate the major issues of the day, scrutinize government policy and administration, hold the government to account, and examine proposals for new legislation. Canadians now need to take note that their highest political tribunal requires their attention and care. A respected and veteran MP recently brought this point home when he pointed out that 'the classic role of the House of Commons, which is to provide oversight to the actions of the government, has basically withered away and died.'[95] If the Commons cannot do this, then it cannot do anything else of substance.

Notes

Chapter 1: Introduction

1 See, among others, Eva Etzioni-Halevy, *Bureaucracy and Democracy: A Political Dilemma* (London: Routledge and Kegan Paul, 1985).

2 Kevin Theakston, *The Civil Service since 1945* (Oxford: Blackwell, 1995), 16.

3 See Ivon Jennings, *Cabinet Government* (Cambridge: Cambridge University Press, 1959), 133.

4 Canada, Privy Council Office, *Responsibility in the Constitution* (Ottawa: Privy Council Office, 1993), 27.

5 House of Commons, *Debates*, 3rd session, 30th Parliament, vol. 1, 15 Nov. 1977, 877–81.

6 Woodrow Wilson, 'The Study of Administration,' *Political Science Quarterly* 2, no. 2 (June 1887), 198.

7 See, among many others, P. Kellner and Lord Crowther-Hunt, *The Civil Servant* (London: Macdonald, 1980).

8 James Q. Wilson, 'The Rise of the Bureaucratic State,' in Nathan Glazer and Irving Kristol, eds., *The American Commonwealth – 1976* (New York: Basic Books, 1976), 77.

9 See, among others, B. Schaffer, *The Administrative Factor* (London: Frank Cass, 1973).

10 *Discussion Paper on Values and Ethics in the Public Service* (Ottawa: CCMD, Dec. 1996), 60.

11 K.C. Wheare, *Federal Government*, 4th ed. (Oxford: Oxford University Press, 1963), 11.

12 C.B. Macpherson, *The Real World of Democracy: The Massey Lectures* (Ottawa: Canadian Broadcasting Corporation, 1965).

13 Robert A. Dahl, *A Preface to Democratic Theory* (Chicago: University of Chicago Press, 1956), 73.
14 See, among others, Richard Johnston et al., *The Challenge of Direct Democracy: The 1992 Canadian Referendum* (Montreal: McGill-Queen's University Press, 1996), and Don Carmichael et al., *Democracy and Rights in Canada* (Toronto: Harcourt Brace-Jovanovich, 1991).
15 See, among many others, Donald J. Savoie, *The Politics of Public Spending in Canada* (Toronto: University of Toronto Press, 1990), chap. 4.
16 Sharon Sutherland, 'Does Westminster Government Have a Future?' (Ottawa: Institute on Governance, Occasional Paper Series, 1996), 1.
17 See Sheldon Ehrenworth, 'A Better Public Service Needs Freedom to Manage Its People,' *Globe and Mail* (Toronto), 15 April 1989, B21.
18 *Rethinking Government 1994: An Overview and Synthesis* (Ottawa: Ekos Research Associates, 1995), 3.
19 Johnston et al., *The Challenge of Direct Democracy*, 3.
20 Jocelyne Bourgon, 'Citizens, Government, Democracy: A New Deal?,' presentation to the International Summit on Public Service Reform, Winnipeg, 11 June 1999, 4.
21 Carolyn Bennett and Reg Alcock, 'Call from Within for Parliamentary Reforms,' *National Post* (Toronto), 27 Jan. 2001, A15.
22 See, among others, R.A.W. Rhodes, *Understanding Governance: Policy Networks, Governance, Reflexivity and Accountability* (Buckingham: Open University Press, 1997), 197.
23 Quoted in Derek Bok, 'A Daring and Complicated Strategy,' *Harvard Magazine* (May–June 1989), 49.
24 Quoted in Christopher Pollitt, *Managerialism and the Public Service: The Anglo-American Experience* (Oxford: Basil Blackwell, 1988), 97.
25 Quoted in Donald J. Savoie, *Thatcher, Reagan, Mulroney: In Search of a New Bureaucracy*, The Pitt Series in Policy and Institutional Studies (Pittsburgh: University of Pittsburgh Press, 1994), 3.
26 Paul Tellier, 'It's Time to Re-engineer the Public Service,' *Public Sector Management* 4, no. 4 (1992), 23.
27 Reagan's quote is from Bok, 'A Daring and Complicated Strategy,' 49, and Thatcher's, from Peter Hennessy, *Whitehall* (London: Fontana, 1989), 592.
28 S.L. Sutherland, 'The Al-Mashat Affair: Administrative Accountability in Parliamentary Institutions,' *Canadian Public Administration* 34, no. 4 (winter 1991), 574.
29 Consultations with Bernard Valcourt, former minister in the Mulroney government.
30 House of Commons, *Debates*, 6 June 1991, 1277.

31 Paul Appleby, *Policy and Administration* (Tuscaloosa: University of Alabama Press, 1949), 170.

32 Luther Gulick, 'Politics, Administration, and the New Deal,' *Annals of the American Academy of Political and Social Science* (Sept. 1933), 61–2.

33 See, for example, D.W. Martin, 'The Fading Legacy of Woodrow Wilson,' *Public Administration Review* 48, no. 1 (March–April 1988), 633.

34 See William D. Richardson, *Democracy, Bureaucracy, and Charter: Founding Thought* (Lawrence: University Press of Kansas, 1997), 41.

35 David Osborne and Ted Gaebler, *Reinventing Government* (New York: Addison-Wesley, 1992).

36 See, for example, Savoie, *Thatcher, Reagan, Mulroney.*

37 See, among others, James G. March and Johan P. Olsen, *Democratic Governance* (New York: Free Press, 1995), 193.

38 Weber, quoted in H.H. Gerth and C. Wright Mills, *From Max Weber* (New York: Oxford University Press, 1946), 278, 232.

39 See, for example, Gordon Osbaldeston, 'The Public Servant and Politics,' *Policy Options* 8, no. 1 (1987), 3–6.

40 See, for example, Jon Pierre, 'Legitimacy, Institutional Change, and the Politics of Public Administration in Sweden,' in B. Guy Peters and Donald J. Savoie, eds., *Governance in a Changing Environment* (Montreal: McGill-Queen's University Press, 1995).

41 Hugh Winsor, 'Jane Lives,' *Globe and Mail* (Toronto), 20 Jan. 2001, A13.

42 Ibid.

43 Etzioni-Halevy, *Bureaucracy and Democracy*, 87.

44 Quoted in 'Unity Trumps Stolen Millions: PM,' *National Post* (Toronto), 31 May 2002, A1.

45 Mel Cappe, *Eighth Annual Report to the Prime Minister on the Public Service of Canada* (Ottawa: Privy Council Office, 2001).

46 E.E. Schattschneider, *The Semisovereign People* (New York: Holt, Rinehart and Winston, 1960), 14.

47 Mel Cappe, 'Making Connections and Meeting the Challenge: E-Government and the Public Service of Canada,' presentation to the ADM Forum, Ottawa, 3 May 2000.

Chapter 2: Creating a Non-partisan Civil Service

1 J.E. Hodgetts, *Pioneer Public Service: An Administrative History of the United Canadas, 1841–1867* (Toronto: University of Toronto Press, 1955), 22.

2 Henry Parris made these comments about the British civil service in *Constitutional Bureaucracy* (London: George Allen & Unwin, 1969), 26.

3 Lord Sydenham, quoted in Hodgetts, *Pioneer Public Service*, 15.

4 Ibid., v.

5 Ibid., 19.

6 Ibid., 23.

7 Ibid., 26.

8 See A.O. Kinchen, *Lord Russell's Canadian Public Policy* (Lubbock: Texas Tech Press, 1945), Appendix 9.

9 Ibid.

10 Hodgetts, *Pioneer Public Service*, 278.

11 Ibid., 18, 21.

12 Adam Shortt, 'The Relations between the Legislative and Executive Branches of the Canadian Government,' *American Political Science Review* 7, no. 21 (May 1913), 187.

13 Hodgetts, *Pioneer Public Service*, 32.

14 Quoted in Peter Hennessy, *Whitehall* (London: Fontana, 1989), 39.

15 See Donald J. Savoie, *Thatcher, Reagan, Mulroney: In Search of a New Bureaucracy* (Pittsburgh: University of Pittsburgh Press, 1994), 45.

16 Hodgetts, *Pioneer Public Service*, 44.

17 Quoted in ibid., 51.

18 Ibid., 70.

19 W.A. Carrothers, 'Problems of the Canadian Federation,' *Canadian Journal of Economics and Political Science* 1, no. 1 (Feb. 1935), 29.

20 See, among others, Sir Edward Bridges, *Portrait of a Profession: The Civil Service Tradition*, The Rede Lecture (Cambridge: Cambridge University Press, 1953).

21 Sir Ivor Jennings, *Cabinet Government* (Cambridge: Cambridge University Press, 1959), 14.

22 Harold Wilson quotes Walter Bagehot to make the point on the role of the prime minister in Harold Wilson, *A Prime Minister on Prime Ministers* (London: Weidenfeld and Nicholson, and Michael Joseph, 1977), 10.

23 Parris, *Constitutional Bureaucracy*, 28.

24 Jennings, *Cabinet Government*, 20.

25 Ibid., 15–16.

26 J.R. Mallory, *The Structure of Canadian Government* (Toronto: Macmillan, 1971), 194–5.

27 Quoted in Sir Norman Chester, *The English Administrative System, 1780–1870* (Oxford: Clarendon Press, 1981), 81.

28 Ibid.

29 Jennings, *Cabinet Government*, 14.

30 Quoted in Parris, *Constitutional Bureaucracy*, 80.

31 At least one leading student of public administration disagrees. See. C.E.S. Franks, 'Not Anonymous: Ministerial Responsibility and the British Accounting Affairs,' *Canadian Public Administration* 40, no. 4 (winter 1997), 626–52.

32 Parris, *Constitutional Bureacracy*, 80.

33 Ibid., 80–1.

34 A.V. Dicey, quoted in ibid., 81.

35 Geoffrey Marshall and Graeme C. Moodie, *Some Problems of the Constitution*, 5th ed. (London: Hutchinson University Library, 1971), 55.

36 Sharon Sutherland, 'Responsible Government and Ministerial Responsibility: Every Reform Is Its Own Problem,' *Canadian Journal of Political Science* 24, no. 1 (March 1991), 95.

37 Ibid., 96.

38 Sir Ivor Jennings, *The Law and the Constitution* (London: University of London Press, 1959), 208.

39 Marshall and Moodie, *Some Problems of the Constitution*, 65.

40 Sutherland, ' Responsible Government and Ministerial Responsibility,' 99.

41 Sharon L. Sutherland and G. Bruce Doern, *Bureaucracy in Canada: Control and Reform*, vol. 43 of Research Studies for the Royal Commission on the Economic Union and Development Prospects for Canada (Ottawa: Minister of Supply and Services, 1985), 20.

42 Hodgetts, *Pioneer Public Service.*

43 See, for example, Chester, *The English Administrative System*, 120–49.

44 Report of the committee on public expenditure, tabled in 1808; quoted in ibid., 149.

45 See, for example, Donald J. Savoie, *The Politics of Public Spending in Canada* (Toronto: University of Toronto Press, 1990), chap. 2.

46 Quoted in Chester, *The English Administrative System*, 26.

47 Quoted in Hennessy, *Whitehall*, 38.

48 Parris, *Constitutional Bureaucracy*, 106.

49 Ibid., 127.

50 Ibid.

51 Hodgetts, *Pioneer Public Service*, 49.

52 See Robert C. Brown, *Robert Laird Bordon: A Biography*, Vol. 1, 1854–1914 (Toronto: Macmillan, 1975), 215.

53 Chester, *The English Administrative System*, 27.

54 Ibid., 370.

55 Quoted in Kevin Theakston, *The Civil Service since 1945* (Oxford: Blackwell, 1995), 176.

56 See, among others, Edward Greenspon and Anthony Wilson-Smith, *Double*

Vision: The Inside Story of the Liberals in Power (Toronto: Doubleday Canada, 1996).

57 Gordon Robertson, *Memoirs of a Very Civil Servant: Mackenzie King to Pierre Trudeau* (Toronto: University of Toronto Press, 2000), 316.

58 R.G. Robertson, 'The Canadian Parliament and Cabinet in the Face of Modern Demands,' *Canadian Public Administration* 11, no. 3 (1968), 275.

59 'Symposium on Ministerial Responsibility,' *Public Administration* 65, no. 1 (spring 1987), 88.

60 Herman Finer, *The British Civil Service* (London: Allen and Unwin, 1937), 196.

Chapter 3: The Traditional Bargain

1 Kenneth McNaught, 'History and the Perception of Politics,' in John H. Redekop, ed., *Approaches to Canadian Politics* (Scarborough: Prentice-Hall of Canada, 1978), 108.

2 Ibid.

3 The observation was made by Ralph Heintzman at a seminar sponsored by the Canadian Centre for Management Development (CCMD) in Ottawa in 1996.

4 Canada, Privy Council Office, *Discussion Paper on Values and Ethics in the Public Service* (Ottawa: PCO, Dec. 1996), 7.

5 See, among others, Peter Aucoin, *The New Public Management: Canada in Comparative Perspective* (Montreal: IRPP, 1995), 40–1. See, in particular, the review of recent management-reform measures and their impact on accountability.

6 John Uhr, 'Parliament and Public Administration,' in J.R. Nethercote, ed., *Parliament and Bureaucracy* (Sydney, NSW: Hale and Iremonger, 1982), 26.

7 Sir Ivor Jennings, *Cabinet Government* (Cambridge: Cambridge University Press, 1969), 133.

8 Geoffrey Marshall, 'Ministerial Responsibility,' *Political Quarterly* 34 (1963), 256.

9 Geoffrey Marshall, *Constitutional Conventions* (Oxford: Oxford University Press, 1984), 209–11.

10 Aucoin, *The New Public Management*, 218.

11 Quoted in V. Seymour Wilson, *Canadian Public Policy and Administration: Theory and Environment* (Toronto: McGraw-Hill Ryerson, 1981), 313.

12 J.R. Mallory, *The Structure of Canadian Government* (Toronto: Macmillan of Canada, 1971), 122.

13 Donald J. Savoie, *Thatcher, Reagan, Mulroney: In Search of a New Bureaucracy* (Pittsburgh: University of Pittsburgh Press, 1994), 26.

14 Herman Finer, *The British Civil Service* (London: Allen and Unwin, 1937), 196.
15 Peter Hennessy, *Whitehall* (London: Fontana Press, 1989), 346.
16 Quoted in H.A. Gert and C. Wright Mills, *From Max Weber: Essays in Sociology* (London: Routledge, 1970), 233–4.
17 Wilson, *Canadian Public Policy and Administration*, 240.
18 Quoted in Hennessy, *Whitehall*, 349.
19 Gordon Robertson, 'Official Responsibility, Private Conscience, and Public Information,' *Optimum* 3, no. 3 (1972), 10.
20 *Responsibility in the Constitution* (Ottawa: Minister of Supply and Services, 1993), 72.
21 K.G. Robertson, *Public Secrets* (London: Macmillan, 1982), 180.
22 James R. Mitchell and Sharon Sutherland, 'Relations between Politicians and Public Servants,' in M. Charih et al., eds., *New Public Management and Public Administration in Canada* (Toronto: IPAC, 1997), 185.
23 Peter Dobell made the observation at '*The Art of the State in a World without Frontiers,*' sponsored by IRPP and CIRRD, Montebello, Quebec, 12–13 Oct. 2001.
24 John Crosbie, *No Holds Barred: My Life in Politics* (Toronto: McClelland and Stewart, 1997), 301.
25 See, among others, Donald J. Savoie, *Governing from the Centre: The Concentration of Power in Canadian Politics* (Toronto: University of Toronto Press, 2001), chap. 7.
26 See ibid., 314.
27 Jean Chrétien, *Straight from the Heart* (Toronto: Key Porter Books, 1985), 18.
28 Ibid.
29 Quoted in ibid., 132–3.
30 Quoted in Donald J. Savoie, *The Politics of Public Spending in Canada* (Toronto: University of Toronto Press, 1990), 223.
31 PCO, *Discussion Paper on Values and Ethics in the Public Service*, 34.
32 See, among others, Joseph Eliot Magnet, 'The Deadly Muzzling of the Public Servants,' *Globe and Mail* (Toronto), 26 Oct. 1982, 7.
33 See, among others, 'Ottawa Blocks MPs' Access to Civil Servants,' *National Post* (Toronto), 7 Aug. 2000, A1 and A8.
34 Access to Information Act, RSC, 1985, c.A-1, p. 39.
35 Public Opinion, *This Morning*, CBC, 3 Dec. 1997.
36 Ibid.
37 Ibid.
38 Consultations with a senior official at the Treasury Board Secretariat, 22 Oct. 2002.

39 Alasdair Robarts, 'Administrative Discretion and the Access to Information
    Act: An Internal Law on Open Government?' *Canadian Public Administration*
    45, no. 2 (summer 2002), 175.
40 Crosbie, *No Holds Barred*, 300.
41 'Cuts Won't Disconnect Government Cell Phones,' *Globe and Mail* (Toronto),
    29 June 1994, A5.
42 See, for example, George Radwaski, *Trudeau* (Toronto: Macmillan, 1978).
43 J.A.G. Griffith and Michael Ryle, *Parliament: Functions, Practice and Procedures*
    (London: Sweet and Maxwell, 1989), 21.
44 C.E.S. Franks, *The Parliament of Canada* (Toronto: University of Toronto
    Press, 1987), 145.
45 Ibid., 146.
46 C.E.S. Franks, 'Not Anonymous: Ministerial Responsibility and the British
    Accounting Officers,' *Canadian Public Administration* 40, no. 4 (1997), 633.
47 In some instances the role is assigned to the second permanent secretary.
48 Gavin Drewey and Tony Butcher, *The Civil Service Today* (Oxford: Basil Black-
    well, 1988), 139.
49 HM Treasury, *The Responsibilities of an Accounting Officer* (London: HMSO,
    1991).
50 Canada, Royal Commission on Financial Management and Accountability,
    Final Report (Ottawa: Minister of Supply and Services, 1979), 374–9.
51 *Responsibility in the Constitution*, 78–9.
52 J.R. Mitchell, 'Reply to C.E.S. Franks,' *Canadian Public Administration* 40, no.
    4 (1997), 656.
53 Kate Jenkins, Karen Caines, and Andrew Jackson, *Improving Management in
    Government: The Next Steps* (London: HMSO, 1988), 3–4, 7.
54 Ibid., 9, 15.
55 Ibid., 15, see annex A, 1.
56 'Prime Minister Announces Change in Way Whitehall Delivers Services,'
    Press Notice (10 Downing Street, 18 Feb. 1987); see also the section 'Notes to
    Editors.'
57 See Geoffrey Fry et al., 'Symposium on Improving Management in Govern-
    ment,' *Public Administration* 55, no. 4 (winter 1988), 443.
58 Butler, cited in House of Commons, London, *Official Report*, 18 Feb. 1988.
    See also Hennessy, *Whitehall*, 621.
59 See S. Trosa, *Next Steps: Moving On* (London: Office of the Public Service,
    1994), 9, and A. Massey, 'Ministers, the Agency Model and Policy Owner-
    ship,' *Public Policy and Administration* 10, no. 2 (1995), 87.
60 Nick Mulder, 'Managing Special Operating Agencies: A Practitioner's Per-
    spectives,' *Optimum* 22, no. 2 (1992), 19.

61 Ian Clark, 'Special Operating Agencies: The Challenges of Innovation,' *Optimum* 22, no. 2 (1992) 17.

62 Savoie, *Thatcher, Reagan, Mulroney,* 240.

63 Alti Rodal, 'Special Operating Agencies: Issues for Parent Departments and Central Agencies' (Ottawa: CCMD, 1996), 5.

64 Professor Evert Lindquist put this question to me when he reviewed this study while it was in manuscript form. I put the same question to senior officials at the Treasury Board Secretariat, and their answer was that no one has been able to demonstrate that programs are better managed in SOAs, and they expressed doubts whether such a question could actually be answered.

65 See David Roth, 'Innovation in Government: The Case of Special Operating Agencies' (Ottawa: Minister of Supply and Services, Consulting and Audit Canada, Sept. 1990), 2–3.

66 *The Special Operating Agency* (Ottawa: Treasury Board Secretariat, n.d.).

67 Michael Prince, 'Banishing Bureaucracy or Hatching a Hybrid? The Canadian Food Inspection Agency and the Politics of Reinventing Government,' *Governance* 13, no. 2 (April 2000), 217.

68 I owe this insight to Nick d'Ombrain, from a meeting to review my manuscript in October 2002. However, some senators raised important issues. Senator Lowell Murray, for example, said: 'If there is a problem with the regulations and the procedures of Treasury Board or the Public Service Commission ... then change the regulations.' He added that reading of the proposed bill 'will convince you that the lines of accountability to Parliament are blurred and will be further blurred.' See *Senate Debates*, 5 Nov. 1998, 2154–7.

69 Franks, 'Not Anonymous,' 652.

70 See, among others, Peter Aucoin, *The New Public Management: Canada in Comparative Perspective* (Montreal: IRPP, 1995).

Chapter 4: Life in the Village

1 Hugh Heclo and Aaron Wildavsky, *The Private Government of Public Money* (London: Macmillan Press, 1981).

2 J.L. Granatstein, *The Ottawa Men: The Civil Service Mandarins, 1935–37* (Toronto: University of Toronto Press, 1982), 12.

3 R.M. Punnett, *The Prime Minister in Canadian Government and Politics* (Toronto: Macmillan of Canada, 1977), 75.

4 Thomas S. Axworthy, 'Of Secretaries to Princes,' *Canadian Public Administration* 31, no. 2 (1998), 250.

5 Gordon Robertson, *Memoirs of a Very Civil Servant: Mackenzie King to Pierre Trudeau* (Toronto: University of Toronto Press, 2000), 87.

6 Granatstein, *The Ottawa* Men, 9–10.

7 Ibid., 10.

8 Ibid., 282.

9 Ibid., 281.

10 Christina Newman, 'The Establishment, That Governs Us,' *Saturday Night* (Toronto), May 1968, 24.

11 A.W. Johnson, *Social Policy in Canada: The Past As It Conditions the Present* (Halifax: Institute for Research on Public Policy, 1987), 1.

12 On how the process worked, see Donald J. Savoie, *Governing from the Centre: The Concentration of Power in Canadian Politics* (Toronto: University of Toronto Press, 1999), chap. 2.

13 See Granatstein, *The Ottawa Men*, and Robertson, *Memoirs of a Very Civil Servant* (Toronto: University of Toronto Press, 2000).

14 Granatstein, *The Ottawa Men*, 278.

15 Long-serving public servants of that era included Clifford Clark, Escott Reid, Gordon Robertson, Norman Robertson, O.D. Skelton, and Graham Towers.

16 Robertson, *Memoirs of a Very Civil Servant*, 255.

17 Granatstein, *The Ottawa Men*, 277.

18 See, among others, James Eayrs, *The Art of the Possible* (Toronto: University of Toronto Press, 1961), 37.

19 Ibid.

20 Ibid., 35.

21 John Hilliker, *Canada's Department of External Affairs: The Early Years*, vol. 1 (Montreal: McGill-Queen's University Press, 1990), 243.

22 See, among others, S.H. Barnes et al., *Political Action: Mass Participation in Five Western Democracies* (London: Sage, 1979), and Aaron Wildavsky, *How to Limit Government Spending* (Berkeley: University of California Press, 1979), 147–8.

23 An excellent example here is John Kenneth Galbraith. See *Dimension* (winter 1986), 13.

24 Quoted in Henry Parris, *Constitutional Bureaucracy* (London: George Allen & Unwin, 1969), 284.

25 See Donald Savoie, *Thatcher, Reagan, Mulroney: In Search of a New Bureaucracy* (Pittsburgh: University of Pittsburgh Press, 1994), 87–8.

26 See, among others, ibid., chap. 3.

27 *Great Britain, The Civil Service*, vol. 1, Report of the Committee 1966–68 (London: Her Majesty's Stationery Office, June 1968), 82. See also Savoie, *Thatcher, Reagan, Mulroney*, 64–70.

28 See Royal Commission on Government Organizations, *Final Report* (Ottawa: Queen's Printer, 1962), 91.

29 Ibid.

30 Donald J. Savoie, *The Politics of Public Spending in Canada* (Toronto: University of Toronto Press, 1990), 4.

31 On public-employment data, see Sutherland and Doern, *Bureaucracy in Canada: Control and Reform*, vol. 43 of Studies for the Royal Commission on the Economic Union and Development Prospects for Canada (Ottawa: Minister of Supply and Services, 1985), 88–105.

32 Ibid., 94.

33 Richard Crossman, *The Diaries of a Cabinet Minister,* vol. 1 (London: Hamilton and Cape, 1975), 90.

34 Christopher Hood, 'De–Sir Humphreyfying the Westminster Model of Bureaucracy: A New Style of Governance,' *Governance* 3, no. 2 (April 1990), 206.

35 Flora MacDonald, 'The Minister and the Mandarins,' in *Policy Options* 1, no. 3 (Sept.–Oct. 1980), 29–31; Jeffrey Simpson, *Discipline of Power* (Toronto: Personal Library Publishers, 1980), 119–20.

36 See, for example, Savoie, *The Politics of Public Spending in Canada*, chap. 9.

37 Quoted in Donald J. Savoie, 'The Minister's Staff: The Need for Reform,' *Canadian Public Administration* 26, no. 4 (1983), 523.

38 Quoted in Thomas A. Hockin, *Government in Canada* (London: Weidenfeld and Nicholson, 1975), 136.

39 This point was made by Gerald Kaufman, *How to Be a Minister* (London: Sidgwick and Jackson, 1980). See also Savoie, *The Politics of Public Spending in Canada*, and Savoie, 'The Minister's Staff.'

40 R.D. Putnam, 'Bowling Alone: America's Declining Social Capital,' *Journal of Democracy* 6 (1995), 65–78.

41 See, for example, John Crosbie, *No Holds Barred: My Life in Politics* (Toronto: McClelland and Stewart, 1997).

42 Quoted in 'Simpson Takes a Swipe at the Year's Political Books,' *Globe and Mail* (Toronto), 31 Dec. 1994, C12.

43 Jeffrey Simpson, 'Finding Harmony on the Linguistic Front,' *Globe and Mail* (Toronto), 9 Oct. 2002, A17.

44 Michael Colsden, 'Read All about Him,' *Globe and Mail* (Toronto), 20 July 2002, D15.

45 See Richard Simeon, 'Globalization and the Canadian Nation-State,' paper presented to a conference sponsored by the C.D. Howe Institute, Toronto, April 1990, 1.

46 Pierre Elliott Trudeau, *Memoirs* (Toronto: McClelland and Stewart, 1993), 110.

47 Robertson, *Memoirs of a Very Civil Servant*, 256.

48 Savoie, *Governing from the Centre.*
49 See B. Guy Peters and D.J. Savoie, 'Politicians and Bureaucrats' (Ottawa: Canadian Centre for Management Development, Oct. 1996), mimeo.
50 See, among others, Savoie, *Thatcher, Reagan, Mulroney.*
51 Ibid.
52 'Up for Grabs,' *Times* (London), 8 April 1991, 41.
53 Canada, Report of the Auditor General of Canada to the House of Commons for Fiscal Year Ended 31 March, 1976 (Ottawa: Minister of Supply and Services, 1976), 10.
54 Quoted in Savoie, *The Politics of Public Spending in Canada,* 35.
55 Canada, 'Andras Announces Royal Commission on Financial Organization and Accountability,' Treasury Board, News Release, 22 Nov. 1976, 2.
56 Canada, Royal Commission on Financial Management and Accountability, *Final Report* (Ottawa: Minister of Supply and Services, 1979), 7.
57 Ibid.
58 See Savoie, *Governing from the Centre,* 207.
59 Progressive Conservative Party of Canada, 'Towards Production Management,' background notes, Ottawa, undated, 1.
60 See, for example, Sutherland, 'The Al-Mashat Affair: Administrative Responsibility in Parliamentary Institutions,' *Canadian Public Administration* 34, no. 2 (winter 1991), 592.
61 See, among many others, Savoie, *The Politics of Public Spending in Canada.*
62 Patrick Boisvert, 'Summaries of Public Sector Reform' (Ottawa: CCMD, 1999), 2.
63 He made this observation about PS 2000 and *La Relève* in his *Reflections on a Decade of Serving Parliament* (Ottawa: CCMD, 2001), 18.

Chapter 5: Diagnosing the Patient

1 Joseph S. Nye Jr, 'Introduction: The Decline of Confidence in Government,' in Nye et al., eds, *Why People Don't Trust Government* (Cambridge, Mass.: Harvard University Press, 1997), 1–2.
2 Neil Nevitte, *The Decline of Deference: Canadian Value Change in Cross-National Perspective* (Peterborough, Ont.: Broadview Press, 1996).
3 Albert O. Hirshman, *Exit, Voice and Loyalty: Responses to Decline in Firms, Organizations and States* (Cambridge, Mass.: Harvard University Press, 1970), 15–16.
4 R. Kenneth Carty et al., *Rebuilding Canadian Party Politics* (Vancouver: UBC Press, 2000), 1 and 9.

5 Jeffrey Simpson quotes political scientist Neil Nevitte to make this point in his 'Canadian Politics and One-Party Government,' *Policy Options* 22, no. 1 (Jan.–Feb. 2001), 15–20.
6 J. Ed Greenspon, 'A Matter of Trust,' *Globe and Mail* (Toronto), 20 March 2001, A4.
7 *Managing Change: The Evolving Role of the Commonwealth's Top Public Servants* (Ottawa: Public Policy Forum, Nov. 1998), 4.
8 See 'Rethinking Government,' Ekos Research Associates, presentation to sponsors, Ottawa, various dates between 1994 and 1997.
9 See, among others, David C. Docherty, *Mr. Smith Goes to Ottawa: Life in the House of Commons* (Vancouver: UBC Press, 1997), 1.
10 37th Parliament, 12t Session, Hansard, number 009, Thursday, 8 Feb. 2001.
11 See, for example, R.J. Dalton, 'Political Support in Advanced Industrial Democracies,' in Pipa Noris, ed., *Critical Citizens* (Oxford: Oxford University Press, 1999), 57–77.
12 Sandford F. Borins, 'Public Choice: Yes Minister Made It Popular, But Does Winning the Nobel Prize Make It True?' *Canadian Public Administration* 33, no. 1 (spring 1988), 22.
13 Donald J. Savoie, *Thatcher, Reagan, Mulroney: In Search of a New Bureaucracy* (Pittsburgh: University of Pittsburgh Press, 1994), 109.
14 Quoted in Peter Hennessy, *Cabinet* (Oxford: Basil Blackwell, 1986), 15.
15 Peter Aucoin, 'Politicians, Public Servants and Public Management: Getting Government Right,' in B. Guy Peters and Donald J. Savoie, eds., *Governance in a Changing Environment* (Montreal: McGill-Queen's University Press, 1995), 113.
16 See, among others, Savoie, *Thatcher, Reagan, Mulroney*, chap. 11.
17 See, among many others, J.A.R. Marriott, *English Political Institutions*, 4th ed. (Oxford: Clarendon Press, 1938).
18 Michael Heseltine, quoted in Simon James, *British Cabinet Government* (London: Routledge, 1992), 33.
19 See, among others, David M. Cameron, 'Power and Responsibility in the Public Service: Summary of Discussions,' *Canadian Public Administration* 2, no. 3 (1978), 361.
20 Arthur Kroeger, 'A Retrospective on Policy Development in Ottawa,' *Canadian Public Administration* 39, no. 4 (winter 1996), 460.
21 David E. Smith, *The Invisible Crown: The First Principle of Canadian Government* (Toronto: University of Toronto Press, 1995), 94.
22 Jacques Bourgault and Stephane Dion, 'The Changing Profile of Federal

Deputy Ministers, 1867 to 1988,' Research Paper no. 2 (Ottawa: Canadian Centre for Management Development, March 1991), 28.

23 Ibid., 39.

24 Frank Swift, *Strategic Management in the Public Service: The Changing Role of the Deputy Minister* (Ottawa: Canadian Centre for Management Development, Nov. 1993), 63.

25 Canada, Privy Council Office, *Discussion Paper on Values and Ethics in the Public Service* (Ottawa: PCO, Dec. 1996), 45.

26 Roméo LeBlanc, 'The Public Service: Connecting with People,' *Management* 8, no. 3 (1997), 8.

27 See, among others, Aucoin, 'Politicians, Public Servants, and Public Management,' 117.

28 Ibid., 118.

29 Quoted in Steven Kelman, 'Public Choice and Public Spirit,' *Public Interest*, no. 87 (1987), 81.

30 Savoie, *Thatcher, Reagan, Mulroney*, 304.

31 Nick d'Ombrain wrote after reading an earlier version of this study that 'immigration in the 1940s, for example, used to require the coordinated policy input of Justice, Agriculture, Labour, Natural Resources, the RCMP and External and still does.'

32 Quoted in B. Guy Peters, *Managing Horizontal Government: The Politics of Coordination* (Ottawa: Canadian Centre for Management Development, 1998), 9.

33 Quoted in Richard Lipsey, 'Macdonald Commission Tells a Vital Tale,' *Financial Post* (Toronto), 26 Oct. 1985, 25.

34 Francis E. Rourke, *Bureaucracy, Politics and Public Policy* (Boston: Little Brown, 1976), 184.

35 Observations made by Bob Rae at a Canada Series Seminar, Harvard University, 3 Dec. 2001.

36 See, among others, B. Guy Peters, *The Politics of Bureaucracy* (New York: Longman, 1984).

37 For an excellent discussion on politicians and bureaucrats, see, among others, Joel D. Aberbach et al., *Bureaucrats and Politicians in Western Democracies* (Cambridge, Mass.: Harvard University Press, 1981).

38 Quoted in Savoie, *Governing from the Centre: The Concentration of Power in Canadian Politics* (Toronto: University of Toronto Press, 1999), 158.

39 See, for example, the views of Flora MacDonald and Lloyd Axworthy in ibid., chap. 7.

40 Peter Aucoin, *The New Public Management Canada in Comparative Perspective* (Montreal: IRPP, 1995), 3.

41 Lord Derek Rayner, *The Unfinished Agenda: Stamp Memorial Lecture*, University of London, Nov. 1984 (London: Athlone Press, 1984), 2 and 9.

42 See Savoie, *Thatcher, Reagan, Mulroney,* 175.
43 Robin Butler, 'Public Management: New Challenges or Familiar Prescriptions,' *Public Administration* 69, no. 3 (autumn 1991), 364. Two public servants report on the importance of the micro-level in their work and argue that 'governments have never had more policy advice.... It has been recognized that one major reason why government programs are frequently not successful is that insufficient attention has been given to their implementation.' See Michael Keating and Malcolm Holmes, 'Reply to Aucoin and Hood,' *Governance* 3, no. 2 (April 1990), 217–18.
44 Paul Tellier, 'Public Service 2000: The Renewal of the Public Service,' *Canadian Public Administration* 33, no. 2 (summer 1990), 123–32.
45 Christopher Pollitt, *Managerialism and the Public Service: The Anglo-American Experience* (Oxford: Basil Blackwell, 1998), vii.
46 John Edwards, manager of PS 2000, 'Revitalization of the Canadian Public Service,' notes for a speaking engagement to the Association of Professional Executives, 11 March 1991, Ottawa, 131.
47 Tellier, 'Public Service 2000,' 131.
48 See Savoie, *Thatcher, Reagan, Mulroney,* and Geoffrey K. Fry, 'The Thatcher Government, the Financial Management Initiative and the New Civil Service,' *Public Administration* 66, no. 2 (spring 1988), 7.
49 United Kingdom, *House of Commons,* 711–12, also Appendix 1, 170–2.
50 See *Reports on Manpower Reductions 1980–81 to the Treasury and Civil Service Committee; Report 1982–83; Report 1983–84* (London: Management and Personnel Office, n.d.).
51 Donald J. Savoie, *The Politics of Public Spending in Canada* (Toronto: University of Toronto Press, 1990), 174.
52 Quoted in Savoie, *Thatcher, Reagan, Mulroney,* 327.
53 See, for example, Savoie, *The Politics of Public Spending in Canada.*
54 Peter Aucoin and Donald J. Savoie, eds., *Managing Strategic Change: Learning from Program Review* (Ottawa: Canadian Centre for Management Development, 1998).
55 Nevil Johnson, 'Management in Government,' in Michael J. Earl, ed., *Perspectives on Management: A Multidisciplinary Analysis* (Oxford: Oxford University Press, 1983), 195.

Chapter 6: Looking Elsewhere for Policy Advice

1 B. Guy Peters and Donald J. Savoie, 'Civil Service Reform: Misdiagnosing the Patient,' *Public Administration Review* 54, no. 5 (Sept.–Oct. 1994), 418.
2 Herbert Kaufman, 'Emerging Conflicts in the Doctrines of Public Administration,' *American Political Science Review* 50 (1972), 1060.

3 See, among others, Peter Wilenski, *Public Power and Public Administration* (Sydney: Hale and Iremonger, 1986).
4 Canada, Privy Council Office, *Discussion Paper on Values and Ethics in the Public Service* (Ottawa: PCO, Dec. 1996).
5 I owe this insight to Evert Lindquist in correspondence with me after he read an earlier version of this study.
6 Patrick Weller, 'Introduction: The Institutions of Governance,' in Michael Keating et al., *Institutions on the Edge?* (St Leonards, Australia: Allen and Unwin, 2000), 4.
7 See, for example, Francis E. Rourke, 'Responsiveness and Neutral Competence in American Bureaucracy,' *Public Administration Review* 52, no. 4 (1992), 541.
8 Jon Pierre, 'Public Consultation and Citizen Participation: Dilemmas of Policy Advice,' in B. Guy Peters and Donald J. Savoie, eds., *Taking Stock: Assessing Public Sector Reforms* (Montreal: McGill-Queen's University Press, 1998), 137.
9 Marcel Massé, *Partners in the Management of Canada: The Changing Roles of Government and the Public Service*, The 1993 John L. Manion Lecture (Ottawa: Canadian Centre for Management Development, 1993), 9.
10 Pierre, 'Public Consultation and Citizen Participation,' 139.
11 Arthur Kroeger, 'The Internet and the Future of Representative Government,' paper at the Conference of the Institute for Public Administration of Canada, Edmonton, 7 May 2001, 1–2.
12 See Alan C. Cairns, *Charter versus Federalism* (Montreal: McGill-Queen's University Press, 1992).
13 Tom Parklington, 'Against Inflating Human Rights,' *The Windsor Yearbook of Access to Justice* (Windsor, Ont.: University of Windsor, 1982), 85.
14 'Canadians Challenging Authority, Report Says,' *National Post* (Toronto), 21 Jan. 2002, A2.
15 Quoted in Sharon L. Sutherland, 'Does Westminster Government Have a Future?' Occasional Paper Series (Ottawa: Institute of Governance, 11 June 1996), 5.
16 See James A. Desveaux, Evert A. Lindquist, and Glen Toner, 'Organizing for Policy Innovation in Public Bureaucracy,' in *Canadian Journal of Political Science* 27, no. 3 (Sept. 1994), 493–528.
17 Massé, *Partners in the Management of Canada*, 5 and 8.
18 Jocelyne Bourgon, *Management in the New Public Sector Culture* (Ottawa: Public Policy Forum, 28 Oct. 1993), 10.
19 Paul Tellier, *First Annual Report to the Prime Minister on the Public Service of Canada* (Ottawa: Privy Council Office, 1992).

20 Jocelyne Bourgon, *Fifth Annual Report to the Prime Minister on the Public Service of Canada* (Ottawa: Privy Council Office, 1998), 10–11.

21 *Government of the Future* (Paris: OECD, 2000), 32.

22 Canada, Task Force on Program Review Private Sector Advisory Committee, *News Release*, Ottawa, 11 March 1986, and Erik Nielsen, *The House Is Not a Home: An Autobiography* (Toronto: Macmillan of Canada, 1989).

23 This is not to suggest, however, that the two authors think that the federal government has been successful in its consultation efforts. See Mark C. Baetz and Brian Tanguay, 'Damned If You Do, Damned If You Don't: Government and the Conundrum of Consultation in the Environmental Sector,' *Canadian Public Administration* 41, no. 3 (Autumn 1998), 396.

24 Arthur Kroeger, 'Reflection on Being a Deputy Minister,' Speech to the Canadian Club, Ottawa, 25 Jan. 1991, 3. See also Evert A. Lindquist, who made a similar observation earlier, in 'Public Managers and Policy Communities: Learning to Meet New Challenges,' *Canadian Public Administration* 35, no. 2 (summer 1992), 127–59.

25 J.R. Mallory, *The Structure of Canadian Government* (Toronto: Macmillan, 1971), 114–15.

26 Walter L. Gordon, *A Political Memoir* (Toronto: McClelland and Stewart, 1977), 97–8.

27 Jeffrey Simpson, *The Friendly Dictatorship: Reflections on Canadian Democracy* (Toronto: McClelland and Stewart, 2001), 31–3.

28 See, for example, Paul Martin's 2001 Budget Speech. See also Evert A. Lindquist, 'A Quarter Century of Canadian Think Tanks: Evolving Institutions, Conditions and Strategies,' in Diane Stone et al., eds., *Think Tanks across Nations: A Comparative Approach* (Manchester: Manchester University Press, 1998), 129–44.

29 IRPP promotes its mission statement in all its publications. See, for example, Donald J. Savoie, *Pulling against Gravity: Economic Development in New Brunswick during the McKenna Years* (Montreal: IRPP, 2001), 1.

30 See, among others, Evert A. Lindquist, 'Think Tanks or Clubs? Assessing the Influence and Roles of Canadian Policy Institutes,' *Canadian Public Administration* 36, no. 4 (winter 1993), 548.

31 The Honourable Paul Martin, *The Budget Speech 2001: Securing Progress in an Uncertain World* (Ottawa: Department of Finance, 10 Dec. 2001).

32 G.B. Doern and R.W. Phidd, *Canadian Public Policy: Ideas, Structure, Process* (Toronto: Methuen, 1983).

33 L.A. Pal, *Public Policy Analysis: An Introduction* (Toronto: Methuen, 1987), 95.

34 Doern and Phidd, *Canadian Public Policy*, 542–3.

35 John W. Langford and K. Lorne Brownsey, 'Think Tanks and Modern Gover-

nance,' in John W. Langford and K. Lorne Brownsey, eds., *Think Tanks and Governance in the Asia Pacific Region* (Halifax: Institute for Research on Public Policy, 1991), 3.

36 Allan Tupper, 'Think Tanks, Public Debt, and the Politics of Expertise in Canada,' *Canadian Public Administration* 36, no. 4 (winter 1994), 545.

37 Quoted in Peter C. Newman, *Titans* (Toronto: Penguin Canada, 1999). The Business Council on National Issues (BCNI), founded in 1976, changed its name to the Canadian Council of Chief Executives in January 2002.

38 Quoted in Donald E. Abelson, 'Public Visibility and Policy Relevance: Assessing the Impact and Influence of Canadian Policy Institutes,' *Canadian Public Administration* 42, no. 2 (summer 1999), 241.

39 G. Bruce Doern and Brian W. Tomlin, *Faith and Fear: The Free Trade Story* (Toronto: Stoddart, 1991), 27.

40 See the special issue on think tanks and research institutes, *Canadian Public Administration* 36, no. 4 (winter 1993).

41 See www.ppforum.com about history.

42 One example is the role that the forum played in the government's handling of a request for financial support of Canada's NHL hockey teams.

43 See www.iog.ca/map.html

44 See www.policyresearch.gc.ca

45 Ibid.

46 *Annual Review, 1999–2000* (Ottawa: Canadian Policy Research Networks, 2001), 29.

47 See www.cprn.com

48 See, for example, 'Judy and Peter Went to Ottawa,' *Globe and Mail* (Toronto), 11 Feb. 1995, A4.

49 Herman Bakvis, 'Rebuilding Policy Capacity in an Era of Virtual Government,' paper presented to the Public Policy and Administration at the Turn of the Century Conference, Lady Margaret Hall, Oxford University, 10–11 July 1998, 29.

50 See R.S. Ritchie, *An Institute for Research on Public Policy: A Study and Recommendations* (Ottawa: Information Canada, 1971).

51 Leslie A. Pal, *Interests of State: The Politics of Language, Multiculturalism, and Feminism in Canada* (Montreal: McGill-Queen's University Press, 1993).

52 See, among others, Edward Heath, Keeling Lecture, Royal Institute of Public Administration, 7 May 1980, London, 2.

53 Quoted in Savoie, *The Politics of Public Spending in Canada* (Toronto: University of Toronto Press, 1990), 216.

54 Ibid.

55 Canada, *Strengthening Our Policy Capacity*, report of the Task Force to the

Coordinating Committee of Deputy Ministers (Policy), Privy Council Office, 3 April 1995, 34.

56 Ibid.

57 See, among others, Bakvis, 'Rebuilding Policy Capacity,' 3.

58 See, among many others, Simpson, *The Friendly Dictatorship.*

59 Bakvis, 'Rebuilding Policy Capacity,' 30.

60 Abelson, 'Public Visibility and Policy Relevance,' 243–4.

61 Ibid., 258 and 264.

62 Michael Howlett, 'Do Networks Matter? Linking Policy Network Structure to Policy Outcomes: Evidence from Four Canadian Policy Sectors, 1990–2000,' *Canadian Journal of Political Science* 25, no. 2 (June 2002), 257–61.

63 James A. Smith, *The Idea Brokers: Think Tanks and the Rise of the New Policy Elite* (New York: Free Press, 1991), 231.

64 Kroeger, 'Reflections on Being a Deputy Minister,' 6.

65 Simpson, *The Friendly Dictatorship,* 174.

66 See 'Lobbyists had role in purchase of PM's New Jets,' *National Post* (Toronto), 23 Sept. 2002, A7.

67 Simpson, *The Friendly Dictatorship,* 46.

68 See, for example, Ignace Snellen, 'Public Service in an Information Society,' in B. Guy Peters and Donald J. Savoie, eds., *Governance in the Twenty-first Century: Revitalizing the Public Service* (Montreal: McGill-Queen's University Press, 2001), 227–43.

69 See, among others, Reg Alcock and Donald G. Levihan, *Opening the E-Government File: Governing in the 21st Century* (Ottawa: Centre for Collaborative Government, Jan. 2001), 8.

70 Quoted in Kroeger, 'The Internet and the Future of Representative Government,' The Conference of the Institute for Public Administration of Canada, Edmonton, 7 May 2001, 1.

71 Quoted in Darin Barney, *Prometheus Wired: The Hope for Democracy in the Age of Network Democracy* (Chicago: University of Chicago Press, 2000), 21.

72 Ibid., 8 and 11.

73 See, for example, 'Caught in the Net,' *Economist,* 24 March 2001, 26.

74 Mel Cappe, 'Remarks to the Arthur Kroeger College of Public Affairs, Leadership Forum Awards Dinner,' Privy Council Office, Ottawa, 6 Feb. 2002, 7.

75 Mel Cappe, *Eighth Annual Report to the Prime Minister on the Public Service of Canada* (Ottawa: Privy Council Office, 2001), 3.

76 Alcock and Levihan, *Opening the E-Government File,* 18.

77 Quoted in Barney, *Prometheus Wired,* 238.

78 Glen Milne, *Making Policy: A Guide to the Federal Government's Policy Process* (Ottawa: Glen Milne, 1999), 32.

79 Ibid., 4.
80 *Building a Higher Quality of Life for All Canadians*, Speech from the Throne to Open the Second Session of the Thirty-Sixth Parliament of Canada, Ottawa, 12 Oct. 1999, 14.
81 Barney, *Prometheus Wired.*
82 Quoted in *Sightings* (Fredericton: University of New Brunswick), no. 39 (autumn 2000), 2.
83 Lawrence K. Grossman, *The Electronic Republic: Reshaping Democracy in the Information Age* (New York: Viking, 1995), 33–4.
84 'A Survey of Government and the Internet,' *Economist*, 24 June 2001.
85 Walter Wriston, *The Twilight of Sovereignty: How the Information Revolution Is Transforming Our World* (New York: Macmillan, 1992), 153, and Barney, *Prometheus Wired*, 20.
86 Roger Gibbins, 'Federalism in a Digital World,' *Canadian Journal of Political Science* 33, no. 4 (Dec. 2000), 668. See also Barry N. Hague and Brian D. Loader, *Digital Democracy: Discourse and Decision Making in the Information Age* (London: Routledge, 1999), and Christine Bellamy and Joyn A. Taylor, *Governing in the Information Age* (Buckingham: Open University Press, 1998).
87 Consultations with officials at the Treasury Board Secretariat, Ottawa, Oct. and Dec. 2001.
88 See, among others, Savoie, *Governing from the Centre.*
89 For an insightful discussion of Trudeau-era changes to the machinery of government, see Richard D. French, *How Ottawa Decides: Planning and Individual Policy Making, 1968–80* (Ottawa: Canadian Institute for Economic Policy, 1980).
90 Gordon Robertson, *Memoirs of a Very Civil Servant* (Toronto: University of Toronto Press, 2001), 255.
91 See Peter Aucoin, 'Politicians, Public Servants and Public Management: Getting Government Right,' in Peters and Savoie, eds., *Governance in the Twenty-first Century*, 121.
92 See Savoie, *Thatcher, Reagan, Mulroney: In Search of a New Bureaucracy* (Pittsburgh: University of Pittsburgh Press, 1994), 224.
93 Peter Aucoin, 'Organizational Change in the Machinery of Canadian Government: From Rational Management to Brokerage Politics,' *Canadian Journal of Political Science* 9, no. 1 (March 1986), 4, 11–27, Savoie, *Thatcher, Reagan, Mulroney*, 226.
94 Quoted in Savoie, *Thatcher, Reagan, Mulroney*, 226.
95 Ibid.
96 Loretta J. O'Connor, 'Chief of Staff,' *Policy Options* (April 1991), 23–5.
97 Bakvis, 'Re-building Policy Capacity,' 11.

98 See Jacques Bourgault and Stéphane Dion, 'Governments Come and Go, But What of Senior Civil Servants? Canadian Deputy Ministers and Transition in Power (1867–1967),' *Governance* 2, no. 2 (1991), 124–51.

99 Quoted in Savoie, *Governing from the Centre: The Concentration of Power in Canadian Politics* (Toronto: University of Toronto Press, 1999).

100 Colin Campbell, *Governments under Stress: Political Executives and Key Bureaucrats in Washington, London, and Ottawa* (Toronto: University of Toronto Press, 1983), 83.

101 Ibid.

102 Robertson, *Memoirs of a Very Civil Servant*, 308–9.

103 *Journal* (Ottawa), 9 Oct. 1974, and Robertson, *Memoirs of a Very Civil Servant*, 309.

104 See Canada, Department of Finance, *Securing Economic Renewal: Budget Papers*, 23 May 1985, 26–7. Dissolved corporations included Canadian Sports Pool Corporation, Canagrex, and Loto Canada.

105 See 'Quote of the Week,' *Globe and Mail* (Toronto), 23 March 2002, A9.

106 Consultations with senior government officials, Ottawa, Nov.–Dec. 2001.

107 O'Connor, 'Chief of Staff,' 24.

108 See, among others, Savoie, *The Politics of Public Spending in Canada* (Toronto: University of Toronto Press, 1990).

109 'The Axworthy Empire,' and 'Transport Ministry Staff Ballooned under Liberals,' *Globe and Mail* (Toronto), 4 Dec. 1984, A1 and A4.

110 My conversation with senior government officials, Ottawa, 28 May 2002.

111 Hon. Paul Martin, *The Budget Speech 2001: Securing Progress in an Uncertain World* (Ottawa: Department of Finance, 10 Dec. 2001), 4.

112 Edward Greenspon and Anthony Wilson-Smith, *Double Vision: The Inside Story of the Liberals in Power* (Toronto: Doubleday, 1996), 67.

113 J.L. Manion, *Dalhousie Conference on Career Public Service: Notes for a Presentation to the Dalhousie Conference on Career Public Service* (Ottawa: Canadian Centre for Management Development, 5 Oct. 1990), 10–11.

114 David Zussman and Jack Jabes, *The Vertical Solitudes* (Montreal: IRPP, 1989), 196.

115 Daryl Copeland, *Foreign Service in the Nineties: Problems and Prospects* (Ottawa: Professional Association of Foreign Service Officials, 1990), 27.

116 My conversations with a senior official at the Treasury Board Secretariat, Ottawa, Dec. 2001.

117 See Savoie, *Thatcher, Reagan, Mulroney*, 341.

118 B. Ostry, 'Making Deals: The Public Official as Politician,' in John W. Langford, ed., *Fear and Ferment: Public Sector Management Today* (Toronto: Institute of Public Administration of Canada, 1987), 171.

119 The observation was made by a senior official in a line department at a CCMD-sponsored seminar held in 1996 to review papers produced for B. Guy Peters and Donald J. Savoie, eds., *Taking Stock: Assessing Public Sector Reforms* (Montreal: McGill-Queen's University Press, 1998).

120 A.W. Johnson, 'The Role of Deputy Ministers: III,' *Canadian Public Administration* 4, no. 4 (Dec. 1961), 373.

121 George Anderson, 'The New Focus on the Policy Capacity of the Federal Government: I,' *Canadian Public Administration* 39, no. 4 (winter 1996), 471.

Chapter 7: Deputy Ministers and Management

1 Quoted in Sharon Sutherland, 'The Al-Mashat Affair: Administrative Responsibility in Parliamentary Institutions,' *Canadian Public Administration* 34, no. 2 (winter 1991), 587.

2 George Post, *Conversations with Canadian Public Service Leaders* (Ottawa: CCMD, March 1996), 13.

3 Gordon Robertson, *Memoirs of a Very Civil Servant* (Toronto: University of Toronto Press, 2001), 38.

4 A.W. Johnson, 'The Role of the Deputy Minister,' *Canadian Public Administration* 4, no. 4 (1961), 363.

5 See, among others, Donald J. Savoie, *The Politics of Public Spending in Canada* (Toronto: University of Toronto Press, 1990), chap. 5.

6 *Reflections on a Decade of Serving Parliament* (Ottawa: Office of the Auditor General, 2001), 2.

7 See, among others, Peter Aucoin, *The New Public Management: Canada in Comparative Perspective* (Montreal: IRPP, 1995).

8 Jacques Bourgault and Stéphane Dion, *The Changing Profile of Federal Deputy Ministers* (Ottawa: CCMD, 1991), v.

9 Ibid., v–vii and 39.

10 A directory of federal deputy ministers, Privy Council Office, Ottawa, Sept. 1981, unpublished.

11 Frank Swift, *Strategic Management in the Public Service: The Changing Role of the Deputy Minister* (Ottawa: CCMD, 1993), 43.

12 Jacques Bourgault, *Le rôle et les défis contemporains des sous-ministres du Gouvernement fédéral du Canada* (Ottawa: Centre canadien de gestion, 2002), 15–40.

13 Consultations with Harrison McCain, Florenceville, New Brunswick, 24 April 2001.

14 J.E. Hodgetts, *The Canadian Public Service: A Physiology of Government, 1867–1970* (Toronto: University of Toronto Press, 1973), 208.

15 Johnson, 'The Role of the Deputy Minister,' 364.
16 The Public Service Employment Act, section 33, states: 'No deputy head ... shall a) engage in work for or against a candidate; b) engage in work for or against a political party; or c) be a candidate.'
17 Canada, Royal Commission on Government Organizations, *Report 1* (1960) 29.
18 Canada, Privy Council Office, *Discussion Paper on Values and Ethics in the Public Service* (Ottawa: PCO, Dec. 1996), 19.
19 Jacques Bourgault, 'La satisfaction des ministres du gouvernement Mulroney face à leur sous-ministre, 1984–1993' (Ottawa: Canadian Centre for Management Development, 1998), 41.
20 Donald J. Savoie, *Governing from the Centre: The Concentration of Power in Canadian Politics* (Toronto: University of Toronto Press, 1999), 280.
21 'Lewis Mackenzie: On Choosing a Chief of Defence Staff,' *Globe and Mail* (Toronto), 27 May 1996, A17.
22 Quoted in Savoie, *Governing from the Centre*, 281.
23 Jacques Bourgault, 'The Mintzberg Model and Some Empirical Evidence: Putting It to the Test,' in Henry Mintzberg and Jacques Bourgault, *Managing Publicly* (Toronto: IPAC, 2000), 159.
24 Ibid., 166.
25 Public Policy Forum, *Managing Change: The Evolving Role of the Commonwealth's Top Public Servants* (Ottawa: Public Policy Forum, Dec. 1998), 46.
26 Bourgault, 'The Mintzberg Model and Some Empirical Evidence,' 167.
27 Jacques Bourgault, 'De Kafka au Net: La lutte incessante du sous-ministre pour contrôler son agenda,' *Gestion* 22, no. 2 (summer 1997), 21–2.
28 Ibid.
29 Quoted in Alasdair Roberts, 'Worrying about Misconduct: The Central Lobby and the PS 2000 Reforms,' *Canadian Public Administration* 39, no. 4 (winter 1996), 504.
30 See, among others, Public Policy Forum, *Managing Change*, 18.
31 Ibid., 13.
32 See Savoie, *Governing from the Centre*, chap. 7.
33 Ibid., 315.
34 Canada, Privy Council Office, *Office of the Deputy Minister* (Ottawa, n.d.), 1.
35 Ibid.
36 The Interpretation Act does not provide power to the deputy minister to make regulations.
37 Hodgetts, *The Canadian Public Service*, 208.
38 See, among others, Herbert R. Balls, 'Decision-Making: The Role of the Deputy Minister,' *Canadian Public Administration* 19, no. 4 (1976), 417–31.

39 Johnson, 'The Role of the Deputy Minister,' 367.

40 Ibid.

41 See Savoie, *Thatcher, Reagan, Mulroney: In Search of a New Bureaucracy* (Pittsburgh: University of Pittsburgh Press, 1994).

42 See, for example, Paul Tellier, 'Public Service 2000: The Renewal of the Public Service,' *Canadian Public Administration* 33, no. 2 (summer 1990), 131.

43 V. Peter Harder, 'The Public Service of Canada: A Key Partner in Productivity,' presentation to the SUMMA Forum on Productivity, Ottawa, 16 March 1999, 3, mimeo.

44 Ralph Heintzman, 'The Effects of Globalization on Management Practices: Should the Public Sector Operate on Different Parameters?' paper presented to the IPAC National Conference, Fredericton, New Brunswick, 31 Aug. 1999, 7–9.

45 Post, *Conversations with Canadian Public Service Leaders*, 21.

46 G.F. Obaldeston, *Keeping Deputy Ministers Accountable* (Toronto: McGraw-Hill Ryerson, 1989), 167.

47 Ibid. See also Frank Swift, *Strategic Management in the Public Service: The Changing Role of the Deputy Minister* (Ottawa: CCMD, 1993), 9–10.

48 D. Quinn Mills, *Rebirth of the Corporation* (New York: J. Wiley, 1991), 253.

49 Frank Swift makes the same observation in *Strategic Management in the Public Service*, 13.

50 Ibid., 13.

51 'Have Zeal, Will Travel,' *Globe and Mail* (Toronto), 15 Feb. 1997, A1.

52 Alasdair Roberts, 'Worrying about Misconduct,' 511.

53 Quoted in ibid., 510.

54 'Minister Blows Gasket over Agency,' *Citizen* (Ottawa), 11 Sept. 1994, A1. See also 'Agency Restructuring over Conflict,' *Globe and Mail* (Toronto), 26 May 1994, A4.

55 Roberts, 'Worrying about Misconduct,' 511.

56 'Public Works Issuing More Window Dressing,' *Citizen* (Ottawa), 13 Jan. 1995, A2.

57 David A. Good, 'The Politics of Public Management: The HRDC Audit of Grants and Contributions' (Victoria: School of Public Administration, Jan. 2002), 17, mimeo.

58 Ibid.

59 Quoted in ibid., 10.

60 Ibid., 18.

61 Ibid., 19.

62 Quoted in ibid., 20.

63 See, among many others, 'Job-Grant Reviews and Accountant's Nightmare,' *National Post* (Toronto), 8 Feb. 2000, A9.

64 'Shovelgate Demands Full Inquiry, *Citizen* (Ottawa), 29 March 2000, A1.

65 Canada, Report of the Auditor General, *Human Resources Development Canada: Grants and Contributions* (Ottawa: Oct. 2000), 5.

66 'Embattled Stewart May Go Dutch,' *Globe and Mail* (Toronto), 2 Aug. 2000, A1.

67 See ibid. and Hugh Winsor, 'Jane Stewart Lives,' *Globe and Mail* (Toronto), 20 Jan. 2001, A13.

68 Canada, Human Resources Development Canada, News Release: Minister Stewart Releases Reports on Grants and Contributions Action Plan, 18 May 2000.

69 Arthur Kroeger, 'Speech to the Canadian Club of Ottawa – The HRDC Affair: Reflections on Accountability in Government,' Ottawa, 12 Dec. 2000, 11–12, mimeo.

70 'Audits Get PR Once-over before Release,' *Citizen* (Ottawa), 29 March 2000, A1.

71 See, among others, 'Multibillion-Dollar Mess Routine, Chrétien Says,' *Globe and Mail* (Toronto), 1 Feb. 2000, A5.

72 Written correspondence sent to the author by a former senior official with the Privy Council Office, Oct. 2002.

73 See, among others, Peter Aucoin, *The New Public Management: Canada in Comparative Perspective* (Montreal: IRPP, 1995).

74 Quoted in 'Ottawa's Missing Mind,' *Globe and Mail* (Toronto), 14 Dec. 1996, D1.

75 Savoie, *Governing from the Centre*, 354.

76 Heintzman, 'The Effects of Globalization on Management Practices,' 8.

77 Harder, 'The Public Service of Canada,' 5.

78 Hugh Winsor, 'Bureaucrats' Resignation: A Warning,' *Globe and Mail* (Toronto), 20 Oct. 1997, A4.

79 James Q. Wilson, *Bureaucracy: What Government Agencies Do and Why They Do It* (New York: Basic Books, 1989), chaps. 7 and 11.

80 Canada, Privy Council Office, *Discussion Paper on Values and Ethics in the Public Service*, 45.

81 Ralph Heintzman, 'The Dialectics of Organizational Design,' in Tom Courchene and Donald J. Savoie, eds., *The Art of the State: Governance in a World without Frontiers* (Montreal: IRPP, 2003), 242.

82 My conversation with a senior official, Ottawa, Nov. 2001.

83 'Innovation in the Federal Government: The Risk Not Taken,' paper prepared by the Public Policy Forum for the Office of the Auditor General, Ottawa, Aug. 1998, 8.

84 My conversation with a government official, Ottawa, Jan. 2002.
85 See, among others, Savoie, *Thatcher, Reagan, Mulroney,* chap. 8. See also Barbara Carroll and David Siegel, *Service in the Field: The World of Field Level Officials* (Montreal: McGill-Queen's University Press, 1999).
86 Privy Council Office, *Discussion Paper on Values and Ethics in the Public Service,* 57.
87 'Fraser Resigns Post,' *Globe and Mail* (Toronto), 24 Sept. 1985, A1.
88 See, among others, John Meisel, 'Science and the Public Trust,' paper presented to the conference 'Science and Public Trust,' Herstmonceaux Castle, Kent, England, 15–18 April 1998.
89 *Blood, Fish and Tears: A Round Table on Credibility and Acceptability of Science Advice for Decision-Making,* 23 Nov. 1998, Public Policy Forum, Ottawa, Summary of Discussions.
90 'Federal Scientists Look for Way to End Bureaucratic Filtering,' *Citizen* (Ottawa), 26 Oct. 1997, A1.
91 'Bureaucrats Sabotage Scientists,' ibid., 21 June 1997, A1.
92 Ibid. For the article by Hutchins and his colleagues, see note 102 below.
93 'DFO Scientists Decry Dishonesty,' *Citizen* (Ottawa), 5 July 1997, A1.
94 'Bureaucrats Sabotage Scientists,' ibid., A2.
95 See, among others, *Getting Science Right in the Public Sector* (Ottawa: Treasury Board Secretariat, 1997).
96 'Bureaucrats Upstage Scientists,' *Citizen* (Ottawa), 27 June 1997, A1.
97 'Health Canada Unsafe: Scientist,' ibid., 3 July 1997, A6.
98 'When Science, Politics Collide: Two Must be Run by Different Bosses, Policy Experts Say,' ibid., 12 July 1997, B1.
99 Quoted in ibid., B2.
100 Peter Aucoin makes a similar point in *Getting Science Right in the Public Sector,* 9.
101 Ibid., 20.
102 Jeffrey Hutchings, Carl Walters, and Richard Haedrich, 'Is Scientific Information Incompatible with Government Information Control?' *Canadian Journal of Fisheries and Aquatic Sciences* 54 (May 1997), 1204.
103 Ibid., 6, 9, and 10.
104 Quoted in *Getting Science Right in the Public Sector,* 18.
105 Ibid., 12.
106 Ibid., 18. The media lost interest in the science-in-government issue, and the controversy died down. From time to time, there is a front-page article on the government's attempt to 'gag' its scientists. The *Globe and Mail* ran such a piece, reporting that Health Canada had 'reimposed a gag order – on its scientists after two of them questioned a decision to have Brazilian

beef. 'See 'Federal Scientists Nuzzled after Two Criticize Beef Ban,' *Globe and Mail* (Toronto), 13 Feb. 2001, A1.

107 See also Gordon F. Osbaldeston, *Keeping Deputy Ministers Accountable* (Scarborough: McGraw-Hill Ryerson Limited, 1989), 5.

108 Barbara S. Romzck and Melvil J. Dubnick, 'Accountability,' in Jay M. Shafritz, ed., *International Encyclopedia of Public Policy and Administration* (New York: Westview Press, 1998), 6.

109 Canada, *Responsibility in the Constitution* (Ottawa: Privy Council Office, 1993), 45; see web site www.pco-bcp.gc.ca

110 See, among many others, Carol Weiss, *Evaluation Research: Methods for Assessing Program Effectiveness* (Englewood Cliffs, NJ: Prentice-Hall, 1972); Aaron Wildavsky, 'The Self-Evaluating Organization,' *Public Administration Review* 32, no. 5 (Sept./Oct. 1972), 509–20; and Wilson, *Bureaucracy.*

111 See Office of the Auditor General, *Annual Report* (Ottawa, 1986).

112 Canada, *Reflections on a Decade of Serving Parliament* (Ottawa: Office of the Auditor General, 2001), 35–6.

113 Savoie, *Governing from the Centre,* 256.

114 See Office of the Auditor General, *Annual Report.*

115 Douglas G. Hartle, 'The Role of the Auditor General of Canada,' *Canadian Tax Journal* 23, no. 3 (1975), 197.

116 See, among others, *To Meet the Needs of the Nations: Staffing the U.S. Civil Service and the Public Service of Canada* (Washington, DC: U.S. Merit Systems Protection Board, 1992). The Office of Personnel Management also produced a number of reports on ways to improve the senior executives' performance-pay initiative.

117 See Savoie, *The Politics of Public Spending in Canada,* 253.

118 Canada, *Strategic Directions for the Public Service of Canada: Priorities for 2001–2002* (Ottawa: Privy Council Office, June 2001), 1–7; see web site www.pco-bcp.gc.ca.

119 There is a COSO process that is supposed to generate systematic assessments and feedback.

120 See, for example, Public Policy Forum, *Managing Change,* 27.

121 Swift, *Strategic Management in the Public Service,* 38.

122 Quoted in Christopher Pollitt, *Managerialism and the Public Service: The Anglo-American Experience* (Oxford: Basil Blackwell, 1988), 97.

123 'Were Mergers Discussed?' *National Post* (Toronto), 4 Dec. 2000, C1.

124 'Cabinet Secrets Stolen from Bureaucrat's Car,' *National Post* (Toronto), 26 Jan. 2001, A7.

125 John L. Manion and Cynthia Williams, 'Transition Planning at the Federal

Level in Canada,' in Donald J. Savoie, ed., *Taking Power: Managing Government Transitions* (Toronto: Institute of Public Administration of Canada, 1993), 109.

126 'Ex-Civil Servant Used to Challenge,' *Globe and Mail* (Toronto), 24 Jan. 2002, B10.

127 See, for example, Nevil Johnson, 'Managing in Government,' in Michael J. Earl, ed., *Perspectives on Management* (Oxford: Oxford University Press, 1983), 179–196.

128 Canada, *Reflections on a Decade of Serving Parliament*, 84.

129 See Frederick C. Mosher, *Democracy and the Public Service*, 2nd ed. (New York: Oxford University Press, 1982), 154.

130 For example, ministers are not allowed for two years to make representations for or on behalf of any other person to any department with which they had direct and significant official dealings. For career officials, the restriction lasts only one year. See Canada, *Conflict of Interest and Past-Employment Code for Public Office Holders* (Ottawa: Office of the Ethics Counsellor, 1994), 17. The code is available on the Government of Canada website under the Industry Department.

131 The committee labels that 'external comparability' and draw its findings from a database of 300 organizations representing all sectors of the economy. See Canada, *Advisory Committee on Senior Level Retention and Compensation, Fourth Report: March 2002* (Ottawa:'Treasury Board Secretariat, 2002), 1.

132 Ibid.

133 'Senior Civil Servants Use Up Entire Budget for Bonuses,' *National Post* (Toronto), 29 Aug. 2002, A1 and A9.

134 C.E.S. Franks, *The Parliament of Canada* (Toronto: University of Toronto Press, 1987), 237.

135 Ekos conducted the survey in May 2001 for Canada, *The Road Ahead: Perceptions of the Public Service* (Ottawa: Public Service Commission, 2002), 1.

Chapter 8: Parliamentarians, Ministers, and Public Servants

1 A. Blais and E. Gidengil, *Making Representative Democracy Work: The Views of Canadians*, Royal Commission on Electoral Reform and Party Financing 14 (Toronto: Dundurn Press, 1991), 36.

2 David C. Docherty, *Mr. Smith Goes to Ottawa: Life in the House of Commons* (Vancouver: UBC Press, 1997), 62.

3 'Liberals Divided over Membership Rules,' *Citizen* (Ottawa), 28 Jan. 2002, A5.

4 Mitchell Sharp, 'Presentation to a Conference Organized by the Canadian Study of Parliament Group,' Ottawa, n.d., 1, mimeo.

5 Quoted in Docherty, *Mr. Smith Goes to Ottawa*, 75.

6 Reg Whitaker, 'Virtual Political Parties and the Decline of Democracy,' *Policy Options* 22, no. 5 (June 2000), 19.

7 Peter Aucoin, 'Politicians, Public Servants and Public Management: Getting Government Rights,' in B. Guy Peters and Donald J. Savoie, eds., *Governance in a Changing Environment* (Montreal: McGill-Queen's University Press, 1995), 115.

8 Platforms for all major parties are accessible on the party's web site. See, for example, www.canadianalliance.ca/platform

9 See, for example, Richard Johnston et al., *Letting the People Decide: Dynamics of a Canadian Election* (Montreal: McGill-Queen's University Press, 1992), 244.

10 Nelson W. Polsby and Aaron Wildavsky, *Presidential Elections: Strategies of American Electoral Politics* (New York: Free Press, 1991), 246.

11 Johnston et al., *Letting the People Decide*, 244.

12 Ibid, 168.

13 Ibid., 225.

14 Quoted in Savoie, *Governing from the Centre: The Concentration of Power in Canadian Politics* (Toronto: University of Toronto Press, 1999), 79.

15 'PM's Camp Beats Tactical Retreat,' *National Post* (Toronto), 2 Feb. 2002, A12.

16 'Iron Fist of PMO,' *The Financial Post* (Toronto), 9 May 1998, 10.

17 Whitaker, 'Virtual Political Parties and the Decline of Democracy,' 21.

18 See, for example, Hugh Winsor, 'How the Liberals Won Again?' *Globe and Mail* (Toronto), 12 Feb. 2001, A4.

19 Harold D. Clarke et al., *Absent Mandate: Interpreting Change in Canadian Elections*, 2nd ed. (Toronto: Gage Educational Publishing Co., 1991), 8, 10.

20 Docherty, *Mr. Smith Goes to Ottawa*, 71.

21 R.K. Carty and L. Erickson, 'Parties and Candidate Selection in the 1988 Canadian General Election,' *Canadian Journal of Political Science* 24, no. 2 (1991), 347.

22 Docherty, *Mr. Smith Goes to Ottawa*, 69.

23 Ibid., 9.

24 C.E.S. Franks, *The Parliament of Canada* (Toronto: University of Toronto Press, 1987), 23–4.

25 See, among many others, Savoie, *Governing from the Centre*, chap. 8.

26 See, among others, Bernard Crick, *The Reform of Parliament* (New York: Doubleday, 1965), x.

27 Ibid., chap. 1. See also Anthony Sampson, *The Changing Anatomy of Britain* (New York: Random House, 1982), chap. 3.

28 See, among others, Docherty, *Mr. Smith Goes to Ottawa.*

29 Franks, *The Parliament of Canada*, 45.

30 Quoted in Savoie, *Governing from the Centre*, 83.

31 Docherty, *Mr. Smith Goes to Ottawa*, 141.

32 See, among others, Peter C. Dobell, 'Stress and the MP,' *Parliamentary Government*, 9 (Nov. 1999), 5.

33 'A Career Marked by Flair for Drama,' *Globe and Mail* (Toronto), 15 Jan. 2002, A5.

34 Docherty, *Mr. Smith Goes to Ottawa*, 131–2.

35 Franks, *The Parliament of Canada*, 97–8.

36 'Mr. Manley on the Move: Is the Sky the Limit?' *National Post* (Toronto), 26 Jan. 2002, B4.

37 'Chrétien Advised to Drop Promise,' ibid., 14 Feb. 2001, A6.

38 Quoted in Savoie, *Governing from the Centre*, 246.

39 Ibid.

40 Quoted in Edward Greenspon and Anthony Wilson-Smith, *Double Vision: The Inside Story of the Liberals in Power* (Toronto: Doubleday, 1966), 209.

41 'Young participera aux audiences publiques sur Via Rail et la loi sur l'assurance-chômage,' *L'Acadie Nouvelle* (Caraquet), 23 July 1989, A3.

42 See, for example, Herman Bakvis, 'Transport Canada and Program Review,' in Peter Aucoin and Donald J. Savoie, eds., *Managing Strategic Change: Program Review and Beyond* (Ottawa: Canadian Centre for Management Development, 1998).

43 Docherty, *Mr. Smith Goes to Ottawa*, 125.

44 'Sending Money Home,' *Toronto Star*, 11 March 2000, H1.

45 Docherety, *Mr. Smith Goes to Ottawa*, 140.

46 The author, a former government MP under the Liberals gave me a copy of the letter.

47 Exchange of material between a minister and his exempt staff and the deputy minister and senior departmental officials. The exchange consists of nine memoranda, and the material was given to me by a former minister.

48 This point was made time and again by MPs whom I consulted for this book, Ottawa, March 2002.

49 See, among others, Ann T. Perkins and C.E.S. Franks, *Accountability and Canada's Federal Public Service* (Ottawa: CCMD, 1992), 30–40, mimeo.

50 Canada, *Annual Report*, Office of the Auditor General of Canada (Ottawa: Supply and Services, 1991), 130.

51 Department of Industry Act, web site: http://lawsjustice@gc.ca

52 W.F. Dawson, *Procedure in the Canadian House of Commons* (Toronto: University of Toronto Press, 1962), 16.

53 Canada, House of Commons, Special Committee on Procedure, *Third Report*, 6 Dec. 1968, 429.

54 J.R. Mallory and P. Thomas, quoted in Canada, 'The Business of Supply: Completing the Circle of Control,' Standing Committee on Procedure and House Affairs, Sixty-fourth Report, n.d., 21.

55 Canada, Report of the Liaison Committee on Committees' Effectiveness, *Parliamentary Government*, no. 43 (June 1993), 4.

56 Canada, House of Commons, *Debates*, 7 Feb. 1994, 962.

57 Robert Giroux, paper presented to 'Changing Nature of Power and Democracy,' IRPP and CIRRD conference, Montebello, Quebec, 12 Oct. 2001, 2.

58 Letter from John L. Manion to the author, 29 Dec. 2001, and John L. Manion, *Information for Parliament on Government Finance*, report prepared for the Office of the Auditor General, 18 April 1992, 23–4.

59 See, among others, D.J. Savoie, *The Politics of Public Spending in Canada* (Toronto: University of Toronto Press, 1990).

60 For an overview of the estimates process, see www.gc.ca-tbs.sct

61 Manion, *Information for Parliament on Government Finance*, 26.

62 Ibid., 27.

63 R.B. Bryce, 'Reflections on the Lambert Report,' *Canadian Public Administration* 22, no. 4 (winter 1979), 673.

64 'Leadership,' notes for an address by J.L. Manion to the Advance Management Program, CCMD, Ottawa, 25 June 1993, 15.

65 My conversation with a government MP, Ottawa, 28 Jan. 2002.

66 I owe this point to Evert Lindquist, who has dealt with this issue in his writings and who emphasized its importance in correspondence with me, Oct. 2002.

67 'Nova Scotia MP Picked to Oversee ACOA,' *Times and Transcript* (Moncton), 10 Jan. 2001, A6.

68 Sharon Sutherland, 'Responsible Government and Ministerial Responsibility: Every Reform Is Its Own Problem,' *Canadian Journal of Political Science* 24, no. 1 (March 1991), 103.

69 In the absence of principles and ideologies, sitting in cabinet becomes the end rather than the means.

70 Quoted in 'In the Spotlight,' *Time*, Canadian edition, 28 Jan. 2002, 17.

71 John M. Reid, 'A Limited Resource,' notes for an address to the Institute of Public Administration, Ottawa, 7 May 1980, 7.

72 See, among others, Savoie, *Governing from the Centre*, chap. 5.

73 Quoted in ibid., 241.

74 James L. Payne and Oliver H. Woshinsky, 'Incentives for Political Participation,' *World Politics* 24 (1972), 519.
75 See 'Dear Minister. A Letter to an Old Friend on Being a Successful Minister,' notes for remarks by Gordon Osbaldeston to the Association of Professional Executives of the Public Service of Canada, Ottawa, 22 Jan. 1988, 2.
76 Ibid., 4.
77 Thomas J. Peters and Robert H. Waterman, Jr, *In Search of Excellence: Lessons from America's Best-Run Companies* (New York: Harper and Row, 1982), chaps. 11 and 12.
78 Canada, *Notes on the Responsibility of Public Servants in Relation to Parliamentary Committees* (Ottawa: Privy Council Office, Dec. 1990), 1.
79 Paul G. Thomas, 'The Changing Nature of Accountability,' in B. Guy Peters and Donald J. Savoie, eds., *Taking Stock: Assessing Public Sector Reforms* (Montreal: McGill-Queen's University Press, 1998), 361.
80 Canada, *Crisis Management* (Ottawa: PCO, n.d.), 5–14.
81 Kevin Theakston, *The Civil Service since 1945* (Oxford: Blackwell, 1995), chap. 1, makes the same case for Britain.
82 See, among many others, Greenspon and Wilson-Smith, *Double Vision*, chap. 2.
83 Ibid., 22.
84 Quoted in ibid., 133.
85 *Creating Opportunity: The Liberal Plan for Canada* (Ottawa: Liberal Party of Canada, 1993).
86 See, for example, Savoie, *Governing from the Centre*, chap. 4.
87 Quoted in ibid., 155.
88 'Le comité de la route 185 veut rencontrer Jean Chrétien,' *L'Acadie Nouvelle* (Caraguet), 7 May 2002, 3.
89 'Penalty Killer PM Plays Rough,' quoted in *Globe and Mail* (Toronto), 1 Dec. 2000, A1.
90 Canada, *Notes on the Responsibilities of Public Servants*, 2–4.
91 My conversation with a deputy minister, Ottawa, 11 Feb. 2002.
92 My conversation with a senior government official, Ottawa, 10 Dec. 2001.
93 My conversation with a former deputy minister, Ottawa, 10 Dec. 2001.
94 Peter Dobell, *Reforming Parliamentary Practice: The Views of MPs*, Policy Matters Series 1, no. 9 (Montreal: IRPP, Dec. 2000), 11.
95 My conversation with an official employed by the Library of Parliament, Ottawa, 11 Feb. 2002.
96 Quoted in Theakston, *The Civil Service since 1945*, 169. Armstrong made the observation in relation to the Peter Wright spy case in Australia.
97 Ibid., 170.

98 See *Public Service Survey – 1999* (Ottawa: Treasury Board Secretariat, 2000). See also 'Treasury Board's Robillard Surveys 190,000 Public Servants,' *Hill Times* (Ottawa), 3 June 2002, 3.

99 'A Totally Dysfunctional Institution,' *National Post* (Toronto), 12 Feb. 2001, A1.

100 Occasional Papers on *Parliamentary Government*, Ottawa, no. 1 (Sept. 1995), 7.

Chapter 9: Reshaping the Bargain

1 See, among others, Sharon Sutherland, *Does Westminster Government Have a Future?* (Ottawa: Institute on Governance, June 1996), 6.

2 Donald J. Savoie, *Governing from the Centre: The Concentration of Power in Canadian Politics* (Toronto: University of Toronto Press, 1999), 302.

3 My conversation with a former deputy minister, Ottawa, Feb. 2002.

4 See www.tbs-sct.gc.ca about the Treasury Board Secretariat.

5 James Douglas, 'Review Article: The Overloaded Crown,' *British Journal of Political Science* 6, no. 3 (1976), 492.

6 See, for example, Thomas S. Axworthy, 'Of Secretaries to Princes,' *Canadian Public Administration* 31, no. 2 (summer 1998).

7 Quoted in Peter Aucoin and Donald J. Savoie, 'Launching and Organizing a Program Review Exercise,' paper prepared for the Canadian Centre for Management Development, Ottawa, 1998, 2.

8 Ibid.

9 See Savoie, *Governing from the Centre.*

10 Donald J. Savoie, *Thatcher, Reagan, Mulroney: In Search of a New Bureaucracy* (Pittsburgh: University of Pittsburgh Press, 1994).

11 See, for example, Peter Aucoin, *The New Public Management: Canada in Comparative Perspective* (Montreal: IRPP, 1995).

12 'Immigration Overload Blind-sides Gagliano,' *Globe and Mail* (Toronto), 2 March 2001, A4.

13 See, for example, Jack Douglas, *The Myth of the Welfare State* (New Brunswick, NJ: Transaction Publishers, 1989), 408, and Anthony Downs, *Inside Bureaucracy* (Boston: Little, Brown, 1967), 264.

14 See also James R. Mitchell and Sharon Sutherland, 'Relations between Politicians and Public Servants,' in M. Charih et al., eds., *New Public Management and Public Administration in Canada* (Toronto: IPAC, 1997), 192.

15 Accenture, *E-government Leadership*, March 2001.

16 Ibid.

17 My conversation with senior officials, Ottawa, Dec. 2001.

18 See Paul C. Light, *Thickening Government: Federal Hierarchy and the Diffusion of Authority* (Washington, DC: Brookings Institution and the Governance Institute, 1995), 64.

19 Alex Himelfarb, 'The Intermestic Challenge: Notes for an Address at the APEX Symposium 2002,' Privy Council Office, Ottawa, 5 June 2002, 5.

20 See, among others, Peter Aucoin, 'Politicians, Public Servants and Public Management,' in B. Guy Peters and Donald J. Savoie, eds., *Governance in a Changing Environment* (Ottawa: Canadian Centre for Management Development, 1995), 129.

21 Others include the Aboriginal Healing Foundation, the Canada Foundation for Sustainable Development Technology, Canada Health Infoway, the Canadian Foundation for Climate and Atmospheric Sciences, the Green Municipal Enabling Fund, and the Green Municipal Investments Fund. See, among others, Canada, *Matters of Special Importance – 2001*, Report of the Auditor General, 4 Dec. 2001, 13.

22 My conversations with senior officials at the Treasury Board Secretariat. Strangway quote: Canada, House of Commons, Standing Committee on Industry, Science, and Technology, *Evidence*, 3 April 2001, 8.

23 Canada, Press Release, Office of the Prime Minister, 25 June 1993.

24 Ibid.

25 My conversation with a former deputy minister, Ottawa, March 2002.

26 See, for example, Arthur Kroeger, 'The Central Agencies and Program Review,' in Peter Aucoin and Donald J. Savoie, eds., *Managing Strategic Change: Learning from Program Review* (Ottawa: CCMD, 1998), 11–38.

27 See Savoie, *The Politics of Public Spending in Canada* (Toronto: University of Toronto Press, 1990), chap. 7.

28 Aucoin and Savoie, eds., *Managing Strategic Change*.

29 Frederick C. Mosher, *Democracy and the Public Service* (New York: Oxford University Press, 1982), 218.

30 'Reforms May Lead to Patronage Problems,' *Edmonton Journal*, 3 March 200 , A5.

31 Consultations with a senior official with the Public Service Commission, Ottawa, 27 May 2002.

32 See, among others, 'Auditor General Asks RCMP to Probe Federal Contracts,' *National Post* (Toronto), 9 May 2002, A1.

33 Quoted in J.E. Hodgetts, *The Canadian Public Service: A Physiology of Government, 1867–1970* (Toronto: University of Toronto Press, 1973), 209.

34 'Ducros Pays Price for Moron Remark,' *Globe and Mail* (Toronto), 26 Nov. 2002, A1.

35 'Ducros Had to Go, But the Rift Remains,' ibid., 27 Nov. 2002, A22.

36 Ian Clark, *Ottawa's Principal Decision-Making and Advisory Committees* (Ottawa: Privy Council Office, Dec. 1993), 15.

37 Savoie, *The Politics of Public Spending in Canada*, 118.

38 Savoie, *Governing from the Centre*, 232.

39 My conversation with a senior official at Treasury Board, Ottawa, Feb. 2002.

40 Based on data provided to me by the Public Service Commission on 23 Oct. 2002.

41 Max Weber, *The Theory of Social and Economic Organization* (New York: Oxford University Press, 1947), 333–7.

42 Michael M. Harmon and Richard T. Mayer, *Organization Theory for Public Administration* (Boston: Little, Brown, 1986), 69.

43 Weber, *The Theory of Social and Economic Organization*, 337.

44 Quoted in Harmon and Mayer, *Organization Theory*, 72.

45 'Treasury Hopes Senior Cuts Will Boost Employee Morale,' *Citizen* (Ottawa), 18 April 1980, A3.

46 My conversation with a deputy minister, Ottawa, 7 March, 2002.

47 '$100 M Wasted Rating PS Jobs,' *Citizen* (Ottawa), 9 May 2002, A1.

48 R. MacGregor Dawson, *The Government of Canada*, 4th ed., rev. Norman Ward (Toronto: University of Toronto Press, 1963), 331.

49 Jennifer Smith, 'Democracy and the Canadian House of Commons at the Millennium,' *Canadian Public Administration* 42, no. 4 (winter 1999), 406.

50 John Stuart Mill, *Considerations on Representative Government* (New York: Harper, 1862), 110.

51 Smith, 'Democracy and the Canadian House of Commons at the Millennium,' 406.

52 Ibid., 406–7.

53 C.E.S. Franks, 'The Decline of the Canadian Parliament,' *Hill Times* (Ottawa), 25 May 1998, 15.

54 Ibid.

55 Ibid.

56 See, among others, 'I'm Not Some Sort of Idiot Bimbo,' interview with Hedy Fry, *Globe and Mail* (Toronto), 23 March 2002, F3.

57 C.E.S. Franks, *The Parliament of Canada* (Toronto: University of Toronto Press, 1987), 146.

58 Quoted in *Occasional Papers on Parliamentary Government* (Ottawa: Parliamentary Centre, Sept. 1996), 11.

59 James Gillies and Jean Pigott, 'Participation in the Legislative Process,' *Canadian Public Administration* 25, no 2 (summer 1982), 260.

60 Franks, *The Parliament of Canada*, 175.

61 'MPs Forcing PM's Hand on Dollar,' *National Post* (Toronto), 10 Jan. 2002, A1.

62 'MPs and Senators Irrelevant, Lobbyists Say,' *Citizen* (Ottawa), 5 Oct. 2000, A1.

63 *Bridging Two Solitudes* (Ottawa: Public Policy Forum, Oct. 2000), 8.

64 Jonathan Malloy, 'Reconciling Expectations and Reality in House of Commons Committees: The Case of the 1989 GST Inquiry,' *Canadian Public Administration* 39, no. 3 (autumn 1996), 318.

65 Anne T. Perkins and C.E. S. Franks, *Accountability and Canada's Federal Public Service: Insight from Great Britain, France, Sweden and the United States* (Ottawa: CCMD, June 1982), 76.

66 See, for example, Bill Curry, 'Parliamentary Library Finds 1980s Produced Blockbuster Reports,' *Hill Times* (Ottawa), 14 Jan. 2002, 1.

67 Hodgetts, *The Canadian Public Service*, 113.

68 My conversation with a deputy minister, Ottawa, 26 March 2002.

69 Canada, *The Canadian Food Inspection Agency Annual Report, 1997–98*, 12 and 30.

70 Canada, Canadian Food Inspection Agency, *2000–2001 Annual Report*, sec. 3.7.

71 See also Kevin Theakston, *The Civil Service 1945* (Oxford: Blackwell, 1995), 169.

72 'HRDC's $16M Computer Bungle,' *Citizen* (Ottawa), Nov. 2002, A1.

73 'MP Doctor Shut Out of Medicare Hearing,' ibid., 26 March 2002, A1 and A7.

74 Jonathan Malloy, 'To Better Serve Canadians: How Technology Is Changing the Relationship between Members of Parliament and Public Servants,' Research study prepared for the Institute of Public Administration of Canada, second draft version, Toronto, 16 May, 2002, 6.

75 Ibid., 35.

76 David Docherty, *Mr. Smith Goes to Ottawa: Life in the House of Commons* (Vancouver: UBC Press, 1997), 73.

77 Robert Stanfield, 'The Present State of the Legislative Process in Canada: Myths and Realities,' in W.A.W. Neilson and J.C. MacPherson, eds., *The Legislative Process in Canada: The Need for Reform* (Toronto: Butterworth, 1978), 47.

78 See, for example, 'Liberals Close Ranks around Defence Minister,' *Globe and Mail* (Toronto), 23 March 2002, A1.

79 'Eggleton Required 3 Briefings to Get Point,' ibid., 27 Feb. 2002, A1.

80 'Why Did Officers Refuse to Take Heat for Political Boss?' ibid., 28 Feb. 2002, A4.

81 Quoted in ibid.

82 'Why the Top Brass Spoke Out,' *Globe and Mail* (Toronto), 28 Feb. 2002, A1.

83 David Cameron, 'Power and Responsibility in the Public Service: Summary of Discussions,' *Canadian Public Administration* 21, no. 3 (1978), 363.

84 'Mandarins Lashed over Russian Diplomat,' *Globe and Mail* (Toronto), 3 Feb. 2001, A.

85 'Anthrax Drug Deal Lands Rock in Hot Water,' *National Post* (Toronto), 20 Oct. 2001, A1.

86 'Ottawa Pays Twice for Cipro,' *Globe and Mail* (Toronto), 25 Oct. 2001, A1.

87 'Rock Rapped for Bungling Cipro Deal,' ibid., 21 Feb. 2002, A9.

88 See, among others, Richard Gwyn, *The Northern Magus: Pierre Trudeau and Canadians* (Toronto: McClelland and Stewart, 1980).

89 'Political Pressure Influenced Loans,' *Globe and Mail* (Toronto), 10 Oct. 1996, A1.

90 Paul Thomas, 'The Changing Nature of Accountability,' in B. Guy Peters and Donald J. Savoie, eds., *Taking Stock: Assessing Public Sector Reforms* (Ottawa: Canadian Centre for Management Development, 1998), 382.

91 Dennis Mills, 'Patronage Fuels Politics: We Need It,' *Globe and Mail* (Toronto), 14 Jan. 2002, A13.

92 Stéphane Dion, 'The Place of Public Administration in a Democracy,' paper presented at a symposium in honour of James Iain Gow, Montreal, May 1999, 5.

93 My conversations with representatives of the 'Human Resources Modernization Task Force,' March 2002, Ottawa.

94 Hood, 'Relationships between Ministers,' 193.

95 Ibid., 196–7.

96 My conversations with government officials, Ottawa, Feb.–March 2002.

97 Reginald Whitaker, *The Government Party: Organizing and Financing the Liberal Party of Canada, 1930–58* (Toronto: University of Toronto Press, 1977).

98 See, among others, 'Don't Abuse the Servants,' *National Post* (Toronto), 21 Oct. 2000, A15.

99 See, among others, 'Foundations Mock the Notion of Public Accountability,' *Globe and Mail* (Toronto), 12 Jan. 2002, B12.

Chapter 10: Redefining Accountability

1 James G. March and Johan P. Olsen, *Democratic Governance* (Toronto: Free Press, 1995), 160.

2 Quoted in *Occasional Papers on Parliamentary Government* (Ottawa: Parliamentary Centre, Sept. 1996).

3 O.C. McSuite, *Legitimacy in Public Administration: A Discourse Analysis* (Thousand Oaks, Calif.: Sage, 1997), 243.

4 My conversations with government officials, Ottawa, 25 June 2002.

5 Andrew Stark, 'What Is the New Public Management?' *Journal of Public Administration Research and Theory* 12, no. 1 (Jan. 2002), 146.

6 See, among others, John M. Kamensky, 'The Role of the Reinventing Government Movement in Federal Management Reform,' *Public Administration Review*, 56 (1996), 252, and Donald J. Savoie, *Thatcher, Reagan, Mulroney: In Search of a New Bureaucracy* (Pittsburgh: University of Pittsburgh Press, 1994).

7 An example is the advisory board to the Atlantic Innovation Fund, which reviews and recommends all proposed projects. See Canada, Atlantic Canada Opportunities Agency, Moncton, www.acoa-apeca.gc.ca

8 March and Olson, *Democratic Governance*, 227.

9 David E. Smith, *The Invisible Crown: The First Principle of Canadian Government* (Toronto: University of Toronto Press, 1995), 82.

10 See Sharon Sutherland, 'Parliament's Unregulated Control Bureaucracy,' *Briefing Notes* (Kingston: Queen's University School of Policy Studies, 2002), 9.

11 Ibid.

12 'Privacy Commissioner Launches Charter Challenge,' News Release (Ottawa: Privacy Commissioner of Canada, 21 June 2002).

13 Ibid.

14 Quoted in Paco Francoli, 'Access Commissioner Reid: Parliament Doesn't Take Me to Task; It's Lost Interest,' *Hill Times* (Ottawa), 28 Oct. 2002, 1.

15 Michelle Falardeau-Ramsay, quoted in *Parliament and Government* nos. 14–15 (Sept. 2002), 17.

16 My conversations with a senior official at the Department of Fisheries and Oceans, Ottawa, May 2002.

17 My conversation with a senior official with the Department of Justice, Ottawa, July 2002.

18 My conversation with a senior government official, Ottawa, 24 Feb. 2002.

19 Ibid.

20 Ibid.

21 Canada, Treasury Board of Canada Secretariat, *Employment Statistics for the Federal Public Service*, 1 April 2000–31 March 2001.

22 'Cabinet Cannot Keep All Its Secrets,' *National Post* (Toronto), 12 July 2002, A1.

23 See, for example, Janet L. Hiebert, *Charter Conflicts: What Is Parliament's Role?* (Montreal: McGill-Queen's University Press, 2002).

24 Smith, *The Invisible Crown*, 89.

25 Mark Considine, 'The End of the Line? Accountable Governance in the Age

of Networks, Partnerships and Joined-Up Services,' *Governance* 15, no. 1 (Jan. 2002), 22.

26 Tom Kent, 'Policy First: Three Case Studies,' paper presented to a joint IRPP and CIRRD conference held at Montebello, Quebec, Oct. 2001.

27 'Parliament's Merit Watchdog Accused of Conflict,' *Citizen* (Ottawa), 10 March 2002, A1.

28 Nevil Johnson, 'Management in Government,' in Michael J. Earl, ed., *Perspectives on Management: A Multidisciplinary Analysis* (Oxford: Oxford University Press, 1983), 182.

29 Peter Aucoin, 'Accountability: The Key to Restoring Public Confidence in Governments,' Timlin Lecture, University of Saskatchewan, Nov. 1997, 10.

30 J.R. Mallory coined this phrase in 'Parliament: Every Reform Creates a New Problem,' *Journal of Canadian Studies* 14, no. 1 (1979), 26–34.

31 See, among others, Charles Hecksher, 'Defining the Post-Bureaucratic Type,' in Charles Heckscher and Anne Donnellon, eds., *The Post Bureaucratic Organization: New Perspective on Organizational Change* (London: Sage Publications, 1994), 14–61.

32 R.A.W. Rhodes, *Understanding Governance: Policy Networks, Governance, Reflexivity and Accountability* (Buckingham: Open University Press, 1997), 127.

33 Paul Light makes this point in the case of the United States in *The True Size of Government* (Washington, DC: Brookings Institution Press, 1999).

34 Ibid., 5.

35 Paul Light, *Thickening Government: Federal Hierarchy and the Diffusion of Accountability* (Washington, DC: Brookings Institution Press, 1995).

36 Smith, *The Invisible Crown*, 63.

37 Some early leaders, however, did see merit in introducing checks and balances to the parliamentary system, including Baldwin, George Brown, Howe, and Lafontaine.

38 Lee Sigelman, quoted in Robert A. Dahl, 'The Science of Public Administration: Three Problems,' *Public Administration Review* 7, no. 1 (1948), 623.

39 Nicholas d'Ombrain, 'Alternative Services Delivery: Governance, Management and Practice,' in *Change, Governance and Public Management* (Ottawa: KPMG and Public Policy Forum, n.d.), 111.

40 See, among many others, Henry Parris, *Constitutional Bureaucracy* (London: George Allen and Unwin, 1969).

41 D'Ombrain, 'Alternative Services Delivery,' 154–5.

42 See, among many others, Sandford Borins, 'The New Public Management is Here to Stay,' *Canadian Public Administration* 38, no. 1 (spring 1995), 122–31.

43 Canada, 'Prime Minister Announces New Ethics Guidelines for the Ministry

and New Appointment Procedure for Ethics Counsellor,' News Release, Office of the Prime Minister, 11 June 2002.

44 D'Ombrain, 'Alternative Services Delivery,' 155.

45 On the work of the accounting officer in Britain, see C.E.S. Franks, *The Parliament of Canada* (Toronto: University of Toronto Press, 1987), chaps. 10 and 11.

46 'Bosses Told Him to Bend Rules, Says Ex-bureaucrat in Ad Furor,' *Globe and Mail* (Toronto), 5 Oct. 2002, A1.

47 'How a Mission to Win Quebec Developed into Scandal,' ibid., 11 Oct. 2002, A4.

48 My conversations with senior career government officials, Ottawa, various dates, 2001 and 2002.

49 My conversation with a senior deputy minister, Ottawa, May 2002.

50 This is not a strictly Canadian phenomenon. See, for example, Ian Marsh, 'Gaps in Policy Making Capacities: Interest Groups, Social Movements, Think Tanks and Media,' in Michael Keating et al., eds., *Institutions on the Edge?* (St Leonards: Allen and Unwin, 2000), 178–204.

51 Franks, *The Parliament of Canada,* 81.

52 Ibid., 10.

53 Smith, *The Invisible Crown,* 95.

54 C.D. Foster made this point in 'Joined-Up Government and Cabinet Governments,' paper presented to the Conference at the British Academy on Joined-Up Conference, London, 30 Oct. 2002, 27. See also Hiebert, *Charter Conflicts.*

55 Paul Martin, 'Notes for an Address on the Democratic Deficit to Students at Osgoode Law School,' 21 Oct. 2002, 12.

56 Canada, 'Prime Minister Announces New Ethics Guidelines,' 3.

57 Albert O. Hirschman, *Exit, Voice and Loyalty: Responses to Decline in Firms, Organizations, and States* (Cambridge, Mass.: Harvard University Press, 1970), 15–16.

58 Ian Clark, quoted in John English and Evert Lindquist, *Performance Management: Linking Results to Public Debate,* New Directions, no. 2 (Toronto: IPAC, 1998), 3.

59 See, among many others, ibid., 9.

60 See, for example, Peter Aucoin, *The New Public Management: Canada in Comparative Perspectives* (Montreal: IRPP, 1995), 247.

61 See, among others, Henry Parris, *Constitutional Bureaucracy* (London: George Allen and Unwin, 1969), chap. 3.

62 B.B. Schaffer, quoted in ibid, 82.

63 See, for example, Robert D. Behn, *Rethinking Democratic Accountability* (Washington, DC: Brookings Institution, 2001).

64 Marsh and Olsen, *Democratic Governance*, 59

65 A. Downs, *Inside Bureaucracy* (Boston: Little, Brown, 1967), 84.

66 See, among others, Considine, 'The End of the Line?'

67 Canada, *Department of Finance Results Based Management: DRI 2001–2002, Appendix C – Financial Performance*, 11 Jan. 2002.

68 See, among others, Carolyn J. Heinrich and Lawrence E. Lynn, 'Means and Ends: A Comparative Study of Empirical Methods for Investigating Governance and Performance,' *Journal of Public Administration and Theory* 11, no. 1 (2001), 109–38.

69 See, for example, 'Where's $12-Billion? Ontario Liberal MP Mills Wants to Know,' *Hill Times* (Ottawa), 3 June 2002, A1.

70 'Lies and Contempt for Parliament at Root of Scandal in Gun Registry,' *Globe and Mail* (Toronto), 4 Dec. 2002, A8.

71 See, among others, 'Commons Wins Scrutiny of $170B,' ibid., 29 May 2002, A11, and 'Panel Targets Parliament's Weakest Link,' *Citizen* (Ottawa), 28 May 2002, A1.

72 My conversations with several central-agency officials, Ottawa, Oct. 2002.

73 See, for example 'Long-Awaited Classification Plan Could Cost Tax Payers Billions,' *Citizen* (Ottawa), 17 Jan. 2001.

74 This is hardly a new idea. Paul Thomas advocated the creation of a parliamentary committee with a mandate to review the activities of the public service and officers in Parliament, in *Relations between Parliamentary Agencies and the Public Service: New Perspectives* (Ottawa: CCMD Action–Research Project, 2002), 15.

75 Aucoin, 'Accountability,' 12.

76 Franks, *The Parliament of Canada*, 23–4.

77 See, for example, Douglas Yates, *Bureaucratic Democracy: The Search for Democracy and Efficiency in American Government* (Cambridge, Mass.: Harvard University Press, 1982), 205.

78 Theodore Lowi, *The End of Liberalism* (New York: Norton, 1969).

79 See, for example, *The Role of the Civil Service: ... Report* (London: HMSO, 1993), vi.

80 Quoted in Louis C. Gowthrop, *Public Service and Democracy: Ethical Imperative for the 21st Century* (New York: Chatham House, 1981), 11.

81 My conversations with a senior official in the Privy Council Office, Oct. 2002. See also Paul Tellier's comments in the *Globe and Mail* after he left government.

82 Canada, 'Prime Minister Announces Formation of Task Force on Moderniz-ing Human Resources Management in the Public Service,' Press Release, Prime Minister's Office, 3 April 2001.

83 D'Ombrain, 'Alternative Services Delivery,' 94.

84 Jon Pierre, 'Externalities and Relationships: Rethinking the Boundaries of the Public Service,' in B. Guy Peters and Donald J. Savoie, eds., *Revitalizing the Public Service: Governance in the Twenty-first Century* (Montreal: McGill-Queen's University Press, 2001), 351.

85 See, among many others, Savoie, *Thatcher, Reagan, Mulroney.* See also the Ekos survey sponsored by the Public Service Commission in 2001, cited in Canada, *The Road Ahead: Recruitment and Retention Challenges for the Public Service* (Ottawa: Public Service Commission, Feb. 2002), 24–5.

86 Ibid.

87 Ibid., 29.

88 Ibid., 31.

89 See Jocelyne Bourgon, 'Citizens, Government, Democracy: A New Deal?' presentation to the International Summit on Public Service Reform, Win-nipeg, 11 June 1999, 5.

90 Quoted in Savoie, *Governing from the Centre*, 148.

91 Quoted in 'PM's Power Threatens to Even Make Cabinet Irrelevant,' *National Post* (Toronto), 16 Oct. 2002, A1.

92 Paul Thomas, 'The Future of Representative Democracy: The Impact of Information Technology,' paper presented to CCMD, Ottawa, undated, mimeo, 14.

93 See, among others, 'Fewer Voters a Sign Public Happy with PM: Liberal,' *National Post* (Toronto), 4 June 2001, A6.

94 D'Ombrain, 'Alternative Services Delivery,' 104.

95 Reg Alcock, quoted in 'MPs Are Not Blameless in Gun Registry,' *Hill Times* (Ottawa), 9 Dec. 2002, 1.

Index